Anti-intellectualism

IN

AMERICAN LIFE

Anti-intellectualism

IN

AMERICAN LIFE

BY

RICHARD HOFSTADTER

NEW YORK ALFRED A. KNOPF

1964

L. C. catalog card number: 63–14086

THIS IS A BORZOI BOOK
PUBLISHED BY ALFRED A. KNOPF, INC.

PUBLISHED MAY 20, 1963
SECOND PRINTING, AUGUST 1963
THIRD PRINTING, JULY 1964

Chapter 7 appeared in somewhat different form as " 'Idealists and Professors and Sore-heads': The Genteel Reformers" in the *Columbia University Forum*. Chapter 14 appeared in somewhat different form as "The Child and the World" in *Daedalus*.

PREFATORY NOTE

❧

WHAT IS ordinarily done in prefaces I have tried to do in my first two chapters, which explain the origin and the intent of this book, as well as its central terms. But one thing should be particularly clear at the beginning: what I have done is merely to use the idea of anti-intellectualism as a device for looking at various aspects, hardly the most appealing, of American society and culture. Despite the fringes of documentation on many of its pages, this work is by no means a formal history but largely a personal book, whose factual details are organized and dominated by my views. The theme itself has been developed in a manner that is by choice rather impulsive and by necessity only fragmentary.

If one is to look at a society like ours from its nether end, so to speak, through scores of consecutive pages, one must resolve to risk wounding the national *amour-propre*, although this can only divert attention from the business at hand, which is to shed a little light on our cultural problems. One must resolve still more firmly to run some slight risk of encouraging the canting and self-righteous anti-Americanism that in Europe today so commonly masquerades as well-informed criticism of this country. For all their bragging and their hypersensitivity, Americans are, if not the most self-critical, at least the most anxiously self-conscious people in the world, forever concerned about the inadequacy of something or other—their national morality, their national culture, their national purpose. This very uncertainty has given their intellectuals a critical function of special interest. The appropriation of some of this self-criticism by foreign ideologues for purposes that go beyond its original scope or intention is an inevitable hazard. But the possibility that a sound enterprise in self-correction may be overheard and misused is the poorest of reasons for suspending it. On this count I admire the spirit of Emerson, who wrote: "Let us honestly state the facts. Our America has a bad name for superficialness. Great men, great nations, have not been boasters and buffoons, but perceivers of the terror of life, and have manned themselves to face it."

R. H.

CONTENTS

❦

PART 1

Introduction

CHAPTER I

Anti-intellectualism
in Our Time

❦

· 1 ·

ALTHOUGH this book deals mainly with certain aspects of the remoter American past, it was conceived in response to the political and intellectual conditions of the 1950's. During that decade the term *anti-intellectualism*, only rarely heard before, became a familiar part of our national vocabulary of self-recrimination and intramural abuse. In the past, American intellectuals were often discouraged or embittered by the national disrespect for mind, but it is hard to recall a time when large numbers of people outside the intellectual community shared their concern, or when self-criticism on this count took on the character of a nation-wide movement.

Primarily it was McCarthyism which aroused the fear that the critical mind was at a ruinous discount in this country. Of course, intellectuals were not the only targets of McCarthy's constant detonations—he was after bigger game—but intellectuals were in the line of fire, and it seemed to give special rejoicing to his followers when they were hit. His sorties against intellectuals and universities were emulated throughout the country by a host of less exalted inquisitors. Then, in the atmosphere of fervent malice and humorless imbecility stirred up by McCarthy's barrage of accusations, the campaign of 1952 dramatized the contrast between intellect and philistinism in the opposing candidates. On one side was Adlai Stevenson, a politician of uncommon mind and style, whose appeal to intellectuals overshadowed anything in recent history. On the other was Dwight D. Eisenhower, conventional in mind, relatively inarticulate, harnessed to the unpalatable Nixon, and waging a campaign whose tone seemed to be set less by the general himself than by his running mate and the McCarthyite wing of his party.

Eisenhower's decisive victory was taken both by the intellectuals themselves and by their critics as a measure of their repudiation by America. *Time*, the weekly magazine of opinion, shook its head in an unconvincing imitation of concern. Eisenhower's victory, it said, "discloses an alarming fact long suspected: there is a wide and unhealthy gap between the American intellectuals and the people." Arthur Schlesinger, Jr., in a mordant protest written soon after the election, found the intellectual "in a situation he has not known for a generation." After twenty years of Democratic rule, during which the intellectual had been in the main understood and respected, business had come back into power, bringing with it "the vulgarization which has been the almost invariable consequence of business supremacy." Now the intellectual, dismissed as an "egghead," an oddity, would be governed by a party which had little use for or understanding of him, and would be made the scapegoat for everything from the income tax to the attack on Pearl Harbor. "Anti-intellectualism," Schlesinger remarked, "has long been the anti-Semitism of the businessman. . . . The intellectual . . . is on the run today in American society." [1]

All this seemed to be amply justified when the new administration got under way. The replacement, in Stevenson's phrase, of the New Dealers by the car dealers seemed to make final the repudiation of intellectuals and their values—they had already been overshadowed by the courthouse politicians of the Truman years. The country was now treated to Charles E. Wilson's sallies at pure research, to stories about Eisenhower's fondness for Western fiction as reading matter, and to his definition of an intellectual as a wordy and pretentious man. But during the Eisenhower administration the national mood reached a turning point: the McCarthyite rage, confronted by a Republican president, burned itself out; the senator from Wisconsin isolated himself, was censured, and deflated. Finally, in 1957, the launching of the Sputnik by the Soviets precipitated one of those periodic surges of self-conscious national reappraisal to which the American public is prone. The Sputnik was more than a shock to American national vanity: it brought an immense amount of attention to bear on the

[1] Arthur Schlesinger, Jr.: "The Highbrow in Politics," *Partisan Review*, Vol. XX (March–April 1953), pp. 162–5; *Time* is quoted here, p. 159.

consequences of anti-intellectualism in the school system and in American life at large. Suddenly the national distaste for intellect appeared to be not just a disgrace but a hazard to survival. After assuming for some years that its main concern with teachers was to examine them for disloyalty, the nation now began to worry about their low salaries. Scientists, who had been saying for years that the growing obsession with security was demoralizing to research, suddenly found receptive listeners. Cries of protest against the slackness of American education, hitherto raised only by a small number of educational critics, were now taken up by television, mass magazines, businessmen, scientists, politicians, admirals, and university presidents, and soon swelled into a national chorus of self-reproach. Of course, all this did not immediately cause the vigilante mind to disappear, nor did it disperse anti-intellectualism as a force in American life; even in the sphere most immediately affected, that of education, the ruling passion of the public seemed to be for producing more Sputniks, not for developing more intellect, and some of the new rhetoric about education almost suggested that gifted children were to be regarded as resources in the cold war. But the atmosphere did change notably. In 1952 only intellectuals seemed much disturbed by the specter of anti-intellectualism; by 1958 the idea that this might be an important and even a dangerous national failing was persuasive to most thinking people.

Today it is possible to look at the political culture of the 1950's with some detachment. If there was then a tendency to see in McCarthyism, and even in the Eisenhower administration, some apocalypse for intellectuals in public life, it is no longer possible, now that Washington has again become so hospitable to Harvard professors and ex-Rhodes scholars. If there was a suspicion that intellect had become a hopeless obstacle to success in politics or administration, it must surely have been put to rest by the new President's obvious interest in ideas and respect for intellectuals, his ceremonial gestures to make that respect manifest in affairs of state, his pleasure in the company and advice of men of intellectual power, and above all by the long, careful search for distinguished talents with which his administration began. On the other hand, if there had ever been an excessive confidence that the recruitment of such talents would altogether transform the conduct of our affairs, time has surely brought its inevitable disenchantment. We have now reached a point at which intellectuals can discuss anti-intellectualism without exaggerated partisanship or self-pity.

• 2 •

The political ferment and educational controversy of the 1950's made the term *anti-intellectual* a central epithet in American self-evaluation; it has slipped unobtrusively into our usage without much definition and is commonly used to describe a variety of unwelcome phenomena. Those who have suddenly become aware of it often assume that anti-intellectualism is a new force in this or that area of life, and that, being a product of recent conditions, it may be expected to grow to overwhelming proportions. (American intellectuals have a lamentably thin sense of history; and modern man has lived so long under the shadow of some kind of apocalypse or other that intellectuals have come to look upon even the lesser eddies of social change as though they were tidal waves.) But to students of Americana the anti-intellectual note so commonly struck during the 1950's sounded not new at all, but rather familiar. Anti-intellectualism was not manifested in this country for the first time during the 1950's. Our anti-intellectualism is, in fact, older than our national identity, and has a long historical background. An examination of this background suggests that regard for intellectuals in the United States has not moved steadily downward and has not gone into a sudden, recent decline, but is subject to cyclical fluctuations; it suggests, too, that the resentment from which the intellectual has suffered in our time is a manifestation not of a decline in his position but of his increasing prominence. We know rather little about all this in any systematic way, and there has not been very much historically informed thinking on the subject. A great deal has been written about the long-running quarrel between American intellectuals and their country, but such writings deal mainly with America as seen by the intellectuals, and give only occasional glimpses of intellect and intellectuals as seen by America.[2]

One reason anti-intellectualism has not even been clearly defined

[2] The only American historian, to my knowledge, who has concerned himself extensively with the problem is Merle Curti, in his suggestive volume, *American Paradox* (New Brunswick, New Jersey, 1956) and in his presidential address before the American Historical Association, "Intellectuals and Other People," *American Historical Review*, Vol. LX (January 1955), pp. 259–82. Jacques Barzun, in *The House of Intellect* (New York, 1959), has dealt with the subject largely in contemporary terms and largely with internal strains within the intellectual and cultural world. An entire number of the *Journal of Social Issues*, Vol. XI, No. 3 (1955), was devoted to discussions of anti-intellectualism by various writers.

is that its very vagueness makes it more serviceable in controversy as an epithet. But, in any case, it does not yield very readily to definition. As an idea, it is not a single proposition but a complex of related propositions. As an attitude, it is not usually found in a pure form but in ambivalence—a pure and unalloyed dislike of intellect or intellectuals is uncommon. And as a historical subject, if it can be called that, it is not a constant thread but a force fluctuating in strength from time to time and drawing its motive power from varying sources. In these pages I have not held myself to a rigorous or narrow definition, which would here be rather misplaced. I can see little advantage in a logically defensible but historically arbitrary act of definition, which would demand singling out one trait among a complex of traits. It is the complex itself I am interested in—the complex of historical relations among a variety of attitudes and ideas that have many points of convergence. The common strain that binds together the attitudes and ideas which I call anti-intellectual is a resentment and suspicion of the life of the mind and of those who are considered to represent it; and a disposition constantly to minimize the value of that life. This admittedly general formulation is as close as I find it useful to venture toward definition.[3]

Once this procedure is adopted, it will be clear that anti-intellectualism cannot be made the subject of a formal history in quite the same way as the life of a man or the development of an institution or a social movement. Dealing as I do with the milieu, the atmosphere, in which American thinking has taken place, I have had to use those impressionistic devices with which one attempts to reproduce a milieu or capture an atmosphere.

Before giving some examples of what I mean by anti-intellectualism, I may perhaps explain what I do *not* mean. I am not dealing, except incidentally, with the internal feuds or contentions of the American intellectual community. American intellectuals, like intellectuals elsewhere, are often uneasy in their role; they are given to moments of self-doubt, and even of self-hatred, and at times they make acidulous and sweeping comments on the whole tribe to which they belong. This internal criticism is revealing and interesting, but it is not my main

---

[3] For an interesting exercise in definition, see Morton White: "Reflections on Anti-Intellectualism," *Daedalus* (Summer, 1962), pp. 457–68. White makes a useful distinction between the anti-intellectual, who is hostile to intellectuals, and the anti-intellectualist, who is critical of the claims of rational intellect in knowledge and in life. He treats at some length the respective strategies of the two, and their points of convergence.

concern. Neither is the ill-mannered or ill-considered criticism that one intellectual may make of another. No one, for example, ever poured more scorn on the American professoriat than H. L. Mencken, and no one has portrayed other writers in fiction with more venom than Mary McCarthy; but we would not on this account dream of classing Mencken with William F. Buckley as an enemy of the professors nor Miss McCarthy with the late senator of the same name.[4] The criticism of other intellectuals is, after all, one of the most important functions of the intellectual, and he customarily performs it with vivacity. We may hope, but we can hardly expect, that he will also do it with charity, grace, and precision. Because it is the business of intellectuals to be diverse and contrary-minded, we must accept the risk that at times they will be merely quarrelsome.

It is important, finally, if we are to avoid hopeless confusion, to be clear that anti-intellectualism is not here identified with a type of philosophical doctrine which I prefer to call anti-rationalism. The ideas of thinkers like Nietzsche, Sorel, or Bergson, Emerson, Whitman, or William James, or of writers like William Blake, D. H. Lawrence, or Ernest Hemingway may be called anti-rationalist; but these men were not characteristically anti-intellectual in the sociological and political sense in which I use the term. It is of course true that anti-intellectualist

---

[4] These considerations serve as a forcible reminder that there is in America, as elsewhere, a kind of intellectual establishment that embraces a wide range of views. It is generally understood (although there are marginal cases) whether a particular person is inside or outside this establishment. The establishment has a double standard for evaluating the criticism of the intellectuals: criticism from within is commonly accepted as having a basically benign intent and is more likely to be heard solely on its merits; but criticism from outside—even the same criticism —will be resented as hostile and stigmatized as anti-intellectual and potentially dangerous. For example, some years ago many intellectuals were critical of the great foundations for devoting too much of their research money to the support of large-budget "projects," as opposed to individual scholarship. But when the Reece Committee was hot on the trail of the foundations, the same intellectuals were not happy to see the same criticism (among others more specious) pressed by such an agency. It was not that they had ceased to believe in the criticism but that they neither liked nor trusted the source.

Of course, not only intellectuals do this; it is a common phenomenon of group life. Members of a political party or a minority group may invoke a similar double standard against criticism, depending on whether it originates from inside or outside the ranks. There is, moreover, some justification for such double standards, in historical fact if not in logic, because the intent that lies behind criticism unfortunately becomes an ingredient in its applicability. The intellectuals who criticized the foundations were doing so in the hope (as they saw it) of constructively modifying foundation policies, whereas the line of inquiry pursued by the Reece Committee might have led to crippling or destroying them. Again, everyone understands that a joke, say, about Jews or Negroes has different overtones when it is told within the group and when it is told by outsiders.

movements often invoke the ideas of such anti-rationalist thinkers (Emerson alone has provided them with a great many texts); but only when they do, and only marginally, is highbrow anti-rationalism a part of my story. In these pages I am centrally concerned with widespread social attitudes, with political behavior, and with middle-brow and low-brow responses, only incidentally with articulate theories. The attitudes that interest me most are those which would, to the extent that they become effective in our affairs, gravely inhibit or impoverish intellectual and cultural life. Some examples, taken from our recent history, may put flesh on the bare bones of definition.

· 3 ·

We might begin with some definitions supplied by those most acutely dissatisfied with American intellectuals.

Exhibit A. During the campaign of 1952, the country seemed to be in need of some term to express that disdain for intellectuals which had by then become a self-conscious motif in American politics. The word *egghead* was originally used without invidious associations,[5] but quickly assumed them, and acquired a much sharper overtone than the traditional *highbrow*. Shortly after the campaign was over, Louis Bromfield, a popular novelist of right-wing political persuasion, suggested that the word might some day find its way into dictionaries as follows: [6]

> *Egghead:* A person of spurious intellectual pretensions, often a professor or the protégé of a professor. Fundamentally superficial. Over-emotional and feminine in reactions to any problem. Supercilious and surfeited with conceit and contempt for the experience of more sound and able men. Essentially confused in thought and immersed in mixture of sentimentality and violent evangelism. A doctrinaire supporter of Middle-European socialism as opposed to Greco-French-American ideas of democracy and liberalism. Subject to the old-fashioned philosophical morality of Nietzsche which frequently leads him into jail or disgrace. A self-

[5] The term was taken up as a consequence of a column by Stewart Alsop, in which that reporter recorded a conversation with his brother John. The columnist remarked that many intelligent people who were normally Republicans obviously admired Stevenson. "Sure," said his brother, "all the egg-heads love Stevenson. But how many egg-heads do you think there are?" Joseph and Stewart Alsop: *The Reporter's Trade* (New York, 1958), p. 188.

[6] Louis Bromfield: "The Triumph of the Egghead," *The Freeman,* Vol. III (December 1, 1952), p. 158.

conscious prig, so given to examining all sides of a question that
he becomes thoroughly addled while remaining always in the
same spot. An anemic bleeding heart.

"The recent election," Bromfield remarked, "demonstrated a number
of things, not the least of them being the extreme remoteness of the
'egghead' from the thought and feeling of the whole of the people."

Exhibit B. Almost two years later President Eisenhower appeared to
give official sanction to a similarly disdainful view of intellectuals.
Speaking at a Republican meeting in Los Angeles in 1954, he reported
a view, expressed to him by a trade-union leader, that the people,
presented with the whole truth, will always support the right cause.
The President added: [7]

> It was a rather comforting thought to have this labor leader
> saying this, when we had so many wisecracking so-called intel-
> lectuals going around and showing how wrong was everybody
> who don't happen to agree with them.
>
> By the way, I heard a definition of an intellectual that I
> thought was very interesting: *a man who takes more words than
> are necessary to tell more than he knows.*

Exhibit C. One of the issues at stake in the controversies of the 1950's
was the old one about the place of expertise in political life. Perhaps
the high moment in the case against the expert and for the amateur
occurred in 1957 when a chain-store president, Maxwell H. Gluck, was
nominated to be ambassador to Ceylon. Mr. Gluck had contributed,
by his own estimate, $20,000 or $30,000 to the Republican campaign
of 1956, but, like many such appointees before him, was not known
for having any experience in politics or diplomacy. Questioned by
Senator Fulbright about his qualifications for the post, Mr. Gluck had
some difficulty: [8]

> FULBRIGHT : What are the problems in Ceylon you think you can
> deal with?
>
> GLUCK : One of the problems are the people there. I believe I
> can—I think I can establish, unless we—again, un-

[7] White House Press Release, "Remarks of the President at the Breakfast
Given by Various Republican Groups of Southern California, Statler Hotel, Los
Angeles . . . September 24, 1954," p. 4; italics added. It is possible that the Presi-
dent had heard something of the kind from his Secretary of Defense, Charles E.
Wilson, who was quoted elsewhere as saying: "An egghead is a man who doesn't
understand everything he knows." Richard and Gladys Harkness: "The Wit and
Wisdom of Charlie Wilson," *Reader's Digest,* Vol. LXXI (August, 1957), p. 197.

[8] *The New York Times,* August 1, 1957.

less I run into something that I have not run into
before—a good relationship and good feeling toward
the United States. . . .

FULBRIGHT :   Do you know our Ambassador to India?

GLUCK :   I know John Sherman Cooper, the previous Ambassador.

FULBRIGHT :   Do you know who the Prime Minister of India is?

GLUCK :   Yes, but I can't pronounce his name.

FULBRIGHT :   Do you know who the Prime Minister of Ceylon is?

GLUCK :   His name is unfamiliar now, I cannot call it off.

Doubts about Mr. Gluck's preparation for the post he was to occupy led to the suggestion that he had been named because of
his contribution to the Republican campaign. In a press conference
held July 31, 1957, a reporter raised the question, whereupon President Eisenhower remarked that an appointment in return for campaign contributions was unthinkable. About his nominee's competence,
he observed: [9]

Now, as to the man's ignorance, this is the way he was appointed: he was selected from a group of men that were recommended highly by a number of people I respect. His business
career was examined, the F.B.I. reports on him were all good.
Of course, we knew he had never been to Ceylon, he wasn't thoroughly familiar with it; but certainly he can learn if he is the
kind of character and kind of man we believe him to be.

It is important to add that Mr. Gluck's service in Ceylon was termi-
nated after a year by his resignation.

Exhibit D. One of the grievances of American scientists was their
awareness that America's disdain for pure science was a handicap not
only to investigation but also to the progress of research and development in the Department of Defense. Examining Secretary of Defense
Charles E. Wilson in 1954 before the Senate Committee on Armed
Services, Senator Stuart Symington of Missouri quoted earlier testimony in which the Secretary had said, among other things, that if
there was to be pure research it should be subsidized by some agency
other than the Department of Defense. "I am not much interested,"
Secretary Wilson had testified, "as a military project in why potatoes
turn brown when they are fried." Pressing Secretary Wilson, Senator
Symington pointed to testimony that had been given about the lack of

[9] Ibid.

sufficient money for research not on potatoes but on bombers, nuclear propulsion, electronics, missiles, radar, and other subjects. The Secretary replied: [1]

> Important research and development is going on in all those areas. . . .
> On the other side, it is very difficult to get these men who are trying to think out ahead all the time to come down to brass tacks and list the projects and what they expect to get. . . . They would just like to have a pot of money without too much supervision that they could reach into. . . .
> In the first place, *if you know what you are doing, why it is not pure research*. That complicates it.

Exhibit E. The kind of anti-intellectualism expressed in official circles during the 1950's was mainly the traditional businessman's suspicion of experts working in any area outside his control, whether in scientific laboratories, universities, or diplomatic corps. Far more acute and sweeping was the hostility to intellectuals expressed on the far-right wing, a categorical folkish dislike of the educated classes and of anything respectable, established, pedigreed, or cultivated. The right-wing crusade of the 1950's was full of heated rhetoric about "Harvard professors, twisted-thinking intellectuals . . . in the State Department"; those who are "burdened with Phi Beta Kappa keys and academic honors" but not "equally loaded with honesty and common sense"; "the American respectables, the socially pedigreed, the culturally acceptable, the certified gentlemen and scholars of the day, dripping with college degrees . . . the 'best people' who were for Alger Hiss"; "the pompous diplomat in striped pants with phony British accent"; those who try to fight Communism "with kid gloves in perfumed drawing rooms"; Easterners who "insult the people of the great Midwest and West, the *heart* of America"; those who can "trace their ancestry back to the eighteenth century—or even further" but whose loyalty is still not above suspicion; those who understand "the Groton vocabulary of the Hiss-Acheson group." [2] The spirit of this rhetorical *jacquerie* was caught by an editorial writer for the *Freeman:* [3]

---

[1] U.S. Congress, 84th Congress, 2nd session, Senate Committee on Armed Services: *Hearings*, Vol. XVI, pp. 1742, 1744 (July 2, 1956); italics added.

[2] This mélange of images is taken from the more extended account of the scapegoats of the 1950's in Immanuel Wallerstein's unpublished M.A. essay: "McCarthyism and the Conservative," Columbia University, 1954, pp. 46 ff.

[3] *Freeman*, Vol. XI (November 5, 1951), p. 72.

The truly appalling phenomenon is the irrationality of the college-educated mob that has descended upon Joseph R. McCarthy. . . . Suppose Mr. McCarthy were indeed the cad the "respectable" press makes him out to be; would this . . . justify the cataclysmic eruptions that, for almost a year now, have emanated from all the better appointed editorial offices of New York and Washington, D.C.? . . . It must be something in McCarthy's personal makeup. He possesses, it seems, a sort of animal negative-pole magnetism which repels alumni of Harvard, Princeton and Yale. And we think we know what it is: This young man is constitutionally incapable of deference to social status.

McCarthy himself found the central reasons for America's difficulties in areas where social status was most secure. The trouble, he said in the published version of his famous Wheeling speech, lay in [4]

the traitorous actions of those who have been treated so well by this Nation. It has not been the less fortunate or members of minority groups who have been selling this Nation out, but rather those who have had all the benefits that the wealthiest nation on earth has had to offer—the finest homes, the finest college education, and the finest jobs in Government we can give. This is glaringly true in the State Department. There the bright young men who are born with silver spoons in their mouths are the ones who have been worst.

Exhibit F. The universities, particularly the better-known universities, were constantly marked out as targets by right-wing critics; but according to one writer in the *Freeman* there appears to have been only an arbitrary reason for this discrimination against the Ivy League, since he considered that Communism is spreading in all our colleges: [5]

Our universities are the training grounds for the barbarians of the future, those who, in the guise of learning, shall come forth loaded with pitchforks of ignorance and cynicism, and stab and destroy the remnants of human civilization. It will not be the subway peasants who will tear down the walls: they will merely do the bidding of our learned brethren . . . who will erase individual Freedom from the ledgers of human thought. . . .

[4] *Congressional Record,* 81st Congress, 2nd session, p. 1954 (February 20, 1950).
[5] Jack Schwartzman: "Natural Law and the Campus," *Freeman,* Vol. II (December 3, 1951), pp. 149, 152.

If you send your son to the colleges of today, you will create the Executioner of tomorrow. The rebirth of idealism must come from the scattered monasteries of non-collegiate thought.

Exhibit G. Right-wing hostility to universities was in part a question of deference and social status, but in part also a reflection of the old Jacksonian dislike of specialists and experts. Here is a characteristic assertion about the equal competence of the common man (in this case the common woman) and the supposed experts, written by the amateur economist, Frank Chodorov, author of *The Income Tax: The Root of All Evil,* and one of the most engaging of the right-wing spokesmen: [6]

A parcel of eminent economists, called into consultation by the Rockefeller Brothers Fund to diagnose the national ailment known as recession, came up with a prescription that, though slightly condensed, covered the better part of two pages in *The New York Times.* The prominence of these doctors makes it presumptuous for one who has not "majored" in economics to examine the ingredients of their curative concoction. Yet the fact is that all of us are economists by necessity, since all of us are engaged in making a living, which is what economics is all about. Any literate housewife, endowed with a modicum of common sense, should be able to evaluate the specifics in the prescription, provided these are extracted from the verbiage in which they are clothed.

Exhibit H. Although the following may well be considered by discriminating readers as anti-cultural rather than anti-intellectual, I cannot omit some remarks by Congressman George Dondero of Michigan, long a vigilant crusader against Communism in the schools and against cubism, expressionism, surrealism, dadaism, futurism, and other movements in art: [7]

The art of the isms, the weapon of the Russian Revolution, is the art which has been transplanted to America, and today, having infiltrated and saturated many of our art centers, threatens to overawe, override and overpower the fine art of our tradition and inheritance. So-called modern or contemporary art in our

[6] "Shake Well before Using," *National Review,* Vol. V (June 7, 1958), p. 544.
[7] *Congressional Record,* 81st Congress, 1st session, p. 11584 (August 16, 1949); see also Dondero's address on "Communism in Our Schools," *Congressional Record,* 79th Congress, 2nd session, pp. A. 3516–18 (June 14, 1946), and his speech, "Communist Conspiracy in Art Threatens American Museums," *Congressional Record,* 82nd Congress, 2nd session, pp. 2423–7 (March 17, 1952).

own beloved country contains all the isms of depravity, decadence, and destruction. . . .

All these isms are of foreign origin, and truly should have no
place in American art. . . . All are instruments and weapons of
destruction.

Exhibit I. Since I shall have much to say in these pages about anti-
intellectualism in the evangelical tradition, it seems important to cite
at least one survival of this tradition. These brief quotations are taken
from the most successful evangelist of our time, Billy Graham, voted
by the American public in a Gallup Poll of 1958 only after Eisenhower,
Churchill, and Albert Schweitzer as "the most admired man in the
world": [8]

Moral standards of yesterday to many individuals are no standard for today unless supported by the so-called "intellectuals."

I sincerely believe that partial education throughout the world
is far worse than none at all, if we only educate the mind without
the soul. . . . Turn that man loose upon the world [who has] no
power higher than his own, he is a monstrosity, he is but halfway
educated, and is more dangerous than though he were not educated at all.

You can stick a public school and a university in the middle of
every block of every city in America and you will never keep
America from rotting morally by mere intellectual education.

During the past few years the intellectual props have been
knocked out from under the theories of men. Even the average
university professor is willing to listen to the voice of the preacher.

[In place of the Bible] we substituted reason, rationalism, mind
culture, science worship, the working power of government,
Freudianism, naturalism, humanism, behaviorism, positivism, materialism, and idealism. [This is the work of] so-called intellectuals. Thousands of these "intellectuals" have publicly stated that
morality is relative—that there is no norm or absolute standard. . . .

Exhibit J. In the post-Sputnik furor over American education, one of
the most criticized school systems was that of California, which had
been notable for its experimentation with curricula. When the San
Francisco School District commissioned a number of professional

[8] William G. McLoughlin, Jr.: *Billy Graham: Revivalist in a Secular Age* (New
York, 1960), pp. 89, 212, 213; on the Gallup Poll, see p. 5.

scholars to examine their schools, the committee constituted for this purpose urged a return to firmer academic standards. Six educational organizations produced a sharp counterattack in which they criticized the authors of the San Francisco report for "academic pettiness and snobbery" and for going beyond their competence in limiting the purposes of education to "informing the mind and developing the intelligence," and reasserted the value of "other goals of education, such as preparation for citizenship, occupational competence, successful family life, self-realization in ethical, moral, aesthetic and spiritual dimensions, and the enjoyment of physical health." The educationists argued that an especially praiseworthy feature of American education had been [9]

the attempt to avoid a highly rigid system of education. To do so does not mean that academic competence is not regarded as highly important to any society, but it does recognize that historically, *education systems which stress absorption of accumulated knowledge for its own sake have tended to produce decadence.* Those who would "fix" the curriculum and freeze educational purpose misunderstand the unique function of education in American democracy.

Exhibit K. The following is an excerpt from a parent's report, originally written in answer to a teacher's complaint about the lax standards in contemporary education. The entire piece is worth reading as a vivid statement by a parent who identifies wholly with the non-academic child and the newer education. As we shall see, the stereotype of the schoolteacher expressed here has deep historical roots.[1]

But kindergarten teachers understand children. Theirs is a child-centered program. School days were one continuous joy of games and music and colors and friendliness. Life rolled merrily along through the first grade, the second grade, the third grade . . . then came arithmetic! Failure like a spectre arose to haunt our days and harass our nights. Father and mother began to attend lectures on psychology and to read about inferiority complexes. We dragged through the fourth grade and into the

[9] *Judging and Improving the Schools: Current Issues* (Burlingame, California, 1960), pp. 4, 5, 7, 8; italics added. The document under fire was William C. Bark et al.: *Report of the San Francisco Curriculum Survey Committee* (San Francisco, 1960).

[1] Robert E. Brownlee: "A Parent Speaks Out," *Progressive Education*, Vol. XVII (October, 1940), pp. 420–41.

fifth. Something had to be done. Even father couldn't solve all the problems. I decided to have a talk with the teacher.

There was no welcome on the mat of that school. No one greeted the stranger or made note of his coming. A somber hallway presented itself, punctuated at regular intervals by closed doors. Unfamiliar sounds came from within. I inquired my way of a hurrying youngster and then knocked at the forbidding threshold. To the teacher I announced my name, smiling as pleasantly as I could. "Oh, yes," she said, as if my business were already known to her and reached for her classbook, quick on the draw like a movie gangster clutching for his gun.

The names of the pupils appeared on a ruled page in neat and alphabetical precision. The teacher moved a bloodless finger down the margin of the page to my daughter's name. After each name were little squares. In the squares were little marks, symbols that I did not understand. Her finger moved across the page. My child's marks were not the same as those of the other children. She looked up triumphantly as if there were nothing more to be said. I was thinking of the small compass into which she had compressed the total activities of a very lively youngster. I was interested in a whole life, a whole personality; the teacher, merely in arithmetical ability. I wished I had not come. I left uninformed and uncomforted.

Exhibit L. The following remarks have already been made famous by Arthur Bestor, but they will bear repetition. After delivering and publishing the address excerpted here, the author, a junior high-school principal in Illinois, did not lose caste in his trade but was engaged for a similar position in Great Neck, Long Island, a post which surely ranks high in desirability among the nation's secondary schools, and was subsequently invited to be a visiting member of the faculty of the school of education of a Midwestern university.[2]

Through the years we've built a sort of halo around reading, writing, and arithmetic. We've said they were for everybody . . . rich and poor, brilliant and not-so-mentally-endowed, ones who

[2] A. H. Lauchner: "How Can the Junior High School Curriculum Be Improved?" *Bulletin of the National Association of Secondary-School Principals,* Vol. XXXV (March, 1951), pp. 299–301. The three dots of elision here do not indicate omissions but are the author's punctuation. The address was delivered at a meeting of this association. See Arthur Bestor's comments in *The Restoration of Learning* (New York, 1955), p. 54.

liked them and those who failed to go for them. Teacher has said that these were something "everyone should learn." The principal has remarked, "All educated people know how to write, spell, and read." When some child declared a dislike for a sacred subject, he was warned that, if he failed to master it, he would grow up to be a so-and-so.

The Three R's for All Children, and All Children for the Three R's! That was it.

We've made some progress in getting rid of that slogan. But every now and then some mother with a Phi Beta Kappa award or some employer who has hired a girl who can't spell stirs up a fuss about the schools . . . and ground is lost. . . .

When we come to the realization that not every child has to read, figure, write and spell . . . that many of them either cannot or will not master these chores . . . then we shall be on the road to improving the junior high curriculum.

Between this day and that a lot of selling must take place. But it's coming. We shall some day accept the thought that it is just as illogical to assume that every boy must be able to read as it is that each one must be able to perform on a violin, that it is no more reasonable to require that each girl shall spell well than it is that each one shall bake a good cherry pie.

We cannot all do the same things. We do not like to do the same things. And we won't. When adults finally realize that fact, everyone will be happier . . . and schools will be nicer places in which to live. . . .

If and when we are able to convince a few folks that mastery of reading, writing, and arithmetic is not the one road leading to happy, successful living, the next step is to cut down the amount of time and attention devoted to these areas in general junior high-school courses. . . .

One junior high in the East has, after long and careful study, accepted the fact that some twenty percent of their students will not be up to standard in reading . . . and they are doing other things for these boys and girls. That's straight thinking. Contrast that with the junior high which says, "Every student must know the multiplication tables before graduation."

These exhibits, though their sources and intentions are various, collectively display the ideal assumptions of anti-intellectualism. Intellectuals, it may be held, are pretentious, conceited, effeminate, and snobbish; and very likely immoral, dangerous, and subversive. The plain sense of the common man, especially if tested by success in some demanding line of practical work, is an altogether adequate substitute for, if not actually much superior to, formal knowledge and expertise acquired in the schools. Not surprisingly, institutions in which intellectuals tend to be influential, like universities and colleges, are rotten to the core. In any case, the discipline of the heart, and the old-fashioned principles of religion and morality, are more reliable guides to life than an education which aims to produce minds responsive to new trends in thought and art. Even at the level of elementary education, a schooling that puts too much stress on the acquisition of mere knowledge, as opposed to the vigorous development of physical and emotional life, is heartless in its mode of conduct and threatens to produce social decadence.

· 4 ·

To avoid some hazards to understanding, it is perhaps necessary to say that a work given single-mindedly to the exploration of such a theme as this must inevitably have the effect of highlighting its importance in a way that would not be warranted in a comprehensive history of American culture. I can only say that I do not suffer from the delusion that the complexities of American history can be satisfactorily reduced to a running battle between the eggheads and the fatheads. Moreover, to the extent that our history can be considered one of cultural and intellectual conflicts, the public is not simply divided into intellectual and anti-intellectual factions. The greater part of the public, and a great part even of the intelligent and alert public, is simply non-intellectual; it is infused with enough ambivalence about intellect and intellectuals to be swayed now this way and now that on current cultural issues. It has an ingrained distrust of eggheads, but also a genuine yearning for enlightenment and culture. Moreover, a book on anti-intellectualism in America can hardly be taken as though it were meant to be a balanced assessment of our culture, any more than a history of bankruptcies could be taken as a full history of our business life. Although I am convinced that anti-intellectualism is pervasive in our culture, I believe that it can rarely be called dominant. Again and again I have noticed, as I hope readers will, that the more mild and benign forms of anti-intellectualism prove to be the most widespread, whereas the most malign forms are found mainly among small if vociferous minority groups. Again, this is not, as it perhaps should be, a comparative study: my concentration on anti-intellectualism in the United States is no more than the result of a special, and possibly parochial, interest in American society. I do not assume that anti-intellectualism does not exist elsewhere. I think that it is a problem of more than ordinary acuteness here, but I believe it has been present in some form and degree in most societies; in one it takes the form of the administering of hemlock, in another of town-and-gown riots, in another of censorship and regimentation, in still another of Congressional investigations. I am disposed to believe that anti-intellectualism, though it has its own universality, may be considered a part of our English cultural inheritance, and that it is notably strong in Anglo-American experience. A few years ago Leonard Woolf remarked that "no people has ever despised and distrusted the intellect and intellectuals more than the British."[3] Perhaps Mr. Woolf had not given sufficient thought to the claims of the Americans to supremacy in this respect (which is understandable, since the British have been tired for more than a century of American boasting); but that a British intellectual so long seasoned and so well informed on the cultural life of his own country could have made such a remark may well give us pause. Although the situation of American intellectuals poses problems of special urgency and poignancy, many of their woes are the common experiences of intellectuals elsewhere, and there are some compensating circumstances in American life.

This book is a critical inquiry, not a legal brief for the intellectuals against the American community. I have no desire to encourage the self-pity to which intellectuals are sometimes prone by suggesting that they have been vessels of pure virtue set down in Babylon. One does not need to assert this, or to assert that intellectuals should get sweeping indulgence or exercise great power, in order to insist that respect for intellect and its functions is important to the culture and the health of any society, and that in ours this respect has often been notably lacking. No one who lives among intellectuals is likely to idealize them unduly; but their relation as fallible persons to the vital function of intellect should remind us of the wisdom of the Church, which holds that although the priesthood is vulnerable to the errors

[3] "G. E. Moore," *Encounter*, Vol. XII (January, 1959), p. 68; the context, it should be said, suggests that Woolf was quite aware of the necessary qualifications to this remark.

and sins of the flesh, the Church itself remains holy. Even here, however, I do not forget that intellect itself can be overvalued, and that
reasonable attempts to set it in its proper place in human affairs
should not be called anti-intellectual. One does not care to dissent
when T. S. Eliot observes that "intellectual ability without the more
human attributes is admirable only in the same way as the brilliance
of a child chess prodigy." [4] But in a world full of dangers, the danger
that American society as a whole will overesteem intellect or assign
it such a transcendent value as to displace other legitimate values is
one that need hardly trouble us.

Possibly the greatest hazard of this venture is that of encouraging
the notion that anti-intellectualism is commonly found in a pure or
unmixed state. It seems clear that those who have some quarrel with
intellect are almost always ambivalent about it: they mix respect and
awe with suspicion and resentment; and this has been true in many
societies and phases of human history. In any case, anti-intellectualism
is not the creation of people who are categorically hostile to ideas.
Quite the contrary: just as the most effective enemy of the educated
man may be the half-educated man, so the leading anti-intellectuals
are usually men deeply engaged with ideas, often obsessively engaged
with this or that outworn or rejected idea. Few intellectuals are without
moments of anti-intellectualism; few anti-intellectuals without single-
minded intellectual passions. In so far as anti-intellectualism becomes
articulate enough to be traced historically or widespread enough to
make itself felt in contemporary controversy, it has to have spokesmen
who are at least to some degree competent. These spokesmen are in
the main neither the uneducated nor the unintellectual, but rather the
marginal intellectuals, would-be intellectuals, unfrocked or embittered
intellectuals, the literate leaders of the semi-literate, full of seriousness
and high purpose about the causes that bring them to the attention of
the world. I have found anti-intellectual leaders who were evangelical
ministers, many of them highly intelligent and some even learned;
fundamentalists, articulate about their theology; politicians, including
some of the shrewdest; businessmen or other spokesmen of the practical demands of American culture; right-wing editors of strong intellectual pretensions and convictions; various marginal writers (*vide*
the anti-intellectualism of the Beatniks); anti-Communist pundits, offended by the past heresies of a large segment of the intellectual community; and, for that matter, Communist leaders, who had much use

[4] *Notes towards the Definition of Culture* (London, 1948), p. 23.

for intellectuals when they could *use* them, but the utmost contempt for what intellectuals are concerned with. The hostility so prominent in the temper of these men is not directed against ideas as such, not even in every case against intellectuals as such. The spokesmen of anti-intellectualism are almost always devoted to some ideas, and much as they may hate the regnant intellectuals among their living contemporaries, they may be devotees of some intellectuals long dead —Adam Smith perhaps, or Thomas Aquinas, or John Calvin, or even Karl Marx.

It would also be mistaken, as well as uncharitable, to imagine that the men and women who from time to time carry the banners of anti-intellectualism are of necessity committed to it as though it were a positive creed or a kind of principle. In fact, anti-intellectualism is usually the incidental consequence of some other intention, often some justifiable intention. Hardly anyone believes himself to be against thought and culture. Men do not rise in the morning, grin at themselves in their mirrors, and say: "Ah, today I shall torment an intellectual and strangle an idea!" Only rarely, and with the gravest of misgivings, then, can we designate an individual as being constitutionally anti-intellectual. In any case, it would be of little value in this enterprise—and certainly it is no concern of mine—to classify or stigmatize individuals; what is important is to estimate the historical tendency of certain attitudes, movements, and ideas.[5] With respect to these, some individuals will appear now on one side and now on another. In fact, anti-intellectualism is often characteristic of forces diametrically opposed to each other. Businessmen and labor leaders may have views of the intellectual class which are surprisingly similar. Again, progressive education has had its own strong anti-intellectual element, and yet its harshest and most determined foes, who are right-wing vigilantes, manifest their own anti-intellectualism, which is, though different in style, less equivocal and more militant.

To be confronted with a simple and unqualified evil is no doubt a kind of luxury; but such is not the case here; and if anti-intellectualism has become, as I believe it has, a broadly diffused quality in our civilization, it has become so because it has often been linked to good, or at least defensible, causes. It first got its strong grip on our ways of thinking because it was fostered by an evangelical religion that

[5] As a case in point, I have found it desirable to discuss the anti-intellectual implications and the anti-intellectual consequences of some educational theories of John Dewey; but it would be absurd and impertinent to say, on this account, that Dewey was *an* anti-intellectual.

also purveyed many humane and democratic sentiments. It made its way into our politics because it became associated with our passion for equality. It has become formidable in our education partly because our educational beliefs are evangelically egalitarian. Hence, as far as possible, our anti-intellectualism must be excised from the benevolent impulses upon which it lives by constant and delicate acts of intellectual surgery which spare these impulses themselves. Only in this way can anti-intellectualism be checked and contained; I do not say eliminated altogether, for I believe not only that this is beyond our powers but also that an unbridled passion for the total elimination of this or that evil can be as dangerous as any of the delusions of our time.

CHAPTER II

On the Unpopularity
of Intellect

❦

· 1 ·

Before attempting to estimate the qualities in our society that make intellect unpopular, it seems necessary to say something about what intellect is usually understood to be. When one hopes to understand a common prejudice, common usage provides a good place to begin. Anyone who scans popular American writing with this interest in mind will be struck by the manifest difference between the idea of intellect and the idea of intelligence. The first is frequently used as a kind of epithet, the second never. No one questions the value of intelligence; as an abstract quality it is universally esteemed, and individuals who seem to have it in exceptional degree are highly regarded. The man of intelligence is always praised; the man of intellect is sometimes also praised, especially when it is believed that intellect involves intelligence, but he is also often looked upon with resentment or suspicion. It is he, and not the intelligent man, who may be called unreliable, superfluous, immoral, or subversive; sometimes he is even said to be, for all his intellect, unintelligent.[1]

Although the difference between the qualities of intelligence and intellect is more often assumed than defined, the context of popular

---

[1] I do not want to suggest that this distinction is made only in the United States, since it seems to be common wherever there is a class that finds intellectuals a nuisance and yet does not want to throw overboard its own claims to intelligence. Thus, in France, after the intellectuals had emerged as a kind of social force, one finds Maurice Barrès writing in 1902: "I'd rather be intelligent than an intellectual." Victor Brombert: *The Intellectual Hero: Studies in the French Novel, 1880–1955* (Philadelphia, 1961), p. 25.

usage makes it possible to extract the nub of the distinction, which seems to be almost universally understood: intelligence is an excellence of mind that is employed within a fairly narrow, immediate, and predictable range; it is a manipulative, adjustive, unfailingly practical quality—one of the most eminent and endearing of the animal virtues. Intelligence works within the framework of limited but clearly stated goals, and may be quick to shear away questions of thought that do not seem to help in reaching them. Finally, it is of such universal use that it can daily be seen at work and admired alike by simple or complex minds.

Intellect, on the other hand, is the critical, creative, and contemplative side of mind. Whereas intelligence seeks to grasp, manipulate, re-order, adjust, intellect examines, ponders, wonders, theorizes, criticizes, imagines. Intelligence will seize the immediate meaning in a situation and evaluate it. Intellect evaluates evaluations, and looks for the meanings of situations as a whole. Intelligence can be praised as a quality in animals; intellect, being a unique manifestation of human dignity, is both praised and assailed as a quality in men. When the difference is so defined, it becomes easier to understand why we sometimes say that a mind of admittedly penetrating intelligence is relatively unintellectual; and why, by the same token, we see among minds that are unmistakably intellectual a considerable range of intelligence.

This distinction may seem excessively abstract, but it is frequently illustrated in American culture. In our education, for example, it has never been doubted that the selection and development of intelligence is a goal of central importance; but the extent to which education should foster intellect has been a matter of the most heated controversy, and the opponents of intellect in most spheres of public education have exercised preponderant power. But perhaps the most impressive illustration arises from a comparison of the American regard for inventive skill as opposed to skill in pure science. Our greatest inventive genius, Thomas A. Edison, was all but canonized by the American public, and a legend has been built around him. One cannot, I suppose, expect that achievements in pure science would receive the same public applause that came to inventions as spectacular and as directly influential on ordinary life as Edison's. But one might have expected that our greatest genius in pure science, Josiah Willard Gibbs, who laid the theoretical foundations for modern physical chemistry, would have been a figure of some comparable acclaim among the educated public. Yet Gibbs, whose work was celebrated in Europe, lived out his life in public and even professional obscurity at Yale, where he taught for thirty-two years. Yale, which led American universities in its scientific achievements during the nineteenth century, was unable in those thirty-two years to provide him with more than a half dozen or so graduate students who could understand his work, and never took the trouble to award him an honorary degree.[2]

A special difficulty arises when we speak of the fate of intellect in society; this difficulty stems from the fact that we are compelled to speak of intellect in vocational terms, though we may recognize that intellect is not simply a matter of vocation. Intellect is considered in general usage to be an attribute of certain professions and vocations; we speak of the intellectual as being a writer or a critic, a professor or a scientist, an editor, journalist, lawyer, clergyman, or the like. As Jacques Barzun has said, the intellectual is a man who carries a brief case. It is hardly possible to dispense with this convenience; the status and the role of intellectuals are bound up with the aggregate of the brief-case-carrying professions. But few of us believe that a member of a profession, even a learned profession, is necessarily an intellectual in any discriminating or demanding sense of the word. In most professions intellect may help, but intelligence will serve well enough without it. We know, for instance, that all academic men are not intellectuals; we often lament this fact. We know that there is something about intellect, as opposed to professionally trained intelligence, which does not adhere to whole vocations but only to persons. And when we are troubled about the position of intellect and the intellectual class in our society, it is not only the status of certain vocational groups which we have in mind, but the value attached to a certain mental quality.

A great deal of what might be called the journeyman's work of our culture—the work of lawyers, editors, engineers, doctors, indeed of some writers and of most professors—though vitally dependent upon ideas, is not distinctively intellectual. A man in any of the learned or quasi-learned professions must have command of a substantial store of frozen ideas to do his work; he must, if he does it well, use them intelligently; but in his professional capacity he uses them mainly as

[2] The situation of Gibbs is often mentioned as a consequence of American attitudes. For the general situation it symbolized, see Richard H. Shryock: "American Indifference to Basic Science during the Nineteenth Century," *Archives Internationales d'Histoire des Sciences,* No. 5 (1948), pp. 50–65.

instruments. The heart of the matter—to borrow a distinction made by Max Weber about politics—is that the professional man lives *off* ideas, not *for* them. His professional role, his professional skills, do not make him an intellectual. He is a mental worker, a technician. He may *happen* to be an intellectual as well, but if he is, it is because he brings to his profession a distinctive feeling about ideas which is not required by his job. As a professional, he has acquired a stock of mental skills that are for sale. The skills are highly developed, but we do not think of him as being an intellectual if certain qualities are missing from his work—disinterested intelligence, generalizing power, free speculation, fresh observation, creative novelty, radical criticism. At home he may happen to be an intellectual, but at his job he is a hired mental technician who uses his mind for the pursuit of externally determined ends. It is this element—the fact that ends are set from some interest or vantage point outside the intellectual process itself—which characterizes both the zealot, who lives obsessively for a single idea, and the mental technician, whose mind is used not for free speculation but for a salable end. The goal here is external and not self-determined, whereas the intellectual life has a certain spontaneous character and inner determination. It has also a peculiar poise of its own, which I believe is established by a balance between two basic qualities in the intellectual's attitude toward ideas—qualities that may be designated as playfulness and piety.

To define what is distinctively intellectual it is necessary to be able to determine what differentiates, say, a professor or a lawyer who is an intellectual from one who is not; or perhaps more properly, what enables us to say that at one moment a professor or a lawyer is acting in a purely routine professional fashion and at another moment as an intellectual. The difference is not in the character of the ideas with which he works but in his attitude toward them. I have suggested that in some sense he lives for ideas—which means that he has a sense of dedication to the life of the mind which is very much like a religious commitment. This is not surprising, for in a very important way the role of the intellectual is inherited from the office of the cleric: it implies a special sense of the ultimate value in existence of the act of comprehension. Socrates, when he said that the unexamined life is not worth living, struck the essence of it. We can hear the voices of various intellectuals in history repeating their awareness of this feeling, in accents suitable to time, place, and culture. "The proper function of the human race, taken in the aggregate," wrote Dante in *De Mon-*

archia, "is to actualize continually the entire capacity possible to the intellect, primarily in speculation, then through its extension and for its sake, secondarily in action." The noblest thing, and the closest possible to divinity, is thus the act of knowing. It is only a somewhat more secular and activist version of the same commitment which we hear in the first sentence of Locke's *Essay Concerning Human Understanding:* "It is the *understanding* that sets man above the rest of sensible beings, and gives him all the advantage and dominion which he has over them." Hawthorne, in a passage near the end of *The Blithedale Romance,* observes that Nature's highest purpose for man is "that of conscious intellectual life and sensibility." Finally, in our own time André Malraux puts the question in one of his novels: "How can one make the best of one's life?" and answers: "By converting as wide a range of experience as possible into conscious thought."

Intellectualism, though by no means confined to doubters, is often the sole piety of the skeptic. Some years ago a colleague asked me to read a brief essay he had written for students going on to do advanced work in his field. Its ostensible purpose was to show how the life of the mind could be cultivated within the framework of his own discipline, but its effect was to give an intensely personal expression to his dedication to intellectual work. Although it was written by a corrosively skeptical mind, I felt that I was reading a piece of devotional literature in some ways comparable to Richard Steele's *The Tradesman's Calling* or Cotton Mather's *Essays to Do Good,* for in it the intellectual task had been conceived as a *calling,* much in the fashion of the old Protestant writers. His work was undertaken as a kind of devotional exercise, a personal discipline, and to think of it in this fashion was possible because it was more than merely workmanlike and professional: it was work at thinking, work done supposedly in the service of truth. The intellectual life has here taken on a kind of primary moral significance. It is this aspect of the intellectual's feeling about ideas that I call his piety. The intellectual is *engagé*—he is pledged, committed, enlisted. What everyone else is willing to admit, namely that ideas and abstractions are of signal importance in human life, he imperatively feels.

Of course what is involved is more than a purely personal discipline and more than the life of contemplation and understanding itself. For the life of thought, even though it may be regarded as the highest form of human activity, is also a medium through which other values are refined, reasserted, and realized in the human community. Collectively, intellectuals have often tried to serve as the moral antennae of the race, anticipating and if possible clarifying fundamental moral issues before these have forced themselves upon the public consciousness. The thinker feels that he ought to be the special custodian of values like reason and justice which are related to his own search for truth, and at times he strikes out passionately as a public figure because his very identity seems to be threatened by some gross abuse. One thinks here of Voltaire defending the Calas family, of Zola speaking out for Dreyfus, of the American intellectuals outraged at the trial of Sacco and Vanzetti.

It would be unfortunate if intellectuals were alone in their concern for these values, and it is true that their enthusiasm has at times miscarried. But it is also true that intellectuals are properly more responsive to such values than others; and it is the historic glory of the intellectual class of the West in modern times that, of all the classes which could be called in any sense privileged, it has shown the largest and most consistent concern for the well-being of the classes which lie below it in the social scale. Behind the intellectual's feeling of commitment is the belief that in some measure the world should be made responsive to his capacity for rationality, his passion for justice and order: out of this conviction arises much of his value to mankind and, equally, much of his ability to do mischief.

· 2 ·

The very suggestion that the intellectual has a distinctive capacity for mischief, however, leads to the consideration that his piety, by itself, is not enough. He may live for ideas, as I have said, but something must prevent him from living for *one idea*, from becoming obsessive or grotesque. Although there have been zealots whom we may still regard as intellectuals, zealotry is a defect of the breed and not of the essence. When one's concern for ideas, no matter how dedicated and sincere, reduces them to the service of some central limited preconception or some wholly external end, intellect gets swallowed by fanaticism. If there is anything more dangerous to the life of the mind than having no independent commitment to ideas, it is having an excess of commitment to some special and constricting idea. The effect is as observable in politics as in theology: the intellectual function can be overwhelmed by an excess of piety expended within too contracted a frame of reference.

Piety, then, needs a counterpoise, something to prevent it from being exercised in an excessively rigid way; and this it has, in most intellectual temperaments, in the quality I would call playfulness. We speak of the play of the mind; and certainly the intellectual relishes the play of the mind for its own sake, and finds in it one of the major values in life. What one thinks of here is the element of sheer delight in intellectual activity. Seen in this guise, intellect may be taken as the healthy animal spirits of the mind, which come into exercise when the surplus of mental energies is released from the tasks required for utility and mere survival. "Man is perfectly human," said Schiller, "only when he plays." And it is this awareness of an available surplus beyond the requirements of mere existence that his maxim conveys to us. Veblen spoke often of the intellectual faculty as "idle curiosity"— but this is a misnomer in so far as the curiosity of the playful mind is inordinately restless and active. This very restlessness and activity gives a distinctive cast to its view of truth and its discontent with dogmas.

Ideally, the pursuit of truth is said to be at the heart of the intellectual's business, but this credits his business too much and not quite enough. As with the pursuit of happiness, the pursuit of truth is itself gratifying whereas the consummation often turns out to be elusive. Truth captured loses its glamor; truths long known and widely believed have a way of turning false with time; easy truths are a bore, and too many of them become half-truths. Whatever the intellectual is too certain of, if he is healthily playful, he begins to find unsatisfactory. The meaning of his intellectual life lies not in the possession of truth but in the quest for new uncertainties. Harold Rosenberg summed up this side of the life of the mind supremely well when he said that the intellectual is one who turns answers into questions.

This element of playfulness infuses products of mind as diverse as Abelard's *Sic et Non* and a dadaist poem. But in using the terms *play* and *playfulness,* I do not intend to suggest any lack of seriousness; quite the contrary. Anyone who has watched children, or adults, at play will recognize that there is no contradiction between play and seriousness, and that some forms of play induce a measure of grave concentration not so readily called forth by work. And playfulness does not imply the absence of practicality. In American public discussion one of the tests to which intellect is constantly submitted when it is, so to speak, on trial is this criterion of practicality. But in principle intellect is neither practical nor impractical; it is extra-practical.

To the zealot overcome by his piety and to the journeyman of ideas concerned only with his marketable mental skills, the beginning and end of ideas lies in their efficacy with respect to some goal external to intellectual processes. The intellectual is not in the first instance concerned with such goals. This is not to say that he scorns the practical: the intrinsic intellectual interest of many practical problems is utterly absorbing. Still less is it to say that he is impractical; he is simply concerned with something else, a quality in problems that is not defined by asking whether or not they have practical purpose. The notion that the intellectual is inherently impractical will hardly bear analysis (one can think so readily of intellectuals who, like Adam Smith, Thomas Jefferson, Robert Owen, Walter Rathenau, or John Maynard Keynes, have been eminently practical in the politician's or businessman's sense of the term). However, practicality is not the essence of his interest in ideas. Acton put this view in rather an extreme form when he said: "I think our studies ought to be all but purposeless. They want to be pursued with chastity, like mathematics."

An example of the intellectual's view of the purely practical is the response of James Clerk Maxwell, the mathematician and theoretical physicist, to the invention of the telephone. Asked to give a lecture on the workings of this new instrument, Maxwell began by saying how difficult it had been to believe, when word first came about it from America, that such a thing had actually been devised. But then, he went on, "when at last this little instrument appeared, consisting, as it does, of parts, every one of which is familiar to us, and capable of being put together by an amateur, the disappointment arising from its humble appearance was only partially relieved on finding that it was really able to talk." Perhaps, then, this regrettable appearance of simplicity might be redeemed by the presence somewhere of "some recondite physical principle, the study of which might worthily occupy an hour's time of an academic audience." But no; Maxwell had not met a single person who was unable to understand the physical processes involved, and even the science reporters for the daily press had almost got it right! [3] The thing was a disappointing bore; it was not recondite, not difficult, not profound, not complex; it was not *intellectually* new.

Maxwell's reaction does not seem to me to be entirely admirable. In looking at the telephone from the point of view of a pure scientist,

[3] W. D. Niven, ed.: *The Scientific Papers of James Clerk Maxwell* (Cambridge, 1890), Vol. II, p. 742.

and not as a historian or a sociologist or even a householder, he was restricting the range of his fancy. Commercially, historically, humanly, the telephone was exciting; and its possibilities as an instrument of communication and even of torture surely might have opened vistas to the imagination. But within his self-limited sphere of concern, that of physics, Maxwell was speaking with a certain stubborn daring about the intellectual interest in the matter. For him, thinking as a physicist, the new instrument offered no possibilities for play.

One may well ask if there is not a certain fatal contradiction between these two qualities of the intellectual temperament, playfulness and piety. Certainly there is a tension between them, but it is anything but fatal: it is just one of those tensions in the human character that evoke a creative response. It is, in fact, the ability to comprehend and express not only different but opposing points of view, to identify imaginatively with or even to embrace within oneself contrary feelings and ideas that gives rise to first-rate work in all areas of humanistic expression and in many fields of inquiry. Human beings are tissues of contradictions, and the life even of the intellectual is not logic, to borrow from Holmes, but experience. Contemplate the intellectuals of the past or those in one's neighborhood: some will come to mind in whom the note of playfulness is dominant; others who are conspicuously pious. But in most intellectuals each of these characteristics is qualified and held in check by the other. The tensile strength of the thinker may be gauged by his ability to keep an equipoise between these two sides of his mind. At one end of the scale, an excess of playfulness may lead to triviality, to the dissipation of intellectual energies on mere technique, to dilettantism, to the failure of creative effort. At the other, an excess of piety leads to rigidity, to fanaticism, to messianism, to ways of life which may be morally mean or morally magnificent but which in either case are not the ways of intellect.[4]

Historically, it may be useful to fancy playfulness and piety as being

[4] It was part of the indictment by Julien Benda in *La Trahison des Clercs* (1927) that so many modern intellectuals had given themselves over to this kind of messianic politics to the grave loss of intellectual values: "Today, if we mention Mommsen, Treitschke, Ostwald, Brunetière, Barrès, Lemaître, Péguy, Maurras, d'Annunzio, Kipling, we have to admit that the 'clerks' now exercise political passions with all the characteristics of passion—the tendency to action, the thirst for immediate results, the exclusive preoccupation with the desired end, the scorn for argument, the excess, the hatred, the fixed ideas." (Translated by Richard Aldington as *The Betrayal of the Intellectuals*, Boston, 1955, p. 32.)

the respective residues of the aristocratic and the priestly backgrounds of the intellectual function. The element of play seems to be rooted in the ethos of the leisure class, which has always been central in the history of creative imagination and humanistic learning. The element of piety is reminiscent of the priestly inheritance of the intellectuals: the quest for and the possession of truth was a holy office. As their legatee, the modern intellectual inherits the vulnerability of the aristocrat to the animus of puritanism and egalitarianism and the vulnerability of the priest to anticlericalism and popular assaults upon hierarchy. We need not be surprised, then, if the intellectual's position has rarely been comfortable in a country which is, above all others, the home of the democrat and the antinomian.

It is a part of the intellectual's tragedy that the things he most values about himself and his work are quite unlike those society values in him. Society values him because he can in fact be used for a variety of purposes, from popular entertainment to the design of weapons. But it can hardly understand so well those aspects of his temperament which I have designated as essential to his intellectualism. His playfulness, in its various manifestations, is likely to seem to most men a perverse luxury; in the United States the play of the mind is perhaps the only form of play that is not looked upon with the most tender indulgence. His piety is likely to seem nettlesome, if not actually dangerous. And neither quality is considered to contribute very much to the practical business of life.

· 3 ·

I have suggested that one of the first questions asked in America about intellect and intellectuals concerns their practicality. One reason why anti-intellectualism has changed in our time is that our sense of the impracticality of intellect has been transformed. During the nineteenth century, when business criteria dominated American culture almost without challenge, and when most business and professional men attained eminence without much formal education, academic schooling was often said to be useless. It was assumed that schooling existed not to cultivate certain distinctive qualities of mind but to make personal advancement possible. For this purpose, an immediate engagement with the practical tasks of life was held to be more usefully educative, whereas intellectual and cultural pursuits were called unworldly, unmasculine, and impractical. In spite of the coarse and philistine rhetoric in which this contention was very often stated, it had a certain rude correspondence to the realities and demands of American life. This skepticism about formally cultivated intellect lived on into the twentieth century. But in our time, of course, American society has grown greatly in complexity and in involvement with the rest of the world. In most areas of life a formal training has become a prerequisite to success. At the same time, the complexity of modern life has steadily whittled away the functions the ordinary citizen can intelligently and comprehendingly perform for himself. In the original American populistic dream, the omnicompetence of the common man was fundamental and indispensable. It was believed that he could, without much special preparation, pursue the professions and run the government. Today he knows that he cannot even make his breakfast without using devices, more or less mysterious to him, which expertise has put at his disposal; and when he sits down to breakfast and looks at his morning newspaper, he reads about a whole range of vital and intricate issues and acknowledges, if he is candid with himself, that he has not acquired competence to judge most of them.

In the practical world of affairs, then, trained intelligence has come to be recognized as a force of overwhelming importance. What used to be a jocular and usually benign ridicule of intellect and formal training has turned into a malign resentment of the intellectual in his capacity as expert. The old idea of the woolly-minded intellectual, so aptly caught in the stereotype of the absent-minded professor, still survives, of course; but today it is increasingly a wishful and rather wistful defense against a deep and important fear. Once the intellectual was gently ridiculed because he was not needed; now he is fiercely resented because he is needed too much. He has become all too practical, all too effective. He is the object of resentment because of an improvement, not a decline, in his fortunes. It is not his abstractness, futility, or helplessness that makes him prominent enough to inspire virulent attacks, but his achievements, his influence, his real comfort and imagined luxury, as well as the dependence of the community upon his skills. Intellect is resented as a form of power or privilege.

It may be said at once that what we really have in mind here is not so much the intellectual as the expert; that many intellectuals are not experts with an important role in public life and that many of them do not impinge very forcefully upon the public consciousness.[5] This is beyond argument; but my point is that the prevailing attitude toward intellectuals is set largely by those intellectuals who do so impinge. In the main, intellectuals affect the public mind when they act in one of two capacities: as experts or as ideologues. In both capacities they evoke profound, and, in a measure, legitimate, fears and resentments. Both intensify the prevalent sense of helplessness in our society, the expert by quickening the public's resentment of being the object of constant manipulation, the ideologue by arousing the fear of subversion and by heightening all the other grave psychic stresses that have come with modernity.

For almost thirty years anyone even moderately informed about public affairs has had to become aware of the machinery through which the expert was making himself felt. At first, during the New Deal the well-publicized brain trust and all the ramifying agencies of control were set up to cope with the depression, and during the war there were the Office of Strategic Services and the Office of Scientific Research and Development. Today the C.I.A., the A.E.C., the Rand Corporation, the President's Council of Economic Advisers, and all the agencies that conduct research on the instruments and strategy of war deal with issues which are beyond the reach of the ordinary man's scrutiny but which can, and often do, determine his fate. A large segment of the public willingly resigns itself to political passivity in a world in which it cannot expect to make well-founded judgments. But in the management of public affairs and private business, where small politicians and small businessmen used to feel that most matters were within their control, these men have been forced, since the days of F.D.R., to confront better educated and more sophisticated experts, to their continuing frustration. Along with the general public, such men now take part less vitally and less knowledgeably in the making of important decisions; the less they understand the inner world of power, the more apt they are to share and arouse popular suspicions of the uses to which power is put. The small-town lawyers and busi-

---

[5] A great deal of internal discussion is heard in the intellectual community as to whether the development of expertise is not also dangerous for intellectuals. The question has been asked whether the intellectual's position as an expert does not in fact destroy his intellectual function by reducing him to a mere mental technician. See, for example, H. Stuart Hughes: "Is the Intellectual Obsolete?" in *An Approach to Peace and Other Essays* (New York, 1962), chapter 10. I shall return to this problem in my final chapter.

nessmen who are elected to Congress cannot hope to expropriate the experts from their central advisory role, but they can achieve a kind of revenge through Congressional investigation and harassment, and, understandably, they carry on this task full of a sense of virtuous mission. There have been, after all, innumerable defeats and failures of expert-initiated policy, and these failures loom in the eyes of millions as the consequences not simply of human error but of cold and cynical manipulation, conspiracy, even treason. The public careers of Alger Hiss and others have given them symbols to which this feeling can be attached, and a few spectacular instances of demonstrated espionage involving scientific knowledge seem to substantiate their image of a world run by the power of secrets and swarming with the stealers of secrets.[6]

The advice of experts in the physical sciences, however suspect many of these experts may be, is accepted as indispensable. Expertise in the social sciences, on the other hand, may be rejected as gratuitous and foolish, if not ominous. One Congressman objected in these words to including the social sciences in the National Science Foundation: [7]

> Outside of myself, I think everyone else thinks he is a social scientist. I am sure that I am not, but I think everyone else seems to believe that he has some particular God-given right to decide what other people ought to do. . . . The average American does not want some expert running around prying into his life and his personal affairs and deciding for him how he should live, and if the impression becomes prevalent in the Congress that this legislation is going to establish some sort of an organization in which there would be a lot of short-haired women and long-haired men messing into everybody's personal affairs and lives, inquiring whether they love their wives or do not love them and so forth, you are not going to get your legislation.

From the politician's point of view, experts were irritating enough in the time of F.D.R., when they seemed to have free access to the White House while the President kept the politicians at arm's length. The situation has grown worse in the age of the cold war, when mat-

---

[6] The atmosphere in which popular politicians confront experts has been explored with much insight by Edward Shils: *The Torment of Secrecy* (Glencoe, Illinois, 1956).

[7] Testimony before a subcommittee of the Committee on Interstate and Foreign Commerce, House of Representatives, 79th Congress, 2nd session, May 28 and 29, 1946, pp. 11, 13.

ters of the highest public interest are susceptible to judgment only by specialists. All this is the more maddening, as Edward Shils has pointed out, in a populistic culture which has always set a premium on government by the common man and through the common judgment and which believes deeply in the sacred character of publicity. Here the politician expresses what a large part of the public feels. The citizen cannot cease to need or to be at the mercy of experts, but he can achieve a kind of revenge by ridiculing the wild-eyed professor, the irresponsible brain truster, or the mad scientist, and by applauding the politicians as they pursue the subversive teacher, the suspect scientist, or the allegedly treacherous foreign-policy adviser. There has always been in our national experience a type of mind which elevates hatred to a kind of creed; for this mind, group hatreds take a place in politics similar to the class struggle in some other modern societies. Filled with obscure and ill-directed grievances and frustrations, with elaborate hallucinations about secrets and conspiracies, groups of malcontents have found scapegoats at various times in Masons or abolitionists, Catholics, Mormons, or Jews, Negroes or immigrants, the liquor interests or the international bankers. In the succession of scapegoats chosen by the followers of this tradition of Know-Nothingism, the intelligentsia have at last in our time found a place.

If some large part of the anti-intellectualism of our time stems from the public's shock at the constant insinuation of the intellectual as expert into public affairs, much of the sensitiveness of intellectuals to their reputation as a class stems from the awkward juxtaposition of their sacred and profane roles. In his sacred role, as prophet, scholar, or artist, the intellectual is hedged about by certain sanctions—imperfectly observed and respected of course, but still effective: he has his privacy, perhaps his anonymity, in the interstices of modern urban civilization; he commands a certain respect for what seem to be his self-denying qualities; he benefits, if he is an academic, from the imperfectly established but operative principle of academic freedom; he has foundations, libraries, publishing houses, museums, as well as universities, at his service. There is a certain measured and genteel dignity about his life. If, in his capacity as expert, he assumes a profane role by mixing in public affairs, he may be horrified to realize that, having become a public figure, he too is vulnerable to the low ethics of controversy which prevail in our politics and the low regard for privacy which governs our entire society. He may even forget that the malice and slander to which he is exposed are not peculiarly directed against him or his kind but are of the same order as almost any working politician of prominence may experience; even some of our greatest statesmen—among them Jefferson, Lincoln, and Franklin D. Roosevelt—were not immune. As Emerson once asked: "Is it not the first attribute and distinction of an American to be abused and slandered as long as he is heard of?" [8]

• 4 •

Compared with the intellectual as expert, who must be accepted even when he is feared, the intellectual as ideologist is an object of unqualified suspicion, resentment, and distrust. The expert appears as a threat to dominate or destroy the ordinary individual, but the ideologist is widely believed to have already destroyed a cherished American society. To understand the background of this belief, it is necessary to recall how consistently the intellectual has found himself ranged in politics against the right-wing mind. This is, of course, no peculiarity of American politics. The modern idea of the intellectuals as constituting a class, as a separate social force, even the term *intellectual* itself, is identified with the idea of political and moral protest. In the broadest signification of the term, there have always been intellectuals, but until the emergence of industrial society and of a kind of market place for ideas, there was little sense of the separateness of the intellectual life as a vocation, and relatively little need for the solidarity, much less for the mobilization, of the intellectuals. Thus, for all that they did in the mid-nineteenth century to prepare the way for the Revolutions of 1848, the liberation of the serfs in Russia, or of the slaves in America, there was still at that time no device widely in use in English to account for them as a group.

The term *intellectual* first came into use in France. It was soon exported—at the time of the Dreyfus case, when so large a part of the intellectual community was aroused to protest against the anti-Dreyfus conspiracy and became involved in an ideological holy war on the French reactionaries.[9] At that time the term came to be used by both

[8] *Journals* (Boston, 1909–1914), Vol. IX (July 1862), p. 436.
[9] On the precursors of the term *intellectual*, and its early use in France, see Victor Brombert: *The Intellectual Hero*, chapter 2. The corresponding Russian term, *intelligentsia*, which came into use after the middle of the nineteenth century, originally meant members of the free professions, but it, too, soon took on the connotation of an opponent of the regime. See Hugh Seton-Watson: "The Russian Intellectuals," *Encounter* (September, 1955), pp. 43–50.

sides—by the right as a kind of insult, by the Dreyfusard intellectuals as a proud banner. "Let us use this word," wrote one of them in 1898, "since it has received high consecration." In the following year William James wrote, in a letter referring to the role of the French intellectuals in the Dreyfus affair: "We 'intellectuals' in America must all work to keep our precious birthright of individualism, and freedom from these institutions [church, army, aristocracy, royalty]. *Every* great institution is perforce a means of corruption—whatever good it may also do. Only in the free personal relation is full ideality to be found."[1] It is significant in our own history that this early use of the term—the first in America of which I am aware—should have been made in the context of just such a "radical," utopian, and anti-institutional statement of purpose. At least from the Progressive era onward, the political commitment of the majority of the intellectual leadership in the United States has been to causes that might be variously described as liberal (in the American use of that word), progressive, or radical.[2] (Of course the American political spectrum is rather foreshortened, and its center lies considerably to the right of that of France, but the position of the intellectuals in relation to the center has been similar.) I am not denying that we have had a number of conservative intellectuals and even a few reactionary ones; but if there is anything that could be called an intellectual establishment in America, this establishment has been, though not profoundly radical (which would be unbecoming in an establishment), on the left side of center. And it has drawn the continuing and implacable resentment of the right, which has always liked to blur the distinction between the moderate progressive and the revolutionary.

As long as the progressivism of the intellectual community remained more or less in harmony with a spirit of protest widely shared by the general public, as it did notably during the Progressive era and the New Deal, its vulnerability to the extreme right has been small. But the allegiance of a large part of the intellectual community to Communism and fellow-traveling in the 1930's gave hostage to its right-wing enemies. Here it is important to do justice to a signal element of reality in the anti-intellectuals' case. It will not do to say that the

[1] *The Letters of William James* (Boston, 1920), Vol. II, pp. 100–1.

[2] On this commitment and its effects, see Seymour M. Lipset: "American Intellectuals: Their Politics and Status," *Daedalus* (Summer, 1959), pp. 460–86. Lipset has many pertinent remarks on the position of American intellectuals, but I am not persuaded by his argument that their status can be described, without qualification, as high.

vulnerability of the intellectuals on this count has already been vastly overexploited in right-wing propaganda; or that the extent of Communist sympathies among the intellectuals of the 1930's has been exaggerated; or even that the most decisively influential intellectuals of the past generation were not Communists or fellow travelers. All these propositions are true, but the case that has been so insistently made against the intellectuals rests on the fact that the appeal of Communism during the 1930's was stronger among intellectuals than among any other stratum of the population; and that in a few spectacular instances faith in Communism led to espionage. One must begin, I believe, with the awareness that the intellectual and moral inconsistencies of Communism and fellow-traveling not only put into the hands of the anti-intellectuals a powerful weapon, but that the sense of shame over past credulity and of guilt over past political involvements induced in many intellectuals a kind of paralysis that caused them to be helpless in the face of the Great Inquisition of the 1950's and even at times to indulge in bitter mutual recriminations. One remembers, for example, with some pain and difficulty, that in August 1939, on the eve of the Nazi-Soviet pact, some four hundred liberal intellectuals appended their signatures to a manifesto denouncing the "fantastic falsehood that the U.S.S.R. and the totalitarian states are basically alike," and describing the Soviet Union as a "bulwark" of peace. This document was reproduced in the *Nation* the week that the Hitler-Stalin pact was signed.[3] Intellectuals thus caught out were not in the best historical, moral, or psychological position to make a vigorous response to McCarthyism.

What I believe is important, however, to anyone who hopes to understand the impulse behind American anti-intellectualism is that this grievance against intellectuals as ideologues goes far beyond any reproaches based on actual Communism or fellow-traveling. The practical intellectuals of the New Deal—Rexford Guy Tugwell is the best example—who had nothing to do with the Communists were as objectionable as the fellow travelers. And today, when Communism has been reduced to a negligible quantity in American domestic life, the cry for a revival of this scapegoat is regularly heard in the land, and investigators who are unable to turn up present Communist affiliations have resorted to stirring up the dead husks of fellow-traveling memories or to obscuring as completely as possible the differences between

[3] *Nation*, Vol. 149 (August 19, 1939), p. 228.

liberals and Communists. The truth is that the right-winger needs his Communists badly, and is pathetically reluctant to give them up.[4] The real function of the Great Inquisition of the 1950's was not anything so simply rational as to turn up spies or prevent espionage (for which the police agencies presumably are adequate) or even to expose actual Communists, but to discharge resentments and frustrations, to punish, to satisfy enmities whose roots lay elsewhere than in the Communist issue itself. This was why it showed such a relentless and indiscriminate appetite for victims and why it seemed happier with respectable and powerful targets than with the occasional obscure Bolshevik it turned up. The McCarthyist fellow travelers who announced that they approved of the senator's goals even though they disapproved of his methods missed the point: to McCarthy's true believers what was really appealing about him were his methods, since his goals were always utterly nebulous. To them, his proliferating multiple accusations were a positive good, because they widened the net of suspicion and enabled it to catch many victims who were no longer, or had never been, Communists; his bullying was welcomed because it satisfied a craving for revenge and a desire to discredit the type of leadership the New Deal had made prominent.

Had the Great Inquisition been directed only against Communists, it would have tried to be more precise and discriminating in its search for them: in fact, its leading practitioners seemed to care little for the difference between a Communist and a unicorn. Real Communists were usually too insignificant to warrant lengthy pursuit; McCarthy did not trouble himself much over an obscure radical dentist promoted by the army when he could use the case to strike at the army itself, and beyond the army at the Eisenhower administration. The inquisitors were trying to give satisfaction against liberals, New Dealers, reformers, internationalists, intellectuals, and finally even against a Republican administration that failed to reverse liberal policies. What was involved, above all, was a set of political hostilities in which the New Deal was linked to the welfare state, the welfare state to socialism, and socialism to Communism. In this crusade Communism was not the target but the weapon, and it is for this reason that so many of the most ardent hunters of impotent domestic Communists were

[4] This reluctance has been nowhere more candidly and ingratiatingly expressed than by Senator Barry Goldwater, who affirmed in July 1959: "I am not willing to accept the idea that there are no Communists left in this country; I think that if we lift enough rocks, we will find some." Quoted by James Wechsler: *Reflections of an Angry Middle-Aged Editor* (New York, 1960), p. 44.

altogether indifferent to efforts to meet the power of international Communism where it really mattered—in the arena of world politics.

The deeper historical sources of the Great Inquisition are best revealed by the other enthusiasms of its devotees: hatred of Franklin D. Roosevelt, implacable opposition to New Deal reforms, desire to banish or destroy the United Nations, anti-Semitism, Negrophobia, isolationism, a passion for the repeal of the income tax, fear of poisoning by fluoridation of the water system, opposition to modernism in the churches. McCarthy's own expression, "twenty years of treason," suggested the long-standing grievances that were nursed by the crusaders, though the right-wing spokesman, Frank Chodorov, put it in better perspective when he said that the betrayal of the United States had really begun in 1913 with the passage of the income-tax amendment.

Clearly, something more is at stake for such people than the heresies of the 1930's and the security problems of the cold war—something more even than the terrible frustration of the Korean War: the McCarthyist era brought to a head several forces engaged in a long-standing revolt against modernity. The older America, until the 1890's and in some respects until 1914, was wrapped in the security of continental isolation, village society, the Protestant denominations, and a flourishing industrial capitalism. But reluctantly, year by year, over several decades, it has been drawn into the twentieth century and forced to cope with its unpleasant realities: first the incursions of cosmopolitanism and skepticism, then the disappearance of American isolation and easy military security, the collapse of traditional capitalism and its supplementation by a centralized welfare state, finally the unrelenting costs and stringencies of the Second World War, the Korean War, and the cold war. As a consequence, the heartland of America, filled with people who are often fundamentalist in religion, nativist in prejudice, isolationist in foreign policy, and conservative in economics, has constantly rumbled with an underground revolt against all these tormenting manifestations of our modern predicament.

One cannot, even if one does not like their responses, altogether withhold one's sympathies from the plight of a people, hitherto so preoccupied with internal material development and in many ways so simple, who have been dragged away from their "normal" concerns, thrust into an alien and demanding world, and forced to try to learn so much in so short a time. Perhaps the truly remarkable thing about the most common American response to the modern world has been its patience and generosity. Within only two generations the village

Protestant individualist culture still so widely observable before the First World War was repeatedly shocked by change. It had to confront modernism in religion, literature, and art, relativity in morals, racial equality as a principle of ethics and public law, and the endless sexual titillation of our mass communications. In rapid succession it was forced to confront Darwinism (*vide* the Scopes trial), Freudianism, Marxism, and Keynesianism, and to submit in matters of politics, taste, and conscience to the leadership of a new kind of educated and cosmopolitan American.

The intellectual as ideologist, having had a leading role in purveying to the country each innovation and having frequently hastened the country into the acceptance of change, is naturally felt to have played an important part in breaking the mold in which America was cast, and in consequence he gets more than his share of the blame. In earlier days, after all, it had been our fate as a nation not to have ideologies but to be one. As European antagonisms withered and lost their meaning on American soil in the eighteenth and nineteenth centuries, the new nation came to be conceived not as sharing the ideologies which had grown out of these antagonisms but as offering an alternative to them, as demonstrating that a gift for compromise and plain dealing, a preference for hard work and common sense, were better and more practical than commitments to broad and divisive abstractions. The great American failure, in this respect, the one capitulation to divisive convictions, resulted in the Civil War; and this had the effect of confirming the belief that it was better to live without too much faith in political abstractions and ideological generalities. Americans continued to congratulate themselves on their ability to get on without the benefit of what are commonly called "foreign isms," just as they had always congratulated themselves on their ability to steer clear of European "corruption" and "decadence."

But in the past few decades the American public has become painfully aware that the breakdown of political and military isolation entails a breakdown of intellectual isolationism, that there are at large in the world powerful forces called ideologies whose consequences we cannot escape, that millions of people are everywhere set in motion by convictions about colonialism, racism, nationalism, imperialism, socialism, communism, and fascism. In all this there is a certain irony that we are ill-equipped to appreciate. The original American hope for the world—in so far as the older America thought about the world at all —was that it might save itself by emulating the American system—

that is, by dropping formal ideologies, accepting our type of democracy, applying itself to work and the arduous pursuit of happiness, and by following the dictates of common sense. The irony is that Americans now suffer as much from the victory as from the defeat of their aspirations. What is it that has taken root in the world, if it is not the spirit of American activism, the belief that life can be made better, that colonial peoples can free themselves as the Americans did, that poverty and oppression do not have to be endured, that backward countries can become industrialized and enjoy a high standard of living, that the pursuit of happiness is everybody's business? The very colonial countries that belligerently reject our leadership try to follow our example, and the Russians themselves in the midst of their challenge to American power have not ceased to admire American industrialization. But this emulation has become tinted with ideologies we do not recognize and has brought consequences we never anticipated. The American example of activism has been imitated: what we call the American way of life has not.

To the most insular type of American mind it seemed that only peoples blinded by abstractions and dead to common sense could fail to see and appropriate all the virtues of the American system, and that some fatal complex of moral weaknesses has prevented the systems of foreign societies from working, not least of these being the acceptance of sinister ideologies. But the persistent strength of the Soviet Union, capped by the Sputnik and other triumphs in space, has given a rude shock to this confidence, for the United States is now confronted by a material power strong enough to pose a perpetual and indestructible challenge. What is more, this material power has unmistakably grown up under the stimulus of one of those fatal foreign isms. The American, so ill at ease in this strange, threatening, and seemingly gratuitous world of ideology, suspects the intellectual for being at home in it. The intellectual is even imagined to have called it into being—and in a certain sense he has. Inevitably, he has been made to bear some share of the irritation of those who cannot believe that the changes of the twentieth century are consequences of anything but a sinister campaign of manipulation and design, or at the very least of a series of fatally stupid errors. Perhaps it is he who has shorn us of the qualities upon which our former strength depended. Certainly he has become a figure in the world just at the time when all these unhappy changes have taken place. If he is not exactly guilty, he will still bear watching.

· 5 ·

To those who suspect that intellect is a subversive force in society, it will not do to reply that intellect is really a safe, bland, and emollient thing. In a certain sense the suspicious Tories and militant philistines are right: intellect *is* dangerous. Left free, there is nothing it will not reconsider, analyze, throw into question.[5] "Let us admit the case of the conservative," John Dewey once wrote. "If we once start thinking no one can guarantee what will be the outcome, except that many objects, ends and institutions will be surely doomed. Every thinker puts some portion of an apparently stable world in peril, and no one can wholly predict what will emerge in its place."[6] Further, there is no way of guaranteeing that an intellectual class will be discreet and restrained in the use of its influence; the only assurance that can be given to any community is that it will be far worse off if it denies the free uses of the power of intellect than if it permits them. To be sure, intellectuals, contrary to the fantasies of cultural vigilantes, are hardly ever subversive of a society as a whole. But intellect is always on the move against something: some oppression, fraud, illusion, dogma, or interest is constantly falling under the scrutiny of the intellectual class and becoming the object of exposure, indignation, or ridicule.

In the course of generations, those who have suffered from the operations of intellect, or who have feared or resented it, have developed a kind of counter-mythology about what it is and the role it plays in society. Those who have made their case against intellect in our time have not found it necessary to originate a single new argument, since this mythology is deeply rooted in our historical experience. The chapters that follow illustrate in some detail how this mythology has grown and perpetuated and expressed itself in the United States. But here I should like to state briefly and in general terms what are the perennial assumptions of the anti-intellectualist case, and in what light I think it ought to be regarded.

The case against intellect is founded upon a set of fictional and wholly abstract antagonisms. Intellect is pitted against feeling, on the

[5] And even, it appears, when not left free; witness the considerable intellectual underground that seems to have grown up in the Soviet Union and its Eastern European satellites.

[6] *Characters and Events* (New York, 1929), p. xi.

ground that it is somehow inconsistent with warm emotion. It is pitted against character, because it is widely believed that intellect stands for mere cleverness, which transmutes easily into the sly or the diabolical.[7] It is pitted against practicality, since theory is held to be opposed to practice, and the "purely" theoretical mind is so much disesteemed. It is pitted against democracy, since intellect is felt to be a form of distinction that defies egalitarianism. Once the validity of these antagonisms is accepted, then the case for intellect, and by extension for the intellectual, is lost. Who cares to risk sacrificing warmth of emotion, solidity of character, practical capacity, or democratic sentiment in order to pay deference to a type of man who at best is deemed to be merely clever and at worst may even be dangerous?

Of course the fundamental fallacy in these fictional antagonisms is that they are based not upon an effort to seek out the actual limits of intellect in human life but rather upon a simplified divorce of intellect from all the other human qualities with which it may be combined. Neither in the development of the individual character nor in the course of history are problems posed in such a simple or abstract fashion. For the same reason it would be pointless to accept the form in which the challenge is put and attempt to make a defense of intellect as *against* emotion or character or practicality. Intellect needs to be understood not as some kind of a claim against the other human excellences for which a fatally high price has to be paid, but rather as a complement to them without which they cannot be fully consummated. Few rational men care to deny that the exercise of intellectual power is one of the fundamental manifestations of human dignity or that it is at the very least a legitimate end among the other legitimate ends of life. If mind is seen not as a threat but as a guide to emotion, if intellect is seen neither as a guarantee of character nor as an inevitable danger to it, if theory is conceived as something serviceable but not

---

[7] "We always preferred an ignorant bad man to a talented one," wrote B. R. Hall of early Indiana society, "and hence attempts were usually made to ruin the moral character of a smart candidate; since unhappily smartness and wickedness were supposed to be generally coupled, and incompetence and goodness." Baynard R. Hall: *The New Purchase, or Seven and a Half Years in the Far West* (1843; ed. Princeton, 1916), p. 170. This occurred even among the Puritans, for all their rationalism and intellectualism. Cf. John Cotton: "The more learned and witty you bee, the more fit to act for Satan will you bee. . . . Take off the fond doting . . . upon the learning of the Jesuites, and the glorie of the Episcopacy, and brave estate of the Prelates. I say bee not deceived with these pompes, and empty shewes, and faire representations of a goodly condition before the eyes of flesh and blood, bee not taken with the applause of these persons." *The Powring Out of the Seven Vials* (London, 1642), The Sixth Vial, pp. 39–40.

necessarily subordinate or inferior to practice, and if our democratic aspirations are defined in such realistic and defensible terms as to admit of excellence, all these supposed antagonisms lose their force. Posed in these rather general terms, this fact may seem obvious; but historically it has been obvious to all too few; and the purpose of this book is to trace some of the social movements in our history in which intellect has been dissevered from its co-ordinate place among the human virtues and assigned the position of a special kind of vice.

In the first instance, anti-intellectualism must be sought out in the framework of our religious history. This is not simply because there is a constant historical tension between rationalism and the requirements of faith—though this in itself is an enduring human problem—but because the patterns of modern thought, both religious and secular, are prefigured in our earlier religious history. To the extent that it becomes accepted in any culture that religion is largely an affair of the heart or of the intuitive qualities of mind, and that the rational mind is irrelevant or worse, so far will it be believed that the rational faculties are barren or perhaps dangerous. And to the extent that a society is suspicious of a learned or professional clergy, so far will it be disposed to repudiate or deprive its intellectual class, whether religious or secular. In modern culture the evangelical movement has been the most powerful carrier of this kind of religious anti-intellectualism, and of its antinomian impulse. Of course, America is not the only society whose culture has been affected by evangelicalism. But in America religious culture has been largely shaped by the evangelical spirit, for here the balance of power between evangelicalism and formal religion was long ago overwhelmingly tipped in the direction of the former. To see how much this was true one need only compare the historical development of religion in Britain, where the Establishment was prepared to absorb and domesticate a large part of the evangelical movement, with that of America, where the evangelicals rapidly subverted, outstripped, or overwhelmed the older liturgical churches.

Akin to the spirit of evangelicalism in its effects has been a kind of primitivism which has won extraordinarily wide credence in America and which requires special attention here, in part because I have not dealt with it in this book as a separate force. Primitivism has had its links on one side with Christianity and on another with paganism; and perhaps some of its pervasive appeal may be attributed to the fact that through primitivism one may be a Christian and enjoy the luxury of a touch of paganism; or, contrarywise, that the basically pagan mind may find in primitivism a consoling element of faith. Primitivism has displayed itself in some quarters as a quest for the spirit of primitive Christianity, but also as a demand to recover the powers of "nature" in man; with it one may be close to Nature or to God—the difference is not always wholly clear. But in it there is a persistent preference for the "wisdom" of intuition, which is deemed to be natural or God-given, over rationality, which is cultivated and artificial.

In various guises primitivism has been a constantly recurring force in Western history and in our own national experience. It is likely to become evident wherever men of the intellectual class itself are disappointed with or grow suspicious of the human yield of a rationally ordered life or when they seek to break away from the routine or apathy or refinement that arise with civilization. In America primitivism has affected the thinking of many men too educated and cultivated to run with the frontier revivalists but sympathetic to their underlying distrust for civilized forms. It is visible in Transcendentalism—which sometimes set itself up as the evangelicalism of the highbrows.[8] It is a

---

[8] Cf. George Ripley in his attack of 1839 on Unitarianism and the Harvard faculty of divinity: "I have known great and beneficial effects to arise from the simple exhibition of the truth of the Gospel to the heart and conscience, by earnest men, who trusted to the intuitive power of the soul, for the perception of its divinity. . . . Much as I value a sound logic in its proper place, I am sure it is not the instrument which is mighty through God to the pulling down of the strong holds of sin. It may detect error; but it cannot give so much as a glimpse of the glory of Christ. It may refute fallacies; but it cannot bind the heart to the love of holiness. . . . You maintain, that 'extensive learning' is usually requisite for those who would influence their fellow men on religious subjects. But Jesus certainly did not take this into consideration in the selection of the twelve from the mass of the disciples; he committed the promulgation of his religion to 'unlearned and ignorant' men; the sublimest truths were entrusted to the most common minds; and, in this way, 'God made foolish the wisdom of the world.' . . . Christ . . . saw that the parade of wisdom, which books impart, was as nothing before 'the light that enlighteneth every human mind.' The whole course of his nation's history was an illustration of the fact 'that poor mechanics are wont to be God's great ambassadors to mankind.' . . . Christ established no college of Apostles; he did not revive the school of the prophets which had died out; he paid no distinguished respect to the pride of learning; indeed, he sometimes intimates that it is an obstacle to the perception of truth; and thanks God, that while he has hid the mysteries of the kingdom of Heaven from the wise and prudent, he has made them known to men as ignorant as babes of the lore of the schools." "The Latest Form of Infidelity Examined," *Letters on the Latest Form of Infidelity* (Boston, 1839), pp. 98–9, 111, 112–13.

The argument in this passage is similar to that commonly used by the evangelicals. One begins with the hardly contestable proposition that religious faith is not, in the main, propagated by logic or learning. One moves on from this to the idea that it is best propagated (in the judgment of Christ and on historical evidence) by men who have been unlearned and ignorant. It seems to follow from this that the kind of wisdom and truth possessed by such men is superior to what learned and cultivated minds have. In fact, learning and cultivation appear to be handicaps

powerful force in our historical writing from Parkman and Bancroft to Turner.[9] It is a persistent theme in the attitude of American writers toward Indians and Negroes. It runs through the popular legend of frontier figures such as Daniel Boone and Davy Crockett down to the heroes of modern Western stories and detective fiction—embracing all those lonely adventurers whose cumulative mythology caused D. H. Lawrence to say, in one of his harsh, luminous hyperboles, that the essential American soul is "hard, isolate, stoic, and a killer." As a sexual mystique, it has become a powerful moving force in American letters, taking its most exaggerated form in recent years among those writers who have been impressed by the theories of Wilhelm Reich. It has been a force in American politics, and its effects have been visible in the public images of figures as diverse as Andrew Jackson, John C. Frémont, Theodore Roosevelt, and Dwight D. Eisenhower.

All this is hardly surprising: America was settled by men and women who repudiated European civilization for its oppressiveness or decadence, among other reasons, and who found the most striking thing on the American strand not in the rude social forms that were taking shape here but in the world of nature and of savages. The escape from civilization to Arcadia, from Europe to nature, was perpetuated in repeated escapes from the East to the West, from the settled world to the frontier. Again and again the American mind turned fretfully against the encroachments of organized society, which were felt to be an effort to reimpose what had been once thrown off; for civilization, though it could hardly be repudiated in its entirety, was still believed to have something pernicious about it.

If evangelicalism and primitivism helped to plant anti-intellectualism at the roots of American consciousness, a business society assured that it would remain in the foreground of American thinking. Since the time of Tocqueville it has become a commonplace among students of America that business activism has provided an overwhelming counter-

---

in the propagation of faith. And since the propagation of faith is the most important task before man, those who are as "ignorant as babes" have, in the most fundamental virtue, greater strength than men who have addicted themselves to logic and learning. Accordingly, though one shrinks from a bald statement of the conclusion, humble ignorance is far better as a human quality than a cultivated mind. At bottom, this proposition, despite all the difficulties that attend it, has been eminently congenial both to American evangelicalism and to American democracy.

[9] On primitivism in Turner, see the penetrating final chapter of Henry Nash Smith: *Virgin Land* (Cambridge, Massachusetts, 1950); there are valuable gleanings on American primitivism in Charles L. Sanford: *The Quest for Paradise* (Urbana, Illinois, 1961).

poise to reflection in this country. Tocqueville saw that the life of
constant action and decision which was entailed by the democratic and
businesslike character of American life put a premium upon rough and
ready habits of mind, quick decision, and the prompt seizure of opportunities—and that all this activity was not propitious for delibera-
tion, elaboration, or precision in thought.[1]

The overwhelming demands of the task of winning a continent and
establishing its industries drew men from pursuits where profits and
honors were less available. But there was more to it than this: business
in America at its highest levels appealed not merely to greed and the
lust for power but to the imagination; alluring to the builder, the
gamester, and the ruler in men, it offered more sport than hunting and
more power than politics. As Tocqueville remarked: "In democracies
nothing is greater or more brilliant than commerce," and its devotees
engaged in it, "not only for the sake of the profit it holds out to them,
but for the love of the constant excitement occasioned by that pursuit." [2] Except in a few older communities, there were no countervailing classes or sets of values—no aristocracy to marry into, no formidable
body of national aspirations outside business aspirations. Business not
only appealed to vigorous and ambitious men but set the dominant
standards for the rest of society, so that members of the professions—
law, medicine, schoolteaching, even the ministry—aped businessmen
and adapted the standards of their own crafts to those of business. It
has in fact been one of the perennial complaints of intellectuals in
America that they cannot have much rapport with the professional
classes as such, because these have been swung into the business orbit.
It was business, finally, that isolated and feminized culture by establishing the masculine legend that men are not concerned with the
events of the intellectual and cultural world. Such matters were to be
left to women—all too often to the type of women of whom Edith
Wharton said that they were so afraid to meet culture alone that they
hunted it in packs.

Both our religion and our business have been touched by the pervasive and aggressive egalitarianism of American life, but the egalitarian spirit is still more effective in politics and education.[3] What we

---

[1] *Democracy in America*, Vol. II, pp. 525–6.

[2] Ibid., pp. 642–3.

[3] Observers of American academia have often asked with some bitterness why
athletic distinction is almost universally admired and encouraged whereas intellectual distinction is resented. I think the resentment is in fact a kind of back-
handed tribute democracy pays to the importance of intellect in our affairs. Ath-

loosely call Jacksonian democracy completed the disestablishment of a patrician leadership that had been losing its grip for some time. At an early date, literature and learning were stigmatized as the prerogative of useless aristocracies—and the argument was not pressed any the less firmly because a large part of the American intellectual class actually supported democratic causes. It seemed to be the goal of the common man in America to build a society that would show how much could be done without literature and learning—or rather, a society whose literature and learning would be largely limited to such elementary things as the common man could grasp and use. Hence, early nineteenth-century America was more noted for a wide range of literacy and for the unusual amount of information, independence, self-respect, and public concern possessed by the ordinary citizen than it was for the encouragement of first-rate science or letters or for the creation of first-rate universities.

Again and again, but particularly in recent years, it has been noticed that intellect in America is resented as a kind of excellence, as a claim to distinction, as a challenge to egalitarianism, as a quality which almost certainly deprives a man or woman of the common touch. The phenomenon is most impressive in education itself. American education can be praised, not to say defended, on many counts; but I believe ours is the only educational system in the world vital segments of which have fallen into the hands of people who joyfully and militantly proclaim their hostility to intellect and their eagerness to identify with children who show the least intellectual promise. The final segments of this book, though necessarily fragmentary as history, will show how this educational force has been built upon widely accepted premises in our thinking—a narrowly conceived preference for utility and "science," a false variety of egalitarianism, and a primitivist view of the child.

---

letic skill is recognized as being transient, special, and for most of us unimportant in the serious business of life; and the tribute given the athlete is considered to be earned because he entertains. Intellect, on the other hand, is neither entertaining (to most men) nor innocent; since everyone sees that it can be an important and permanent advantage in life, it creates against itself a kind of universal fraternity of commonplace minds.

PART 2

The Religion of
the Heart

CHAPTER III

The Evangelical Spirit

❦

· 1 ·

T HE AMERICAN mind was shaped in the mold of early modern
Protestantism. Religion was the first arena for American intellectual
life, and thus the first arena for an anti-intellectual impulse. Anything
that seriously diminished the role of rationality and learning in early
American religion would later diminish its role in secular culture. The
feeling that ideas should above all be made to work, the disdain for
doctrine and for refinements in ideas, the subordination of men of ideas
to men of emotional power or manipulative skill are hardly innovations
of the twentieth century; they are inheritances from American Protestantism.

Since some tension between the mind and the heart, between emotion and intellect, is everywhere a persistent feature of Christian experience, it would be a mistake to suggest that there is anything
distinctively American in religious anti-intellectualism. Long before
America was discovered, the Christian community was perennially
divided between those who believed that intellect must have a vital
place in religion and those who believed that intellect should be subordinated to emotion, or in effect abandoned at the dictates of emotion. I do not mean to say that in the New World a new or more
virulent variety of anti-intellectualist reaction was discovered, but
rather that under American conditions the balance between traditional
establishments and revivalist or enthusiastic movements drastically
shifted in favor of the latter. In consequence, the learned professional
clergy suffered a loss of position, and the rational style of religion they
found congenial suffered accordingly. At an early stage in its history,
America, with its Protestant and dissenting inheritance, became the

scene of an unusually keen local variation of this universal historical struggle over the character of religion; and here the forces of enthusiasm and revivalism won their most impressive victories. It is to certain peculiarities of American religious life—above all to its lack of firm institutional establishments hospitable to intellectuals and to the competitive sectarianism of its evangelical denominations—that American anti-intellectualism owes much of its strength and pervasiveness.

The style of a church or sect is to a great extent a function of social class, and the forms of worship and religious doctrine congenial to one social group may be uncongenial to another. The possessing classes have usually shown much interest in rationalizing religion and in observing highly developed liturgical forms. The disinherited classes, especially when unlettered, have been more moved by emotional religion; and emotional religion is at times animated by a revolt against the religious style, the liturgy, and the clergy of the upper-class church, which is at the same time a revolt against aristocratic manners and morals.[1] Lower-class religions are likely to have apocalyptic or millennarian outbursts, to stress the validity of inner religious experience against learned and formalized religion, to simplify liturgical forms, and to reject the idea of a learned clergy, sometimes of any professional clergy whatsoever.

America, having attracted in its early days so many of Europe's disaffected and disinherited, became the ideal country for the prophets of what was then known to its critics as religious "enthusiasm." The primary impulse in enthusiasm was the feeling of direct personal access to God.[2] Enthusiasts did not commonly dispense with theological beliefs or with sacraments; but, seeking above all an inner conviction of communion with God, they felt little need either for liturgical expression or for an intellectual foundation for religious conviction. They felt toward intellectual instruments as they did toward aesthetic forms: whereas the established churches thought of art and music as leading the mind upward toward the divine, enthusiasts commonly felt them to be at best intrusions and at worst barriers to

---

[1] Cf. H. Richard Niebuhr: "An intellectually trained and liturgically minded clergy is rejected in favor of lay readers who serve the emotional needs of this religion (i.e., of the untutored and economically disfranchised classes) more adequately and who on the other hand, are not allied by culture and interest with those ruling classes whose superior manner of life is too obviously purchased at the expense of the poor." *The Social Sources of Denominationalism* (Meridian ed., 1957), p. 30.

[2] I owe much in my remarks on this subject to Msgr. R. A. Knox's *Enthusiasm* (Oxford, 1950).

the pure and direct action of the heart—though an important exception must be made here for the value the Methodists found in
hymnody. The enthusiasts' reliance on the validity of inward experience always contained within it the threat of an anarchical subjectivism, a total destruction of traditional and external religious authority.

This accounts, in some measure, for the perennial tendency of
enthusiastic religion toward sectarian division and subdivision. But
enthusiasm did not so much eliminate authority as fragment it; there
was always a certain authority which could be won by this or that
preacher who had an unusual capacity to evoke the desired feeling of
inner conviction. The authority of enthusiasm, then, tended to be
personal and charismatic rather than institutional; the founders of
churches which, like the Methodist, had stemmed from an enthusiastic
source needed great organizing genius to keep their followers under a
single institutional roof. To be sure, the stabler evangelical denominations lent no support to rampant subjectivism. They held that the
source of true religious authority was the Bible, properly interpreted.
But among the various denominations, conceptions of proper interpretation varied from those that saw a vital role for scholarship and rational expertise down through a range of increasing enthusiasm and
anti-intellectualism to the point at which every individual could reach
for *his* Bible and reject the voice of scholarship. After the advent of
the higher criticism, the validity of this Biblical individualism became
a matter of life or death for fundamentalists.

When America was still a tiny outpost of England on the fringes of
Western civilization, movements of religious protest in the mother
country began to display qualities that were to become prominent in
American religion. As the English religious reformers became convinced that the Reformation had not gone far enough to meet the social or spiritual demands of their followers, successive waves of Millennarians, Anabaptists, Seekers, Ranters, and Quakers assailed the
established order and its clergy, preached a religion of the poor,
argued for intuition and inspiration as against learning and doctrine,
elevated lay preachers to leadership, and rejected the professional
clergy as "null and void and without authority." At the time of the
Puritan revolution, the preachers of the New Model Army were unsparing in their anti-professional and anti-intellectual broadsides
against the clergy, the university teachers, and the lawyers. Most
Puritans, to be sure, were heartily in favor of an educated ministry; but

the left-wing chaplains, in the line of the Levellers and Diggers, followed Gerrard Winstanley's example in calling the universities "standing ponds of stinking waters," in pointing out that a liberal education did nothing to make men less sinful, and in stirring the egalitarian passions of the poor.[3]

In America the Anglicans, Presbyterians, and Congregationalists, with their severe standards of church organization, and their formally organized and often highly educated clergymen, at first successfully controlled such leveling tendencies. But hardly had these churches been organized when some dissenters began to find fault with them. Many, especially along the Southern frontier, simply drifted away for a time from all church connections. Others criticized and agitated, especially in New England, where religious activism was a major principle of life. For example, before Massachusetts Bay had survived even its first score of years, it was badly shaken by the activities of Mistress Anne Hutchinson, whose hostility to the learned ministers and to university education aroused intense anxiety in the establishment.[4] This unfortunate woman was persecuted in part because of her own courageous intransigence, but largely because the community was persuaded that she was thoroughly subversive. Not until the time of the Great Awakening of the eighteenth century did the enthusiasts win general major victories outside the confines of a single colony. It was then that they set the precedent on American shores not only for the repeated waves of nineteenth-century evangelicalism, but also for the tradition of anti-intellectualism itself, in so far as this tradition was carried within the matrix of religious belief. But to understand the Awakening, one must look at the state of the established clergy in the

[3] On the general aspects of the religion of the disinherited, see Niebuhr: op. cit., chapters 2 and 3. See Leo Solt's suggestive account of "Anti-Intellectualism in the Puritan Revolution," *Church History*, Vol. XXIV (December, 1956), pp. 306–16; and D. B. Robertson: *The Religious Foundations of Leveller Democracy* (New York, 1951), especially pp. 29–40.

[4] As Samuel Eliot Morison has remarked, such hostility among radical Puritans was "an article of faith. Sincere fanatics called the universities 'stews of Anti-Christ,' 'Houses of lies,' that 'stink before God with the most loathsome abomination.'" Edward Johnson saw Anne Hutchinson "and her consorts mightily rayling against learning, perswading all they could to take heed of being spoyled by it." One of her followers had said to him: "Come along with me. . . . I'le bring you to a Woman that Preaches better Gospell then any of your black-coates that have been at the Ninneversity, a Woman of another kinde of spirit, who hath had many Revelations of things to come. . . . I had rather hear such a one that speekes from the meere motion of the spirit, without any study at all, then any of your learned Scollers, although they may be fuller of Scripture." Edward Johnson: *Wonder-Working Providence of Sions Saviour in New England*, ed. by J. F. Jameson (New York, 1910), pp. 127–8.

colonies, and here the position of the Puritan clergy is of special interest; for the Puritan clergy came as close to being an intellectual ruling class—or, more properly, a class of intellectuals intimately as· sociated with a ruling power—as America has ever had.

• 2 •

Like most intellectual groups, the Puritan ministry had serious faults, and these became dangerous when the ministers wielded power. But what is significant for us—and it may serve as a paradigm of the situation of the intellectual in America—is that the Puritan ministry is popularly remembered almost entirely for its faults, even for faults for which it was less culpable than the community in which it lived. It is significant, moreover, that this rather odious image of the Puritan clergy, for which the name of Cotton Mather is a byword, has dominated not only our popular historical lore but also the historical thinking of our intellectuals. The reputation of this, the first class of American intellectuals, has gone down in infamy, and subsequent generations of intellectuals have often led the campaign against them.

It is doubtful that any community ever had more faith in the value of learning and intellect than Massachusetts Bay. It was with only slight and pardonable exaggeration that Moses Coit Tyler wrote, in his history of colonial American literature: [5]

> In its inception New England was not an agricultural community, nor a manufacturing community, nor a trading community: it was a thinking community; an arena and mart for ideas; its characteristic organ being not the hand, nor the heart, nor the pocket, but the brain. . . . Probably no other community of pioneers ever so honored study, so reverenced the symbols and instruments of learning. Theirs was a social structure with its corner-stone resting on a book. . . . Only six years after John Winthrop's arrival in Salem harbor, the people of Massachusetts took from their own treasury the fund from which to found a university; so that while the tree-stumps were as yet scarcely weather-browned in their earliest harvest fields, and before the nightly howl of the wolf had ceased from the outskirts of their villages, they had made arrangements by which even in that wilderness their young men could at once enter upon the study of Aristotle and Thucydides, of Horace

[5] *A History of American Literature, 1607–1765* (Ithaca, New York: 1949), pp. 85–7.

and Tacitus, and the Hebrew Bible. . . . The learned class was
indeed an order of nobility among them.

Among the first generation of American Puritans, men of learning
were both numerous and honored. There was about one university-
trained scholar, usually from Cambridge or Oxford, to every forty or
fifty families. Puritans expected their clergy to be distinguished for
scholarship, and during the entire colonial period all but five per cent
of the clergymen of the New England Congregational churches had
college degrees. These Puritan emigrants, with their reliance upon the
Book and their wealth of scholarly leadership, founded that intellectual
and scholarly tradition which for three centuries enabled New England to lead the country in educational and scholarly achievement.

It must not be imagined that the earliest generations of Harvard
graduates were given nothing but a narrow theological education. The
notion has become widespread that Harvard and the other colonial
colleges were at their inception no more than theological seminaries—
and the fear expressed by the Puritan fathers of the development of an
"illiterate ministry" seems to give support to the idea. In fact, however,
the Oxford and Cambridge colleges which trained the men who
founded Harvard College had long since been thoroughly infused with
humanist scholarship. The founding fathers of colonial education saw
no difference between the basic education appropriate for a cleric and
that appropriate for any other liberally educated man. The idea of a
distinctively theological seminary is a product of modern specialism,
sectarian competition, and of a reaction to the threat of secularism in
the colleges. Such an idea was outside their ken. They felt the need of
learned ministers more acutely than learned men in other professions,
but they intended their ministers to be educated side by side and in
the same liberal curriculum with other civic leaders and men of
affairs. As it turned out, this was precisely what happened; in Harvard's first two generations, only about half the graduates became
ministers and the remainder went into secular occupations.

Having established a learned and literary class, the Puritan community gave this class great scope for the realization of their gifts. The
Puritan ministry was well served by the community, and it served
the community well in return. As the country became more settled, the
clergy found sufficient leisure to express themselves in writing; the
productivity shown by some of them is astounding. Puritanism, as a
religion of the Book, placed a strong emphasis upon interpretation and

rational discourse and eschewed ranting emotionalism. Puritan sermons combined philosophy, piety, and scholarship; and it was one of the aims of Puritan popular education to train a laity capable of understanding such discourses. In the early days, at least, this seems to have been achieved.

But a great deal more was achieved. In estimating the intellectual accomplishments of the Puritan colonists it is necessary to bear in mind that even in 1700, after more than seventy years of settlement, the population numbered only about 106,000, much of it very thinly spread; that Boston, the largest town, had only about 7,000 souls in 1699; and that during the 1670's they were ravaged by a serious and costly war with the Indians in which one of every sixteen men of military age was killed and half their towns suffered damage. Despite isolation, poverty, and other handicaps, they established a college which graduated scores of civic leaders and ministers, and whose degrees soon after its founding were accepted *ad eundem gradem* at Oxford and Cambridge. It was a college, too, where young men learned not merely to read and interpret the Bible and theological works, but to read Hesiod, Homer, Sophocles, Aristophanes, and other classical writers. There is every evidence that the learned class of Massachusetts Bay became cultivated men, interested in humane letters as well as theology, and that they successfully brought to the New World much of the best of the heritage of European civilization. In addition to Harvard College, their leaders established a system of grammar and elementary schools, a printing press, and some creditable libraries. The ministers produced a remarkable literature of sermons, histories, and verse, and, in time, a literature of political speculation and controversy which germinated into the political writing of the Revolutionary era. They laid the basis of an educational system and, one might add, of a community morale in matters of study which made New England and the New England mind distinguished in the history of American culture for three centuries. The clergy spread enlightenment as well as religion, fostered science as well as theology, and provided models of personal devotion to things of the mind in tiny villages where such examples might otherwise not have been seen.[6]

[6] For a spirited defense and appreciation of these early cultural achievements, see Samuel Eliot Morison: *The Intellectual Life of Colonial New England* (New York, 1956); cf. Thomas G. Wright: *Literary Culture in Early New England* (Cambridge, 1920); Kenneth Murdock: *Literature and Theology in Colonial New England* (Cambridge, 1949).

The most common modern conception of the Puritan clergy is that they not only shared the faults of their community but also led in its persecutions. This judgment needs severe qualification. It is true that theirs was, by the standards of the enlightened modern mind, an intolerant age, and that the clergy shared its intolerances. Moreover, the clergy displayed, especially in the first generation, a weakness to which intellectuals are prone at times in political affairs—that is, they imagined that they might be able to commit an entire civil society to the realization of transcendent moral and religious standards, and that they could maintain within this society a unified and commanding creed. They had risked the Atlantic and the wilderness to show that this was possible; and of course in the end they failed, after having committed a number of excesses in the attempt to realize their vision.

But the fairest way to assess any intellectual group like the Puritan ministry is not to put them to the test of the most advanced standards of tolerance and enlightenment, but to measure them against their own times, the community in which they lived, and the laymen they served. The modern liberal mind tends to assume that, as leaders of the community the clergy were the prime movers in those acts, like the Salem witchcraft trials, which are most disturbing to our minds; and that the essential responsibility for the excesses of that community rests with them.

The truth is more complex. The clergy were themselves not a homogeneous group, for with the passing of the first generation and the enlargement of the community they had become diversified.[7] Perhaps the most important points of diversity were those of generation and of location. The older clergy, and especially those in the more remote rural communities, clung to the hard orthodoxies in which the Puritan community had begun. But by the end of the seventeenth century there had also arisen a group of young clergymen who were cosmopolitan in outlook, relatively liberal in religious tendency, and conversant with the latest intellectual influences from Europe. Most of these ministered to the growing towns of the seaboard.

There is ample evidence that, as an intellectual class, the members of the more learned and more cosmopolitan clergy (which includes such men as Increase and Cotton Mather) earned their privileged position. Their leadership was far from fully effective or controlling;

[7] On the state of the clergy during the period 1680–1725, see Clifford K. Shipton: "The New England Clergy of the 'Glacial Age,'" *Colonial Society of Massachusetts Publications*, Vol. XXXII (Boston, 1937), pp. 24–54.

but such influence as they had they used to encourage greater tolerance, a broader pursuit of learning, the cultivation of science, and the
restraint of some of the bigoted tendencies of the leading country
laymen, the public, and the less enlightened clergy. By the close of the
seventeenth century, the leading clergymen were much more liberal
in thought than the elderly uneducated laymen who controlled a great
many of the rural congregations or the provincial politicians who often
invoked religious fundamentalism because it was popular with the
growing electorate.

After 1680, the Puritan ministry was more tolerant and more accommodating to dissenters such as Baptists and Quakers than was
the Boston public at large; and the influential Boston ministers—
including the Mathers—were more liberal in this respect than the
older preachers in the countryside. While the cosmopolitan clerics
were importing the latest latitudinarian books from England and year
by year making more departures from the harsher traditions of
Calvinism, leading laymen were often resisting these changes. So far as
the encouragement of science is concerned, this was almost entirely in
clerical sponsorship before about the middle of the eighteenth century (Harvard had its first lay scientist in Professor John Winthrop,
who began to teach in 1738). In the most controversial and stirring of
all scientific questions of the day, that of the adoption of inoculation
for smallpox, outstanding clerical intellectuals once again took the
lead in defending innovation. Not least of them was Cotton Mather,
who held to his position even though a bomb was thrown into his
study by anti-inoculation agitators. Even with respect to the much-
mooted witchcraft trials, the record of the clergy, though mixed, is
better than that of the lay judges and the public. Most of the clerics
gave credence to the idea of witchcraft itself—as did some of the
distinguished minds of the Western world—but they were strongly
opposed to the extremely loose criteria of evidence that were admitted
in the terrible Salem trials, and many clerics exercised a restraining
influence.[8]

Toward the end of the seventeenth century, certain strains were

---

[8] After the first hanging had taken place and when many suspects were await-
ing trial, a group of clergymen wrote to the governor and council pointing to the
"need of a very critical and Exquisite *Caution*, lest by too much *Credulity* for
Things received only on the Devils Authority, there be a Door opened for a long
Train of miserable Consequences." When the lay authorities ignored this protest
and went on accepting what was called "spectral evidence" against suspects,
leading ministers continued to complain, and fourteen of them petitioned Governor
Phips. At their insistence Phips began to call a halt to the proceedings. Shipton:
"The New England Clergy," p. 42.

already evident in Puritan religious sensibility which affected the lives
and the position of the ministry. Puritanism had always required a
delicate balance between intellect, which was esteemed as essential to
true religion in New England, and emotion, which was necessary to
the strength and durability of Puritan piety. This balance proved to
be precarious, and there developed a tendency toward a split in the
religious community itself. One side of the church tended to be socially
correct, and sophisticated, liberal, and latitudinarian in its intellectual
outlook, but religiously cold and formal. The other side, which was to
prove vulnerable to revivalism, was moved both by ideas and by
religious fervor; but its partisans, in their most fervent moments,
turned antinomian and anti-intellectual. Jonathan Edwards stood out
almost alone among the leading clergymen as exemplifying the old
intellectualism and piety of New England and combining with them
the ability to deal creatively with new ideas. By the middle of the
eighteenth century, the religion of New England, like that of the other
colonies, was ripe for an awakening that would have profound consequences for the position of the learned clergy.

· 3 ·

The first major episode in which the educated clergy was roundly
repudiated came during the Great Awakening of the mid-eighteenth
century. These religious revivals, to be sure, did not have an un-
ambiguously bad effect on intellect and learning; but they set an important precedent for later attacks upon the learned clergy and for
movements to make religion less formal and its leadership less professional.

The American Awakening was a counterpart of similar religious
changes in Europe, notably the rise of German pietism and English
Methodism, but America was especially ripe for religious reawaken-
ing. Large numbers of Americans either were dissenters—Baptists, for
instance, living restively under established Anglican or Congregational
churches—or were unchurched, without affiliations or the habit of
church attendance. The population had moved beyond the reach of
the ministry, either geographically or spiritually. In some areas, notably
in Virginia, a large portion of the Anglican clergy was especially remote and ineffective. Even the religion of New England had cooled.
By the 1730's and 1740's the Congregational churches of New England
(and often the Presbyterian churches of the Middle Colonies and

elsewhere) had lost much of their pristine morale and had settled into dull repositories of the correct faith of the established classes. Abstract and highly intellectual in their traditions, they had lost the power to grip simple people; the Reformation controversies out of which the doctrinal commitments of these churches had grown had lost much of their meaning.[9] The zealots of the first Puritan generation and their well-schooled sons had long since gone to their graves. The ministers themselves had lost much of the drive, and therefore the prestige, of their earlier days. They were highly civilized, often versatile men; but they were in some cases too civilized, too versatile, too worldly, to play anything like their original role. Their sermons, attended by sleepy congregations, were often dull and abstruse exercises in old dogmatic controversies. As the Awakener, George Whitefield, said, "the reason why Congregations have been so dead is because dead Men preach to them." [1] From Massachusetts southward to Virginia and beyond, the latent religious energies of the people thus lay ready for any preacher who had the skill to reach them.

The Great Awakenings began in 1720, when the members of the Dutch Reformed Church in New Jersey began to be aroused by the sermons of a young preacher, Theodore Frelinghuysen, who had come to the New World inspired by English and Dutch Puritanism. His revival in New Jersey led to a second among the Scotch-Irish Presbyterians of the Middle Colonies. In 1726 one of them, William Tennent, established at Neshaminy, Pennsylvania, his "Log College," a sort of rudimentary theological school, and there, for the next twenty years, he trained about a score of young men to carry the revivalist spirit into the Presbyterian ministry. In 1734 revivalism appeared independently in New England. Jonathan Edwards, a unique figure among the awakening preachers, combined the old Puritan regard for doctrine and the Puritan custom of the written sermon with the passion and religious zeal of the revivalists. Edwards's revival sermons, though they inflamed the town of Northampton and the surrounding country during 1734 and 1735, were limited in their reach compared with those of George Whitefield, an eloquent young associate of the Wesleys in England, who came to America on evangelistic missions in 1738 and

---

[9] Perry Miller has written a brilliant account of the institutional and doctrinal aspects of this decline in *The New England Mind: from Colony to Province* (Cambridge, Massachusetts, 1953).

[1] Quoted by Edwin Scott Gaustad: *The Great Awakening in New England* (New York, 1957), p. 27.

1739. His second campaign began in Georgia and twice brought him northward; he finally came to New England in the fall of 1740. Whitefield, who, David Garrick said, could send an audience into paroxysms by pronouncing "Mesopotamia," met with a wildly enthusiastic response to his preaching in America. Thousands flocked from the countryside to the towns where he chose to talk, and great numbers were seized with a realization of sin and experienced spiritual rebirth. Whitefield's first visit to New England was followed by that of William Tennent's son, Gilbert, who brought the revival to a degree of frenzy distasteful to many persons who had welcomed the earlier signs of a spiritual awakening.

Representative of the more enthusiastic antics of revivalism was the work of James Davenport, a Long Island minister and a graduate of Yale, who toured Connecticut and Massachusetts in 1742 and 1743, pouring such invective upon the established ministers and committing such other outrages upon decorum (singing, for example, on his way to meeting) that he fell afoul of the authorities. In the summer of 1742 he was tried in Connecticut for breach of the peace under the guise of holding religious meetings, but was charitably spared graver punishment than deportation from the province because he was deemed "disturbed in the rational Faculties of his Mind." A few months later he turned up in Boston, where he was jailed for slandering the ministers, but was again released as *non compos mentis*, and returned to Long Island to be tried for neglecting his own parish. After one more gaudy episode in New London, Connecticut, he was at last persuaded to quit, and in 1744 he wrote a somewhat inconsistent testimonial of repentance. The fact that Davenport was repudiated and sharply condemned by Gilbert Tennent, whose preachings had helped to unsettle him in the first place, suggests that the middle-of-the-road awakeners were almost as much alarmed by the barking and howling that the movement had unleashed as were the regular ministers.[2]

As for the regular ministers, at first the overwhelming majority of them welcomed the itinerant revivalists as agents who would bring a warmer spirit to the religion of their parishioners; this welcome was extended even by such outstanding liberal highbrows as Benjamin Colman of Boston. It was only after the Awakening was well under

[2] On Davenport see Gaustad: op. cit., pp. 36–41. Edwards himself, in his *Treatise Concerning Religious Affections* (1746), expressed at length his disapproval of such manifestations.

way that the regular ministers began to realize that the awakeners did not regard them as fellow workers in a common spiritual task but as competitors—and very inferior ones at that.

Gilbert Tennent expressed the revivalists' view of the older clergy (those "orthodox, Letter-learned and regular Pharisees") in a sermon on *The Danger of an Unconverted Ministry;* he attacked them as crafty, cruel, cold-hearted, bigoted, faithless hypocrites who held the people in contempt. Tennent found the motives and the piety of the unawakened ministers suspect, and he regarded them not as co-workers but as enemies. ("If they coud help it, they wo'dn't let one faithful Man come into the Ministry; and therefore their Opposition is an encouraging Sign.") Tennent's approach was hardly ingratiating, but he believed that he was raising a real issue, and it would be hard to deny that what he was advocating could be called religious democracy. If, under existing church organization, a congregation had a cold and unconverted minister, and if it was forbidden to receive an awakened one except with the consent of the unconverted, how would the congregation ever win access to "a faithful Ministry"?[3] Like a true Protestant, Tennent was once again addressing himself to a major problem—how the faith could be propagated under conditions of religious monopoly. To the standing ministry, the problem presented itself in quite another guise: how, under the conditions to which they were bound by inherited church principles, could they compete with inspired preachers like Tennent and Whitefield, if these men took it into their heads to treat the regular ministry as foes?

In truth, the established ministers found it difficult to cope with the challenge of the awakeners. The regular ministers, living with their congregations year in and year out under conditions devoid of special religious excitement, were faced with the task of keeping alive the spiritual awareness of their flocks under sober everyday circumstances. Confronted by flaming evangelists of Whitefield's caliber, and even by such lesser tub-thumpers and foot-stampers as Gilbert Tennent and Davenport, they were at somewhat the same disadvantage as an aging housewife whose husband has taken up with a young hussy from the front line of the chorus. The revivalists, with the prominent exception of Edwards, who was an intellectual largely out of rapport with his own congregation, felt little or no necessity to work upon the reason of their audiences or to address themselves to knotty questions

[3] Gilbert Tennent, *The Danger of an Unconverted Ministry Considered in a Sermon on Mark VI, 34* (Boston, 1742), pp. 2–3, 5, 7, 11–13.

of doctrine. They dispensed (again one must except Edwards) with written sermons, and confronted their listeners with the spontaneity of direct intercourse. They dealt directly with the ultimate realities of religious experience—the sense of sin, the yearning for salvation, the hope for God's love and mercy—and rarely hesitated to work upon the sensibilities of the audience; the fits and seizures, the shrieks and groans and grovelings, the occasional dementia characteristic of later revivalism made their appearance. Tennent, for instance, commonly frightened his listeners into conversions, as he stamped up and down and finally lapsed into incoherence. Performances like his were evidently in demand; on his three-months' tour of New England, when he often preached in foot-deep snow, he sent his converts groveling to the ground. As Timothy Cutler, a rather prejudiced Anglican witness, reported it: "After him [Whitefield] came one Tennent—a monster! impudent and noisy—and told them all they were *damned, damned, damned!* This charmed them; and in the most dreadful winter I ever saw, people wallowed in snow, night and day, for the benefit of his beastly brayings; and many ended their days under these fatigues." [4]

Before long, it became clear that the extreme exponents of revivals were challenging every assumption of the settled churches, whether Congregational, Dutch Reformed, Presbyterian, or Anglican. The Congregationalists of New England, and their Presbyterian counterparts elsewhere, had assumed, as I have said, that ministers must be learned professional men. Traditionally their ministers had commanded respect not merely for their learning but also for their piety and their spiritual qualities. But learning was held to be essential because learning and the rational understanding of doctrine were considered vital to religious life. Moreover, the regular churches were conducted in an orderly fashion. Ministers had to be invited and commissioned; their relations with their congregations were stable, solemn, orderly marriages. Unlicensed preachers were not to be thought of, and uninvited preaching simply was not done.

All these assumptions were now challenged. The most extreme revivalists were undermining the dignity of the profession by their personal conduct; they were invading and dividing the allegiances of the established ministers' congregations; they were trying to discredit

---

[4] L. Tyerman: *The Life of the Rev. George Whitefield* (London, 1847), Vol. II, p. 125. See Eugene E. White: "Decline of the Great Awakening in New England: 1741 to 1746," *New England Quarterly*, Vol. XXIV (March, 1951), p. 37.

the standing ministry by denouncing it as cold and unregenerate; [5]
many of them were preaching that not learning but the spirit was important to salvation; and finally (despite the disapproval of some awakeners like Tennent), they were threatening to undermine the professional
basis of the ministry by commissioning laymen—lay exhorters, as they
were called—to carry on the work of conversion. Before long many
congregations were split in two; and major denominations like the
Congregationalists and Presbyterians were divided into quarreling factions. Plainly the thing had got out of hand. As Ezra Stiles recalled
nearly twenty years later: "Multitudes were seriously, soberly and
solemnly out of their wits." [6]

· 4 ·

It was not long before the awakeners wore out their welcome from the
established ministry. By 1743 the ministers themselves had fallen out
—not over such extravagances as the commissioning of laymen or the
uninvited invading of parishes, acts which were defended by no one
of consequence, but over the meaning of the Awakening itself. A
strong minority (perhaps as many as a third) held that, for all its
defects, it was "a happy revival of religion," but the majority had come
to look upon it as a fit of superstitious enthusiasm, an anti-intellectualist
uprising against traditional and rational authority. The most extensive
tract against the awakeners was written by one of their most intransigent foes, Charles Chauncy, a somewhat stuffy but liberal-
minded leader of the Boston clergy. His *Seasonable Thoughts on the
State of Religion in New England,* published in 1743, shows his outrage at the *insolence* of the upstarts from miscellaneous occupations
who had come to challenge the ministry—men totally unqualified but
of overweening pride and assertiveness. The revivals had opened the
door, he complained, to lay exhorters: "Men of all Occupations who are

[5] Charles Chauncy compiled a catalogue of some of the epithets Gilbert Tennent
used against the established ministry: "Hirelings; Caterpillars; Letter-Learned
Pharisees; Men of the craft of Foxes, and the Cruelty of Wolves; plaistered Hypocrites; Varlets; seed of the Serpent; foolish Builders, whom the Devil drives into the
Ministry; dry Nurses; dead Dogs that cannot bark; blind Men; dead Men; Men
possessed of the Devil; Rebels and Enemies of god; Guides that are Stone-blind
and Stone deaf; children of Satan . . . murderous Hypocrites." *Seasonable
Thoughts on the State of Religion in New England* (Boston, 1743), p. 249. Most
of these examples appear to have been taken from Tennent's *Danger of an Unconverted Ministry.*
[6] Gaustad: op. cit., p. 103.

vain enough to think themselves fit to be Teachers of others; Men who, though they have no Learning, and but small Capacities, yet imagine they are able, and without Study too, to speak to the spiritual Profit of such as are willing to hear them." [7]

"Without study too"! Here we are close to one of the central issues of the Great Awakening. An error of "former Times" was now being revived, Chauncy asserted, the error of the heretics and popular preachers who said that "they needed no Books but the Bible." "They pleaded there was no Need of Learning in preaching, and that one of them could by the SPIRIT do better than the Minister by his Learning; as if the SPIRIT and Learning were Opposites." This, Chauncy thought, was the fundamental error of the revivalists: [8]

> Their depending on the Help of the SPIRIT as to despise Learning. To this it is owing, that so many speak slightly of our Schools and Colleges; discovering a Good-Will, were it in their Power, to rase them to their Foundations. To the same Cause it may be ascrib'd, that such Swarms of Exhorters have appear'd in the Land, and been admir'd and run after, though many of them could scarce speak common Sense . . . and to the same Cause still it must be attributed that so many Ministers preach, not only without Book, but without Study; and justify their doing so, lest, by previous Preparation, they should stint the Spirit.

To the exponent of a religion of the book, for whom a correct reading of the Bible was a vital concern, this was the ultimate heresy: that one who was possessed of the Spirit could, without study and without learning, interpret the word of God effectively enough to be an agent of the salvation of others. And here we have the nub of the difference between the awakeners and the spokesmen of establishments: whether it was more important to get a historically correct and rational understanding of the Book—and hence of the word of God—or to work up a proper emotion, a proper sense of inner conviction and of relation to God.

An association of revivalist ministers put their case in these terms: [9]

> That every brother that is qualified by God for the same has a right to preach according to the measure of faith, and that the

---

[7] *Seasonable Thoughts*, p. 226.

[8] Ibid., pp. 256–8.

[9] Leonard W. Labaree: "The Conservative Attitude toward the Great Awakening," *William and Mary Quarterly*, 3rd ser., Vol. I (October, 1944), pp. 339–40, from Tracy: *Great Awakening*, p. 319.

essential qualification for preaching is wrought by the Spirit of
God; and that the knowledge of the tongues and liberal sciences
are not absolutely necessary; yet they are convenient, and will
doubtless be profitable if rightly used, but if brought in to supply
the want of the Spirit of God, they prove a snare to those that use
them and all that follow them.

Conservatives found in this a complete repudiation of the role of
learning in religion; and in the emotional kind of religion that came
from the preaching of men so disposed, they saw the destruction of
all rationality in religious life. "As none but rational creatures are
capable of religion," wrote a Southern opponent of evangelism,[1]

so there is no true religion but in the use of reason; there will
always be these two things in the former, which the latter must
judge of, namely the *Truth* and the *Meaning*. The virtue of our
religion must consist in the inward persuasion of our mind, for
if we owe our religion to birth, humor, interest, or any external
circumstances or motive whatever, we bring all religions upon a
level; and though by the happiness of education we should pro-
fess the true religion, yet if we do not make it our own by understanding the reasons for it, it will not be profitable to us; we offer
to God the *Sacrifice of Fools*, in which he has no pleasure.

Understandably, many of the conservative ministers in the affected
colonies, who had at first expected good results for religion from the
revivals, soon began to abhor them as a threat to their own position, to
the churches themselves, and to all true religion. Fundamental tenets
were being neglected, the organized ministry was being bypassed
and traduced. Extemporized preaching threatened to dissolve all rational elements in religion, for many of the evangelists admitted that
their preaching came by "the immediate impression of the Holy
Ghost putting a long chain of thoughts into their minds and words into
their mouths." Conservatives considered this bad practice even in a
properly educated minister, but it was much more dangerous in the
lay exhorters, who were "private persons of no education and but low
attainment in knowledge and in the great doctrines of the Gospel."[2]
Finally, not only had these irruptions created divisions and quarrels
within a great many congregations, but the established ministers

---

[1] Quoted by Labaree: op. cit., p. 345, from *South Carolina Gazette* (September
12–19, 1741).
[2] Ibid., p. 336.

feared that the evangelists would strike at the very source of the educated ministry by circumventing the colleges and the usual process of ministerial training.

The fear was exaggerated, but the revivalists had tried to bully the colleges and at a few moments of extremism they had gone in for book-burning. Even the moderate Whitefield had urged that certain books be burned and had succeeded in persuading some of his followers to commit them to the flames. In March 1743, James Davenport urged the people of New London to collect for burning their jewelry and objects of personal luxury, as well as books and sermons written by Increase Mather, Benjamin Colman, Charles Chauncy, and other regular ministers. And one Sunday morning a large pyre was consumed on the town wharf while Davenport and his followers sang *Gloria Patri* and *Hallelujah* and chanted this invocation: "The smoak of the torments of such of the authors . . . as died in the same belief, as when they set them out, was now ascending in hell in like manner, as the smoak of these books rise." [3]

The immediate effects of the Awakening on education were mixed. In an organization like the Presbyterian Church, manned as it was by many well-trained ministers from the Scottish universities, even a revivalist was likely to be sensitive to the charge that his work was hostile to learning. William Tennent trained a number of capable scholars at his "Log College," and his son Gilbert was not the ignorant lout that has often been pictured. More important, the revivalist Presbyterians established the College of New Jersey (later Princeton) in 1746, to assure that they would have their own center of learning; and in time other institutions—Brown, Rutgers, and Dartmouth— were founded by men influenced by the revivals. Only later did the revivalist tradition become consistently hostile to education. It must be added, however, that the effect of the Awakening was to subordinate education to religious factionalism and to consolidate the tradition of sectarian control of colleges. What the ardent religious factionalists wanted most of all were not centers of learning, but *their own* instruments of teaching; they pushed doctrinal and pietistic considerations forward, at the expense of humane learning. Even the learned Jonathan Edwards once attacked Harvard and Yale for failing to be "nurseries of piety" and for taking more pains "to teach the scholars human learning" than to educate them in religion.[4]

[3] White: op. cit., p. 44.
[4] *Works* (New York, 1830), Vol. IV, pp. 264–5.

Whitefield himself, another responsible evangelist, was also dissatisfied with the two New England colleges. The light of these colleges, he complained, had become "darkness, darkness that may be felt." When he returned to New England in 1744, most of the ministers who had opened their pulpits to him on his first visit now kept them resolutely closed, and the faculties of both Yale and Harvard issued pamphlets denouncing him, denying his charges against the colleges, and submitting a bill of countercharges. There is no reason to accept the view of some of Whitefield's more suspicious opponents that he intended to "vilify and subvert" the colleges of New England in order to overthrow its established ministers and create wholly new ways of training their successors. But at a time when scores of local pastors were being denounced to their own congregations by awakeners as lacking in true piety, if not as agents of the devil, the fear of thoroughgoing subversion was an understandable response.[5]

The burning of books and the baiting of colleges, to be sure, were examples not of the characteristic behavior of the awakeners, but of their excesses. The awakeners had not started out to divide the churches, attack the colleges, or discredit intellect and learning; in so far as they did so, it was only to serve their fundamental purpose, which was to revive religion and bring souls to God. And, for all the tart animadversions of men like Chauncy, the anti-intellectual effects of the New England and Middle Colony Awakenings, taking place as they did within the framework of the powerful Congregational and Presbyterian respect for learning and rationality, were distinctly limited. But the Great Awakening, even in New England, revealed the almost uncontrollable tendency of such revivals toward extremes of various kinds. Opponents, with Chauncy, said that the emotional fevers and the anti-intellectualism of the Awakening were its essence, but the friends of revival thought these things were merely the incidental defects of a fundamentally good movement toward Christian conversion. In the short run, and in the restrained milieu of the New England churches, the friends of the Awakening were probably right; but their opponents divined more correctly what the inner tendency and future direction of such revivals would be—especially when revivalism got away from the traditions and restraints of New England into the great American interior. The most recent historian of the New

England Awakening, who writes of it with evident sympathy, still concludes that it "demonstrated the feasibility of and made fashionable a fervent evangelism without intellectual discipline," and observes that "the discrediting of 'human learning,' characteristic of only a minority during the Awakening, later became typical of a majority of Protestantism." [6]

There can be little doubt that the conventional judgment is right: by achieving a religious style congenial to the common man and giving him an alternative to the establishments run by and largely for the comfortable classes, the Awakening quickened the democratic spirit in America; by telling the people that they had a right to hear the kind of preachers they liked and understood, even under some circumstances a right to preach themselves, the revivalists broke the hold of the establishments and heightened that assertiveness and self-sufficiency which visitor after visitor from abroad was later to find characteristic of the American people. Moreover, the impulse given to humanitarian causes—to anti-slavery and the conversion of slaves and Indians—must also be chalked up to the credit of the Great Awakening. There was no soul to whose welfare the good awakener was indifferent. But the costs (in spite of the newly formed colleges) to the cause of intellect and learning in religion must also be reckoned. The awakeners were not the first to disparage the virtues of mind, but they quickened anti-intellectualism; and they gave to American anti-intellectualism its first brief moment of militant success. With the Awakenings, the Puritan age in American religion came to an end and the evangelical age began. Subsequent revivals repeated in an ever larger theater the merits and defects of the revivals of the eighteenth century.

· 5 ·

As later revivalism moved from New England and the Middle Colonies and from the Congregational and Presbyterian denominations out into the saddlebag and bear-meat country of the South and West, it became more primitive, more emotional, more given to "ecstatic" manifestations. The preachers were less educated, less inclined to restrain physical responses as an instrument of conversion; and the grovelings, jerkings, howlings, and barkings increased. From the beginning, Whitefield's work had been effective in the Southern colonies; the

[6] Gaustad: op. cit., pp. 129, 139.

evangelical movement, spurred by his preaching and by the overflow of Middle-Colony Presbyterian revivalists, spread into Virginia, North Carolina, and the deeper South in the 1740's and 1750's. There revivalists found a large unchurched population; and there, where the rusticated Anglican clergymen sometimes went to seed, the grounds for an indictment of the established ministry were considerably better than they had been in the North. There also, because the Anglican establishment was linked with the upper classes, the democratic and dissenting implications of revivalism were sharper. In the South, despite the activity of such a distinguished Presbyterian preacher as Samuel Davies, later to be president of Princeton, a major part was played by Baptists and later by Methodists, groups less committed than the Presbyterians and Congregationalists to a learned ministry. There only weak obstacles stood in the way of such revival phenomena as unpaid itinerant ministers, laymen preaching to the people, and denunciations of the established clerics.

The Southern revivalists carried the light of the gospel to a people who were not only unchurched but often uncivilized. The Reverend Charles Woodmason, an Anglican minister who traveled extensively in the Carolina back-country during the 1760's and 1770's left a chilling picture of the savagery of the life he found there and a suggestive if rather jaundiced record of "these roving Teachers that stir up the Minds of the People against the Establish'd Church, and her Ministers—and make the Situation of any Gentleman extremely uneasy, vexatious, and disagreeable."

> Few or no Books are to be found in all this vast Country, beside the Assembly, Catechism, Watts Hymns, Bunyans Pilgrims Progress—Russells—Whitefields and Erskines Sermons. Nor do they delight in Historical Books or in having them read to them, as do our Vulgar in England, for these People despise Knowledge, and instead of honouring a Learned Person, or any one of Wit or Knowledge, be it in the Arts, Sciences, or Languages, they despise and Ill treat them—And this Spirit prevails even among the Principals of this Province.

Of the revivalist or New Light faction among the Baptists he reported a few years later that they were altogether opposed to authority and, having made successful assaults upon the established church, were now trying to destroy the state. "The Gentlemen of the Law, seem now to engage their Attention: Like *Straw* and *Tyler*, of old [John Rackstraw and Wat Tyler of the English Peasants' Revolt of 1381], they want for to demolish all the Learned Professions. Human Learning being contrary to the spirit of God." [7]

What Woodmason observed on the Carolina frontier in the eighteenth century was an example, somewhat exaggerated, of the conditions in which the shifting population increasingly found itself. As the people moved westward after the Revolution, they were forever outrunning the institutions of settled society; it was impossible for institutions to move as fast or as constantly as the population. The trans-Allegheny population, which was about 100,000 in 1790, had jumped to 2,250,000 thirty years later. Many families made not one but two or three moves in a brief span of years. Organizations dissolved; restraints disappeared. Churches, social bonds, and cultural institutions often broke down, and they could not be reconstituted before the frontier families made yet another leap into the wilderness or the prairie. Samuel J. Mills, later one of the chief organizers of the American Bible Society, took two companions on Western trips during 1812–15 and found community after community which had been settled many years but which had no schools and no churches and little interest in establishing either. In Kaskaskia, the capital of Illinois territory, they could not find a single complete Bible. [8]

John Mason Peck, the first Baptist missionary to work in the Illinois and Missouri region, later recalled "a specimen of the squatter race found on the extreme frontiers" in 1818 in an extremely primitive condition": [9]

About nine o'clock I found the family to which I was directed. As this family was a specimen of the squatter race found on the extreme frontiers in early times, some specific description may amuse the reader, for I do not think a duplicate can now [1864] be found within the boundaries of Missouri. The single log-cabin,

[7] Richard J. Hooker, ed.: *The Carolina Backcountry on the Eve of the Revolution* (Chapel Hill, 1953), pp. 42, 52–3, 113, on cultural conditions in the Southern back-country. See also Carl Bridenbaugh: *Myths and Realities: Societies of the Colonial South* (Baton Rouge, 1952), chapter 3.

[8] Colin B. Goodykoontz: *Home Missions on the American Frontier* (Caldwell, Idaho, 1939), pp. 139–43. It was not merely Protestant denominations that suffered this breakdown of religious practice in the process of migration. An Indiana priest wrote in 1849 of Irish immigrants in his vicinity: "They scarcely know there is a God; they are ashamed to attend Catechism, and when they do come they do not understand the instruction." Sister Mary Carol Schroeder: *The Catholic Church in the Diocese of Vincennes, 1847–1877* (Washington, 1946), p. 58.

[9] Rufus Babcock, ed.: *Forty Years of Pioneer Life: Memoir of John Mason Peck, D.D.* (Philadelphia, 1864), pp. 101–3.

of the most primitive structure, was situated at some distance within the cornfield. In and around it were the patriarchal head and his wife, two married daughters and their husbands, with three or four little children, and a son and daughter grown up to manhood and womanhood. The old man said he could read but "mighty poorly." The old woman wanted a *hyme* book, but could not read one. The rest of this romantic household had no use for books or "any such trash." I had introduced myself as a Baptist preacher, traveling through the country preaching the gospel to the people. The old man and his wife were Baptists, at least had been members of some Baptist church when they lived "in the settlements." The "settlements" with this class in those days meant the back parts of Virginia and the Carolinas, and in some instances the older sections of Kentucky and Tennessee, where they had lived in their earlier days. But it was "a mighty poor chance" for Baptist preaching where they lived. The old man could tell me of a Baptist meeting he had been at on the St. François, and could direct me to Elder Farrar's residence near St. Michael. The old woman and the young folks had not seen a Baptist preacher since they had lived in the territory some eight or ten years. Occasionally they had been to a Methodist meeting. This was the condition of a numerous class of people then scattered over the frontier settlements of Missouri. The "traveling missionary" was received with all the hospitality the old people had the ability or knew how to exercise. The younger class were shy and kept out of the cabin, and could not be persuaded to come in to hear the missionary read the Scriptures and offer a prayer. There was evidence of backwardness, or some other propensity, attending all the domestic arrangements. . . .

Not a table, chair, or any article of furniture could be seen. These deficiencies were common on the frontiers; for emigrations from the "settlements" were often made on pack-horses, and no domestic conveniences could be transported, except the most indispensable cooking-utensils, bedding, and a change or two of clothing. But the head of the family must be shiftless indeed, and void of all backwoods' skill and enterprise, who could not make a table for family use. There were two fashions of this necessary article in the time to which I refer. One was a slab, or "puncheon," as then called, split from a large log, four feet long, and from fifteen to eighteen inches wide, and hewn down to the thickness of a plank. In this were inserted four legs, after the fashion of a stool or bench, at the proper height. The other was a rough frame, in which posts were inserted for legs, and covered with split clap-boards shaved smooth, and fastened with small wooden pins. We found one of these descriptions of tables in hundreds of log cabins where neatness, tidiness, and industry prevailed. . . .

The viands now only need description to complete this accurate picture of real squatter life. The rancid bacon when boiled could have been detected by a foetid atmosphere across the yard, had there been one. The snap-beans, as an accompaniment, were not half-boiled. The sour buttermilk taken from the churn, where the milk was kept throughout the whole season, as it came from the cow, was "no go." The article on which the traveler made a hearty breakfast, past ten o'clock in the morning, was the corn, boiled in fair water.

At times, the missionaries were simply overwhelmed. One wrote of his difficulties in the town of China, Indiana, in 1833: [1]

Ignorance & her squalid brood. A universal dearth of intellect. Total abstinence from literature is very generally practiced. Aside from br. Wilder and myself, there is not a literary man of any sort in the bounds. There is not a scholar in grammar or geography, or a *teacher capable* of *instructing* in *them*, to my knowledge. There are some neighborhoods in which there has *never been a school* of *any* kind. Parents and children are one dead level of ignorance. Others are supplied a few months in the year with the most antiquated & unreasonable forms of teaching reading, writing & cyphering. Master Ignoramus is a striking facsimile of them. They are never guilty of teaching any thing but "pure *school-master larnin*." Of course there is no kind of ambition for improve-ment; & it is no more disgrace for man, woman or child to be un-able to read, than to have a long nose. Our own church the other day elected a man to the eldership who is unable to read the bible. I don't know of ten families who take any kind of paper, political or religious, & the whole of their revenue to the Post office de-partment is not as much as mine alone. Need I stop to remind you of the host of loathsome reptiles such a stagnant pool is fitted to breed! Croaking jealousy; bloated Bigotry; coiling suspicion; wormish blindness; crocodile malice! . . .

[1] Goodykoontz: op. cit., p. 191.

But men and women living under conditions of poverty and exacting toil, facing the hazards of Indian raids, fevers, and agues, and raised on whisky and brawling, could not afford education and culture; and they found it easier to reject what they could not have than to admit the lack of it as a deficiency in themselves.

Another worker in a nearby Indiana town wrote more sympathetically at about the same time that "the people are poor & far from market labouriously engaged in improving & cultivating their new land." But the cultural conditions he found were somewhat the same: [2]

> Society here is in an unformed state composed of persons from every part of the Union. . . . Religious sects are numerous & blind guides enough to swallow all the camels in Arabia—Some of these cant read—Some labour to preach down the Sabbath! & others to rob *Christ of His divinity!* and all harmoniously unite in decrying education—as requisite for a public teacher & in abusing the learned clergy who take wages for their services. When shall this reign of ignorance & error cease in the West?

Of course, to describe the condition of this country is to provide the evangelists with their best defense. It must be said that they were not lowering the level of a high culture but trying to bring the ordinary restraints and institutions of a civilized society into an area which had hardly any culture at all. The best of them were clearly the intellectual and cultural superiors of their environment, and the poorest of them could hardly have made it worse. The home missionaries sent out by the religious organizations were constantly fighting against one manifestation or another of the process of social dissolution—against the increasing numbers of unchurched and non-religious people, against "marriages" unsanctified in the church, and against unregulated lives, wild drinking, and savage fighting. Though often welcomed, they still had to carry on their work under opposition that at the least came to heckling and at the worst was really hazardous. The most famous of the circuit-riding Methodist preachers, Peter Cartwright, reported that camp meetings were attended by rowdies armed with knives, clubs, and horsewhips, determined to break up the proceedings. One Sunday morning, when his sermon was interrupted by toughs, Cartwright himself had to lead his congregation in a counterassault. Those who undertook the hard task of bringing religion westward, as it were, in their

[2] Ibid., pp. 191–2. For an account of similar conditions in early Indiana, see Baynard R. Hall: *The New Purchase* (1843; ed. Princeton, 1916), p. 120.

saddlebags, would have been ineffective had they been the sort of pastors who were appropriate to the settled churches of the East. They would have been ineffective in converting their moving flocks if they had not been able to develop a vernacular style in preaching, and if they had failed to share or to simulate in some degree the sensibilities and prejudices of their audiences—anti-authority, anti-aristocracy, anti-Eastern, anti-learning. The various denominations responded in different ways to this necessity: but in general it might be said that the congregations were raised and the preachers were lowered. In brief, the elite upon which culture depended for its transmission was being debased by the demands of a rude social order. If our purpose were to pass judgment on the evangelical ministers, a good case could be made for them on the counts of sincerity, courage, self-sacrifice, and intelligence. But since our primary purpose is to assess the transit of civilization and the development of culture, we must bear in mind the society that was emerging. It was a society of courage and character, of endurance and practical cunning, but it was not a society likely to produce poets or artists or savants.

CHAPTER IV

Evangelicalism
and the Revivalists

❦

• 1 •

IT SEEMS evident in retrospect, as indeed it did to some contemporaries, that the conditions of early nineteenth-century American development created a new and distinctive form of Christianity in which both the organization of the churches and the standards of the ministry were unique. For centuries the first tradition of Christianity had been not the tradition of multiple religious "denominations" but the tradition of *the* Church. But from the beginning the American colonies were settled by a variety of immigrant groups representing the wide range of confessional commitments that had grown up in post-Reformation Europe—the religions of the "left" as well as those of the "right." It became clear at an early date that the maintenance on these shores of a monopolistic and coercive establishment would be extremely difficult; and by the middle of the eighteenth century the colonials were well on the way to learning the amenities of religious accommodation and the peaceful possibilities of a legal policy of toleration.

As religious disunity was followed by religious multiplicity, Americans uprooted church establishments and embraced religious liberty. Under the broad liberty prevailing in the American states at the close of the eighteenth century and the beginning of the nineteenth, religious groups that had begun as dissenting sects developed into firm organizations, less formal than the churches of the past, but too secure and well-organized to be considered sects. The promoted sects and the demoted establishments, now operating more or less on a par in a voluntary and freely competitive religious environment, settled down into what has come to be called denominationalism.[1] The essence of American denominationalism is that churches became *voluntary* organizations. The layman, living in a society in which no church enjoyed the luxury of compulsory membership and in which even traditional, inherited membership was often extraordinarily weak, felt free to make a *choice* as to which among several denominations should have his allegiance. In the older church pattern, the layman was born into a church, was often forced by the state to stay in it, and received his religious experiences in the fashion determined by its liturgical forms. The American layman, however, was not simply born into a denomination nor did he inherit certain sacramental forms; the denomination was a voluntary society which he chose to join often after undergoing a transforming religious experience.

There was nothing fictional about this choice. So fluid had been the conditions of American life toward the end of the eighteenth century, and so disorganizing the consequences of the Revolution, that perhaps as many as ninety per cent of the Americans were unchurched in 1790. In the subsequent decades this astonishing condition of religious anarchy was to a considerable degree remedied. The religious public sorted itself out, as it were, and much of it fell into line in one denomination or another. But in this process the decision to join a church had been made over and over again by countless individuals. And what the layman chose was a religious denomination already molded by previous choices and infused with the American's yearning for a break with the past, his passion for the future, his growing disdain for history. In the American political creed the notion prevailed that Europe represented corruptions of the past which must be surmounted. The Protestant denominations were based on a similar view of the Christian past.[2] It was commonly believed that the historical development of Christianity was not an accretion of valuable institutional forms and practices but a process of corruption and degeneration in which the purity of primitive

[1] Readers who are familiar with Sidney E. Mead's brilliant essays on American religious history will recognize my great indebtedness to him in the following pages, especially to his penetrating account of "Denominationalism: The Shape of Protestantism in America," *Church History*, Vol. XXIII (December, 1954), pp. 291–320; and "The Rise of the Evangelical Conception of the Ministry in America (1607–1850)," in Richard Niebuhr and Daniel D. Williams, ed.: *The Ministry in Historical Perspectives* (New York, 1956), pp. 207–49.

[2] For a stimulating exploration of the desire to surmount the past in nineteenth-century American letters, see R. W. B. Lewis: *The American Adam* (Chicago, 1955).

Christianity had been lost. The goal of the devout, then, was not to preserve forms but to strike out anew in order to recapture this purity. "This is an age of freedom," wrote the distinguished evangelical Presbyterian, Albert Barnes, in 1844, "and men *will* be free. The religion of forms is the stereotyped wisdom or folly of the past, and does not adapt itself to the free movements, the enlarged views, the varying plans of this age." [3]

The objective was to return to the pure conditions of primitive Christianity, to which Scripture alone would give the key. Even those who disliked this tendency in American religion could see how central it was. In 1849 a spokesman of the German Reformed Church remarked that the appeal of the sects to private judgment and to the Bible [4]

> involves, of necessity, a protest against the authority of all previous history, except so far as it may seem to agree with what is thus found to be true; in which case, of course, the only real measure of truth is taken to be, not this authority of history at all, but the mind, simply, of the particular sect itself. . . . A genuine sect will not suffer itself to be embarrassed for a moment, either at its start or afterwards, by the consideration that it has no proper root in past history. Its ambition is rather to appear in this respect *autochthonic*, aboriginal, self-sprung from the Bible, or through the Bible from the skies. . . . The idea of a historical continuity in the life of the Church, carries with it no weight whatever for the sect consciousness.

It is significant, then, that the bond that held most denominations together need not be a traditional, inherited confessional bond—that is, not a historical system of doctrinal belief—but goals or motives more or less newly constituted and freshly conceived. Since there need be only a shadow of confessional unity in the denominations, the rational discussion of theological issues—in the past a great source of intellectual discipline in the churches—came to be regarded as a distraction, as a divisive force. Therefore, although it was not abandoned, it was subordinated to practical objectives which were conceived to be far more

---

[3] "The Position of the Evangelical Party in the Episcopal Church," *Miscellaneous Essays and Reviews* (New York, 1855), Vol. I, p. 371. This essay is a thoroughgoing attack on religious forms as being inconsistent with the evangelical spirit.

[4] John W. Nevin: "The Sect System," *Mercersburg Review*, Vol. I (September, 1849), pp. 499–500.

important.[5] The peculiar views or practices of any denomination, if they were not considered good for the general welfare or the common mission enterprise, were sacrificed to this mission without excessive regret.[6] And the mission itself was defined by evangelism. In a society so mobile and fluid, with so many unchurched persons to be gained for the faith, the basic purpose of the denominations, to which all other purposes and commitments were subordinated, was that of gaining converts.

The denominations were trying to win to church allegiance a public which, for whatever reason, had *not* been held by the traditional sanctions of religion and which had lost touch both with liturgical forms and with elaborate creeds. It was unlikely that an appeal mediated by such forms and creeds could now regain the people. What did seem to work was a restoration of the kind of primitive emotional appeal that the first Christian proselytizers had presumably used in the early days of the faith. Revivalism succeeded where traditionalism had failed. Emotional upheavals took the place of the coercive sanctions of religious establishments. Simple people were brought back to faith with simple ideas, voiced by forceful preachers who were capable of getting away from the complexities and pressing upon them the simplest of alternatives: the choice of heaven or hell. Salvation, too, was taken as a matter of choice: the sinner was expected to "get religion"—it was not thought that religion would get him. Whatever device worked to

[5] This historical background may go far to explain what Will Herberg has found to be such a prominent characteristic of contemporary American religion— a strong belief in the importance of religion-in-general coupled with great indifference to the content of religion. (Cf. Eisenhower in 1952: "Our government makes no sense, unless it is founded in a deeply felt religious faith—and I don't care what it is.") This generalized faith in faith is the product, among other things, of centuries of denominational accommodation. See Herberg: *Protestant, Catholic, Jew* (Anchor ed., New York, 1960), chapter 5, especially pp. 84–90.

[6] Even in 1782 Crèvecoeur found that in America, "if the sectaries are not settled close together, if they are mixed with other denominations, their zeal will cool for want of fuel, and will be extinguished in a little time. Then the Americans will become as to religion what they are as to country, allied to all. . . . All sects are mixed as well as all nations; thus religious indifference is imperceptibly disseminated from one end of the continent to the other; which is at present one of the strongest characteristics of the Americans. Where this will reach no one can tell, perhaps it may leave a vacuum fit to receive other systems. Persecution, religious pride, the love of contradiction, are the food of what the world commonly calls religion. These motives have ceased here; zeal in Europe is confined; here it evaporates in the great distance it has to travel; there it is a grain of powder enclosed, here it burns away in the open air, and consumes without effect." *Letters from an American Farmer* (New York, 1957), pp. 44, 47. Of course, in the decades after 1790 some of the religious enthusiasm was restored, but the passion for distinguishing sectarian differences was restored in nothing like the same manner.

bring him back into the fold was good. As that indefatigable saver of souls, Dwight L. Moody, once put it: "It makes no difference how you get a man to God, provided you get him there." [7] Long before pragmatism became a philosophical creed, it was formulated, albeit in a crude way, by the evangelists. For the layman the pragmatic test in religion was the experience of conversion; for the clergyman, it was the ability to induce this experience. The minister's success in winning souls was taken as the decisive evidence that he preached the truth.[8]

The ministry itself was metamorphosed by the denominational system and the regnant evangelical spirit. The churches, whatever their denominational form or plan of organization, tended in varying degrees to move in the direction of a kind of congregationalism or localism. The combined forces of localism and revivalism greatly strengthened the hand of the heretic or the schismatic: so long as he could produce results, who could control him? They also strengthened the hand of the layman. The minister, pulled away from the sustaining power of a formidable central church, was largely thrown on his own resources in working out his relationship with his congregation. He did claim and establish as much authority as he could, but the conditions of American life favored an extraordinary degree of lay control. In the South even the colonial Anglican church, with its traditions of clerical authority, had found that an extraordinary measure of control passed into the hands of its vestrymen. Everywhere the American ministers seemed to be *judged* by the laymen, and in a sense used by them. Even in the eighteenth century, Crèvecoeur had commented on the attitude of the Low Dutchman who "conceives no other idea of a clergyman than that of an hired man; if he does his work well he will pay him the stipulated sum; if not he will dismiss him, and do without his sermons, and let his house be shut up for years." [9]

[7] Quoted in William G. McLoughlin: *Billy Sunday Was His Real Name* (Chicago, 1955), p. 158. A more sophisticated preacher like Washington Gladden could also say that his own theology "had to be hammered out on the anvil for daily use in the pulpit. The pragmatic test was the only one that could be applied to it: 'Will it work?'" *Recollections* (Boston, 1909), p. 163.

[8] One of the chapters in Charles G. Finney's *Lectures on Revivals of Religion* (New York, 1835) is headed: "A Wise Minister Will Be Successful," and cites Proverbs XI, 30: "He that winneth souls is wise."

[9] Crèvecoeur: op. cit., p. 45. This should not be taken as suggesting that the ministers were not respected. They did not *have* respect by virtue of their office, but they could and often did *win* respect. Timothy Dwight said of the early Connecticut clergy that they had no official power but much influence. "Clergymen, here, are respected for what they are, and for what they do, and not for anything adventitious to themselves, or their office." Mead: "The Rise of the Evangelical Conception of the Ministry," p. 236.

The ministers, in turn, unable to rely as much as in the Old World upon the authority of their churches and their own positions, became, when they were most successful, gifted politicians in church affairs, well versed in the secular arts of manipulation. Moreover, there was a premium upon ministers capable of a mixed kind of religious and nationalistic statecraft, whose object was to reform the country and win the West for Christianity. Concerning the apparatus of societies devoted to such purposes which sprang up between 1800 and 1850, one minister complained: "The minister is often expected to be, for the most part, a manager of social utilities, a wire-puller of beneficent agencies," whose character was too often judged by "the amount of visible grinding that it can accomplish in the mill of social reform. . . ."[1] As a consequence, Sidney E. Mead has pointed out, "the conception of the minister practically lost its priestly dimension as traditionally conceived, and became that of a consecrated functionary, called of God, who directed the purposive activities of the visible church."[2]

Finally, the work of the minister tended to be judged by his success in a single area—the saving of souls in measurable numbers. The local minister was judged either by his charismatic powers or by his ability to prepare his congregation for the preaching of some itinerant ministerial charmer who would really awaken its members.[3] The "star" system prevailed in religion before it reached the theater. As the evangelical impulse became more widespread and more dominant, the selection and training of ministers was increasingly shaped by the revivalist criterion of ministerial merit. The Puritan ideal of the minister as an intellectual and educational leader was steadily weakened in the face of the evangelical ideal of the minister as a popular crusader and exhorter. Theological education itself became more instrumental. Simple dogmatic formulations were considered sufficient. In considerable

[1] Andrew P. Peabody: *The Work of the Ministry* (Boston, 1850), p. 7. It was the patriotic and statesmanlike concern of the Protestant clergy for the Christianization of the West that caused Tocqueville to remark that "if you converse with these missionaries of Christian civilization, you will be surprised to hear them speak so often of the goods of this world, and to meet a politician where you expected to find a priest." *Democracy in America*, ed. by Phillips Bradley (New York, 1945), Vol. I, pp. 306–7.

[2] "The Rise of the Evangelical Conception of the Ministry," p. 228.

[3] This reliance upon the charismatic power of the minister has never ceased to be important. "Truth through Personality," said Phillips Brooks, "is our description of real preaching." And one of his contemporaries, William Jewett Tucker, agreed: "The law is, the greater the personality of the preacher, the larger the use of his personality, the wider and deeper the response of men to truth." See Robert S. Michaelsen: "The Protestant Ministry in America: 1850 to the Present," in Niebuhr and Williams: op. cit., p. 283.

measure the churches withdrew from intellectual encounters with the
secular world, gave up the idea that religion is a part of the whole life
of intellectual experience, and often abandoned the field of rational
studies on the assumption that they were the natural province of
science alone. By 1853 an outstanding clergyman complained that
there was "an impression, somewhat general, that an intellectual
clergyman is deficient in piety, and that an eminently pious minister is
deficient in intellect."[4]

• 2 •

All the foregoing is in the nature of broad generalization, always somewhat hazardous where American religion is concerned, because of
regional differences and the diversity of American religious practices.
But I think these generalizations roughly describe the prevalent pattern of American denominational religion, and the characteristic effects of evangelicalism. There were, of course, important conservative
churches largely or wholly uninfluenced by the evangelicals. Some of
them, like the Roman Catholic Church and the Lutherans, were unaffected except in external ways by the currents of evangelicalism;
others, like the Episcopalian, were affected in varying degrees from
place to place; others, like the Presbyterian and Congregational, were
internally divided by the evangelical movement.

If one compares American society at the close of the Revolution, still
largely hemmed in east of the Alleghenies, with the much vaster American society of 1850, when the denominational pattern was basically
fixed, one is impressed by the gains of the groups committed to evangelicalism. At the end of the Revolution the three largest and strongest
denominations were the Anglicans, the Presbyterians, the Congregationalists. Two of these had once been established in one place or another, and the third had a strong heritage in America. By 1850, the
change was striking. The largest single denomination was then the
Roman Catholic. Among Protestant groups the first two were now the
Methodists and the Baptists, once only dissenting sects. They were followed by the Presbyterians, Congregationalists, and Lutherans, in that

[4] Bela Bates Edwards: "Influence of Eminent Piety on the Intellectual Powers,"
Writings (Boston, 1853), Vol. II, pp. 497–8. "Are we not apt to dissociate the
intellect from the heart, to array knowledge and piety against each other, to exalt
the feelings at the expense of the judgment, and to create the impression extensively, that eminent attainments in knowledge and grace are incompatible?" Ibid.,
pp. 472–3.

order. The Episcopal Church had fallen to eighth place—a significant token of its inability, as an upper-class conservative church, to hold its own in the American environment.[5]

By and large, then, the effort to maintain and extend Protestant Christianity, both in the fresh country of the West and in the growing cities, was carried on successfully by the popular, evangelical denominations, not by the liturgical churches. The sweeping gains of the Methodists and Baptists were evidence of their ability to adapt to the conditions of American life. The extent to which the evangelicals had taken over such denominations as the Congregationalists and the Presbyterians is also evidence of the power of the evangelical impulse to transform older religious structures.

The evangelists were the main agents of the spread of Protestant Christianity, religious revival its climactic technique. From the closing years of the eighteenth century, and well on into the nineteenth, successive waves of revivals swept over one or another part of the country. A first wave, running roughly from about 1795 to 1835, was particularly powerful in the New West of Tennessee and Kentucky, then in western New York and the Middle Western states. Its fevers had not long died out when a new wave, beginning about 1840, swept into the towns and cities, demonstrating (as later revivalists like Dwight L. Moody, Billy Sunday, and Billy Graham were to understand) that revivalism need not be only a country phenomenon. This revival reached its climax in the troubled years 1857 and 1858, when great outpourings of the spirit affected New York, Boston, Philadelphia, Cincinnati, Pittsburgh, Rochester, Binghamton, Fall River, and a host of smaller towns.[6]

Revivals were not the sole instruments of this effort. By the third

[5] For an excellent statement about the numbers, schismatic divisions, theological commitments, and mutual relations of the various denominations, see Timothy L. Smith: *Revivalism and Social Reform* (New York and Nashville, 1958), chapter 1, "The Inner Structure of American Protestantism." In 1855 all Methodist groups (including North and South) had 1.5 million members; all Baptists groups 1.1 million; all Presbyterian groups 490,000; all Lutheran, German Reformed and similar groups, 350,000. The Congregationalists numbered about 200,000; the Episcopalians, only about 100,000.

[6] My treatment of revivalism owes much to William G. McLoughlin's excellent survey of the whole movement: *Modern Revivalism* (New York, 1959); to Timothy L. Smith's *Revivalism and Social Reform*, already cited, which is particularly good on the period after 1840 and on the urban revivals; to Charles A. Johnson's account of *The Frontier Camp Meeting* (Dallas, 1955), which is especially illuminating with regard to the primitive frontier conditions of 1800–1820; and to Bernard Weisberger's *They Gathered at the River* (Boston, 1958).

decade of the century, the evangelicals had founded a number of mission societies, Bible and tract societies, education societies, Sunday-school unions, and temperance organizations, most of them organized on interdenominational lines. These agencies were prepared to assist in a crusade whose first objective would be to Christianize the Mississippi Valley and save it from religious apathy, infidelity, or Romanism, and whose ultimate purpose was to convert every American and then, quite literally, the world. For a long time denominational differences were subordinated in this drive against the common foes of skepticism, passivity, and Romanism. Where denominations did not co-operate as such, the benevolent societies gave scope to individuals who were interested in a common effort; they also offered opportunities for assertive laymen to take the lead in joint benevolent enterprises where clergymen were reluctant. The evangelical groups maintained their co-operation through most of the great revival upsurge of 1795 to 1835. But by about 1837 the common effort had lost its impetus; in part it was checked by resurgent disputes between the sects and by schisms within them; but it declined also because the evangelizing crusade had already succeeded in achieving its main objectives.[7]

Successful it was, by any reasonable criteria. The figures show a remarkable campaign of conversion carried out under inordinately difficult circumstances. In the mid-eighteenth century, America had a smaller proportion of church members than any other nation in Christendom. American religious statistics are notoriously unreliable, but it has been estimated that in 1800 about one of every fifteen Americans was a church member; by 1850 it was one of seven. In 1855 slightly more than four million persons were church members in a population of over twenty-seven million. To the twentieth-century American, accustomed to see a great majority of the population enrolled as church members, these figures may not seem impressive; but it is important to remember that church membership, now bland and often meaningless, was then a more serious and demanding thing; all the evangelizing sects required a personal experience of conversion as well as a fairly stern religious discipline. There were many more church-goers than church members—at least if we are to judge by the twenty-six million church seating accommodations reported in 1860 for a population

---

[7] On the common effort of this period, and its recession, see Charles I. Foster: *An Errand of Mercy: The Evangelical United Front, 1790–1837* (Chapel Hill, 1960).

of thirty-one million.[8] The most imposing achievements of all the denominations were those of the Methodists and Baptists, who together had almost seventy per cent of all Protestant communicants.

· 3 ·

As the evangelical tide at first swept westward, and then into the growing cities, it became clear that the religious conquest of America was mainly in the hands of three denominations: the Methodists, the Baptists, and the Presbyterians. A look at these denominations will tell us much about the cultural evangelization of the continent.

Among the evangelical groups, the strongest intellectual tendencies were shown by the Presbyterians, who carried westward the traditions of both New England Congregationalism and colonial Presbyterianism. Under the terms of their Plan of Union of 1801, the Presbyterians and the Congregationalists had co-ordinated their activities in such a way that Congregationalism largely lost its identity outside New England. The Plan of Union was based upon the common Calvinist-derived theology of the two churches; and since most Congregationalists outside of Massachusetts had no profound objection to the Presbyterian form of church organization, Congregational associations in New York and the Middle West tended to be absorbed into Presbyteries. But Congregationalism contributed a distinct cultural leaven and a strong New England flavor to the Presbyterian Church in the Middle West.

The Presbyterians were often fiercely doctrinaire. Appealing to the enterprising and business classes as they did, they also became the elite church among the untraditional denominations.[9] The Presbyterians were much concerned with fostering an instrumental form of higher education and using it for their sectarian interests. In time they fell victim to their own doctrinal passions and underwent a schism. Much influenced by their Congregational allies and recruits, a portion of the Presbyterian ministry began to preach what was

[8] The estimate for 1800 is that of Winfred E. Garrison: "Characteristics of American Organized Religion," *Annals of the American Academy of Political and Social Science*, Vol. CCLVI (March, 1948), p. 20. The figures for 1855 and 1860 are in Timothy L. Smith: op. cit., pp. 17, 20–1. The proportion of the population having church membership rose roughly from about 15 per cent in 1855 to 36 per cent in 1900, 46 per cent in 1926, and 63 per cent in 1958. Will Herberg: *Protestant, Catholic, Jew*, pp. 47–8.

[9] There is a bit of Protestant folklore which sheds light on the social position of the various churches. A Methodist, it was said, is a Baptist who wears shoes; a Presbyterian is a Methodist who has gone to college; and an Episcopalian is a Presbyterian who lives off his investments.

known as the New Haven theology, a considerably liberalized version of Calvinism, which offered a greater hope of divine grace to a larger portion of mankind and lent itself more readily to the spirit and practice of evangelical revivals. The stricter Calvinists of the Old School, more in the Scottish and Scotch-Irish tradition, and based on Princeton College and Princeton Theological Seminary, could not accept the New School ideas. From 1828 to 1837 the church was shaken by controversies and heresy trials. Leaders of Presbyterian evangelism such as Albert Barnes, Lyman Beecher, Asa Mahan, and Lyman Beecher's son Edward were among those charged with heresy. Finally, in 1837, the Old School ousted the New School, and henceforth synods and presbyteries throughout the country had to line up with one or the other of the two factions. Aside from theological differences, the Old School found the New School altogether too sympathetic to interdenominational missionary societies, and in a lesser measure objected to abolitionist sympathizers and agitators, who were strong in New School ranks. Yale, Oberlin College, and Lane Theological Seminary in Cincinnati were the main intellectual centers of New School evangelism. Its great figure was Charles Grandison Finney, the outstanding revivalist in America between the days of Edwards and Whitefield and those of Dwight L. Moody.

The case of Charles Grandison Finney provides a good illustration of the ambiguities of what has been called "Presbygational" evangelism and of the difficulty involved in any facile classification of religious anti-intellectuals. Finney and his associates, being heirs to the intellectual tradition of New England, were often very much concerned with the continuation, if not the development, of learning. The heritage of such excellent transplanted Yankee colleges as Oberlin and Carleton College is a testimony to the persistent vitality of their tradition. It would be difficult to find among other evangelical groups many such literate and intelligent men as Finney, Asa Mahan, or Lyman Beecher; and one may well wonder how many evangelists of the period since the Civil War could have written an autobiography comparable to Finney's *Memoirs*. The minds of these men had been toughened by constant gnawing on Calvinist and neo-Calvinist theology and disciplined by the necessity of carving out their own theological fretwork. But their culture was exceptionally narrow; their view of learning was extremely instrumental; and instead of enlarging their intellectual inheritance, they steadily contracted it.

Finney himself, although now remembered only by those who have a keen interest in American religious or social history, must be reckoned among our great men. The offspring of a Connecticut family which was caught up in the westward movement, he spent his childhood first in Oneida County in central New York and later near the shore of Lake Ontario. After a brief turn at schoolteaching in New Jersey, he qualified for the bar in a small town not far from Utica. His conversion happened when he was twenty-nine. As he tells it, he was praying for spiritual guidance in a darkened law office when he "received a mighty baptism of the Holy Ghost," the first of several such mystical confrontations that he was to have during his life. The following morning he told a client: "I have a retainer from the Lord Jesus Christ to plead his cause, and I cannot plead yours." [1] From that time forward, he belonged entirely to the ministry. In 1824 he was ordained in the Presbyterian church, and from 1825 to 1835 he launched a series of revivals that made him pre-eminent among the evangelical preachers of his time and established him as one of the most compelling figures in the history of American religion.

Finney was gifted with a big voice and a flair for pulpit drama. But his greatest physical asset was his intense, fixating, electrifying, madly prophetic eyes, the most impressive eyes—except perhaps for John C. Calhoun's—in the portrait gallery of nineteenth-century America. The effect upon congregations of his sermons—alternately rational and emotional, denunciatory and tender—was overpowering. "The Lord let me loose upon them in a wonderful manner," he wrote of one of his most successful early revivals, and "the congregation began to fall from their seats in every direction, and cried for mercy. . . . Nearly the whole congregation were either on their knees or prostrate." [2]

In his theology Finney was a self-made man, an individualistic village philosopher of the sort whose independence impressed Tocqueville with the capacity of the American to strike out in pursuit of untested ideas. As a candidate for the Presbyterian ministry he politely rejected the offer of a group of interested ministers to send him to Princeton to study theology: "I plainly told them that I would not put myself under such an influence as they had been under; that I was confident they had been wrongly educated, and they were not ministers that met my ideal of what a minister of Christ should be." An admitted

---

[1] *Memoirs* (New York, 1876), pp. 20, 24; there is an illuminating account of Finney and enthusiasm in western New York in Whitney R. Cross: *The Burned-Over District* (Ithaca, 1950).

[2] *Memoirs*, pp. 100, 103.

novice in theology, he still refused to accept instruction or correction when it did not correspond with his own views. "I had read nothing on the subject except my Bible; and what I had there found upon the subject, I had interpreted as I would have understood the same or like passages in a law book." Again: "I found myself utterly unable to accept doctrine on the ground of authority. . . . I had no where to go but directly to the Bible, and to the philosophy or workings of my own mind. . . ." [3]

Finney carried from the law into the pulpit an element of the old Puritan regard for rationality and persuasion (he once said he spoke to congregations as he would to a jury), which he used especially when he confronted educated middle-class congregations. For all his emotional power, he was soon regarded as too rational by some of his evangelical associates, who warned him in 1830 that his friends were asking about him: "Is there not danger of his turning into an intellectualist?" [4] But Finney was proud of his ability to adapt his preaching style to the sensibilities of his public, stressing emotion in the little country villages and adding a note of rational persuasion in more sophisticated Western towns such as Rochester. "Under my preaching, judges, and lawyers, and educated men were converted by scores." [5]

At any rate, there was no danger of Finney's turning into an "intellectualist." In the main, he was true to the revival tradition both in his preaching methods and in his conception of the ministry. He did not admire ignorance in preachers, but he admired soul-winning *results,* no matter how achieved; he scorned the written sermon, because it lacked spontaneity; and he looked upon secular culture as a potential threat to salvation.

Finney had little use for ministerial education or for the kind of preaching he believed the educated clergy were doing. Not having enjoyed, as he said, "the advantages of the higher schools of learning," he was acutely conscious of being regarded as an amateur by the ministry, and he was aware of being considered undignified. Early in his career, he learned that it was widely believed "that if I were to succeed in the ministry, it would bring the schools into disrepute." After some

---

[3] Ibid., pp. 42, 45–6, 54. This independence persisted, although Finney was aware that he lacked the learning to interpret the Bible independently. In time he learned some Latin, Greek, and Hebrew, but he "never possessed so much knowledge of the ancient languages as to think myself capable of independently criticising our English translation of the Bible." Ibid., p. 5.

[4] McLoughlin: *Modern Revivalism,* p. 55.

[5] *Memoirs,* p. 84; cf. pp. 365–9.

experience in preaching, he became convinced that "the schools are to a great extent spoiling the ministers," who were being given a great deal of Biblical learning and theology but who did not know how to use it. Practice was all: "A man can never learn to preach except by preaching." The sermons of the school-trained ministers "degenerate into literary essays. . . . This reading of elegant literary essays is not preaching. It is gratifying to literary taste, but not spiritually edifying." [6]

Finney was against all forms of elegance, literary or otherwise. Ornamentation in dress or efforts to improve one's domestic furnishings or taste or style of life were the same to him as the depraved tastes and refinements of smoking, drinking, card-playing, and theater-going. As to literature: "I cannot believe that a person who has ever known the love of God can relish a secular novel." "Let me visit your chamber, your parlor, or wherever you keep your books," he threatened. "What is here? Byron, Scott, Shakespeare, and a host of triflers and blasphemers of God." Even the classical languages, so commonly thought necessary to a minister, were of dubious benefit. Students at Eastern colleges would spend "four years . . . at *classical* studies and no God in them," and upon graduation such "learned students may understand their *hic, haec, hoc,* very well and may laugh at the humble Christian and call him ignorant, although he may know how to win more souls than five hundred of them." [7] Looking upon piety and intellect as being in open enmity, Finney found young ministers coming "out of college with hearts as hard as the college walls." The trouble with the "seminaries of learning" was that they attempted to "give young men intellectual strength, to the almost entire neglect of cultivating their moral feelings." "The race is an intellectual one. The excitement, the zeal, are all for the intellect. The young man . . . loses the firm tone of spirituality. . . . His intellect improves, and his heart lies waste." [8]

[6] These opinions are all from Finney's *Memoirs*, chapter 7, "Remarks Upon Ministerial Education," pp. 85–97; cf. Finney's *Lectures on Revivals of Religion*, pp. 176–8.

[7] McLoughlin: *Modern Revivalism*, pp. 118–20. The one field in which education had Finney's approval, McLoughlin points out, was science. Like the Puritans of old, he saw science not as a threat to religion but as a means of glorifying God. The Middle Western church colleges have continued this regard for science, and have produced a great many academic scientists. On the reasons for this, see the stimulating discussion by R. H. Knapp and H. B. Goodrich: *Origins of American Scientists* (Chicago, 1952), chapter 19.

[8] *Lectures on Revivals of Religion*, pp. 435–6.

It is difficult to say whether Finney's description of American ministerial education was accurate, but certainly his sentiments represented the prevailing evangelical view. However prosperous the state of intellect was among fledgling ministers, he was against it.

· 4 ·

I have spoken of Finney at this length because he is a fair representative of the Presbygational evangelical movement: he was neither the most cultivated nor the crudest of its preachers. The effect of the evangelical impulse, of the search for a new religious style to reach the people and save souls, was to dilute the strong intellectual and educational traditions of the Presbyterians and the Congregationalists. The history of the Methodists, the largest church body and one vastly more successful than the Presbyterians in converting the benighted Americans, presents an interesting contrast. The American Methodists began without an intellectualist tradition and with little concern for education or a highly trained ministry; but as time went on, as they lost much of their sectarian spirit and became a settled church, they attracted a membership whose concern for education grew with the years. Before the middle of the nineteenth century, the church was intermittently shaken by controversy between those who looked back nostalgically to the days of the ignorant but effective circuit-riding preachers and those who looked forward to the day when a better-educated clergy would minister to a respectable laity. The history of both the Methodists and the Baptists is an instructive illustration of the divided soul of American religion. On one hand, many of the members of the church gave free expression to a powerfully anti-intellectual evangelism; on the other, in any large church there was always a wing which gave strong voice to a wistful respect for polite, decorative, and largely non-controversial learning. In this regard, that division between the redskin and the paleface which Philip Rahv has characterized as a feature of American letters was prefigured in American religion.

John Wesley himself, an Oxford-trained cleric and a voracious reader, combined in a curious way an extraordinary intellectual vigor with a strong strain of credulity; he had set creditable intellectual standards for Methodism, but his American followers were not vitally interested in sustaining them. The nature of the evangelical spirit itself no doubt made the evangelical revival anti-intellectualist, but American conditions provided a particularly liberating milieu for its anti-intellectual impulse.[9]

Both Wesley himself and Francis Asbury, the first organizer of American Methodism, were itinerant preachers, committed to itinerancy not out of convenience but out of principle. It was their belief that a resident clergy (as in many an English vicarage) tended to go dead and lose its grip on congregations, but itinerants could bring new life to religion. On American soil the practice of itinerancy was a strategic asset that made the Methodists particularly adept at winning the mobile American population back to Christianity. The bulwark and the pride of the early American Methodists were the famous circuit-riding preachers who made up in mobility, flexibility, courage, hard work, and dedication what they might lack in ministerial training or dignity. These itinerants were justly proud of the strenuous sacrifices they made to bring the gospel to the people. Ill-paid and overworked, they carried out their mission in all weathers and under excruciating conditions of travel. (During a particularly ferocious storm it used to be said: "There's nobody out tonight but crows and Methodist preachers.") Their very hardships seemed testimony enough to their sincerity,[1] and their

---

[9] "It is a fundamental principle with us," Wesley declared in answer to an early detractor of Methodism, "that to renounce reason is to renounce religion, that religion and reason go hand in hand, and that all irrational religion is false religion." R. W. Burtner and R. E. Chiles: *A Compend of Wesley's Theology* (New York, 1954), p. 26. But, as Norman Sykes has remarked, the influence of the evangelical revival was nonetheless intellectually retrograde, for it rose partly from a reaction against the rationalistic and Socinian tendencies that had grown out of the latitudinarian movement in theology. By comparison with the leading theological liberals, Wesley was "almost superstitious in his notions of the special interventions of Providence attendant upon the most ordinary details of his life," Sykes remarks, and "with Whitefield the situation was much worse, for he lacked altogether the education and cultured influence of his colleague. . . ." Norman Sykes: *Church and State in England in the Eighteenth Century* (Cambridge, 1934), pp. 398–9.

A. C. McGiffert writes of the evangelical revival in England: "It turned its face deliberately toward the past instead of toward the future in its interpretation of man and his need. It sharpened the issue between Christianity and the modern age, and promoted the notion that the faith of the fathers had no message for their children. Becoming identified in the minds of many with Christianity, its narrowness and mediaevalism, its emotionalism and lack of intellectuality, its crass supernaturalism and Biblical literalism, its want of sympathy with art and science and secular culture in general, turned them permanently against religion. In spite of the great work accomplished by evangelicalism, the result in many quarters was disaster." *Protestant Thought before Kant* (New York, 1911), p. 175. On the intellectual limitations of early American Methodism, see S. M. Duvall: *The Methodist Episcopal Church and Education up to 1869* (New York, 1928), pp. 5–8, 12.

[1] One thing these early churchmen understood was how much of their strength lay in the fact that they were not differentiated from the laymen they served either in culture or in style of living. An English visitor, accustomed to the dignity

achievements in reclaiming the unchurched were often truly extraordinary. It was mainly by their efforts that American Methodism grew from a little sect of some 3,000 members in 1775, four years after Asbury's arrival, to the largest Protestant denomination, with over a million and a half members eighty years later.

Whatever claims might be made for the more educated ministry of the high-toned denominations, the circuit-riders knew that their own way of doing things worked. They evolved a kind of crude pietistic pragmatism with a single essential tenet: their business was to save souls as quickly and as widely as possible. For this purpose, the elaborate theological equipment of an educated ministry was not only an unnecessary frill but in all probability a serious handicap; the only justification needed by the itinerant preacher for his limited stock of knowledge and ideas was that he got results, measurable in conversions. To this justification very little answer was possible.

The Methodist leaders were aware, as their critics often observed, that they appealed to the poor and the uneducated, and they proposed to make a virtue of it. Francis Asbury, who was offended by the students at Yale because they were "very genteel," found even the Quakers too "respectable"—"Ah, there is death in that word." [2] In the country at large the Methodists easily outstripped the other denominations in the race for conversions. It was significant that for them New England, where the more settled populace was still somewhat more acquainted with the standards of an educated ministry, presented the stoniest soil, and that they made least headway there. But even there the Methodists began to make incursions upon religious life in the early nineteenth century. At first they ran up their banner in a fashion reminiscent of the New England Awakening: "We have always been more anxious to preserve a *living* rather than a *learned* ministry." [3] Jesse Lee, the leader of New England Methodism, when challenged about his

---

of Anglican bishops, was astounded at his introduction to an Indiana Methodist bishop in 1825. He was surprised to find that the bishop's residence was a common farmhouse. As he waited with some impatience for the bishop to appear, he was told by one of the American ministers that Bishop Roberts was coming. "I see a man there, but no Bishop," he said. "But that is certainly the Bishop," said the American. "No! no! that cannot be, for the man is in his shirtsleeves." Bishop Roberts had been at work on his property. Charles E. Elliott: *The Life of the Rev. Robert R. Roberts* (New York, 1844), pp. 299–300. On the frontier bishop, see Elizabeth K. Nottingham: *Methodism and the Frontier* (New York, 1941), chapter 5.

[2] George C. Baker, Jr.: *An Introduction to the History of Early New England Methodism, 1789–1839* (Durham, 1941), p. 18.

[3] Ibid., p. 14.

education (a familiar experience there for Methodists competing with the learned clergy), would simply reply that he had education enough to get him around the country.[4] In time, New England became a test case for the adaptability of the Methodists, and they were not found wanting. A process of accommodation to respectability, gentility, and education set in among them which was to herald later and less spectacular adaptations elsewhere.

The Methodists of Norwich, Connecticut, for instance, were described by a pamphleteer of 1800 as being "the most weak, unlearned, ignorant, and base part of mankind."[5] But toward the middle of the nineteenth century, a Congregationalist recalled the changes that had taken place in the Methodist church of nearby Ridgefield in words that might have applied widely elsewhere.[6]

> Though, in its origin, it seemed to thrive upon the outcasts of society—its people are now as respectable as those of any other religious society in the town. No longer do they choose to worship in barns, schoolhouses, and by-places; no longer do they affect leanness, long faces, and loose, uncombed hair; no longer do they cherish bad grammar, low idioms, and the euphony of a nasal twang in preaching. . . . The preacher is a man of education, refinement and dignity.

As Methodism diffused throughout the country, along the frontier and into the South, in a milieu less demanding of educational performance, its original dissent from the respectable, the schooled, and the established kept reasserting itself, but its own success again compelled it to wage a battle against the invading forces of gentility. In a more decentralized church, each locality might have been more free to set its own character, but in a denomination with the formidable

---

[4] Ibid., p. 72. Cf. these words from a Methodist sermon reported to have been delivered in Connecticut: "What I insist upon, my brethren and sisters, is this: larnin isn't religion, and eddication don't give a man the power of the Spirit. It is grace and gifts that furnish the real live coals from off the altar. St. Peter was a fisherman—do you think he ever went to Yale College? Yet he was the rock upon which Christ built his church. No, no, beloved brethren and sisters. When the Lord wanted to blow down the walls of Jericho, he didn't take a brass trumpet, or a polished French horn; no such thing; he took a ram's horn—a plain, natural ram's horn—just as it grew. And so, when he wants to blow down the walls of Jericho . . . he don't take one of your smooth, polite, college learnt gentlemen, but a plain, natural ram's horn sort of a man like me." S. G. Goodrich: *Recollections of a Lifetime* (New York, 1856), Vol. I, pp. 196–7.

[5] Baker: op. cit., p. 16.

[6] Goodrich: op. cit., p. 311.

centralization of the Methodists, the fight over the cultural tone of the church became general. One can follow changing views within the church through one of its highbrows organs, *The Methodist Magazine and Quarterly Review*, and its successor, entitled after 1841 *The Methodist Quarterly Review*. During the early 1830's, it is clear, the Methodists were still acutely aware of being the butt of attacks by the more established religious groups; they were agitated by a difference between those on the one hand who stood for the kind of preaching represented by the itinerants and on the other hand laymen and educated preachers who wanted reforms.[7] In 1834 the controversy was brought to a head by an article by Reverend La Roy Sunderland, which in effect proposed to undercut the very existence of the itinerants by requiring a good education of all Methodist preachers. "Has the Methodist Church," he asked heatedly,

> any usage or practice in any department of her membership from which one might be led to infer that an education of any kind is indispensably necessary before one can be licensed as a preacher of the Gospel? Nay, are not many of her usages the most directly calculated to give the impression that an education is not necessary? Do we not say in the constant practice of our . . . conferences, that, if one has gifts, grace, and a sound understanding, it is enough?

Sunderland was answered by a spokesman of the old school who said that those who demanded an elaborate theological education were guilty of looking upon preaching as "a 'business,' a trade, a secular profession like '*law* and *medicine*,' requiring a similar 'training.'" The existing ministry was not in fact ignorant, and to say so was merely to "confirm all that our enemies have said." Had not the Methodists opened their own academies, colleges, even their university? "All our young men may now be educated, without having their morals endangered by corrupt and infidel teachers; and without having their Methodism ridiculed out of them, by professors or presidents."[8] As

[7] *Methodist Magazine and Quarterly Review*, Vol. XII (January, 1830), pp. 16, 29–68; Vol. XII (April, 1830), pp. 162–97; Vol. XIII (April, 1831), pp. 160–87; Vol. XIV (July, 1832), pp. 377 ff.

[8] La Roy Sunderland: "Essay on a Theological Education," *Methodist Magazine and Quarterly Review*, Vol. XVI (October, 1834), p. 429. David M. Reese: "Brief Strictures on the Rev. Mr. Sunderland's 'Essay on Theological Education,'" *Methodist Magazine and Quarterly Review*, Vol. XVII (January, 1835), pp. 107, 114, 115.

time went on, the periodical itself reflected the victory of the reformers over the old guard, since it ran fewer reminiscences of the old-fashioned itinerant ministers, which had long been a large part of its stock-in-trade, and more essays on fundamental theological subjects and matters of general intellectual interest.

The church, in fact, was in the throes of a significant change during the 1830's and 1840's. The passion for respectability was winning significant victories over the itinerating-evangelical, anti-intellectualist heritage from the previous generations. Again, the policy toward education, both for laymen and for ministers, was a focal issue. Earlier Methodist efforts in education had been on the whole rather pathetic.[9] In its earliest days, the church was handicapped in its educational efforts not only by a lack of numbers but also by a lack of interest which seemed to pervade it from the lowliest laymen up to Asbury himself.[1] Most Methodist laymen could not afford to do much for general education in any case, and theological education seemed a waste of time for a ministry whose work it would be to preach a simple gospel to a simple people.

Such early schools as were launched tended to fail for lack of sup-

[9] The fate of the first Methodist "college," Cokesbury College in Abingdon, Maryland, may serve as an illustration. The project was the pet idea of Dr. Thomas Coke, Wesley's emissary, who brought to America his alien Oxford-inspired notions of education and succeeded in persuading the Methodists that they should found a college, in spite of the objections of Asbury, who would have preferred a general school such as Wesley had founded at Kingswood. Founded in 1787, the college was combined at the beginning (as was so often the case with early American colleges) with a preparatory school, which was far the more successful of the two. Within a year of its founding, the college lost all three faculty members by resignation. In 1794 the collegiate department was closed, leaving only the lower school; plans to re-found the college were interrupted by two fires in 1795 and 1796, which put an end to the project altogether. Asbury felt that it had been a waste of time and money. "The Lord called not Mr. Whitefield nor the Methodists to build colleges. I wished only for schools. . . ." *The Journal and Letters of Francis Asbury*, ed. by Elmer T. Clark et al. (London and Nashville, 1958), Vol. II, p. 75. See also Sylvanus M. Duvall: *The Methodist Episcopal Church and Education up to 1869* (New York, 1928), pp. 31–6. The Virginia Episcopal evangelist, Devereux Jarratt, who knew something of the educational standards of the Anglican ministry, was appalled by the Methodist effort at Abingdon: "Indeed, I see not, how any considerate man could expect any great things from a seminary of learning, while under the supreme direction and controul of tinkers and taylors, weavers, shoemakers and country mechanics of all kinds—or, in other words, of men illiterate and wholly unacquainted with colleges and their contents." *The Life of the Reverend Devereux Jarratt Written by Himself* (Baltimore, 1806), p. 181.

[1] Nathan Bangs, the first noted historian of the church, remarked that early Methodist hostility to learning became proverbial, and justly so. *A History of the Methodist Episcopal Church* (New York, 1842), Vol. II, pp. 318–21.

port. But after the death of Asbury in 1816, a group of strong-minded educational reformers, mainly from New England, went to work on the increasingly numerous and receptive body of laymen. Their efforts began to bear fruit in the late 1820's, and Methodists began to sponsor several academies and a few creditable little colleges. Wesleyan in Connecticut, founded in 1831, was followed by Dickinson College (taken over from the Presbyterians in 1833), Allegheny College (1833), Indiana Asbury (founded in 1833, later DePauw), and Ohio Wesleyan (1842), to mention only the most outstanding. From 1835 to 1860 the church started more than two hundred schools and colleges. As in the past, many of the schools were but poorly supported and maintained. The prevailing Methodist view of education was no doubt mainly instrumental—but it represented an advance over the period when learning was not considered to be even of instrumental value to religion. The passion of some of the leading ministers for a more educated clergy, and the growing need to defend their theological position from increasingly subtle critics,[2] finally broke through the Methodist suspicion of a learned ministry. Theological seminaries were still suspect, as fountainheads of heresy; so the first two Methodist seminaries were founded under the name of "Biblical Institutes." Again, the leadership came from New England—not where the Methodists were strongest or most numerous, but where the competing educational standards were most formidable.[3]

The old guard never became reconciled to the newly emerging Methodist church, with its apparatus of academies, colleges, seminaries, and magazines. The most famous of the circuit-riders, Peter Cartwright, included in his remarkable autobiography, written in 1856, a full and forthright statement of the old-fashioned evangelical view of the ministry which deserves quotation at length as a perfect embodiment of the anti-intellectualist position.[4]

Suppose, now, Mr. Wesley had been obliged to wait for a literary and theologically trained band of preachers before he moved

[2] Ibid., Vol. III, pp. 15–18.
[3] The first such seminary was not founded until 1847: it was the Methodist General Biblical Institute, organized at Concord, New Hampshire, and later transferred to Boston as the School of Theology of Boston University. It was followed by the Garrett Biblical Institute, at Evanston, Illinois, in 1854. The third such institution, Drew Theological Seminary, awaited the generosity of the famous Wall Street pirate, Daniel Drew; it was founded in 1867.
[4] Charles L. Wallis, ed.: *Autobiography of Peter Cartwright* (New York, 1956), pp. 63–5, 266–8.

in the glorious work of his day, what would Methodism have been in the Wesleyan connection today? . . . If Bishop Asbury had waited for this choice literary band of preachers, infidelity would have swept these United States from one end to the other. . . .

The Presbyterians, and other Calvinistic branches of the Protestant Church, used to contend for an educated ministry, for pews, for instrumental music, for a congregational or stated salaried ministry. The Methodists universally opposed these ideas; and the illiterate Methodist preachers actually set the world on fire (the American world at least) while they were lighting their matches! . . .

I do not wish to undervalue education, but really I have seen so many of these educated preachers who forcibly reminded me of lettuce growing under the shade of a peach-tree, or like a gosling that had got the straddles by wading in the dew, that I turn away sick and faint. Now this educated ministry and theological training are no longer an experiment. Other denominations have tried them, and they have proved a perfect failure. . . .

I awfully fear for our beloved Methodism. Multiply colleges, universities, seminaries, and academies; multiply our agencies, and editorships, and fill them with all our best and most efficient preachers, and you localize the ministry and secularize them too; then farewell to itinerancy; and when this fails we plunge right into Congregationalism, and stop precisely where all other denominations started. . . .

Is it not manifest that the employing so many of our preachers in these agencies and professorships is one of the great causes why we have such a scarcity of preachers to fill the regular work? Moreover, these presidents, professors, agents, and editors get a greater amount of pay, and get it more certainly too, than a traveling preacher, who has to breast every storm, and often falls very far short of his disciplinary allowance. Here is a great temptation to those who are qualified to fill those high offices to seek them, and give up the regular work of preaching and trying to save souls. . . .

Perhaps, among the thousands of traveling and local preachers employed and engaged in this glorious work of saving souls, and building up the Methodist Church, there were not fifty men that had anything more than a common English education, and scores of them not that; and not one of them was ever trained in a theological school or Biblical institute, and yet hundreds of them preached the Gospel with more success and had more seals to their ministry than all the sapient, downy D.D.'s in modern times, who, instead of entering the great and wide-spread harvest-field of souls, sickle in hand, are seeking presidencies or professorships in colleges, editorships, or any agencies that have a fat salary, and are trying to create newfangled institutions where good livings can be monopolized, while millions of poor, dying sinners are thronging the way to hell without God, without Gospel. . . .

I will not condescend to stop and say that I am a friend to learning, and an improved ministry, for it is the most convenient way to get rid of a stubborn truth, for these learned and gentlemanly ministers to turn about and say that all those ministers that are opposed to the present abuses of our high calling, are advocates for ignorance, and that ignorance is the mother of devotion. What has a learned ministry done for the world, that have studied divinity as a science? Look, and examine ministerial history. It is an easy thing to engender pride in the human heart, and this educational pride has been the downfall and ruin of many preeminently educated ministers of the Gospel. But I will not render evil for evil, or railing for railing, but will thank God for education, and educated Gospel ministers who are of the right stamp, and of the right spirit. But how do these advocates for an educated ministry think the hundreds of commonly educated preachers must feel under the lectures we have from time to time on this subject? It is true, many of these advocates for an improved and educated ministry among us, speak in rapturous and exalted strains concerning the old, illiterate pioneers that planted Methodism and Churches in early and frontier times; but I take no flattering unction to my soul from these extorted concessions from these velvet-mouthed and downy D.D.'s; for their real sentiments, if they clearly express them, are, that we were indebted to the ignorance of the people for our success.

This was, no doubt, exactly the sentiment that some of the critics of the itinerants meant to express; but Cartwright might well have seen fit to concede that there was some truth in their case. Not all his evangelical brothers would have denied it. As one group of evangelical workers had put it years earlier to Finney: "It is more difficult to labour with educated men, with cultivated minds and moreover predisposed to skepticism, than with the uneducated." [5]

• 5 •

In many respects the history of the Baptists recapitulates that of the Methodists; but since the Baptists were much less centralized, still more uncompromising, still more disposed to insist on a ministry without educational qualifications and even without salary, they yielded to change later and less extensively than the Methodists. As William Warren Sweet observes: "Among no other religious body was the prejudice against an educated and salaried ministry so strong as among the Baptists, and this prejudice prevailed not only among frontier Baptists, but pretty generally throughout the denomination in the early years of the nineteenth century." [6]

The Baptists, of course, had had bitter experiences with educated ministers and established churches, both in Congregational Massachusetts and Anglican Virginia, where they had been much persecuted. Characteristically, they supplied their ministry from the ranks of their own people. The Baptist preacher might be a farmer who worked on his land or a carpenter who worked at his bench like any other layman, and who left his work for Sunday or weekday sermons or for baptisms and funerals. He had little or no time for books. Such hard-working citizens did not relish competition from other preachers, and they resisted with the most extraordinary ferocity even the home missionary societies which attempted to join with them in spreading the gospel throughout the hinterland. In this resistance to "outside" interference and centralized control they indoctrinated their followers. The word went out that anyone who had to do with the missionary societies would not be welcomed into the Baptist Associations. "We cannot receive into fellowship either churches or members who join one of those unscriptural societies," declared a Kentucky Baptist Association. And an Illinois group, manifesting in its almost paranoid

---

[5] Charles C. Cole: *The Social Ideas of Northern Evangelists, 1826–1860* (New York, 1954), p. 80. Sam Jones, one of the most successful revivalists of the Gilded Age, later said that he preferred to work in the South: "I find the people further South are more easily moved. They haven't got the intellectual difficulties that curse the other portions of the country." McLoughlin: *Modern Revivalism*, pp. 299–300.

[6] *Religion in the Development of American Culture* (New York, 1952), p. 111.

extreme a suspicion against authority, declared in a circular letter: "We further say to the churches, have nothing to do with the Bible Society, for we think it dangerous to authorize a few designing men to translate the holy Bible. Stand fast in the liberty wherewith Christ has set you free, and be not entangled with the yoke of bondage." [7] One should, I think, check one's impulse to wonder whether the Bible was to be translated by a national convention, and remember that Baptist suspicions had been kept alive by the memory of early persecutions and cruel ridicule. [8]

Baptists opposed missions in good part because they opposed the centralization of authority. Any concession to central church organization, they felt, would be a step toward "the Pope of Rome and the Mother of Harlots." Their uneducated and unsalaried ministers inevitably resented the encroachments of a better-educated and better-paid ministry. It was easy for an unpaid preacher to believe that the educated missionaries from the East were working only for the money it brought them. [9] A contemporary observer concluded that the uneducated preachers were thoroughly aware of their own limitations. But "instead of rejoicing that the Lord had provided better gifts to promote the cause, they felt the irritability of wounded pride, common to narrow and weak minds." This diagnosis was confirmed by the candid retort of a Baptist preacher to a moderator who pointed out that, after all, no one was compelled to listen to missionaries or to give them money unless he chose. "Well, if you must know, Brother Moderator, you know the big trees in the woods overshadow the little ones; and these missionaries will be all great men, and the people will all go to hear them preach, and we shall be all put down. That's the objection." [1]

The Baptists, however, like the old-guard Methodists, could not absolutely resist the pressure for an educated ministry. Here the desire

[7] W. W. Sweet, ed.: *Religion on the American Frontier—The Baptists, 1783–1830* (New York, 1931), p. 65n.
[8] Cf. an early Virginia version of the Baptists: "Some of them were hair-lipped, others were blear-eyed, or hump-backed, or bow-legged, or clump-footed; hardly any of them looked like other people." Walter B. Posey: *The Baptist Church in the Lower Mississippi Valley, 1776–1845* (Lexington, Kentucky, 1957), p. 2.
[9] Sweet: *Religion on the American Frontier*, p. 72. "Money and Theological learning seem to be the pride, we fear, of too many preachers of our day." Ibid., p. 65.
[1] Ibid., pp. 73–4. On the intellectual condition of Baptist preachers and the resistance of preachers and laymen to education, see Posey: op. cit., chapter 2.

for self-respect and for the respect of others went hand in hand. A Virginia Baptist Association, seeking to found a seminary as early as 1789, gave the following reason: [2]

> Our brethren of other denominations around us Could no longer curse us for not knowing the Law, or discard and Reprobate a great deal of our Teaching for not knowing our Mother tongue, much less the original languages, and if we (in this as we ought in everything), do it with a single eye to The glory of God, and the advancement of the Redeemer's interest Then shall we have sufficient to hope we shall meet with heaven's approbation.

The Baptist laymen were divided between their desire for respectability and their desire for a congenial and inexpensive ministry. By 1830 Baptist leaders had made considerable progress toward providing an educated and salaried ministry, as well as toward raising the educational level of the laity itself. But it was slow work to transform the original bias of the Baptist churches, and it required a constant struggle against entrenched revivalist influences.[3]

· 6 ·

After the Civil War, important structural changes occurred in the position of the churches. Bringing Christianity to the people of the growing cities became more and more urgent; it became increasingly difficult as well, since the churches had to find ways of adapting to the sensibilities of the urban worker and of coping with his poverty, as well as holding migrants from the countryside. The interest of revivalists in the cities, which had risen markedly even in the 1840's and 1850's, now took on special urgency. From the time of Dwight L. Moody to that of Billy Graham, success in making conversions in the big cities—and on an international scale—has been the final test of an evangelist's importance. The exhorter whose appeal was limited to the countryside and the small towns was never more than third rate.

Moody was by far the most imposing figure between Finney and Billy Sunday. The son of a poor brickmason in Northfield, Massachusetts, he lost his father at an early age, and was converted at eighteen by a Congregational pastor who had been an itinerant evan-

---

[2] Wesley M. Gewehr: *The Great Awakening in Virginia, 1740–1790* (Durham, North Carolina, 1930), p. 256.

[3] For efforts in behalf of education, see Posey: op. cit., chapter 8.

gelist. In his early twenties Moody was already involved in the religious and welfare activity that had begun in the cities in the decade before the Civil War. Although very successful as a wholesale shoe salesman in Chicago, he decided in 1860 to give up business for independent mission work. During the war he was active in the Y.M.C.A., and soon after the war's end he became president of the Chicago branch. Unschooled since his thirteenth year, he never sought ordination, and never became a minister.

Before 1873, Moody's main achievements were in Y.M.C.A. and Sunday-school work, though he had demonstrated enterprise and curiosity by twice making trips to Great Britain to look into the methods of Christian leaders there. In 1873 he had his first major success when he was invited by British acquaintances to come and conduct a series of evangelical meetings. Taking with him his organist and singer, Ira D. Sankey, he launched in the summer of 1873 upon a two-year series of meetings that brought him to York, Edinburgh, Glasgow, Belfast, Dublin, Manchester, Sheffield, Birmingham, Liverpool, and London. It was estimated that over two and a half millions heard Moody in London alone. Britain had not known such impressive preaching since the days of Wesley and Whitefield. He had left America in obscurity, and he returned in the full blaze of fame; from 1875 to his death in 1899 he was not only the unchallenged leader of a new phase in American evangelism but the greatest figure in American Protestantism.

Moody was quite unlike Finney. Whereas Finney overwhelmed audiences with an almost frightening power, Moody was a benign and lovable man, much happier holding out the promise of heaven than warning of the torments of hell. Short, corpulent, and full-bearded, he resembled General Grant, and the resemblance was more than physical. Like Grant, Moody was inordinately simple, yet of powerful will; and his sieges of souls showed some of the same determined capacity for organization that went into the siege of Vicksburg. Like Grant, he could bring overwhelming superiority in force to bear at the point of weakness, until resistance wore down. Like Grant, he hid his intensity behind an unpretentious façade. Here the resemblance ends. Grant did what he had to do, in spite of an inner lack of confidence; he had been lost in the business world before his war career and he was to be lost again in politics afterwards. Moody's self-confidence was enormous. He had been well on his way toward a fortune when, still very young, he gave up business for religion; and it is hard to imagine him failing in any practical sphere of life in which endurance, shrewdness, decision, simple manliness, and a human touch were the prime requisites. He was immensely ignorant—ignorant even of grammar, as critics of his sermons were forever saying; but he knew his Bible and he knew his audiences. Unsensational, untiring, he repeatedly confronted them with his inevitable question: "Are you a Christian?" and swept them along toward salvation with breathless torrents of words uttered in a voice that easily filled the huge auditoriums in which he flourished.

Moody's message was broad and nondenominational—it is significant that he had the endorsement at one time or another of practically every denomination except the Roman Catholics, the Unitarians, and the Universalists [4]—and he cared not a whit for the formal discussion of theological issues ("My theology! I didn't know I had any. I wish you would tell me what my theology is.").[5] The knowledge, the culture, the science of his time meant nothing to him, and when he touched upon them at all, it was with a note as acid as he was ever likely to strike. In this respect, he held true to the dominant evangelical tradition. Although he had no desire to undermine the established ministry or its training, he cordially approved of laymen in religious work and felt that seminary-educated ministers "are often educated away from the people." [6] He denigrated all education that did not serve the purposes of religion—for secular education, he said, instead of telling men what a bad lot they are, flatters them and tells them "how angelic they are because they have some education. An educated rascal is the meanest kind of rascal." Aside from the Bible, he read almost nothing. "I have one rule about books. I do not read any book, unless it will help me to understand *the* book." Novels? They were "flashy. . . . I have no taste for them, no desire to read them; but if I did I would not do it." The theater? "You say it is part of one's education to see good plays. Let that kind of education go to the four winds." Culture? It is "all right in its place," but to speak of it before a man is born of God is "the height of madness." Learning? An encumbrance to the man of spirit: "I would rather have zeal without knowledge; and there is a good deal of knowledge without zeal." Science? It had become, by Moody's time, a threat to religion rather than a means for the discovery and glorification of God. "It is a great deal easier to believe that man was made after the image of God than to believe, as some young men

[4] McLoughlin: *Modern Revivalism*, pp. 219–20.
[5] Gamaliel Bradford: *D. L. Moody: A Worker in Souls* (New York, 1927), p. 61.
[6] McLoughlin: *Modern Revivalism*, p. 273.

and women are being taught now, that he is the offspring of a monkey." [7]

True to the evangelical tradition in his attitude toward intellect and culture, Moody nevertheless marked for his generation a new departure in the history of revivalism, a departure not from goals or attitudes but from methods. In the days of Jonathan Edwards and his contemporaries, it had been customary to look upon revivals as the consequence of divine visitations. Edwards had referred to the Northampton revival, in the title of his first great work, as a "surprising work of God"; and it was the adjective here that suggested the Northampton preacher's conception that the affair was not altogether in the control of human will. Whitefield, one surmises, knew better; as a veteran promoter of revivals, he must have had more than an inkling that human will had something to do with it. The preferred theory, none the less, was that divine intervention was the essential active agent and that the human will was relatively passive. By the time of Finney, this notion was in decline, and the voluntarism characteristic of the American evangelical tradition was in the ascendant. *"Religion is the work of man,"* Finney insisted. It is true, he admitted, that God interposes his spirit to make men obey His injunctions. But the spirit is always at work—it is, as we would now say, a constant; the human response is the variable. Revivals take place when the human will rises to the occasion. A revival of religion, Finney asserted, "is not a miracle, or dependent on a miracle, in any sense. It is a purely philosophical result of the right use of the constituted means." Hence, it was false and slothful to sit and wait for the miraculous reoccurrence of revivals. "You see why you have not a revival. It is only because you don't want one." [8]

Finney's *Lectures on Revivals of Religion* were wholly devoted to showing what the right means were and how revivals could be produced, so to speak, at will. But it is noteworthy that the means about which Finney was speaking were not simply mechanical; they were not mere techniques; they were a series of instructions as to how the heart, the mind, and the will could all be marshaled to the great end of reviving religion. Here is where Moody and his generation, adapting

---

[7] Bradford: *Moody,* pp. 24, 25–6, 30, 35, 37, 64, 212.

[8] *Lectures on Revivals of Religion,* pp. 9, 12, 32. I have hardly done justice to the full range of Finney's argument for the role of human agency in bringing about revivals; it is stated cogently in the first chapter of his book.

revivalism to the spirit of the new industrial age, made their departure. It would be impertinent to suggest that a man of Moody's force and sincerity lacked the necessary inward psychic resources; but it is important to note that he added something else—the techniques of business organization. Finney's revivalism belonged to the age of Andrew Jackson and Lyman Beecher; Moody's belonged to the age of Andrew Carnegie and P. T. Barnum.

Finney's revivals, though carefully planned, had been conducted without much apparatus. Moody's brought an imposing machinery into play.[9] Advance agents were sent to arrange invitations from local evangelical ministers. Advertising campaigns were launched, requiring both display posters and newspaper notices (the latter inserted in the amusement pages). Churches, even the largest, could no longer seat the crowds. Large auditoriums had to be found, and where there were none they had to be erected. If temporary, they were afterwards sold and scrapped for what they would bring. The building for Moody's Boston meetings cost $32,000. To defray his imposing expenses—a series of meetings in one city might require from $30,000 (New York) to $140,000 (London)—finance committees were established; through them the resources of local businessmen could be tapped. But Moody did not have to depend only upon small businessmen. Cyrus McCormick and George Armour helped him in Chicago, Jay Cooke and John Wanamaker in Philadelphia, J. P. Morgan and Cornelius Vanderbilt II in New York. The meetings required staffs of local ushers to handle the crowds, staffs of assistants for follow-ups on the spiritual condition of Moody's converts in after-sermon "inquiry" sessions. Then there were the arrangements for the music—Sankey's singing and his organ, the recruitment of teams of local singers for choirs of from 600 to 1,000 persons for each city. Like almost anything else in business, the results of Moody's meetings became the object of measurement. At first Moody himself objected to making estimates of the numbers of souls saved—3,000, they said, in London, 2,500 in Chicago, 3,500 in New York—but in later years he began to use "decision cards" to record systematically the names and addresses of those who came to the inquiry room.

Finney, we have seen, was proud that some of his legal training carried over into his most rational sermons. Perhaps less self-consciously,

[9] See the excellent account of Moody's revival machinery, in McLoughlin: *Modern Revivalism*, chapter 5, "Old Fashioned Revival with the Modern Improvements."

Moody's preaching revealed his early business experience. At times he talked like a salesman of salvation. He seemed still to be selling a product when he mounted a chair at an "inquiry" meeting to say: "Who'll take Christ now? That's all you want. With Christ you have eternal life and everything else you need. Without Him you must perish. He offers Himself to you. Who'll take Him?" [1] Or when he was heard to say: "If a man wants a coat he wants to get the best coat he can for the money. This is the law the world around. If we show men that religion is better than anything else, we shall win the world," one can only concur with the judgment of Gamaliel Bradford that this is "the dialect of the shoe-trade." [2] The point was not lost on contemporaries. "As he stood on the platform," Lyman Abbott wrote of Moody, "he looked like a business man; he dressed like a business man; he took the meeting in hand as a business man would; he spoke in a business man's fashion." [3]

Whereas Finney had been a radical on at least one major social issue, that of slavery, Moody was consistently conservative; the union between the evangelical and the business mind which was to characterize subsequent popular revivalists was, to a great extent, his work. His political views invariably resembled those of the Republican businessmen who supported him, and he was not above making it clear how useful the Gospel was to the propertied interests. "I say to the rich men of Chicago, their money will not be worth much if communism and infidelity sweep the land." Again: "There can be no better investment for the capitalists of Chicago than to put the saving salt of the Gospel into these dark homes and desperate centers. . . ." But it would be wrong to suggest that he was pandering. His conservatism was a reflection of his pre-millennialist beliefs, which in him engendered a thoroughgoing social pessimism. Man was naturally and thoroughly bad, and nothing was to be expected of him on earth. "I have heard of reform, reform, until I am tired and sick of the whole thing. It is regeneration by the power of the Holy Ghost that we need." As a consequence, Moody showed no patience for any kind of sociological discussion.[4] Man was, and always had been, a failure in all his works. The true task was to get as many souls as possible off the sinking ship of this world.

[1] Bernard Weisberger: *They Gathered at the River*, p. 212.
[2] Op. cit., p. 243.
[3] *Silhouettes of My Contemporaries* (New York, 1921), p. 200.
[4] McLoughlin: *Modern Revivalism*, pp. 167, 269, 278; Bradford: op. cit., pp. 220–1.

· 7 ·

In one important respect, the revivalism of Moody's era had to be more controlled than its predecessors. The "enthusiastic" manifestations of the old-time revivals—the shriekings, groanings, faintings, howlings, and barkings—were now inadmissible. It was not merely that pietism had grown more restrained, but that the city revivals took place under the critical eye of the urban press and nothing could be allowed to happen that would lose the sympathetic interest of the public. The loss of control that had been permissible in village churches and at camp meetings might also have created dangerous scenes in the huge auditoriums of the big-time revivals. The most intelligent sympathizers of revivals had always found the extreme manifestations of enthusiasm an embarrassment. Finney, though he regularly induced them, thought of them as necessary encumbrances and evils. Moody, determined to have done with them, would interrupt a sermon to have ushers remove a disturbed member of the audience. Even an excess of "Amens" or "Hallelujahs" would bring him to call out: "Never mind, my friend, I can do all the hollering." [5] His successor, Billy Sunday, believing that "a man can be converted without any fuss," held a stern hand over audiences, and instructed ushers to throw out disorderly manifestants. "Two can't windjam at once, brother; let me do it," he once yelled. And on another occasion: "Just a minute, sister, hold your sparker back and save a little gasoline." [6] Decorum—of a sort—was to be kept; and there must be no distractions from the performance of the star.

Although the conditions of city evangelism demanded restraint in audiences, they seem to have released the preachers. For the historian of popular sensibilities, one of the most arresting aspects of the development of evangelicalism is the decline of the sermon from the vernacular to the vulgar. The conception that preaching should be plain, unaffected, unlearned, and unadorned, so that it would reach and move simple people, had always been central to pietism. Finney had argued that the truly good sermon, like the truly good life, would be trimmed of elegance and pretense. He had spoken movingly for the vernacular style in sermons, and preferred the extemporane-

[5] McLoughlin: *Modern Revivalism*, p. 245; cf. Bradford: op. cit., p. 223.
[6] McLoughlin: *Modern Revivalism*, p. 433-4; also *Billy Sunday Was His Real Name*, pp. 127-8.

ous to the written sermon because spontaneous utterance would be
more direct and closer to common speech. When men are entirely in
earnest, he said, "their language is in point, direct and simple. Their
sentences are short, cogent, powerful." They appeal to action and get
results. "This is the reason why, formerly, the ignorant Methodist
preachers, and the earnest Baptist preachers produced so much more
effect than our most learned theologians and divines. They do so
now." [7]

One can hardly resist the cogency of Finney's pleas for the vernacular sermon. Is there not, after all, an element of the vernacular in most
good preaching? One thinks, for example, of Luther visualizing the
Nativity for his listeners with the utmost directness and intimacy: [8]

> Bad enough that a young bride married only a year could not
> have had her baby at Nazareth in her own house instead of mak-
> ing all that journey of three days when heavy with child! . . .
> The birth was still more pitiable. No one regarded this young wife
> bringing forth her first-born. No one took her condition to heart.
> . . . There she was without preparation: no light, no fire, in the
> dead of night, in thick darkness. . . . I think myself if Joseph and
> Mary had realized that her time was so close she might perhaps
> have been left in Nazareth. . . . Who showed the poor girl what
> to do? She had never had a baby before. I am amazed that the lit-
> tle one did not freeze.

Perhaps, too, the plain style of Finney's own utterance was no more
than an inheritance from the best Puritan preaching. Surely the greatest image in the history of American preaching was Jonathan Edwards's image of the soul as a spider held over the fire in the kitchen
stove, suspended by a silken thread at the mercy of God. And is it not
the vernacular note itself which has given American literature much
of its originality and distinction?

All true enough, and justification enough for Finney's own conception of the sermon. The problem for later evangelism was to stabilize
the vernacular style at some point before it would merely confirm, or

[7] *Memoirs*, pp. 90–1. Finney's conception of preaching is expounded at length in
Lectures on Revivals of Religion, chapter 12. Among his rules for the manner of
ministerial discourse were these: "It should be *conversational.*" "It must be in the
language of common life." It should be parabolical—that is, illustrations should be
drawn from real or supposed incidents of common life, and "from the common
business of society." It should be repetitious, but without monotony.

[8] Roland H. Bainton: *Here I Stand: A Life of Martin Luther* (New York and
Nashville, 1940), p. 354.

even exaggerate, the coarsest side of popular sensibility. A contemporary of Finney's, Jabez Swan, was no doubt merely adding a racy colloquial touch when he described Jonah's fish in these terms: [9]

> The great fish splashed, foamed, and pitched up and down, here and there, and everywhere, to get rid of his burden. At length, growing more and more sick, as well he might, he made for the shore and vomited the nauseous dose out of his mouth.

Moody's preaching, spilled out at 220 words a minute, was colloquial without being coarse, though Moody, as befitted his time, introduced a heavy note of sentimentality that Finney might have found strange. Like Finney, Moody was impatient with what he called "essay preaching." "It is a stupid thing to try to be eloquent," he said.[1] Conventional audiences were put off by his folkish informality ("Everyone is going to be disappointed in these meetings if he ain't quickened himself") and the London *Saturday Review* found him "simply a ranter of the most vulgar type."[2] But in the main, his sermons stopped short of vulgarity. Younger contemporaries, such as Sam Jones, were striking a broader and more aggressive tone: "Half of the literary preachers in this town are A.B.'s, Ph.D's, D.D.'s, LL.D.'s, and A.S.S.'s." "If anyone thinks he can't stand the truth rubbed in a little thicker and faster than he ever had it before, he'd better get out of here."[3] It was this note, and not Moody's, that was to be imitated by Billy Sunday.

With the arrival of Billy Sunday, whose career as an evangelist spans the years 1896 to 1935, one reaches the nadir in evangelical rhetoric. By comparison, a contemporary of ours like Billy Graham seems astonishingly proper and subdued. Sunday's career in some ways parallels Moody's. His father had been an Iowa bricklayer who died in the Union Army in 1862. Sunday had a rather poverty-stricken country boyhood, left high school before graduating, and was picked up in 1883 by a scout for the Chicago White Stockings baseball team. From 1883 to 1891, Sunday made his living as a ballplayer. His later career sounds as though one of the ineffable egomaniac outfielders of Ring Lardner's stories had got religion and turned to evangelism. Like Moody, Billy Sunday went into evangelical work through the Y.M.C.A.

[9] McLoughlin: *Modern Revivalism*, p. 140.
[1] Bradford: op. cit., p. 101. On his preaching style, see also McLoughlin: *Modern Revivalism*, pp. 239 ff.; there is a wide range of illustrative matter in J. Wilbur Chapman: *The Life and Work of Dwight L. Moody* (Boston, 1900).
[2] Bradford: op. cit., p. 103.
[3] McLoughlin: *Modern Revivalism*, p. 288.

A convert in 1886, he began to give Y.M.C.A. talks, worked as a Y.M.C.A. secretary after leaving baseball, and started preaching in 1896. Unlike Moody, who accepted his own lay status, Sunday hungered for ordination, and in 1903 faced a board of examiners of the Chicago Presbytery. After a series of answers in the general tenor of "That's too deep for me," the examination was waived on the ground that Sunday had already made more converts than all his examiners, and he was elevated to the ministry without further inquiry.

After 1906 Sunday left the small towns of the Midwest, where he had his early successes, and began to reach the medium-sized towns. By 1909 he was an established big-time evangelist in the major cities, the heir to Moody's mantle. In one way or another, political leaders like Bryan, Wilson, and Theodore Roosevelt gave him their blessings; tycoons opened their coffers to him, as they had to Moody; the respectable world found him respectable; and millions came to hear him. In 1914 the readers of the *American Magazine,* responding to a poll on the question: "Who is the greatest man in the United States?" put him in eighth place, tied with Andrew Carnegie. He conducted his evangelical enterprise in most external respects in a manner similar to Moody's; but there were two important differences. Moody had needed and sought the invitations of local ministers; Sunday went further and often bulldozed reluctant clerics until they fell in line. And Moody had lived comfortably but without great wealth, whereas Sunday became a millionaire, and replied to critics of the cost of his revivals by saying: "What I'm paid for my work makes it only about $2 a soul, and I get less proportionately for the number I convert than any other living evangelist." Both men were immensely businesslike, but Moody's personal indulgence was limited to heavy meals, and Sunday wore ostentatious clothes. With his striped suits, hard collars, diamond pins and studs, shiny patent-leather shoes, and spats, he resembled a hardware drummer out to make time with the girls. Like Moody, he had his musical accompanist, Homer A. Rodeheaver; but Sankey had sung sweetly, and Rodeheaver began to jazz the hymns.[4]

Finney would have marveled at Sunday's style, and at the elements of entertainment in the work of this revivalist, who hired a circus giant as a doorman, broke into broad imitations of his contemporaries (one of Finney's most solemn injunctions had been against levity), shed his coat and vest during a heated sermon, and punctuated

---

[4] On Sunday's life, see William G. McLoughlin's thorough and perceptive biography: *Billy Sunday Was His Real Name.*

his harangues with feats of physical agility on the platform. Sunday was proud of his slanginess. "What do I care if some puff-eyed little dibbly-dibbly preacher goes tibbly-tibbling around because I use plain Anglo-Saxon words? I want people to know what I mean and that's why I try to get down where they live." Literary preachers, he said, tried "to please the highbrows and in pleasing them miss the masses." The language used by Moody, simple though it was, lacked savor enough for Sunday. Moody had said: "The standard of the Church is so low that it does not mean much." Sunday asserted: "The bars of the Church are so low that any old hog with two or three suits of clothes and a bank roll can crawl through." Moody had been content with: "We don't want intellect and money-power, but the power of God's word." Sunday elaborated: "The church in America would die of dry rot and sink forty-nine fathoms in hell if all members were multimillionaires and college graduates." [5]

Classic folkish preaching had tried to treat Biblical stories in realistic intimacy; Sunday had the powers of darkness and light talking in current small-town lingo. In his sermons the Devil tempted Jesus with these words: "Turn some of these stones into bread and get a square meal! Produce the goods!" and he told the miracle of the loaves in this way:

> But Jesus looked around and spied a little boy whose ma had given him five biscuits and a couple of sardines for his lunch, and said to him, "Come here, son, the Lord wants you." Then He told the lad what He wanted, and the boy said, "It isn't much, Jesus, but what there is you're mighty welcome to it."

Those who were appalled in the 1920's by the vulgarity of Bruce Barton's *The Man Nobody Knows* may not have realized how much Sunday had done to pave the way for Barton's portrayal of Christ as a go-getter: "Jesus could go some; Jesus Christ could go like a six-cylinder engine, and if you think Jesus couldn't, you're dead wrong." He felt it important also to establish the point that Jesus "was no dough-faced, lick-spittle proposition. Jesus was the greatest scrapper that ever lived." [6]

---

[5] McLoughlin: *Billy Sunday*, pp. 164, 169.

[6] Weisberger: *They Gathered at the River*, p. 248; McLoughlin: *Billy Sunday*, pp. 177, 179. Sunday's language here expresses a new violence of expression, very common among the clergy during the First World War. See Ray H. Abrams: *Preachers Present Arms* (New York, 1933).

CHAPTER V

The Revolt against Modernity

🏵

· 1 ·

B ILLY SUNDAY's rhetorical coarseness was a surface phenomenon, less important for itself than for what it revealed about the position of evangelism in his time. Underlying the slang and the vulgarity was a desperately embattled spirit that would have been quite unfamiliar to Finney or Moody. It is true that these earlier evangelists were also embattled—embattled with the forces of hell, and militant in the saving of souls. But Sunday was embattled in addition—and at times one suspects even primarily—with the spirit of modernism. Quite aside from purely personal temperament, which has its importance too, his tone derives its significance and popularity from the travail of fundamentalism in a waning phase of its history.

As we move into the twentieth century, we find the evangelical tradition rapidly approaching a crisis. The first part of this crisis was internal: it was no longer possible to put off or avoid a choice between the old religious ways and modernism, since the two had come into more open and more universal confrontation. Fundamentalists, both lay and clerical, were anguished to see a large portion of the great evangelical denominations, the Baptists and Methodists, succumb at least in part to modernist ideas, and their resentment against these defectors added to their bitterness. The second part was external: secular challenges to religious orthodoxy were older than the nation itself, but the force of Darwinism, combined with the new urban style, gave such challenges an unprecedented force. Moreover, the expanding education and the mobility of the whole country, and the development of a nationwide market in ideas, made it increasingly difficult for the secular, liberated thought of the intelligentsia and the scriptural faith of the fundamentalists to continue to move in separate grooves. So long as secularism in its various manifestations was an elite affair, fundamentalists could either ignore it or look upon it as a convenient scapegoat for militant sermons. But now the two were thrown into immediate and constant combat—this was the first consequence for religion of the development of a mass culture, and of its being thrown into contact with high culture.

I do not want to suggest that a kind of quiet religious withdrawal from the mental environment of secular culture ceased to be possible; but for many combative types it ceased to be desirable. Religion, for many individuals or groups, may be an expression of serene belief, personal peace, and charity of mind. But for more militant spirits it may also be a source or an outlet for animosities. There is a militant type of mind to which the hostilities involved in any human situation seem to be its most interesting or valuable aspect; some individuals live by hatred as a kind of creed, and we can follow their course through our own history in the various militant anti-Catholic movements, in anti-Masonry, and a variety of crank enthusiasms. There are both serene and militant fundamentalists; and it is hard to say which group is the more numerous. My concern here is with the militants, who have thrown themselves headlong into the revolt against modernism in religion and against modernity in our culture in general. We are here dealing, then, with an ever smaller but still far from minuscule portion of the whole body of the evangelical tradition—a type which has found that it can compensate with increasing zeal and enterprise for the shrinkage in its numbers.

The two new notes which are evident in a most striking form in Billy Sunday's rhetoric, the note of toughness and the note of ridicule and denunciation, may be taken as the signal manifestations of a new kind of popular mind. One can trace in Sunday the emergence of what I would call the one-hundred per cent mentality—a mind totally committed to the full range of the dominant popular fatuities and determined that no one shall have the right to challenge them. This type of mentality is a relatively recent synthesis of fundamentalist religion and fundamentalist Americanism, very often with a heavy overlay of severe fundamentalist morality.[1] The one-hundred percenter, who will tolerate no ambiguities, no equivocations, no reservations, and no criticism, considers his kind of committedness an evidence of toughness and masculinity. One observer remarked of Sunday that no man of the time, "not even Mr. Roosevelt himself, has insisted so much on his personal, militant masculinity." Jesus was a scrapper, and his disciple Sunday would destroy the notion that a Christian must be "a sort of dishrag proposition, a wishy-washy sissified sort of galoot that lets everybody make a doormat out of him." "Lord save us from off-handed, flabby-cheeked, brittle-boned, weak-kneed, thin-skinned, pliable, plastic, spineless, effeminate ossified three-karat Christianity." Sunday wanted to kill the idea "that being a Christian takes a man out of the busy whirl of the world's life and activity and makes him a spineless, effeminate proposition." He struck a Rooseveltian note in his assertion: "Moral warfare makes a man hard. Superficial peace makes a man mushy"; and he summed up his temper when he confessed: "I have no interest in a God who does not smite." [2]

To assess the historical significance of this growing militancy, let us go back to the earlier history of the evangelical movement. Sidney E. Mead has remarked that, after about 1800, "Americans have in effect been given the hard choice between being intelligent according to the standards prevailing in their intellectual centers, and being religious according to the standards prevailing in their denominations." [3] But this choice was not nearly so clear nor the problem so acute after 1800 as it was after 1860, and particularly after 1900. Up to about 1800 there was, as Mead himself has pointed out, a kind of informal understanding between the pietist and the rationalist mind, based chiefly on a common philanthropism and on a shared passion for religious liberty. One thinks, for example, of Benjamin Franklin listening to Whitefield's preaching in Philadelphia, emptying his pockets for the support of one

---

[1] Very commonly a sexual fundamentalism—thoroughgoing in its fear both of normal sex and of deviation—is linked with the other two. One frequently gets the feeling from later fundamentalist sermons that they were composed for audiences terrified of their own sexuality. It would be instructive in this respect to trace the treatment of dancing and prostitution in evangelical literature. Sunday felt that "the swinging of corners in the square dance brings the position of the bodies in such attitude that it isn't tolerated in decent society," and proposed a law preventing children over twelve from attending dancing schools and another prohibiting dancing until after marriage. McLoughlin: *Billy Sunday*, pp. 132, 142.

[2] McLoughlin: *Billy Sunday*, pp. 141–2, 175, 179.

[3] "Denominationalism: the Shape of Protestantism in America," p. 314.

of the Awakener's favored charities, and, after the regular clergy had refused their pulpits to Whitefield, contributing to the erection of a meeting house that would be available to any preacher. This rapprochement between pietism and rationalism reached a peak at the time of Jefferson's presidency, when the dissenting groups, notably the Baptists, gladly threw their support behind a man who, rationalist or not, stood so firmly for religious freedom.[4]

It is true, of course, that in the 1790's, when the influence of Deism reached its peak in America, there was a great deal of frightened talk about the incursions of infidelity. These alarms mainly affected the members of the established denominations whose colleges and defecting believers were involved.[5] It is also true that Voltaire and Tom Paine served as whipping boys for preachers during the revivals that broke out after 1795.[6] But most early evangelists were far too realistic to imagine that a learned and intellectually self-conscious skepticism was a real menace to the simple public they were trying to reach. They knew that the chief enemy was not rationalism but religious indifference, that their most important work was not with people who had been exposed to Tom Paine's assaults on the Bible but with those who had never been exposed to the Bible. As evangelicals made increasingly impressive gains from 1795 to 1835, and as Deism lapsed into relative quiescence, the battle between pietism and rationalism fell into the background. There was much more concern among evangelicals with rescuing the vast American interior from the twin

[4] See, for instance, on the Republicanism of New England Baptists, William A. Robinson: *Jeffersonian Democracy in New England* (New Haven, 1916) pp. 128–41.

[5] The most vivid account of the hysteria over revolution and infidelity that followed the French Revolution is that of Vernon Stauffer in *New England and the Bavarian Illuminati* (New York, 1918). Although a gentle variety of philosophical skepticism was indeed widespread among the American elite at the close of the eighteenth century, it was mainly a private creed without any bent toward proselytizing. After the French Revolution and the rise of Jeffersonian democracy, upper-class rationalists were less disposed than ever to propagate their rationalism among the public. A crusading skeptic like Elihu Palmer, who wanted to unite republicanism and skepticism for the middle and lower classes, found it very hard going, though there were a few Deistic societies in New York, Philadelphia, Baltimore, and Newburgh. See G. Adolph Koch: *Republican Religion* (New York, 1933).

[6] Catherine C. Cleveland: *The Great Revival in the West, 1797–1805* (Chicago, 1916), p. 111. Martin E. Marty, in *The Infidel* (Cleveland, 1961), argues that infidelity was much too weak in America to be of grave importance in itself, but that it became important as a scare word in the orthodox sermon and in theological recriminations between the religious groups.

evils of Romanism and religious apathy than there was with dispelling the rather faint afterglow of the Enlightenment.

After the Civil War, all this changed, and rationalism once more took
an important place among the foes of the evangelical mind. The coming of Darwinism, with its widespread and pervasive influence upon
every area of thinking, put orthodox Christianity on the defensive;
and the impact of Darwinism was heightened by modern scholarly
Biblical criticism among the learned ministry and among educated
laymen. Finally, toward the end of the century, the problems of industrialism and the urban churches gave rise to a widespread movement
for a social gospel, another modernist tendency. Ministers and laymen
alike now had to choose between fundamentalism and modernism;
between conservative Christianity and the social gospel.

As time went on, a great many clerics—including a substantial number with evangelical sympathies—became liberal.[7] Those who did not
found themselves in the distressing situation of having to live in the
same world with a small minority of rationalist skeptics, and of seeing
constant defections from orthodox Christianity to modernism: from a
Christianity essentially bound up with the timeless problem of salvation to one busied with such secular things as labor unions, social settlements, and even the promotion of socialism. By the end of the century it was painfully clear to fundamentalists that they were losing
much of their influence and respectability. One can now discern among
them the emergence of a religious style shaped by a desire to strike
back against everything modern—the higher criticism, evolutionism,
the social gospel, rational criticism of any kind. In this union of social
and theological reaction, the foundation was laid for the one hundred
per cent mentality.

The gradual stiffening can be seen in a comparison of Moody and his
most prominent successor. Moody's views were akin to those later
called fundamentalist, but his religious style had already been formed
by the early 1870's, when the incursions of modernism were still largely
restricted to highbrow circles. His references to the emerging conflict between fundamentalism and modernism were determined partly
by his personal benignity and partly by the general state of the conflict
itself in his formative years. The Bible is the inspired word of God, he

[7] On divergent patterns in the ministry, see Robert S. Michaelson: "The Protestant Ministry in America: 1850 to the Present," in H. Richard Niebuhr and
D. D. Williams: op. cit., pp. 250–88.

insisted; there is nothing in it that is not wise, nothing that is not good, and any attempt to undermine any part of it is the Devil's work. "If there was one portion of the Scripture untrue, the whole of it went for nothing." It was still possible simply to dismiss science, and even rational efforts to interpret the Bible—"the Bible was not made to understand." Talk about figurative language and symbolic meanings made him impatient. "That's just the way men talk now and just figure away everything." [8] For all this, there was a notable freedom from bigotry and militancy in Moody's utterances. He preferred to keep peace with those religious liberals whom he respected; he was glad to have them at his Northfield Conferences, and he disliked hearing them called infidels by other conservatives. It is indicative of the character of his inheritance that of the two educational centers founded under his auspices, one, the Moody Bible Institute at Chicago, later became fundamentalist, whereas the other, Northfield Seminary in Massachusetts, became modernist; both claimed that they were carrying on in the spirit of Moody's work.

With Sunday it was quite another matter. He brooked no suggestion that fundamentalism was not thoroughgoing, impregnable, and tough. He turned his gift for invective as unsparingly on the higher criticism and on evolution as on everything else that displeased him. "There is a hell and when the Bible says so don't you be so black-hearted, low-down, and degenerate as to say you don't believe it, you big fool!" Again: "Thousands of college graduates are going as fast as they can straight to hell. If I had a million dollars I'd give $999,999 to the church and $1 to education." "When the word of God says one thing and scholarship says another, scholarship can go to hell!" [9]

· 2 ·

The note of petulance became increasingly shrill. The challenge to orthodoxy had grown too formidable and penetrated too many focal centers of social power and respectability to be taken lightly. Presumably, the fundamentalists themselves were afflicted on occasion by nagging doubts about the adequacy of their faith, which was now being questioned everywhere. As Reinhold Niebuhr has remarked: "Extreme orthodoxy betrays by its very frenzy that the poison of skepti-

[9] McLoughlin: *Billy Sunday*, pp. 125, 132, 138.
[8] Bradford: op. cit., pp. 58–60; McLoughlin: *Modern Revivalism*, p. 213; on Moody's pragmatic tolerance, see pp. 275–6.

cism has entered the soul of the church; for men insist most vehemently upon their certainties when their hold upon them has been shaken. Frantic orthodoxy is a method for obscuring doubt." [1]

The feeling that rationalism and modernism could no longer be answered in debate led to frantic efforts to overwhelm them by sheer violence of rhetoric and finally by efforts at suppression and intimidation which reached a climax in the anti-evolution crusade of the 1920's. The time had come, as Sunday himself asserted in a sermon of that decade, when "America is not a country for a dissenter to live in." [2] But unfortunately for the fundamentalists, *they* had become the dissenters; they lacked the power to intimidate and suppress their critics; they were afloat on a receding wave of history. Even within the large evangelical denominations, they had lost much of their grip. Large numbers of Methodists, and of Baptists at least in the North, were themselves taken with religious liberalism. Having lost their dominance over the main body of evangelicism itself, many fundamentalists began to feel desperate.

The 1920's proved to be the focal decade in the *Kulturkampf* of American Protestantism. Advertising, radio, the mass magazines, the advance of popular education, threw the old mentality into a direct and unavoidable conflict with the new. The older, rural and small-town America, now fully embattled against the encroachments of modern life, made its most determined stand against cosmopolitanism, Romanism, and the skepticism and moral experimentalism of the intelligentsia. In the Ku Klux Klan movement, the rigid defense of Prohibition, the Scopes evolution trial, and the campaign against Al Smith in 1928, the older America tried vainly to reassert its authority; but its only victory was the defeat of Smith, and even that was tarnished by his success in reshaping the Democratic Party as an urban and cosmopolitan force, a success that laid the groundwork for subsequent Democratic victories. [3]

One can hear in the anguished cries of the 1920's a clear awareness that the older American type was passé, and the accusation that it

[1] *Does Civilization Need Religion?* (New York, 1927), pp. 2–3. I trust that it will be clear to readers that my discussion deals with fundamentalism as a mass movement and not with the more thoughtful critics of modernism. For an example of the latter, see J. Gresham Machen: *Christianity and Liberalism* (New York, 1923). On the intellectual development of fundamentalism, see Stewart G. Cole: *The History of Fundamentalism* (New York, 1931).

[2] McLoughlin: *Billy Sunday,* p. 278.

[3] On this aspect of Smith's achievement, see my essay: "Could a Protestant Have Beaten Hoover in 1928?" *The Reporter,* Vol. 22 (March 17, 1960), pp. 31–3.

was the intelligentsia who were trying to kill it. In 1926 Hiram W. Evans, the Imperial Wizard of the Ku Klux Klan, wrote a moving essay on the Klan's purposes, in which he portrayed the major issue of the time as a struggle between "the great mass of Americans of the old pioneer stock" and the "intellectually mongrelized 'Liberals.'" All the moral and religious values of the "Nordic Americans," he complained, were being undermined by the ethnic groups that had invaded the country, and were being openly laughed at by the liberal intellectuals. "We are a movement," Evans wrote,[4]

of the plain people, very weak in the matter of culture, intellectual support, and trained leadership. We are demanding, and we expect to win, a return of power into the hands of the everyday, not highly cultured, not overly intellectualized, but entirely unspoiled and not de-Americanized, average citizen of the old stock. Our members and leaders are all of this class—the opposition of the intellectuals and liberals who hold the leadership, betrayed Americanism, and from whom we expect to wrest control, is almost automatic.

This is undoubtedly a weakness. It lays us open to the charge of being "hicks" and "rubes" and "drivers of second-hand Fords." We admit it. Far worse, it makes it hard for us to state our case and advocate our crusade in the most effective way, for most of us lack skill in language. . . .

Every popular movement has suffered from just this handicap. . . .

The Klan does not believe that the fact that it is emotional and instinctive, rather than coldly intellectual, is a weakness. All ac-

[4] "The Klan's Fight for Americanism," *North American Review*, Vol. CCXXIII (March–April–May, 1926), pp. 38 ff. Cf. Gerald L. K. Smith in 1943: "Our people frequently do not express themselves because there are only a few of us who speak with abandon in times like this, but in the hearts of our people are pent-up emotions which go unexpressed because they fear their vocabularies are insufficient." Leo Lowenthal and Norbert Guterman: *Prophets of Deceit* (New York, 1949), p. 110.

This feeling that the American public is sound at heart but that spokesmen of the old American values somehow lack the means to compete with the smart-alecks of modernism runs through the utterances of the right wing. Cf. Senator Barry Goldwater in *The Conscience of a Conservative* (New York, 1960), pp. 4–5: "Our failure . . . is the failure of the Conservative demonstration. Though we Conservatives . . . feel sure that the country agrees with us, we seem unable to demonstrate the practical relevance of Conservative principles to the needs of the day. . . . Perhaps we suffer from an over-sensitivity to the judgments of those who rule the mass communications media. We are daily consigned by 'enlightened' commentators to political oblivion."

tion comes from emotion, rather than from ratiocination. Our emotions and the instincts on which they are based have been bred into us for thousands of years; far longer than reason has had a place in the human brain. . . . They are the foundations of our American civilization, even more than our great historic documents; they can be trusted where the fine-haired reasoning of the denatured intellectuals cannot.

This is not an altogether irrelevant statement of the case, and not immoderate in tone. The difficulty was to find any but immoderate means of putting it into action. On this count, the shabby history of the Klan speaks eloquently. So does the panic of the fundamentalists. The Georgia assemblyman who said:

> Read the Bible. It teaches you how to act. Read the hymn-book. It contains the finest poetry ever written. Read the almanac. It shows you how to figure out what the weather will be. There isn't another book that it is necessary for anyone to read, and therefore I am opposed to all libraries.

may seem too obscure to be worth notice; but one can hardly say the same of a former Secretary of State and three-time candidate for the presidency who could proclaim, as Bryan did in a speech before Seventh-Day Adventists in 1924: "All the ills from which America suffers can be traced back to the teaching of evolution. It would be better to destroy every other book ever written, and save just the first three verses of Genesis." [5]

It was in the crusade against the teaching of evolution that the fundamentalist movement reached its climax and in the Scopes trial that it made its most determined stand. The trial afforded a perfect dramatization of everything at stake in the confrontation of the fundamentalist and the modernist mind. That the issue centered over the place of evolution in the public high school was itself evidence of the degree to which modernism had been brought down from the level of elite consciousness and made a part of popular experience. The battle over evolution in education had been fought out once before, in the colleges and universities, where conservative clergymen had tried

---

[5] Both quotations are in Maynard Shipley: *The War on Modern Science* (New York, 1927), pp. 130, 254–5. Such remarks are in the main tradition of evangelicalism, but they reflect its increasing shrillness in this period. Cf. the milder expression of the pre-Civil War Methodist preacher, James B. Finley: "I have wondered if the great multiplication of books has not had a deleterious tendency, in diverting the mind from the Bible." *Autobiography* (Cincinnati, 1854), p. 171.

during the three decades after 1860 to stem the tide of Darwinism. But there it had taken place at the elite level, and the inevitable losses sustained by the anti-evolutionists did not touch the vitals of the fundamentalists. Few of the true believers, after all, then attended college, and those who did could still seek out the backwater schools that had been kept pure from the infections of *The Origin of Species*. By the 1920's, however, the teaching of evolution, moving down the educational ladder, had overtaken high schools, and the high schools had begun to reach the people. In the fifteen years before the First World War, the number of high schools had more than doubled, and this growth continued apace after the war. The high-school diploma was clearly becoming the point to which vast numbers of American children would be educated—the point to which they must be educated if they were to be equipped for the scramble for success. Masses of pious and aspiring Americans were now beginning to feel that their children ought to go to high school, and to realize that they were all but certain to be menaced there by evolutionism. It was over the use of an evolutionist textbook, George Hunter's *Civic Biology*, that John T. Scopes came to trial in Tennessee. This book had been adopted by the state textbook commission in 1919 and had been in use in schools of the state as far back as 1909, fifteen years before it was found dangerous.

To the fundamentalists of Tennessee and elsewhere, the effort to stop the teaching of evolution represented an effort to save the religion of their children—indeed, to save all the family pieties—from the ravages of the evolutionists, the intellectuals, the cosmopolitans.[6] If the fundamentalists deserve any sympathy—and I think they do—it must be on this count. A good deal of their ferocity is understandable if one realizes that they saw (and still see) the controversy as a defense of their homes and families. John Washington Butler, the Primitive Baptist Tennessee legislator who introduced the law against the teaching of evolution in that state, did so because he had heard of a young woman in his own community who had gone to a university and returned an evolutionist. This set him to worrying about what would

[6] "The greatest menace to the public school system today is . . . its Godlessness," Bryan remarked in *The Commoner*, February, 1920, p. 11. Bryan was disturbed by the reports he kept receiving from parents throughout the country that the state schools were undermining the faith of their children. *Memoirs* (Chicago, 1925), p. 459. On this theme in the anti-evolutionist literature, see Norman F. Furniss: *The Fundamentalist Controversy, 1918–1931* (New Haven, 1954), pp. 44–5.

happen to his own five children, and led at last to his success in 1925 in getting his wishes enacted into law in his state. "Save our children for God!" cried a member of the Tennessee Senate in the debate on Butler's bill. When Clarence Darrow said at Scopes's trial that "every child ought to be more intelligent than his parents," he was raising the specter that frightened the fundamentalists most. This was precisely what they did *not* want, if being more intelligent meant that children were expected to abandon parental ideas and desert parental ways. "Why, my friend," said William Jennings Bryan during the trial, "if they believe [evolution], they go back to scoff at the religion of their parents. And the parents have a right to say that no teacher paid by their money shall rob their children of faith in God and send them back to their homes, skeptical, infidels, or agnostics, or atheists." "Our purpose and our only purpose," he announced before the trial began, "is to vindicate the right of parents to guard the religion of their children. . . ." [7] To Bryan and his followers it was patent that Darrow was trying to pull apart the skeins of religion and family loyalties. "Damn you," said one Tennessean, shaking his fist under Darrow's nose, "don't you reflect on *my mother's Bible*. If you do I will tear you to pieces." [8]

It was appropriate that the national leadership of the anti-evolution crusade should have fallen to Bryan, a layman who combined in his person the two basic ancestral pieties of the people—evangelical faith and populistic democracy. In his mind, faith and democracy converged in a common anti-intellectualist rationale. On one side were the voices of the people and the truths of the heart; on the other were the intellectuals, a small arrogant elite given over to false science and mechanical rationalism—variously described by him as a "scientific soviet" and a "little irresponsible oligarchy of self-styled 'intellectuals.'" [9] Religion, he pointed out, had never belonged exclusively to an elite: "Christianity is intended for *all*, not for the so-called 'thinkers' only." Mind, being mechanical, needs the heart to direct it. Mind can plan the commission of crimes as well as deeds for the benefit of

---

[7] Leslie H. Allen, ed.: *Bryan and Darrow at Dayton* (New York, 1925), p. 70; this work is edited from the trial record and other sources.

[8] Italics added here; see Ray Ginger's excellent study of the Scopes trial: *Six Days or Forever?* (Boston, 1958), pp. 2, 17, 64, 134, 181, 206.

[9] Ginger: op. cit., pp. 40, 181; cf. Bryan's *Famous Figures of the Old Testament*, p. 195; *Seven Questions in Dispute*, pp. 78, 154; *In His Image* (New York, 1922), pp. 200–2; *The Commoner*, August, 1921, p. 3; November, 1922, p. 3.

society. "Mind worship is the great sin in the intellectual world today." Only the heart—which is the province of religion—can bring discipline to the things of the mind so that they work for good.

Here is the crux of the matter: the juncture between populistic democracy and old-fashioned religion. Since the affairs of the heart are the affairs of the common man, and since the common man's intuition in such matters is as good as—indeed better than—that of the intellectuals, his judgment in matters of religion should rule. Where there appeared to be a conflict between religion and science, it was the public, Bryan believed, and not "those who measure men by diplomas and college degrees," who should decide. As Walter Lippmann observed, the religious doctrine that all men will at last stand equal before the throne of God was somehow transmuted in Bryan's mind into the idea that all men were equally good biologists before the ballot box of Tennessee. In effect, Bryan proposed to put the question of evolution to the vote of Christians, and the issue was metamorphosed into a question of the rights of the majority.[1]

The Bible condemns evolution, theistic evolution as well as materialistic evolution, if we can trust the judgment of Christians as to what the Bible means. Not one in ten of those who accept the Bible as the Word of God have ever believed in the evolutionary hypothesis as applied to man. Unless there is some rule by which a small fraction can compel the substitution of their views for the views entertained by the masses, evolution must stand condemned as contrary to the revealed will of God.

In Bryan's mind the question of the teaching of evolution in the schools was a challenge to popular democracy. "What right have the evolutionists—a relatively small percentage of the population—to

[1] Bryan: *Orthodox Christianity versus Modernism* (New York, 1923), pp. 14, 26, 29–30, 32, 42; cf. Ginger: op. cit., pp. 35, 40, 181. "The one beauty about the word of God," said Bryan, "is that it does not take an expert to understand it." When some metropolitan newspapers suggested that a jury of Dayton residents might not be competent to pass on the issues at stake, Bryan commented: "According to our system of government, the people are interested in everything and can be trusted to decide everything, and so with our juries." As he saw it, the case raised the question, "can a minority use the courts to force its ideas on the schools?" In this controversy, poor Bryan, so long starved for victory, made another of his great miscalculations. He appears to have expected to win. "For the first time in my life," he told a fundamentalist conference, "I'm on the side of the majority." Ginger: op. cit., pp. 44, 90. For an astute contemporary statement on the relation between Bryan's version of democracy, his evangelical sympathies, and his anti-intellectualism, see John Dewey: "The American Intellectual Frontier," *New Republic*, Vol. XXX (May 10, 1922), pp. 303–5.

teach *at public expense* a so-called scientific interpretation of the
Bible when orthodox Christians are not permitted to teach an orthodox
interpretation of the Bible?" Bryan was not convinced, in any case,
that the science of the evolutionists was sound; but even so, he said,
they ignored "the science of government," in which "rights are determined by the *majority*," except for those rights safeguarded to the
minority by the Constitution. To prevent the minority from teaching
their doctrines in the *public* schools would not infringe on their rights.
"They have no right to demand pay for teaching that which the parents
and the taxpayers do not want taught. The hand that writes the pay-
check rules the school." Christians had to build their own schools and
colleges in which to teach Christianity. "Why should not atheists and
agnostics be required to build their own schools and colleges in which
to teach their doctrines?" [2] So, if Bryan had had his way, the public
schools would have banned evolutionary biology altogether, and the
teaching of modern science would have been confined to a small number of secularist private schools. This would have been a catastrophe
for American education, but Bryan, who saw no contradiction between
sound education and orthodox faith, knew what the choice must be, if
it had to be made. An educated man without religion is a ship without
a pilot. "If we have to give up either religion or education, we should
give up education." [3]

· 3 ·

Today the evolution controversy seems as remote as the Homeric era
to intellectuals in the East, and it is not uncommon to take a condescending view of both sides. In other parts of the country and in
other circles, the controversy is still alive. A few years ago, when the
Scopes trial was dramatized in *Inherit the Wind,* the play seemed on
Broadway more like a quaint period piece than a stirring call for freedom of thought. But when the road company took the play to a small
town in Montana, a member of the audience rose and shouted
"Amen!" at one of the speeches of the character representing Bryan.
Today intellectuals have bogies much more frightening than fundamentalism in the schools; but it would be a serious failure of imagina-
tion not to remember how scared the intellectuals of the 1920's were.
Perhaps not quite so much appeared to be at stake as in the McCarthy-

[2] *Orthodox Christianity versus Modernism,* pp. 29, 45–6; cf. "Darwinism in
Public Schools," *The Commoner,* January, 1923, pp. 1–2.
[3] Ginger: op. cit., p. 88.

ist crusade of the 1950's, but the sense of oppressive danger was no less real. One need only read Maynard Shipley's contemporary survey of the anti-evolution movement, *The War on Modern Science,* to recapture a sense of the genuine alarm of the intellectuals. The Scopes trial, like the Army-McCarthy hearings thirty years later, brought feeling to a head and provided a dramatic purgation and resolution. After the trial was over, it was easier to see that the anti-evolution crusade was being contained and that the fears of the intellectuals had been excessive. But before the trial, the crusade had gained a great deal of strength in many states, including several outside the South. In the South, as W. J. Cash, who observed it at first hand, remarked, it was, like the Klan, an authentic folk movement, which had the "active support and sympathy of the overwhelming majority of the Southern people," not only among the masses but among influential lay and clerical leaders.[4] If the highbrows had nothing to fear for themselves in their more secure centers of learning, they could fear with some reason that the country's system of secondary education might be ruined. Nor did they altogether have their way in its defense. To this day, the language of most secondary-school biology texts is guarded, and evolution is taught in many places only by indirection. Just a few years ago, in a poll of representative adolescent opinion throughout the country, only about a third of the sample responded affirmatively to the statement: "Man was evolved from lower forms of animals." [5]

The evolution controversy and the Scopes trial greatly quickened the pulse of anti-intellectualism. For the first time in the twentieth century, intellectuals and experts were denounced as enemies by leaders of a large segment of the public. No doubt, the militant fundamentalists were a minority in the country, but they were a substantial minority; and their animus plainly reflected the feelings of still larger numbers, who, however reluctant to join in their reactionary crusade, none the less shared their disquiet about the trend of the times, their fear of the cosmopolitan mentality, of critical intelligence, of experimentalism in morals and literature.[6] Bryan's full-throated as-

[4] W. J. Cash: *The Mind of the South* (New York, 1941), pp. 337–8.

[5] In this poll, 40 per cent checked "No," 35 per cent "Yes," and 24 per cent "Don't know." H. H. Remmers and D. H. Radler: *The American Teenager* (Indianapolis, 1957). Cf. the pressures against the teaching of evolution in the 1930's as reported by Howard K. Beale in *Are American Teachers Free?* (New York, 1936), pp. 296–7.

[6] This concern with morals might bear further examination. As fundamentalists saw it, the loss of faith among their children would be only the preliminary to a loss of morals. They had a good deal to say about the "sensuality" inherent in the

saults upon the "experts" were symbolic of the sharply deviating paths being taken by the two sides. It had not always been so. In the Progressive era the intellectuals had felt themselves to be essentially in harmony with the basic interests and aspirations of the people. Now it was evident once more that this harmony was neither pre-established nor guaranteed. The more spiritually earnest the great religious public was, the more violently it might differ from the views of the majority of intellectuals. As for the fundamentalists, it would be a mistake to forget that being routed in the main contest did not cause them to capitulate or disappear. They retired sullenly, some of them looking for other spheres in which modernists might be more vulnerable. They could not eclipse modernism or secularism in the religious controversy itself, but they might find other areas in which to rise and smite again.

The events of the Great Depression gave them scant comfort. Their theological isolation from the main body of the big evangelical churches was doubly oppressive, for the evangelicals in overwhelming numbers now became politically liberal or left.[7] However, the laymen did not go so far as the clergy, and many conservative laymen felt that the development of a new social-gospel movement had created a new "priestly class" (as one right-wing churchman put it) out of harmony with the sentiments of many people in their congregations. Their heightened sense of isolation and impotence helped to bring many of the dwindling but still numerically significant fundamentalists into the ranks of a fanatical right-wing opposition to the New Deal. The fundamentalism of the cross was now supplemented by a fundamentalism of the flag. Since the 1930's, fundamentalism has been a significant component in the extreme right in American politics, whose cast of thought often shows strong fundamentalist filiations.[8] The spokesmen

---

notion that man has descended from lower forms of life, and their rhetoric suggests to what a degree sexual fears, as well as others, were mobilized in this controversy.

[7] I am indebted here to two excellent studies of the social crosscurrents in American religion: Paul Carter's *The Decline and Revival of the Social Gospel* (Ithaca, 1954) and Robert Moats Miller's *American Protestantism and Social Issues* (Chapel Hill, 1958).

[8] The several authors, including myself, of the essays assessing *The New American Right* (New York, 1955), ed. by Daniel Bell, have either ignored or given only casual attention to the place of fundamentalism in right-wing extremism. But see some of the more recent essays in the new edition, *The Radical Right* (New York, 1963). The most informative work on the subject is Ralph Lord Roy's *Apostles of Discord* (Boston, 1953), which is written in a mood of muckraking and exposure but has an extensive scholarly documentation. On recent developments, see David Danzig: "The Radical Right and the Rise of the Fundamentalist Minority," *Commentary*, Vol. XXXIII (April, 1962), pp. 291–8.

of this trend in political fundamentalism have kept alive the folkish anti-intellectualism of the evolution controversy. "I do not understand political science, as an authority from an academic viewpoint," one of their leaders proclaimed. "I am not familiar with the artistic master-pieces of Europe, but I do say this tonight: I understand the hearts of the American people." And he went on to denounce their betrayers: "The Scribes and Pharisees of the Twentieth Century . . . [who] provide a nation with its dominant propaganda, including seasonal fashions in politics, religious attitudes, sub-standard ethics and half-caste morals." It is an ancient and indigenous refrain, echoed in the simplest terms by another: "We are going to take this government out of the hands of these city-slickers and give it back to the people that still believe two plus two is four, God is in his Heaven, and the Bible is the Word." [9]

Although no one has ever tried to trace in detail the historic links be-tween the radical right of the depression and post-depression periods and the fundamentalism of the 1920's, there are some suggestive con-tinuities among the leaders. Many of the leaders of right-wing groups have been preachers, or ex-preachers, or sons of preachers with rigid religious upbringings. Some of the men associated with Billy Sunday in the mid-thirties later turned up as right-wing or quasi-fascist agitators. Gerald Winrod of Kansas, one of the most prominent right-wing prophets of our time, began his career of agitation as a crusading anti-evolutionist. Another, Gerald L. K. Smith, was a minister's son and a preacher for the Disciples of Christ. The late J. Frank Norris, a Southern Baptist preacher in the forefront of the anti-evolution crusade in Texas, later became one of the most colorful right-wing messiahs. Carl McIntire, a leading organizer of contemporary right-wing opposition to modernism, was originally a protégé of the high-brow fundamentalist, J. Gresham Machen.[1] The more recent resur-gence of the right wing in the John Birch Society and various "Christian Crusades" has made the fundamentalist orientation of a large segment of the right wing more conspicuous than at any time in the past; the movement has been led, to a great extent, by preachers

---

[9] Leo Lowenthal and Norbert Guterman: *Prophets of Deceit* (New York, 1949), pp. 109–10; the quotations are from Gerald L. K. Smith and Charles B. Hudson.

[1] On Winrod, Smith, Norris, and McIntire, see Roy: op. cit., *passim;* Carter: op. cit., chapter 4; Miller: op. cit., chapter 11; and McLoughlin: *Billy Sunday,* pp. 290, 310. On fundamentalism and the John Birch Society, see *The New York Times,* April 23 and October 29, 1961; Tris Coffin: "The Yahoo Returns," *New Leader,* April 17, 1961.

and ex-preachers. The literature of the extreme right also shows a significant continuity in style—indicative of the degree to which the pattern of fundamentalism has become the pattern of militant nationalism. (It was with an appropriate sense of this continuity that Gerald L. K. Smith named his paper *The Cross and the Flag.*)

It is not mere opportunism that causes the politically minded fundamentalist to gravitate toward the far right. No less than others, fundamentalists like to feel that they have a comprehensive world view, and their minds are more satisfied when religious and political antipathies can be linked together. They have developed a gift for combining seemingly irrelevant animosities so as to make them mutually re-enforcing. For example, just as contemporary fundamentalists have linked their religious sentiments to the cold war, the fundamentalists of the twenties responded to the issues of the First World War and to residual anti-German feeling. It was one of their most common arguments against the modernists that higher criticism of the Bible has received its strongest impetus from German scholarship; they were thus able to forge a link between the German amorality supposedly revealed by wartime atrocity stories and the destructive moral effects of Biblical criticism. This case was argued at various levels of sophistication, perhaps most simply and informally by Billy Sunday: "In 1895 at the Potsdam Palace the Kaiser called his statesmen together and outlined his plan for world domination, and he was told that the German people would never stand by and endorse it, as it was not in line with the teaching of Martin Luther. Then the Kaiser cried, 'We will change the religion of Germany then,' and higher criticism began." [2]

There seems to be such a thing as the generically prejudiced mind. Studies of political intolerance and ethnic prejudice have shown that zealous church-going and rigid religious faith are among the important correlates of political and ethnic animosity.[3] It is the existence of this

---

[2] McLoughlin: *Billy Sunday*, p. 281.

[3] The most interesting work I know of on the generically prejudiced mind is that of E. L. Hartley, who asked college students to rate various nations and races according to their acceptability. He had in his list the names of three fictitious ethnic groups, the Daniereans, Pireneans, and Wallonians. There was a high correlation between expressed prejudice against actual ethnic groups and prejudice against these fictitious ones, bespeaking a set of mind that is prepared to react with a certain hostility to anything. See E. L. Hartley: *Problems in Prejudice* (New York, 1946). On the relation between religious orthodoxy and forms of intolerance, see Samuel A. Stouffer: *Communism, Conformity, and Civil Liberties* (New York, 1955), pp. 140–55; and T. A. Adorno et al.: *The Authoritarian Personality* (New York, 1950), chapters 6 and 18.

type of mind that sets the stage for the emergence of the one-hundred percenter and determines the similarity of style between the modern right wing and the fundamentalist. In fact, the conditions of the cold war and the militant spirit bred by the constant struggle against world Communism have given the fundamentalist mind a new lease on life. Like almost everything else in our world, fundamentalism itself has been considerably secularized, and this process of secularization has yielded a type of pseudo-political mentality whose way of thought is best understood against the historical background of the revivalist preacher and the camp meeting. The fundamentalist mind has had the bitter experience of being routed in the field of morals and censorship, on evolution and Prohibition, and it finds itself increasingly submerged in a world in which the great and respectable media of mass communication violate its sensibilities and otherwise ignore it. In a modern, experimental, and "sophisticated" society, it has been elbowed aside and made a figure of fun, and even much of the religious "revival" of our time is genteel and soft-spoken in a way that could never have satisfied the old-fashioned fundamentalist zeal. But in politics, the secularized fundamentalism of our time has found a new kind of force and a new punitive capacity. The political climate of the post-war era has given the fundamentalist type powerful new allies among other one-hundred percenters: rich men, some of them still loyal to a fundamentalist upbringing, stung by the income tax and still militant against the social reforms of the New Deal; isolationist groups and militant nationalists; Catholic fundamentalists, ready for the first time to unite with their former persecutors on the issue of "Godless Communism"; and Southern reactionaries newly animated by the fight over desegregation.

One reason why the political intelligence of our time is so incredulous and uncomprehending in the presence of the right-wing mind is that it does not reckon fully with the essentially theological concern that underlies right-wing views of the world. Characteristically, the political intelligence, if it is to operate at all as a kind of civic force rather than as a mere set of maneuvers to advance this or that special interest, must have its own way of handling the facts of life and of forming strategies. It accepts conflict as a central and enduring reality and understands human society as a form of equipoise based upon the continuing process of compromise. It shuns ultimate showdowns and looks upon the ideal of total partisan victory as unattainable, as merely another variety of threat to the kind of balance with which it is familiar. It is sensitive to nuances and sees things in degrees. It is essentially relativist and skeptical, but at the same time circumspect and humane.

The fundamentalist mind will have nothing to do with all this: it is essentially Manichean; it looks upon the world as an arena for conflict between absolute good and absolute evil, and accordingly it scorns compromises (who would compromise with Satan?) and can tolerate no ambiguities. It cannot find serious importance in what it believes to be trifling degrees of difference: liberals support measures that are for all practical purposes socialistic, and socialism is nothing more than a variant of Communism, which, as everyone knows, is atheism. Whereas the distinctively political intelligence begins with the political world, and attempts to make an assessment of how far a given set of goals can in fact be realized in the face of a certain balance of opposing forces, the secularized fundamentalist mind begins with a definition of that which is absolutely right, and looks upon politics as an arena in which that right must be realized. It cannot think, for example, of the cold war as a question of mundane politics—that is to say, as a conflict between two systems of power that are compelled in some degree to accommodate each other in order to survive—but only as a clash of faiths. It is not concerned with the realities of power—with the fact, say, that the Soviets have the bomb—but with the spiritual battle with the Communist, preferably the domestic Communist, whose reality does not consist in what he does, or even in the fact that he exists, but who represents, rather, an archetypal opponent in a spiritual wrestling match. He has not one whit less reality because the fundamentalists have never met him in the flesh.

The issues of the actual world are hence transformed into a spiritual Armageddon, an ultimate reality, in which any reference to day-by-day actualities has the character of an allegorical illustration, and not of the empirical evidence that ordinary men offer for ordinary conclusions. Thus, when a right-wing leader accuses Dwight D. Eisenhower of being a conscious, dedicated agent of the international Communist conspiracy, he may seem demented, by the usual criteria of the political intelligence; but, more accurately, I believe, he is quite literally out of this world. What he is trying to account for is not Eisenhower's actual political behavior, as men commonly understand it, but Eisenhower's place, as a kind of fallen angel, in the realm of ultimate moral and spiritual values, which to him has infinitely greater reality than mundane politics. Seen in this light, the accusation is no longer quite so willfully perverse, but appears in its proper character as a kind of sublime nonsense. *Credo quia absurdum est.*

· 4 ·

A NOTE ON AMERICAN CATHOLICISM

In these pages I have been mainly concerned with the relationship between Protestant evangelicism and American anti-intellectualism, simply because America has been a Protestant country, molded by Protestant institutions. It would be a mistake, however, to fail to note the distinctive ethos of American Catholicism, which has contributed in a forceful and decisive way to our anti-intellectualism. Catholicism in this country over the past two or three generations has waxed strong in numbers, in political power, and in acceptance. At the middle of the nineteenth century it was, though a minority faith, the largest single church in the country and was steadily gaining ground despite anti-Catholic sentiment. Today the Church claims almost a fourth of the population, and has achieved an acceptance which would have seemed surprising even thirty years ago.

One might have expected Catholicism to add a distinctive leaven to the intellectual dialogue in America, bringing as it did a different sense of the past and of the world, a different awareness of the human condition and of the imperatives of institutions. In fact, it has done nothing of the kind, for it has failed to develop an intellectual tradition in America or to produce its own class of intellectuals capable either of exercising authority among Catholics or of mediating between the Catholic mind and the secular or Protestant mind. Instead, American Catholicism has devoted itself alternately to denouncing the aspects of American life it could not approve and imitating more acceptable aspects in order to surmount its minority complex and "Americanize" itself. In consequence, the American Church, which contains more communicants than that of any country except Brazil and Italy, and is the richest and perhaps the best organized of the national divisions of the Church, lacks an intellectual culture. "In no Western society," D. W. Brogan has remarked, "is the intellectual prestige of Catholicism lower than in the country where, in such respects as wealth, numbers, and strength of organization, it is so powerful." In the last two decades, which have seen a notable growth of the Catholic middle

class and the cultivated Catholic public, Catholic leaders have become
aware of this failure; a few years ago, Monsignor John Tracy Ellis's
penetrating brief survey of American Catholic intellectual impoverishment had an overwhelmingly favorable reception in the Catholic
press.[4]

Two formative circumstances in the development of early American Catholicism made for indifference to intellectual life. First in importance was the fiercely prejudiced Know-Nothing psychology
against which it had to make its way in the nineteenth century. Regarded as a foreign body that ought to be expelled from the national
organism, and as the agent of an alien power, the Church had to fight
to establish its Americanism. Catholic laymen who took pride in their
religious identity responded to the American milieu with militant
self-assertion whenever they could, and Church spokesmen seemed to
feel that it was not scholarship but vigorous polemicism which was
needed.[5] The Church thus took on a militant stance that ill accorded
with reflection; and in our time, when the initial prejudice against it
has been largely surmounted, its members persist in what Monsignor
Ellis calls a "self-imposed ghetto mentality." A second determining
factor was that for a long time the limited resources of the American
Church were pre-empted by the exigent task of creating the institutions necessary to absorb a vast influx of immigrants—almost ten
million between 1820 and 1920—and to provide them with the rudiments of religious instruction. So much was taken up by this pressing
practical need that little was left over for the higher culture, in so far as
there were members of the Church who were concerned with Catholic
culture.

[4] These paragraphs owe much to Monsignor Ellis's article, "American Catholics
and the Intellectual Life," *Thought*, Vol. XXX (Autumn, 1955), pp. 351–88. Information and quotations not otherwise identified are taken from this essay. See
also, among Catholic writers, the discussions of related issues in Thomas F.
O'Dea: *American Catholic Dilemma: An Inquiry Into Intellectual Life* (New
York, 1958); and Father Walter J. Ong, S. J.: *Frontiers in American Catholicism*
(New York, 1957); and, among non-Catholic writers, Robert D. Cross: *Liberal
Catholicism in America* (Cambridge, Massachusetts, 1958), which examines at
length some of the tensions within the Church caused by adaptation to America.

[5] As Father Ong (op. cit., p. 38) points out, it is all but impossible for American
Catholics to understand "how this evident devotion [of educated French Catholics]
can be nurtured in the twentieth century without courses in apologetics of the sort
which American Catholic Colleges and universities feature but which are quite
unknown at the Institut Catholique (Catholic University faculty) in Paris,
Toulouse, or elsewhere. American Catholics are lost when they find that the French
apologetic tends to train the youthful mind to think *through* modern problems in
Catholic ways. . . ."

Catholicism was, moreover, the religion of the immigrant.[6] To American Catholics, the *true* Church seemed to be in Europe; and they were content to leave the cultivation of intellectual life to the more sophisticated Europeans—all the while developing an exaggerated and unwarranted deference to such Catholic writers as Belloc and Chesterton. Non-English-speaking immigrants showed a high degree of passivity before clerical leadership, as well as before American society as a whole. What is perhaps most important—though it receives less than its proper share of attention from Catholic analysts of the Church's cultural problems here—is the fact that the Irish became the primary catalysts between America and the other immigrant groups. The Irish, taking advantage of their knowledge of English and their prior arrival, constructed the network of political machines and Church hierarchy through which most Catholic arrivals could make a place for themselves in American life. And more than any other group, the Irish put their stamp on American Catholicism; consequently the American Church absorbed little of the impressive scholarship of German Catholicism or the questioning intellectualism of the French Church, and much more of the harsh Puritanism and fierce militancy of the Irish clergy.

Cut off by language and class from easy entrance into the mainstream of Protestant Anglo-Saxon culture, immigrant working-class Catholics were in no position to produce intellectual spokesmen. It is significant that many of the intellectual leaders of the Church in America were not, in national origin, typical of the mass of American Catholics, but were rather native Anglo-Americans converted to the Church, like Orestes Brownson and Father Isaac Hecker. The social origins and cultural opportunities of Church officials were well characterized by Archbishop Cushing in 1947 when he said that "in all the American hierarchy, resident in the United States, there is not known

---

[6] The immigrant character of the Church brings into focus a problem that has existed for all immigrant faiths and indeed for all upwardly mobile American groups, Protestant or Catholic, immigrant or native. It is that the process of education, instead of becoming a reinforcing bond between generations, constitutes an additional barrier between them and adds greatly to the poignance of parenthood. Within a stable social class, attendance at the same schools can often provide a unifying set of experiences for parents and children. But in a country in which millions of children of almost illiterate parents have gone to high school and millions more whose parents have only modest educations have gone to college, the process of education is as much a threat to parents as a promise. This has added force to the desire to put, so to speak, a ceiling on the quality and range of education. Parents often hope to give their children the social and vocational advantages of college without at the same time infusing in them cultural aspirations too remote from those of the home environment in which they have been reared.

to me one Bishop, Archbishop or Cardinal whose father or mother was a college graduate. Every one of our Bishops and Archbishops is the son of a working man and a working man's wife." The hierarchy, which has been drawn from this culturally underprivileged background, is of course educated, but primarily in a vocational way. As Bishop Spalding pointed out at the Third Plenary Council of Baltimore: "the ecclesiastical seminary is not a school of intellectual culture, either here in America or elsewhere, and to imagine that it can become the instrument of intellectual culture is to cherish a delusion." So, even in this most ancient of Christian churches, the American environment has prevailed and the American problem has reasserted itself in an acute form: culturally one began *de novo*. So lacking in scholarly distinction were American Catholics that when the Catholic University of America was opened by the American hierarchy in 1889, with the hope of remedying this situation, six of its original eight-man faculty had to be recruited from Europe, and the two native members were converts who had been educated outside the folds of the Church.

For a long time the proportion of lay Catholics wealthy enough to give significant patronage to intellectual institutions was small, as compared with other faiths. The emergence of the modern Catholic millionaire has not changed this situation as much as it might have done. Monsignor Ellis remarks, concerning one case in point, that the Catholic University of America received, during the first sixty-six years of its existence, only about ten bequests of $100,000 or more, and only one of these approached the kind of munificence that has made the American private secular university possible. With the increasing upward mobility of a large part of the Catholic population, Catholics, like Protestants, have sent their children to colleges in growing numbers. But both Catholic educators and non-Catholic friends like Robert M. Hutchins have been dismayed to see Catholic schools commonly reproducing the vocationalism, athleticism, and anti-intellectualism which prevails so widely in American higher education as a whole. The intellectual achievement of Catholic colleges and universities remains startlingly low, both in the sciences and in the humanities. Robert H. Knapp and his collaborators, surveying the collegiate origins of American scientists in 1952, remarked that Catholic institutions are "among the least productive of all institutions and constitute a singularly unproductive sample." Their record in the humanities, surprisingly, is worse: "Catholic institutions, though exceptionally unproductive in all areas of scholarship, achieve their best record in the sciences." [7]

As one might have expected, the way of the Catholic intellectual in this country has been doubly hard. He has had to justify himself not only as a Catholic to the Protestant and secular intellectual community but also as an intellectual to fellow Catholics, for whom his vocation is even more questionable than it is to the American community at large. Catholic scholars and writers tend to be recognized belatedly by their co-religionists, when they are recognized at all. [8]

All of this concerns, of course, not so much the anti-intellectualism of American Catholicism as its cultural impoverishment, its non-intellectualism. But it will serve as background for a more central point: a great many Catholics have been as responsive as Protestant fundamentalists to that revolt against modernity of which I have spoken, and they have done perhaps more than their share in developing the one-hundred per cent mentality. In no small measure this has been true because their intellectual spokesmen—who are now growing in numbers and influence—have not yet gained enough authority in the Catholic community to hold in check the most retrograde aspects of that revolt, including its general suspicion of mind and its hostility to intellectuals. A great deal of the energy of the priesthood in our time has been directed toward censorship, divorce, birth control, and other issues which have brought the Church into conflict with the secular and the Protestant mind time and again; some of it has also gone into ultra-conservative political movements, which are implacable enemies of the intellectual community. Catholic intellectuals on the whole have opposed the extreme and (from the point of view of the faith) gratuitous aspects of this enmity, but they have been unable to restrain it. [9]

Indeed, one of the most striking developments of our time has been the emergence of a kind of union, or at least a capacity for co-operation, between Protestant and Catholic fundamentalists, who share a common puritanism and a common mindless militancy on

[7] Robert H. Knapp and H. B. Goodrich: *Origins of American Scientists* (Chicago, 1952), p. 24; Robert H. Knapp and Joseph J. Greenbaum: *The Younger American Scholar: His Collegiate Origins* (Chicago, 1953), p. 99.

[8] Harry Sylvester's article, "Problems of the Catholic Writer," *Atlantic Monthly*, Vol. CLXXXI (January, 1948), pp. 109–13, contains a stimulating discussion of the subject.

[9] For evidence that Catholic clergy and laymen alike are unusually hostile to freedom of thought and criticism, even on subjects remote from dogma, see Gerhardt Lenski: *The Religious Factor* (New York, 1960), especially p. 278.

what they imagine to be political issues, which unite them in opposition to what they repetitively call Godless Communism. Many Catholics seem to have overcome the natural reluctance one might expect them to have to join hands with the very type of bigoted Protestant who scourged their ancestors. It seems a melancholy irony that a union which the common bonds of Christian fraternity could not achieve has been forged by the ecumenicism of hatred. During the McCarthy era, the senator from Wisconsin had wide backing both from right-wing Protestant groups and from many Catholics, who seemed almost to believe that he was promulgating not a personal policy but a Catholic policy. It mattered not a bit that the organs of Catholic intellectuals, like *Commonweal* and the Jesuits' *America*, vigorously condemned him. More recently the John Birch Society, despite its heavy Protestant fundamentalist aura, has attracted enough Catholics to cause at least one member of the hierarchy to warn them against it. For Catholics there is a dangerous source of gratification in the present indiscriminately anti-Communist mentality of the country. After more than a century of persecution, it must feel luxurious for Catholics to find their Americanism at last unquestioned, and to be able to join with their former persecutors in common pursuit of a new international, conspiratorial, un-American enemy with a basically foreign allegiance—this time not in Rome but in Moscow. The pursuit is itself so gratifying that it does not much matter that the menacing domestic Communist has become a phantom. These Catholics will not thank anyone, not even thinkers of their own faith, for interrupting them with such irrelevancies at a time when they feel as though they have Cromwell's men themselves on the run.

PART 3

The Politics of Democracy

CHAPTER VI

The Decline of the
Gentleman

❦

· 1 ·

WHEN THE United States began its national existence, the relationship between intellect and power was not a problem. The leaders
were the intellectuals. Advanced though the nation was in the development of democracy, the control of its affairs still rested largely in a
patrician elite: and within this elite men of intellect moved freely and
spoke with enviable authority. Since it was an unspecialized and
versatile age, the intellectual as expert was a negligible force; but the
intellectual as ruling-class gentleman was a leader in every segment of
society—at the bar, in the professions, in business, and in political
affairs. The Founding Fathers were sages, scientists, men of broad
cultivation, many of them apt in classical learning, who used their wide
reading in history, politics, and law to solve the exigent problems of
their time. No subsequent era in our history has produced so many men
of knowledge among its political leaders as the age of John Adams,
John Dickinson, Benjamin Franklin, Alexander Hamilton, Thomas
Jefferson, James Madison, George Mason, James Wilson, and George
Wythe. One might have expected that such men, whose political
achievements were part of the very fabric of the nation, would have
stood as permanent and overwhelming testimonial to the truth that
men of learning and intellect need not be bootless and impractical as
political leaders.

It is ironic that the United States should have been founded by
intellectuals; for throughout most of our political history, the intellec-

tual has been for the most part either an outsider, a servant, or a scapegoat. The American people have always cherished a deep historical piety, second only to that felt for Lincoln, for what Dumas Malone has called "the Great Generation," the generation which carried out the Revolution and formed the Constitution. We may well ask how a people with such beginnings and such pieties so soon lost their high regard for mind in politics. Why, while most of the Founding Fathers were still alive, did a reputation for intellect become a political disadvantage?

In time, of course, the rule of the patrician elite was supplanted by a popular democracy, but one cannot blame the democratic movement alone for the decline in regard for intellect in politics. Soon after a party division became acute, the members of the elite fell out among themselves, and lost their respect for political standards. The men who with notable character and courage led the way through the Revolution and with remarkable prescience and skill organized a new national government in 1787–88 had by 1796 become hopelessly divided in their interests and sadly affected by the snarling and hysterical differences which were aroused by the French Revolution.[1] The generation which wrote the Declaration of Independence and the Constitution also wrote the Alien and Sedition Acts. Its eminent leaders lost their solidarity, and their standards declined. A common membership in the patrician class, common experiences in revolution and statemaking, a common core of ideas and learning did not prevent them from playing politics with little regard for decency or common sense. Political controversy, muddied by exaggerated charges of conspiracies with French agents or plots to subvert Christianity or schemes to restore monarchy and put the country under the heel of Great Britain, degenerated into demagogy. Having no understanding of the uses of political parties or of the function of a loyal opposition, the Founding Fathers surrendered to their political passions and entered upon a struggle in which any rhetorical weapon would do.

Not even Washington was immune from abuse and slander; however, the first notable victim of a distinctively anti-intellectualist broadside was Thomas Jefferson, and his assailants were Federalist leaders and members of the established clergy of New England. The assault on Jefferson is immensely instructive because it indicates the qualities his enemies thought could be used to discredit him and

[1] See Marshall Smelser: "The Federalist Period as an Age of Passion," *American Quarterly*, Vol. X (Winter, 1958), pp. 391–419.

establishes a precedent for subsequent anti-intellectualist imagery in our politics. In 1796, when it seemed that Jefferson might succeed Washington, the South Carolina Federalist congressman, William Loughton Smith, published an anonymous pamphlet attacking Jefferson and minimizing his qualifications for the presidency. Smith tried to show how unsettling and possibly even dangerous Jefferson's "doctrinaire" leadership would be. Jefferson was a philosopher and, Smith pointed out, philosophers have a way of being doctrinaires in politics —witness Locke's impracticable constitution for the Carolinas, Condorcet's "political follies," and Rittenhouse's willingness to lend his name to the Democratic Society of Philadelphia! [2]

> The characteristic traits of a philosopher, when he turns politician, are, timidity, whimsicalness, and a disposition to reason from certain principles, and not from the true nature of man; a proneness to predicate all his measures on certain abstract theories, formed in the recess of his cabinet, and not on the existing state of things and circumstances; an inertness of mind, as applied to governmental policy, a wavering of disposition when great and sudden emergencies demand promptness of decision and energy of action.

What was needed was not intellect but character, and here too Jefferson was found wanting: philosophers, the pamphleteer argued, are extremely prone to flattery and avid of repute, and Jefferson's own abilities "have been more directed to the acquirement of literary fame than to the substantial good of his country." Washington—there was a man, no nonsense about him: "The great WASHINGTON was, thank God, no philosopher; had *he* been one, we should never have seen his great military exploits; we should never have prospered under his wise administration." Smith hit upon a device that was to become standard among the critics of intellect in politics—portraying the curiosity of the active mind as too trivial and ridiculous for important affairs. He mocked at Jefferson's skills in "impaling butterflies and insects, and

[2] [William Loughton Smith]: *The Pretensions of Thomas Jefferson to the Presidency Examined* (n.p., 1796), Part I, pp. 14–15. No one wishes to say that he is opposed to "genuine" learning and wisdom but only to an inferior or debased version. Smith thought Jefferson a bogus philosopher, not a "real" one. He had only the external and inferior characteristics of a philosopher, which meant, in politics, "a want of steadiness, a constitutional indecision and versatility, visionary, wild, and speculative systems, and various other defective features." Ibid., p. 16. Those who remember Adlai Stevenson's campaigns will find in these quotations a familiar ring.

contriving turn-about chairs" and also suggested that no real friend of Jefferson, or of the country, would "draw this calm philosopher from such useful pursuits" to plunge him into the ardors of politics. In language almost identical with that used a generation later against John Quincy Adams, Smith suggested that Jefferson's merits "might entitle him to the Professorship of a college, but they would be as compatible with the duties of the presidency as with the command of the Western army." [3]

In Smith's attack, certain other preoccupations appear which foreshadow the tone of later political literature. There was the notion that military ability is a test of the kind of character which is good for political leadership. It was assumed that a major part of civic character resides in military virtue; even today an intellectual in politics can sometimes counteract the handicap of intellect by pointing to a record of military service.

In the campaign of 1800 all inhibitions broke down. The attempt to score against Jefferson on the ground that he was a man of thought and learning was, of course, only one aspect of a comprehensive attack upon his mind and character designed to show that he was a dangerous demagogue without faith or morals—or, as one critic put it, of "no Conscience, no Religion, no Charity." It was charged that he kept a slave wench and sired mulattoes; that he had been a coward during the American Revolution; that he had started the French Revolution; that he had slandered Washington; that he was ambitious to become a dictator, another Bonaparte; that he was a visionary and a dreamer, an impractical doctrinaire, and, to make matters worse, a French doctrinaire.[4]

The campaign against Jefferson became at the same time an attempt to establish as evil and dangerous the qualities of the speculative mind. Learning and speculation had made an atheist of Jefferson, it was said; had caused him to quarrel with the views of the theologians about the age of the earth and to oppose having school children read the Bible. Such vagaries might be harmless in a closet philosopher, but to allow him to bring these qualities of mind into the presidency would be dangerous to religion and to society.[5] His abstractness of mind and

[3] Ibid., pp. 4, 6, 16; Part II, p. 39.

[4] For a summary of the worst assaults on Jefferson, see Charles O. Lerche, Jr.: "Jefferson and the Election of 1800: A Case Study of the Political Smear," *William and Mary Quarterly*, 3rd ser., Vol. V (October, 1948), pp. 467–91.

[5] [William Linn]: *Serious Considerations on the Election of a President* (New York, 1800).

his literary interests made him unfit for practical tasks. He tended always to theorize about government: "All the ideas which were derived from Experience were hooted at." [6] "I am ready to admit," said one Federalist pamphleteer, "that he is distinguished for shewy talents, for theoretic learning, and for the elegance of his *written* style." He went on: [7]

> It was in France, where he resided nearly seven years, and until the revolution had made some progress, that his disposition to theory, and his skepticism in religion, morals, and government, acquired full strength and vigor. . . . Mr. Jefferson is known to be a theorist in politics, as well as in philosophy and morals. He is a *philosophe* in the modern French sense of the word.

Eminent contemporaries agreed. Fisher Ames thought that Jefferson, "like most men of genius . . . has been carried away by systems, and the everlasting zeal to generalize, instead of proceeding, like common men of practical sense, on the low, but sure foundation of matter of fact." [8] The Federalist writer, Joseph Dennie, saw in him a favorite pupil of the "dangerous, Deistical, and Utopian" school of French philosophy. "The man has talents," Dennie conceded, [9]

> but they are of a dangerous and delusive kind. He has read much and can write plausibly. He is a man of letters, and should be a retired one. His closet, and not the cabinet, is his place. In the first, he might harmlessly examine the teeth of a non-descript monster, the secretions of an African, or the almanac of Banneker. . . . At the seat of government his abstract, inapplicable, metaphysico-politics are either nugatory or noxious. Besides, his principles relish so strongly of Paris and are seasoned with such a profusion of French garlic, that he offends the whole nation. Better for Americans that on their extended plains "thistles should grow, instead of wheat, and cockle, instead of barley," than that a philosopher should influence the councils of the country, and that his admiration of the works of Voltaire and Helvetius should induce him to wish a closer connexion with Frenchmen.

[6] *Connecticut Courant,* July 12, 1800, quoted in Lerche: op. cit., p. 475.
[7] *Address to the Citizens of South Carolina on the Approaching Election of a President and Vice-President of the United States. By a Federal Republican* (Charlestown, 1800), pp. 9, 10, 15.
[8] Seth Ames, ed.: *The Life and Works of Fisher Ames* (Boston, 1854), Vol. II, p. 134.
[9] *The Lay Preacher,* ed. by Milton Ellis (New York, 1943), p. 174; the essay originally appeared in the *Port Folio,* Vol. I (1801).

Charles Carroll of Carrollton thought Jefferson "too theoretical and fanciful a statesman to direct with prudence the affairs of this extensive and growing confederacy." [1] The implication seemed clear: the young confederacy must learn to keep men of intellectual genius out of practical affairs.

The demagogic attacks made on Jefferson by the established clergy may be explained also by the fact that he had forged a singular, and to them obnoxious, coalition. Jefferson, although a Deist and a man of secular learning, had roused many supporters among the evangelical and pietistic denominations, particularly among the Baptists. Not only were they impressed by Jefferson's reputation for democratic sentiments, but as dissenters they were also impressed by his espousal of toleration. They were far less troubled by the charges of infidelity hurled at him than by the disabilities imposed on themselves by the established churches. Jefferson and other secular intellectuals thus joined the pietistic denominations in a curious political alliance based upon common hostility to established orthodoxy. Both groups appealed to standards of authority alien to the established churches: the secular liberals to rationalist criticism, the pietists to intuition. For the moment, under the pressure of their common dislike of established dogma, the liberals and pietists chose to ignore their own differences, and to set aside the fact that the one objected to all dogma and the other to all establishments.[2]

To drive a wedge into this alliance, the established clergy tried to demonstrate that Jefferson was a threat to all Christians—a charge that many of them in their partisan anguish no doubt sincerely believed. In time the alliance between the pietists and the enlightened liberals did break up; a gap was opened between the common man and the intellectual which has seldom since been satisfactorily bridged. But at the time of Jefferson's election the alliance between liberal intellect and evangelical democracy still held good. When the break finally occurred, when the upsurging forces of popular democracy were released from the restraining hand of enlightened patrician leadership, the forces of evangelicalism produced an anti-intellectualism

[1] In a letter to Alexander Hamilton, in J. C. Hamilton, ed.: *The Works of Alexander Hamilton* (New York, 1850–51), Vol. VI, pp. 434–5. Hamilton himself understood that Jefferson, far from being a thoroughgoing doctrinaire, was a temporizing and opportunistic statesman.

[2] On the nature of this alliance and the consequences of its ultimate dissolution, see Sidney E. Mead's penetrating essay, "American Protestantism during the Revolutionary Epoch," *Church History*, Vol. XII (December, 1953), pp. 279–97.

every bit as virulent and of far more effect than that employed by the established clergy against Jefferson.

· 2 ·

The shabby campaign against Jefferson, and then the Alien and Sedition Acts, manifested the treason of many wealthy and educated Federalists against the cultural values of tolerance and freedom. Unfortunately, it did not follow that more popular parties under Jeffersonian or Jacksonian leadership could be counted on to espouse these values. The popular parties themselves eventually became the vehicles of a kind of primitivist and anti-intellectualist populism hostile to the specialist, the expert, the gentleman, and the scholar.

Even in its earliest days, the egalitarian impulse in America was linked with a distrust for what in its germinal form may be called political specialization and in its later forms expertise. Popular writers, understandably proud of the political competence of the free man, were on the whole justifiably suspicious of the efforts of the cultivated and wealthy to assume an exclusive or excessively dominant role in government. Their suspicions did not stop there, however, but led many of them into hostility to all forms of learning. A current of anti-intellectualism can be found in some of the earliest expressions of popular political thought. In the revolutionary era, some popular writers assumed that efforts to limit the power of the rich and well-born would have to include their allies, the learned classes, as well. A rural delegate to the convention elected in Massachusetts to decide on the ratification of the Constitution in 1788 explained his opposition to the document in these words: [3]

These lawyers, and men of learning, and moneyed men, that talk so finely, and gloss over matters so smoothly, to make us poor illiterate people swallow down the pill, expect to get into Congress themselves; they expect to be the managers of this constitution, and get all the power and all the money into their own hands, and then they will swallow up all us little folks, like the great *Leviathan*, Mr. President; yes, just as the whale swallowed up *Jonah*. This is what I am afraid of.

We are fortunate to have, from the hands of a plain New England farmer, William Manning of North Billerica, Massachusetts, a political

[3] Jonathan Elliot: *Debates* (Philadelphia, 1863), Vol. II, p. 102.

pamphlet showing what one shrewd, militantly democratic American thought when he turned his mind to the philosophy of government. This spirited Jeffersonian document, *The Key of Libberty*, was written in 1798 at a time when party passions were at a high pitch. Noteworthy here is the central place accorded by Manning ("not a Man of Larning my selfe for I never had the advantage of six months schooling in my life") to learning as a force in the political struggle. The opening words of his manuscript proclaim: "Learning & Knowledg is essential to the preservation of Libberty & unless we have more of it amongue us we Cannot Seporte our Libertyes Long." [4] But to Manning learning and knowledge were of interest mainly as class weapons.

At the heart of Manning's philosophy was a profound suspicion of the learned and property-holding classes. Their education, their free time, and the nature of their vocations made it possible, he saw, for the merchants, lawyers, doctors, clergymen, and executive and judicial officers of state to act together in pursuit of their ends, as the laboring man could not. Among these classes there is, he thought, a general dislike of free government: they constantly seek to destroy it because it thwarts their selfish interests.

> To efect this no cost nor pains is spared, but they first unite their plans and schemes by asotiations, conventions & corraspondances with each other. The Marchents asotiate by themselves, the Phitisians by themselves, the Ministers by themselves, the Juditial and Executive Officers are by their professions often called together & know each others minds, & all letirary men & the over grown rich, that can live without labouring, can spare time for consultation. All being bound together by common interest, which is the strongest bond of union, join in their secret correspondance to counter act the interests of the many & pick their pockets, which is efected ondly for want of the meens of knowledg amongue them.

Since learning is an instrument for the pursuit of one's interests, "the few" naturally favor the institutions that serve their own class: "the few are always crying up the advantages of costly collages, national acadimyes & grammer schools, in ordir to make places for men to live without work and so strengthen their party. But are always opposed to

[4] Samuel Eliot Morison, ed.: *The Key of Libberty* (Billerica, Mass., 1922). The work is reprinted in *William and Mary Quarterly*, 3rd ser., Vol. XIII (April, 1956), pp. 202–54, and quotations in the following paragraphs are from pp. 221, 222, 226, 231–2.

cheep schooles & woman schooles, the ondly or prinsaple means by which larning is spred amongue the Many." In the colleges (Manning no doubt had Federalist Harvard in mind) the principles of republicanism are criticized, and the young are indoctrinated with monarchical notions. Manning also observed that the graduates of these institutions "are taught to keep up the dignity of their professions"—and to this he objected because it made them set too high a value on their services, and thus made religious and educational services expensive to the many: "For if we apply for a preacher or a School Master, we are told the price, So Much, & they cant go under, for it is agreed upon & they shall be disgrased if they take less." As Manning saw it, the schoolmaster ought to become what in fact he did become in America—an inexpensive hired laborer of very low status.

Here, then, is the key to Manning's educational strategy. Education was to be made cheap for the common man; and higher education, such as there was, would be organized simply to serve elementary education—to provide inexpensive instructors for the common schools. "Larning . . . aught to be promoted in the cheepest and best manner possable"—in such a way, that is, that "we should soone have a plenty of school masters & misstrises as cheap as we could hire other labour, & Labour & Larning would be connected together & lessen the number of those that live without work." It must be said that Manning's prescription, offered at a time when the vaunted common school system of Massachusetts was being neglected, had its point. But in the interests of the lower reaches of the educational system he proposed to strip the upper reaches, to reduce their functions to that of producing cheap academic labor. Advanced learning Manning considered to have no intrinsic value worth cultivating. Academies and classical studies that went beyond what was necessary "to teach our Children a b c" were "ondly to give imploy to gentlemens sons & make places for men to live without worke. For their is no more need for a mans haveing a knowledge of all the languages to teach a Child to read write & cifer than their is for a farmer to have the marinors art to hold plow." Education had been for a long time the instrument of the few; Manning hoped to make it, so far as possible, the instrument of the many. Of its instrumental, and hence subservient, character he had no doubt; nor did he worry about the consequence of his policy for high culture—which was, after all, the prerogative of those who lived without work.

The place of education, in this controversy between the few and the many, is a perfect paradigm of the place of high culture in American politics. Education was caught between a comfortable class only imperfectly able to nourish it, and a powerful, upsurging, egalitarian public chiefly interested in leveling status distinctions and in stripping the privileged of the instruments of privilege. Understandably, the common man wanted to protect his interests and use education to expand his social opportunities; no one seemed able to show him how to do this without damage to intellectual culture itself.

That there was a certain rough justice in Manning's contentions cannot be denied. The Federalists had indeed appropriated Harvard College; why should the democrats not retaliate by appropriating as far as they could the instruments of common education? If they could have their way, there would be no more Harvard Colleges. If a learned class could do nothing but support privilege, there need be no learned class. Almost half a century after Manning wrote his essay, Horace Greeley argued that the American yeoman did in fact appreciate and respect talent and learning; but that all too often he found them "directed to the acquisition of wealth and luxury by means which add little to the aggregate of human comforts, and rather subtract from his own especial share of them." [5] Hence, as the demand for the rights of the common man took form in nineteenth-century America, it included a program for free elementary education, but it also carried with it a dark and sullen suspicion of high culture, as a creation of the enemy.

· 3 ·

Something was missing in the dialectic of American populistic democracy. Its exponents meant to diminish, if possible to get rid of, status differences in American life, to subordinate educated as well as propertied leadership. If the people were to rule, if they aspired to get along with as little leadership as possible from the educated and propertied classes, whence would their guidance come? The answer was that it could be generated from within. As popular democracy gained strength and confidence, it reinforced the widespread belief in the superiority of inborn, intuitive, folkish wisdom over the cultivated, oversophisticated, and self-interested knowledge of the literati and the well-to-do. Just as the evangelicals repudiated a learned religion and a formally constituted clergy in favor of the wisdom of the heart and direct access to God, so did advocates of egalitarian politics pro-

[5] In an address at Hamilton College, January 23, 1844, quoted in Merle Curti: *American Paradox* (New Brunswick, 1956), p. 20; cf. pp. 19–24.

pose to dispense with trained leadership in favor of the native practical sense of the ordinary man with its direct access to truth. This preference for the wisdom of the common man flowered, in the most extreme statements of the democratic creed, into a kind of militant popular anti-intellectualism.

Even Jefferson, who was neither an anti-intellectual nor a dogmatic egalitarian, seemed at times to share this preference. To his nephew, Peter Carr, he wrote in 1787: "State a moral case to a ploughman and a professor. The former will decide it as well, and often better than the latter, because he has not been led astray by artificial rules." [6] Jefferson was simply expressing a conventional idea of eighteenth-century thinking: the idea that God had given man certain necessary *moral* sentiments. It would not have occurred to him to assert the intellectual superiority of the plowman. But one need only go one step further than Jefferson, and say that political questions were in essence moral questions,[7] to lay a foundation for the total repudiation of cultivated knowledge in political life. For if the plowman understood morals as well as the professor, he would understand politics equally well; and he was likely to conclude (here Jefferson would not have agreed) that he had little to learn from anyone, and had no need of informed leaders. Push the argument just a bit further and it would support the assertion that anyone who had anything of the professor about him made an inferior leader; and that political leaders should be sought from among those who in this respect resembled the untutored citizen. Ironically, Jefferson himself was to suffer from this notion. Later it became one of the rallying cries of Jacksonian democracy.

The first truly powerful and widespread impulse to anti-intellectualism in American politics was, in fact, given by the Jacksonian movement. Its distrust of expertise, its dislike for centralization, its desire to

---

[6] *Writings*, A. E. Bergh, ed., Vol. VI (Washington, 1907), pp. 257–8, August 10, 1787. Jefferson was advising his nephew on the conduct of his education, and his chief concern was to establish the point that much study of moral philosophy was "lost time." If moral conduct were a matter of science rather than sound impulse, he pointed out, the millions who had no formal learning would be less moral than the few who had. Clearly, God had not left men without a moral sense, and a very small stock of reason or common sense would be needed to implement it. This was, of course, a familiar doctrine. Jefferson may well have been led to it by the writings of Lord Kames. One may wonder, however, if the study of moral philosophy was useless, why Jefferson had read so widely in this field. On the problems created in his thinking by this doctrine, see Adrienne Koch: *The Philosophy of Thomas Jefferson* (New York, 1943), chapter 3.

[7] As, a century after Jefferson, William Jennings Bryan most explicitly did: "The great political questions are in their final analysis great moral questions." Paxton Hibben: *The Peerless Leader* (New York, 1929), p. 194.

uproot the entrenched classes, and its doctrine that important functions were simple enough to be performed by anyone, amounted to a repudiation not only of the system of government by gentlemen which the nation had inherited from the eighteenth century, but also of the special value of the educated classes in civic life. In spite of this, many intellectuals and men of letters, particularly the young, supported the Jacksonian cause—enough, indeed, to belie the common charge that the educated classes regularly withheld their sympathies from movements meant to benefit the common man. It is true that the leading literary quarterlies were devoted to gentility and remained in the hands of the Whig opposition; but when John L. O'Sullivan founded the *Democratic Review* he was able to get contributions from a distinguished roster of writers of varying political persuasions. It is also true that the leading New England Transcendentalists were largely aloof or hostile. But writers like Orestes Brownson, William Cullen Bryant, George Bancroft, James Fenimore Cooper, Nathaniel Hawthorne, James Kirke Paulding, and Walt Whitman supported the new democracy with varying degrees of cordiality and persistence.[8]

The support of such men was welcomed in Jacksonian ranks, and was sometimes greeted with pride, but on the whole, intellectuals were not accorded much recognition or celebrity. The most outstanding exception was George Bancroft, the historian. In Massachusetts the Democrats felt the need of literary and intellectual leadership to counter the distinguished array of talent in the ranks of the opposition, and Bancroft assumed prominence in his party when he was still in his thirties. He was appointed Collector of the Port of Boston, became Secretary of the Navy under Polk (a post also given to Paulding by Van Buren), and was later minister to Great Britain. His influence enabled him to find a job for Hawthorne in the Boston Custom House and for Brownson (to Bancroft's prompt regret) as steward of the Marine Hospital there. The situation of Hawthorne represents the other side of the picture. He was constantly honored with jobs considerably slighter than his merits or his desperate needs would have dictated. In the Custom House he was no more than a weigher and gauger, and the post (a "grievous thraldom," he called it) was a poor substitute for the position he had actually sought as historian to an expedition to the Antarctic. Later he sought the postmastership of Salem and was made instead surveyor of the port. And finally, after writing a campaign

[8] On the relation of Jacksonian democracy and the intellectuals, see Arthur Schlesinger, Jr.: *The Age of Jackson* (Boston, 1945), especially chapter 29.

biography of his friend and college classmate, Franklin Pierce, he was awarded a consulate—but at Liverpool. On the whole, the record of Jacksonian democracy in achieving a *rapprochement* between the intellectual or man of letters and the popular mind was inferior to that later achieved by Progressivism and the New Deal.

The contests in 1824 and 1828 between Jackson and John Quincy Adams provided a perfect study in contrasting political ideals. Adams's administration was the test case for the unsuitability of the intellectual temperament for political leadership in early nineteenth-century America. The last President to stand in the old line of government by gentlemen, Adams became the symbol of the old order and the chief victim of the reaction against the learned man. He had studied in Paris, Amsterdam, Leyden, and The Hague, as well as at Harvard; he had occupied Harvard's chair of rhetoric and oratory; he had aspired to write epic poetry; like Jefferson, he was known for his scientific interests; he had been head for many years of the American Academy of Arts and Sciences; and as Monroe's Secretary of State he had prepared a learned scientific report on systems of weights and measures which is still a classic. Adams believed that if the new republic failed to use its powers to develop the arts and sciences it would be "hiding in the earth the talent committed to our charge—would be treachery to the most sacred of trusts." It was his hope—as it had been Washington's, Jefferson's and Madison's—that the federal government would act as the guide and center of a national program of educational and scientific advancement. But in proposing that Washington be developed as a cultural capital, he mobilized against himself the popular dislike of centralization.

In his first annual message to Congress, Adams proposed a system of internal improvements—roads and canals—advantageous to business interests, and also asked for several things desired chiefly by men of the learned classes: a national university at Washington, a professional naval academy, a national observatory, a voyage of discovery to the Northwest to follow upon the expedition of Lewis and Clark, an efficient patent office, federal aid to the sciences through a new executive department.

It was characteristic of Adams to offend the same bumptious popular nationalism to which Jackson so perfectly appealed. Adams pointed out that European countries, though less happily blessed with freedom than America, were doing more for science; and he had the temerity to suggest that some policies of the governments of France, Great

Britain, and Russia could well be emulated here. Then, as now, such intellectual cosmopolitanism was unpopular. Having thus flouted national *amour-propre*, Adams went on to flout democratic sentiment by urging generous appropriations for scientific purposes; he even suggested in an inflammatory phrase that Congressional leaders should not "fold up our arms and proclaim to the world that we are palsied by the will of our constituents." Worse still, Adams referred provocatively to the many observatories built under the patronage of European governments as "lighthouses of the skies." Congress snickered at this phrase, and the lighthouses were thrown back at Adams time and again. His own Cabinet saw that the President's program would shock the country—Clay, for instance, found the proposal of a national university "certainly hopeless," and doubted that Adams could get five votes in the House for his proposed executive department—and in the end Adams had to give it up. He represented a kind of leadership which had outlived its time. Hamilton, Washington, even Jefferson, had been interested in a measure of centralization within some kind of national plan, and had expressed the desire common among the gentlemen of the Eastern seaboard to give some order to the expansion of America. But the country grew too fast for them, and would accept no plan and no order. As their type became obsolete in politics, the position of the man of intellect also deteriorated.[9] Adams was the last nineteenth-century occupant of the White House who had a knowledgeable sympathy with the aims and aspirations of science or who believed that fostering the arts might properly be a function of the federal government.

As Adams embodied the old style, Andrew Jackson embodied the new; and the opposition between these two in the politics of the 1820's symbolized what America had been and what it would become. In headlong rebellion against the European past, Americans thought of "decadent" Europe as more barbarous than "natural" America; they feared that their own advancing civilization was "artificial" and might estrange them from Nature. Jackson's advocates praised him as the representative of the natural wisdom of the natural man. Among his other gifts as a national leader, the hero of New Orleans, the conqueror of the "barbaric" army of cultivated Britain was able to offer

[9] For Adams's program, see J. R. Richardson: *Messages and Papers of the Presidents* (New York, 1897), Vol. II, pp. 865–83, and the comments of A. Hunter Dupree: *Science in the Federal Government* (Cambridge, 1957), pp. 39–43; cf. Samuel Flagg Bemis: *John Quincy Adams and the Union* (New York, 1956), pp. 65–70.

reassurances as to the persistence of native vigor and the native style. Jackson, it was said, had been lucky enough to have escaped the formal training that impaired the "vigour and originality of the understanding." Here was a man of action, "educated in Nature's school," who was "artificial in nothing"; who had fortunately "escaped the training and dialectics of the schools"; who had a "judgement unclouded by the visionary speculations of the academician"; who had, "in an extraordinary degree, that native strength of mind, that practical common sense, that power and discrimination of judgement which, for all useful purposes, are more valuable than all the acquired learning of a sage"; whose mind did not have to move along "the tardy avenues of syllogism, nor over the beaten track of analysis, or the hackneyed walk of logical induction," because it had natural intuitive power and could go "with the lightning's flash and illuminate its own pathway." [1]

George Bancroft, who must have believed that his own career as a schoolmaster had been useless, rhapsodized over Jackson's unschooled mind: [2]

> Behold, then, the unlettered man of the West, the nursling of the wilds, the farmer of the Hermitage, little versed in books, unconnected by science with the tradition of the past, raised by the will of the people to the highest pinnacle of honour, to the central post in the civilization of republican freedom. . . . What policy will he pursue? What wisdom will he bring with him from the forest? What rules of duty will he evolve from the oracles of his own mind?

Against a primitivist hero of this sort, who brought wisdom straight out of the forest, Adams, with his experience at foreign courts and his elaborate education, seemed artificial. Even in 1824, when Adams won a freakish four-way election, Jackson was by far the more popular candidate; when the General returned to challenge him four years later, there could be no doubt of the outcome. Adams was outdone in every section of the country but New England, in a battle fought unscrupulously on both sides and described as a contest between

> John Quincy Adams who can write
> And Andrew Jackson who can fight.

[1] The quotations from Jacksonian literature are from John William Ward: *Andrew Jackson: Symbol for an Age* (New York, 1955), pp. 31, 49, 52, 53, 68. I am much indebted to Professor Ward's brilliant study of Jacksonian imagery.

[2] Ward: op. cit., p. 73.

The main case made by Jackson's spokesmen against Adams was that he was self-indulgent and aristocratic and lived a life of luxury. And, what is most relevant here, his learning and political training were charged up not as compensating virtues but as additional vices. A group of Jackson's supporters declared that the nation would not be much better off for Adams's intellectual accomplishments: [3]

> That he is *learned* we are willing to admit; but his *wisdom* we take leave to question. . . . We confess our attachment to the homely doctrine: thus happily expressed by the great English poet:
>> That not to know of things remote
>> From use, obscure and subtle, but to know
>> That which before us lies in daily life,
>> Is the prime wisdom.
>
> That wisdom we believe Gen. Jackson possesses in an eminent degree.

Another Jacksonian, speaking of the past record of the two, said: "Jackson made law, Adams quoted it." [4]

Jackson's triumph over Adams was overwhelming. It would be an exaggeration to say that this was simply a victory of the man of action over the man of intellect, since the issue was posed to the voters mainly as a choice between aristocracy and democracy. But as the two sides fashioned the public images of the candidates, aristocracy was paired with sterile intellect, and democracy with native intuition and the power to act. [5]

[3] *Address of the Republican General Committee of Young Men of the City and County of New York* (New York, 1828), p. 41.

[4] Ward: op. cit., p. 63.

[5] Electoral appeals on both sides were lacking in truth and delicacy; and Adams never repudiated the viler aspersions cast by the Adams propagandists upon Jackson's life with Mrs. Jackson. Adams seems to have been persuaded that these were justified. In 1831 he wrote in his diary that "Jackson lived in open adultery with his wife." Most of the Brahmin world found itself unable to embrace Jackson as President. Harvard did award him an honorary degree of Doctor of Laws at its 1833 commencement, but Adams refused to attend. "I *would not* be present," he wrote, "to see my darling Harvard disgrace herself by conferring a Doctor's degree upon a barbarian and savage who can scarcely spell his own name." Bemis: op. cit., p. 250; see also Adams's *Memoirs*, Vol. VIII (Philadelphia, 1876), pp. 546–7. Adams was told by President Quincy of Harvard that he was well aware how "utterly unworthy of literary honors Jackson was," but that after a degree had been awarded to Monroe it would be necessary to honor Jackson to avoid the show of "party spirit." At the occasion itself, Jackson appears to have charmed the hostile audience. But the rumor went about, and was widely believed by the credulous in Cambridge and Boston, that Jackson had responded to the ceremonies, which were in Latin, by rising and saying: *"Caveat emptor: corpus*

• 4 •

Although the Jacksonians appealed powerfully to both egalitarian and anti-intellectual sentiments, they had no monopoly on either. It was not merely Jacksonianism that was egalitarian—it was the nation itself. The competitive two-party system guaranteed that an irresistible appeal to the voters would not long remain in the hands of one side, for it would be copied. It was only a question of time before Jackson's opponents, however stunned by the tactics of his supporters in 1828, would swallow their distaste for democratic rhetoric and learn to use it. Party leaders who could not or would not play the game would soon be driven off the field.

A persistent problem facing party organizers who were linked to men of affairs—to promoters of canals, banks, turnpikes, and manufacturing enterprises—was to manage to identify themselves with the people and to find safe popular issues which they could exploit without risk to their interests. There was a premium on men who could keep touch with the common people and yet move comfortably and function intelligently in the world of political management and business enterprise.[6] Henry Clay was so gifted, and he had many of the qualities of a major public hero as well; but by the beginning of the 1830's he had been on the national scene too long; his views were too well known, and he was too closely associated with the discredited Adams to be of use. Most notable among the new party bosses with a good grasp of the problem was Thurlow Weed, who used the violently egalitarian passions of anti-Masonry to ride into prominence, and who became one of the greatest of the Whig, and then Republican, party organizers. But the anti-Jacksonians, for all they may have learned in 1828, did not find the figure who set quite the right style for them until Davy Crockett bolted from the ranks of the Jacksonians.

Frontiersman, hunter, fighter, and spokesman of the poor Western squatter, Crockett became a major American folk symbol, and his autobiography a classic of American frontier humor. Unembarrassed by wealth or education, Crockett was drawn into politics by the force

---

delicti: *ex post facto: dies irae: e pluribus unum: usque ad nauseam: Ursa Major: sic semper tyrannis: quid pro quo: requiescat in pace.*" See the recollections of Josiah Quincy: *Figures of the Past* (Boston, 1926), pp. 304–7.

[6] Cf. the analysis of the situation in Glyndon G. Van Deusen: *Thurlow Weed: Wizard of the Lobby* (Boston, 1947), pp. 42–4; and Whitney R. Cross: *The Burned-Over District* (Ithaca, 1950), pp. 114–17.

of his own appeal. When he was about thirty, and newly arrived at a small settlement on Shoal Creek in Tennessee, he was appointed justice of the peace, was soon elected colonel of the militia regiment organized in his district, and then sent to the state legislature. In 1826, after it had been casually suggested to him that he run for Congress, he waged a campaign enlivened by funny stories, and found himself elected. Tennessee now had a representative in Congress who could "wade the Mississippi, carry a steam-boat on his back, and whip his weight in wild cats," and who was not afraid, for all his simplicity, to address the House because he could "whip any man in it."

It was Crockett's pride to represent the native style and natural intuition. In his autobiography, published in 1834, Crockett boasted of the decisions he handed down from the Tennessee bench at a time when he "could just barely write my own name." "My judgments were never appealed from, and if they had been they would have stuck like wax, as I gave my decisions on the principles of common justice and honesty between man and man, and relied on natural born sense, and not on law learning to guide me; for I had never read a page in a law book in all my life." [7] This ingenuous confidence in the sufficiency of common sense may have been justified by Crockett's legal decisions, but he was not content to stop here: he had a considered disdain for the learned world. At one point in his Congressional career, Crockett reported: [8]

> There were some gentlemen that invited me to go to Cambridge, where the big college or university is; where they keep ready-made titles or nicknames to give people. I would not go, for I did not know but they might stick an LL.D. on me before they let me go; and I had no idea of changing "Member of the House of Representatives of the United States," for what stands for "lazy lounging dunce," which I am sure my constituents would have translated my new title to be, knowing that I had never taken any degree, and did not own to any, except a small degree of good sense not to pass for what I was not. . . .

Crockett, who had fought under Jackson in the Creek War in 1813–14, first went to Congress as a member of the Jacksonian group

[7] Hamlin Garland, ed.: *The Autobiography of Davy Crockett* (New York, 1923), p. 90.

[8] Ibid., p. 180. The main butt of the humor here was Andrew Jackson, who had already received his Harvard degree. "One *digniterry,*" said Crockett, "was enough from Tennessee."

from Tennessee and as a representative of the poor Western squatters
of the state, whose condition was very much what his had once been.
Before long, he found these two loyalties in conflict. A group of Ten-
nesseeans, led by James K. Polk, was attempting to get the United
States to cede to the state some unappropriated Western District lands
as an endowment for education. The interests of education and the
interests of the poorer classes seemed unfortunately to be thrown into
conflict at this time, and Crockett, as the representative of the squatters, naturally looked askance at Polk's land bill. Land warrants held
by the University of North Carolina had already caused some of his
constituents to lose their homes. Crockett concluded that the proposal
to use part of the land proceeds for a college in Nashville would in the
same way hurt others. His constituents, he pointed out, would not be
compensated by the development of colleges, for none of them could
use them. If, he remarked, "we can only get a common country, or as
College Graduates sometimes deridingly call it, a B-a school, convenient enough to send our Big Boys in the winter and our little ones
all the year, we think ourselves fortunate, especially if we can raise
enough Coon-Skins and one little thing or other to pay up the teacher
at the end of every quarter." [9]

Explaining in Congress that he was not an opponent of education,
Crockett pointed out that he felt obliged, none the less, to defend the
interests of the people he represented, who had "mingled the sweat of
their brows with the soil they occupied," and who were now to have
their "humble cottages" taken away from them by "the Legislature of
the State, for the purpose of raising up schools for the children of the
rich." [1]

I repeat, that I was utterly opposed to this, not because I am
the enemy of education, but because the benefits of education are
not to be dispensed with an equal hand. This College system
went into practice to draw a line of demarcation between the
two classes of society—it separated the children of the rich from
the children of the poor. The children of my people never saw

[9] Quoted in Charles Grier Sellers, Jr.: *James K. Polk, Jacksonian: 1795–1843*
(Princeton, 1957), pp. 123–4. On the land bill, see ibid., pp. 122–8; James A.
Shackford: *David Crockett, the Man and the Legend* (Chapel Hill, 1956),
pp. 90–9.

[1] *Register of Debates,* 20th Congress, 2nd session, pp. 162–3 (January 5, 1829).
In raising the question of the diversion of funds for the use of colleges, Crockett
was here using a false issue, since Polk had already attempted to mollify Crockett
by inserting a requirement that the proceeds of land sales be used only for common
schools.

the inside of a college in their lives, and never are likely to do so.
. . . If a swindling machine is to be set up to strip them of what
little the surveyors, and the colleges, and the warrant holders,
have left them, it shall never be said that I sat by in silence, and
refused, however humbly, to advocate their cause.

We hear in this an echo of Manning's idea that common schools serve
the people and colleges the rich. For American society it was tragic
that the interests of higher education and those of the ordinary citizen
should thus be allowed to appear to be in conflict. But to the Adams-
Clay men, always under severe pressure from the Jackson forces, the
split in the ranks of the Tennessee Jacksonians came as a gift from
heaven. Before long, the astute opposition organizers, realizing that
to have a pioneer democrat in their ranks would give them a magnificent counterpoise to Jackson, approached Crockett and took advantage
of his alienation from the Jackson men in his state and his long-standing
personal resentment of the President to bring him around to the opposition. This alliance between Crockett and the national anti-Jackson
forces, negotiated by Matthew St. Clair Clarke, a friend of Nicholas
Biddle, the president of the United States Bank, was apparently in the
making as early as 1829 and was clearly consolidated by 1832. Crockett's Congressional speeches began to be written for him, and various
parts of his famous *Autobiography* were also ghost-written, though
they have about them the air of Crockett's own dictation.[2] In 1835
Crockett published an assault upon Martin Van Buren that prefigured
the full-blown demagogy of the Whig campaign of 1840.

By 1840 the conquest of the Whig Party by the rhetoric of populism
was complete. Crockett, who was too provincial and too unreliable to
have presidential stature, had gone off to Texas, had been killed in the
defense of the Alamo, and had begun to be transformed into a demi-
god; but in the presidential election of 1836 William Henry Harrison,
like Jackson a hero of early Indian campaigns, had been found to have
a similar public appeal. It mattered little that his famous victory over
Tecumseh's forces at Tippecanoe in 1811 had been something of a
fiasco; with skillful publicity and some lapse of memory on the part
of the public, it could be glorified into a feat comparable, almost, to
Old Hickory's victory at New Orleans. The common touch was supplied in 1840 by the log-cabin and hard-cider theme, although Harrison lived in a rather substantial mansion on the banks of the Ohio. It

[2] The most satisfactory account of Crockett's *rapprochement* with the Eastern
conservatives and the authorship of his speeches and autobiographical writings is
that of Shackford: op. cit., pp. 122–9.

seems in fact to have been the depression that tipped the scales against Van Buren, but the Whigs tried to assure their victory by using against him the same techniques of ballyhoo and misrepresentation that the Jacksonians had used against John Quincy Adams twelve years earlier. Representative Charles Ogle of Pennsylvania struck the keynote of the campaign in April when he delivered in the House his masterful address on "The Regal Splendor of the President's Palace," which was distributed as a pamphlet in thousands of copies. Speaking against a trifling appropriation of some $3,600 for alterations and repairs in the White House and its grounds, Ogle entertained the House with a fantastic account of the luxurious life of Martin Van Buren, easily eclipsing similar claims that had been made against Adams in 1828. This tirade reached a climax when Ogle denounced Van Buren for having installed in the White House some bathtubs which, in Ogle's opulent phrases, took on the dimensions of the baths of Caracalla.[3]

A Whig banner of 1840 proclaimed, with all too much truth: "WE STOOP TO CONQUER." Cultivated and hitherto fastidious men, once opposed to universal manhood suffrage, now proclaimed themselves friends of the people and gave their consent to the broadest and most irrational campaign techniques. Eminent politicians, raised on the controversies of an earlier and somewhat more restrained era, may have gagged, but they went along with the use of what one newspaper called "The Davy Crockett Line." A reserved and cultivated Southern aristocrat, Hugh Swinton Legaré, swallowed his distaste and went on a speaking tour. Daniel Webster was inspired to say that although he had not had the good fortune to be born in a log cabin, "my elder brother and sisters were. . . . That cabin I annually visit, and thither I carry my children, that they may learn to honor and emulate the stern and simple virtues that there found their abode. . . ." Anyone who called him an aristocrat was "not only a LIAR but a COWARD," and must be prepared to fight if Webster could get at him. Henry Clay, for his part, said privately that he "lamented the necessity, real or imagined . . . of appealing to the feelings and passions of our Countrymen, rather than to their reasons and judgments," and then did exactly that.

Sensitive men in the Whig ranks may have shrunk from the rhetoric of the log-cabin, hard-cider campaign, but if they wanted to stay in politics they could not shrink too long. The gentleman as a force in American politics was committing suicide. John Quincy Adams, watch-

[3] Charles Ogle: *The Regal Splendor of the President's Palace* (n.p., 1840), especially p. 28.

ing the discouraging spectacle from Washington, found in this boisterous election "a revolution in the habits and manners of the people." [4] The process set in motion decades earlier, and poignantly symbolized by his own expulsion from the White House in 1829, had reached its fulfillment. "This appears to be the first time in our history," Morgan Dix commented, "in which a direct appeal was made to the lower classes by exciting their curiosity, feeding the desire for amusement, and presenting what is low and vulgar as an inducement for support. Since that day the thing has been carried farther, until it is actually a disadvantage to be of good stock and to have inherited 'the grand old name of gentleman.' " [5]

· 5 ·

The withdrawal of the soberer classes from politics went on, hastened by the new fevers aroused by slavery and sectional animosities. As early as 1835 Tocqueville had commented on the "vulgar demeanor" and the obscurity of the members of the House; he would have found the deterioration quite advanced, had he returned in the 1850's. "Do you remark," wrote Secretary of the Navy John Pendleton Kennedy to his uncle in the 1850's, "how lamentably destitute the country is of men in public station of whom we may speak with any pride? . . . How completely has the conception and estimate of a *gentleman* been obliterated from the popular mind! Whatever of that character we have seems almost banished from the stage." [6] In 1850, Francis Bowen, writing in the *North American Review*, found that both Houses of Congress had been "transformed into noisy and quarrelsome debating clubs." [7]

> Furious menaces and bellowing exaggeration take the place of calm and dignified debate; the halls of the capitol often present scenes which would disgrace a bear-garden; and Congress attains the unenviable fame of being the most helpless, disorderly, and inefficient legislative body which can be found in the civilized world.

[4] For this campaign and the quotations, see Robert G. Gunderson: *The Log-Cabin Campaign* (Lexington, 1957), especially pp. 3, 7, 101–7, 134, 162, 179–86, 201–18.

[5] *Memoirs of John A. Dix* (New York, 1883), Vol. I, p. 165.

[6] Henry T. Tuckerman: *Life of John Pendleton Kennedy* (New York, 1871), p. 187.

[7] "The Action of Congress on the California and Territorial Questions," *North American Review*, Vol. LXXI (July, 1850), pp. 224–64.

Representative Robert Toombs of Georgia concurred. The present Congress, he wrote to a friend, "furnishes the worst specimens of legislators I have ever seen here. . . . There is a large infusion of successful jobbers, lucky serving men, parishless parsons and itinerant lecturers among them who are not only without wisdom or knowledge but have bad manners, and therefore we can have but little hope of good legislation." [8] By 1853 it was deemed necessary to forbid Congressmen by law to take compensation for prosecuting any claim against the government, and to prescribe penalties against bribery.[9] Deterioration reached the point of outright helplessness in 1859, when the House found itself almost unable to agree on a Speaker. Young Charles Francis Adams was in Washington that year visiting his father, who was then a Congressman. As he later recalled: [1]

> I remember very well the Senate and House at that time. Neither body impressed me. The House was a national bear-garden; for that was, much more than now, a period of the unpicturesque frontiersman and the overseer. Sectional feeling ran high, and bad manners were conspicuously in evidence; whiskey, expectoration and bowie-knives were the order of that day. They were, indeed, the only kind of "order" observed in the House, over which poor old Pennington, of New Jersey, had as a last recourse been chosen to preside, probably the most wholly and all-round incompetent Speaker the House ever had.

In the earlier days of the Republic it had been possible for men in high places to add to their ranks with confidence other men of talents and distinction. This process was not as undemocratic as it may sound, since those who were thus co-opted were often men without advan-

[8] U. B. Phillips, ed.: *The Correspondence of Robert Toombs, Alexander H. Stephens, and Howell Cobb,* American Historical Association *Annual Report,* 1911, Vol. II, p. 188.

[9] Leonard D. White: *The Jacksonians,* p. 27. On deterioration in Congress and the public service, see pp. 25–7, 325–32, 343–6, 398–9, 411–420.

[1] *An Autobiography* (Boston, 1916) pp. 43–4. This was, of course, only a few years after the famous assault on Sumner by Brooks; during the same year a Congressman shot and killed a waiter out of annoyance with hotel dining-room service in Washington. On the state of Congress in the 1850's, see Roy F. Nichols: *The Disruption of American Democracy* (New York, 1948), pp. 2–3, 68, 188–91, 273–6, 284–7, 331–2. On the background of governmental decline, David Donald's Harmsworth Inaugural Lecture, "An Excess of Democracy: The American Civil War and the Social Process" (Oxford, 1960), is most stimulating. The decline of political leadership in the South has been particularly well traced in Clement Eaton: *Freedom of Thought in the Old South* (Durham, 1940), and Charles S. Sydnor: *The Development of Southern Sectionalism, 1819–1848* (Baton Rouge, 1948), especially chapter 12.

tages of birth and wealth. In 1808 it had been possible, for instance, for President Jefferson to write to William Wirt, a distinguished lawyer and essayist who had been born the son of an immigrant tavern-keeper, the following letter: [2]

> The object of this letter . . . is to propose to you to come into Congress. That is the great commanding theatre of this nation, and the threshold to whatever department or office a man is qualified to enter. With your reputation, talents, and correct views, used with the necessary prudence, *you will at once be placed at the head of the republican body in the House of Representatives;* and after obtaining the standing which a little time will ensure you, you may look, at your own will, into the military, the judiciary, the diplomatic, or other civil departments, *with a certainty of being in either whatever you please.* And in the present state of what may be called the eminent talents of our country, you may be assured of being engaged through life in the most honourable employments.

A few years after Jefferson's death, the confident assumptions of this letter were no longer conceivable. The techniques of advancement had changed; the qualities that put an aspiring politician into rapport with the public became more important than those that impressed his peers or superiors. More men were pushed up from the bottom than selected from the top.

The change in the standards of elected personnel was paralleled by the fate of the public service. The first tradition of the American civil service, established for the Federalists by Washington and continued by both Federalists and Jeffersonians until 1829, was a tradition of government by gentlemen.[3] By contemporary European standards of administration, Washington's initial criteria for appointments to Federal offices, although partisan, had been high. He demanded competence, and he also placed much emphasis both on the public repute and on the personal integrity of his appointees, in the hope that to name

---

[2] *Writings,* edited by Bergh, Vol. XI (Washington, 1904), pp. 423–4; italics are mine.

[3] My conclusions with regard to the history of the civil service have followed Leonard D. White's invaluable histories: *The Federalists* (New York, 1948), *The Jeffersonians* (New York, 1951), *The Jacksonians,* already cited, and *The Republican Era 1869–1901* (New York, 1958). Paul P. Van Riper, in his *History of the United States Civil Service* (Evanston, Illinois, 1958), p. 11, remarks: "During the formative years of the American national government its public service was one of the most competent in the world. Certainly it was one of the freest from corruption."

"such men as I conceive would give dignity and lustre to our National Character" would strengthen the new government. The impersonal principle of geographical distribution of appointments was observed from the beginning, but nepotism was ruled out. By 1792 political allegiance began to play more of a role in appointments, but it was still a modest role, as indicated by the remark of Washington's successor, John Adams, that the first President had appointed "a multitude of democrats and jacobins of the deepest die." [4] The greatest obstacle to recruitment into public service was that rural opinion kept federal salaries low, and from the beginning the prestige of public service was not high enough to be consistently attractive, even to men chosen for cabinet posts. When the Jeffersonians replaced the Federalists, Jefferson tried partly to calm the political hysteria of the previous years by avoiding wholesale public-service removals for political reasons alone; the most outspoken, intransigent, and active Federalist office-holders were fired, but the quieter ones retained their jobs. The caliber of public officers remained the same, although Jefferson advanced the idea that the offices should be more or less equally divided between the parties. The old criteria of integrity and respectability prevailed, and whatever else may be said about Jefferson's "Revolution of 1800," it brought no revolution in administrative practice. Indeed, in this respect, the remarkable thing was the continuity of criteria for choosing personnel.[5]

In the meantime, however, partisan use of patronage was becoming standard practice in some states, notably in Pennsylvania and New York. The idea of rotation in office spread from elective to appointive positions. With the rise of universal suffrage and egalitarian passions, older traditions of administration gave way during the 1820's to a more candid use of patronage for partisan purposes. The principle of rotation in office, which was considered the proper democratic creed, was looked upon by Jacksonians not as a possible cause of the deterioration of administrative personnel but rather as a social reform. Jacksonians saw the opportunity to gain office as yet another opportunity

[4] John Adams: *Works* (Boston, 1854), Vol. IX, p. 87. This was not said in complete disapproval. Adams himself did not propose to proscribe the opposition, lest he exclude "some of the ablest, most influential, and best characters in the Union."

[5] Van Riper remarks that, so far as partisanship is concerned, Jefferson proscribed enough public employees to be considered, as much as Jackson, the founder of the national spoils system, but that, so far as the caliber and social type of appointees are concerned, neither he nor his chief associates "made any real indentation on the essentially upper-class nature of the federal civil service." Op. cit., p. 23.

available to the common man in an open society. The rotation of office-holders, they held, would make it impossible for an undemocratic, permanent officeholding class to emerge. Easy removals and easy access to vacancies were not considered administrative weaknesses but democratic merits. This conception was expressed most authoritatively by Andrew Jackson in his first annual message to Congress in December, 1829.

Jackson argued that even when personal integrity made corruption unthinkable, men who enjoyed long tenure in office would develop habits of mind unfavorable to the public interest. Among long-standing officeholders, "office is considered as a species of property, and government rather as a means of promoting individual interests than as an instrument created for the service of the people." Sooner or later, whether by outright corruption or by the "perversion of correct feelings and principles," government is diverted from its legitimate ends to become "an engine for the support of the few at the expense of the many." The President was not troubled by the thought of the numbers of inexperienced and untried men that rotation would periodically bring. "The duties of all public officers are, or least admit of being made, so plain and simple that men of intelligence may readily qualify themselves for their performance"; and more would be lost by keeping men in office for long periods than would be gained as a result of their experience. In this, and in other passages, one sees Jackson's determination to keep offices open to newcomers as a part of the democratic pattern of opportunity, and to break down the notion that offices were a form of property. The idea of rotation in office he considered "a leading principle in the republican creed." [6]

The issue was clearly drawn: offices were in fact regarded by all as a kind of property, but the Jacksonians believed in *sharing* such property. Their approach to public offices was a perfect analogue of their anti-monopolistic position on economic matters. In a society whose energy and vitality owed so much to the diffusion of political and economic opportunities, there may have been more latent wisdom in this than Jackson's opponents were willing to admit. But the Jacksonian conviction that the duties of government were so simple that almost

[6] J. D. Richardson, ed.: *Messages and Papers of the Presidents* (New York, 1897), Vol. III, pp. 1011–12. Several historians have pointed out that the actual number of Jackson's removals was not very great. His administration was perhaps more notable for providing a rationale for removals. In later years, addiction to the spoils system became so acute that it invaded the factions within the parties. In the 1850's the Buchanan Democrats were throwing out the Pierce Democrats.

anyone could execute them downgraded the functions of the expert
and the trained man to a degree which turned insidious when the
functions of government became complex.[7] Just as the gentleman was
being elbowed out of the way by the homely necessities of American
elections, the expert, even the merely competent man, was being
restricted by the demands of the party system and the creed of rotation
into a sharply limited place in the American political system. The
estrangement of training and intellect from the power to decide and to
manage had been completed. The place of intellect in public life had,
unfortunately, been made dependent upon the gentleman's regard for
education and training and had been linked too closely to his political
fortunes. In nineteenth-century America this was a losing cause.

[7] In fact, the principle of rotation could not be quite so fully realized as
Jacksonian pronunciamentos suggested. What emerged was what Leonard D.
White has called a "dual system," in which a patronage system and a career
system existed side by side. Patronage clerks came and went, while a certain core of
more permanent officers remained. See *The Jacksonians*, pp. 347–62.

CHAPTER VII

The Fate of the Reformer

• 1 •

By mid-century, the gentlemen had been reduced to a marginal role in both elective and appointive offices in the United States, and had been substantially alienated from American politics. For a time the Civil War submerged their discontents. The war was one of those major crises that suspend cultural criticism. It was a cause, a distraction, a task that urgently had to be done, and, on the whole, Northerners of the patrician class rallied to the support of their country without asking whether the political culture they proposed to save was worth saving. Lincoln, as they came to know him, was reassuring, and he pleased them by appointing men of learning and letters to diplomatic posts—Charles Francis Adams, Sr., John Bigelow, George William Curtis, William Dean Howells, and John Lothrop Motley. If American democratic culture could produce such a man, it was possible that they, after all, had underestimated it.

But when the war was over, the failure of the system seemed only to have been dramatized. Hundreds of thousands of lives had been lost to redeem the political failures of the pre-war generation, and during the terrible fiasco of Reconstruction, it became clear that beyond the minimal goal of saving the Union nothing had been accomplished and nothing learned. The new generation of entrepreneurs was more voracious than the old, and politics appeared to have been abandoned to bloody-shirt demagogy, to dispensing the public domain to railroad barons, and to the tariff swindle. The idealistic Republican Party of 1856 had become the party of men like Benjamin F. Butler and Ben

Wade, and the creature of the scandalmakers of the Grant administration.

Many reformers saw how the tide of events was running as early as 1868, when Richard Henry Dana, Jr., tried to oust Benjamin F. Butler from his Massachusetts Congressional seat. For them the issue was sharply drawn: in the Bay State, the heart and center of the Brahmin class and the moral and intellectual wellspring of the patrician type, one of their own kind was now trying to remove from the political scene the man who had become the pre-eminent symbol of candid cynicism in politics. This was, *The New York Times* thought, "a contest between the intelligent, sober-minded, reflective men of the district, and the unthinking, reckless, boisterous don't-care-a-damnative portion of the community." [1] It proved also to be a contest between a tiny minority and the overwhelming majority of the immigrants and workers, marked by the almost classic ineptitude of Dana's electioneering techniques.[2] The dismal prospects of men of Dana's kind were harshly clarified by the election; Dana got less than ten per cent of the votes.

The humiliation of Dana was the first of a series of shocks. The reformers' friends were faring badly. Motley, on the strength of a rumor, was forced out of his diplomatic post by Andrew Johnson; reappointed by Grant, he was ditched once again because Grant wanted to strike through him at Sumner. Judge Ebenezer R. Hoar's nomination for the Supreme Court was rejected mainly because the politicians didn't like him. ("What could you expect," asked Simon Cameron, "from a man who had snubbed seventy Senators?") The able economist, David A. Wells, was cut out of his office as special revenue agent because of his free-trade views. Jacob Dolson Cox, a leading advocate of civil-service reform, felt impelled by lack of presidential support to resign as Grant's Secretary of the Interior. By 1870, Henry Adams, explaining why he had left Washington to teach at Harvard, wrote: "All my friends have been or are on the point of being driven out of the

[1] *The New York Times*, October 24, 1868. For years Butler used the Brahmins' hatred of him as a political asset. A supporter in 1884 declared that he won elections because "all the snobs and all the dilettantes hate him, and Harvard College won't make him a doctor of laws." H. C. Thomas: *Return of the Democratic Party to Power in 1884* (New York, 1919), p. 139.

[2] It was in this campaign that Butler, driving a wedge between Dana and working-class constituencies, accused Dana of wearing white gloves. Dana admitted that he did at times wear white gloves and clean clothes, but assured his audience, the workingmen of Lynn, that when he spent two years before the mast as a young sailor, "I was as dirty as any of you." Benjamin F. Butler: *Butler's Book* (Boston, 1892), pp. 921–2.

government and I should have been left without any allies or sources of information." [3]

The young men who had hoped that the party of Lincoln and Grant might bring about a reform no longer had any illusions. As the grim shape of the new America emerged out of the smoke of the war, there emerged with it a peculiar American underground of frustrated aristocrats, a type of genteel reformer whose very existence dramatized the alienation of education and intellect from significant political and economic power. The dominant idea of the genteel reformers was public service; their chief issue, civil-service reform; their theoretical spokesman, E. L. Godkin of the *Nation;* their most successful political hero, Grover Cleveland. Their towering literary monument proved to be that masterpiece in the artistry of self-pity, Henry Adams's *Education.*

The historian, looking back upon the genteel reformers and realizing how many grave social issues they barely touched upon and how many they did not touch at all, may be inclined to feel that their blood ran thin, and to welcome the appearance among them in later days of such a bold and distracted figure as John Jay Chapman. But this class represented the majority of the politically active educated men of the community; and the place of mind in American politics, if mind was to have any place at all, rested mainly upon their fortunes. This they understood themselves; it was what Lowell meant when he begged Godkin to protest in the *Nation* against "the queer notion of the Republican Party that they can get along without their brains"—and Charles Eliot Norton when he made his pathetic if rather parochial plaint that "the *Nation* & Harvard & Yale College seem to me almost the only solid barriers against the invasion of modern barbarism & vulgarity." [4]

The reform type was not national or representative. As a rule, the genteel reformers were born in the Northeast—mainly in Massachusetts, Connecticut, New York, and Pennsylvania—although a scattered few lived in those parts of the Middle West which had been colonized by Yankees and New Yorkers. Morally and intellectually these men were the heirs of New England, and for the most part its heirs by

[3] Adams to C. M. Gaskell, October 25, 1870, in W. C. Ford, ed.: *Letters of Henry Adams* (Boston, 1930), p. 196.
[4] J. R. Lowell to Godkin, December 20, 1871, in Rollo Ogden, ed.: *Life and Letters of Edwin Lawrence Godkin* (New York, 1907), Vol. II, p. 87; C. E. Norton to Godkin, November 3, 1871, in Ari Hoogenboom: *Outlawing the Spoils* (Urbana, Illinois, 1961), p. 99.

descent. They carried on the philosophical concerns of Unitarianism and transcendentalism, the moral animus of Puritanism, the crusading heritage of the free-soil movement, the New England reverence for education and intellectualism, the Yankee passion for public duty and civic reform.

They struck the Yankee note, one must add, of self-confidence and self-righteousness; most of the genteel reformers were certain of their own moral purity. "Each generation of citizens," declared the publisher George Haven Putnam, describing them in his autobiography, "produces a group of men who are free from self-seeking and who, recognizing their obligations to the community, are prepared to give their work and their capacities for doing what may be in their power for the service of their fellow-men." [5] This capacity for disinterested service was founded upon financial security and firm family traditions. The genteel reformers were not usually very rich, but they were almost invariably well-to-do. Hardly any were self-made men from obscure or poverty-stricken homes; they were the sons of established merchants and manufacturers, lawyers, clergymen, physicians, educators, editors, journalists, and publishers, and they had followed their fathers into business and the professions. Their education was far above the ordinary: at a time when college diplomas were still rare, there were among them an impressive number with B.A.'s, and most of those who lacked B.A.'s had law degrees. Several were historians, antiquarians, and collectors; others wrote poetry, fiction, or criticism. A high proportion of the college men had gone to Harvard or Yale, or to such outposts of the New England educational tradition as Amherst, Brown, Williams, Dartmouth, and Oberlin. Those whose religious affiliations can be determined belonged (aside from a few independents and skeptics) to the upper-class denominations, and especially those most affected by the New England tradition or those which appealed to mercantile patricians—Congregationalists, Unitarians, and Episcopalians.[6]

Politically and morally, as Henry Adams so poignantly demonstrated,

[5] George Haven Putnam: *Memories of a Publisher* (New York, 1915), p. 112.

[6] My generalizations about the reformers are based on an analysis of factors in the careers of 191 men in an unpublished master's essay at Columbia University written by James Stuart McLachlan: *The Genteel Reformers: 1865–1884* (1958). His conclusions are similar to those in Ari Hoogenboom's analysis of civil-service reformers, op. cit., pp. 190–7. Cf. his essay, "An Analysis of Civil Service Reformers," *The Historian,* Vol. XXIII (November, 1960), pp. 54–78. Paul P. Van Riper emphasizes the prior abolitionist sympathies of these reformers, and their preoccupation with individual liberty and political morality; op. cit., pp. 78–86.

the genteel reformers were homeless. They had few friends and no allies. Almost everywhere in American life—in business as well as in politics—an ingenuous but coarse and ruthless type of person had taken over control of affairs, a type Adams found in possession when he returned to Washington from England after the Civil War: [7]

> In time one came to recognize the type in other men [than Grant], with differences and variations, as normal; men whose energies were the greater, the less they wasted on thought; men who sprang from the soil to power; apt to be distrustful of themselves and of others; shy; jealous, sometimes vindictive; more or less dull in outward appearance, always needing stimulants; but for whom action was the highest stimulant—the instinct of fight. Such men were forces of nature, energies of the prime, like the *Pteraspis,* but they made short work of scholars. They had commanded thousands of such and saw no more in them than in others. The fact was certain; it crushed argument and intellect at once.

Wherever men of cultivation looked, they found themselves facing hostile forces and an alien mentality. They resented the new plutocracy which overshadowed them in business and in public affairs—a plutocracy they considered as dangerous socially as it was personally vulgar and ostentatious; for it consisted of those tycoons about whom Charles Francis Adams, Jr., said that after years of association he had not met one that he would ever care to meet again, or one that could be "associated in my mind with the idea of humor, thought or refinement." [8] No less vulgar were the politicians—"lewd fellows of the baser sort," Godkin called them [9]—who compounded their vulgarity with inefficiency, ignorance, and corruption. Henry Adams had not long returned to Washington when a Cabinet officer told him how pointless it was to show patience in dealing with Congressmen: "You can't use tact with a Congressman! A Congressman is a hog! You must take a stick and hit him on the snout!" Everyone in Boston, New England, and New York agreed in warning Adams that "Washington was no place for a respectable young man," and he could see for himself that the

[7] *The Education of Henry Adams* (New York: Modern Library edition; 1931), p. 265.

[8] Charles Francis Adams: *An Autobiography* (Boston, 1916), p. 190.

[9] E. L. Godkin: "The Main Question," *Nation,* Vol. IX (October 14, 1869), p. 308.

place had no tone, no society, no social medium through which the ideas of men of discernment and refinement could influence affairs.[1]

Society seemed hardly more at home than he. Both Executive and Congress held it aloof. No one in society seemed to have the ear of anybody in Government. No one in Government knew any reason for consulting any one in society. The world had ceased to be wholly political, but politics had become less social. A survivor of the Civil War—like George Bancroft, or John Hay—tried to keep footing, but without brilliant success. They were free to do or say what they liked, but no one took much notice of anything said or done.

The genteel reformers were as much alienated from the general public as they were from the main centers of power in the business corporations and the political machines. They had too much at stake in society to campaign for radical changes and too much disdain for other varieties of reformers to make political allies. The discontented farmers, with their cranky enthusiasms and their monetary panaceas, inspired in them only distaste. Snobbishness and gentility, as well as class interest, estranged them from the working class and the immigrants. Charles Francis Adams, Jr., expressed a feeling common to his class when he said: "I don't associate with the laborers on my place"; and he was no doubt doubly right when he added that such association would not be "agreeable to either of us." [2] As for the immigrants, the reformers considered their role in the misgovernment of cities to be one of the chief sources of the strength of the bosses. Reformers were sometimes skeptical about the merits of unrestricted democracy and universal manhood suffrage, and toyed with the thought of education tests or poll taxes that would disfranchise the most ignorant in the electorate.[3]

Thus estranged from major social interests which had different needs from their own, the genteel reformers were barred from useful political alliances and condemned to political ineffectuality. They had

[1] Adams: *Education*, pp. 261, 296, 320. Cf. James Bryce: "Why the Best Men Do Not Go into Politics," *The American Commonwealth* (New York, 1897), Vol. II, chapter 57.

[2] *Autobiography*, pp. 15–16.

[3] See "The Government of our Great Cities," *Nation*, Vol. III (October 18, 1866), pp. 312–13; *North American Review*, Vol. CIII (October, 1866), pp. 413–65; Arthur F. Beringause: *Brooks Adams* (New York, 1955), pp. 60, 67; Barbara M. Solomon: *Ancestors and Immigrants* (Cambridge, Mass., 1956). On the outlook of the reformers, see Geoffrey T. Blodgett's sensitive account of "The Mind of the Boston Mugwump," *Mississippi Valley Historical Review*, Vol. XLVIII (March, 1962), pp. 614–34.

to content themselves with the hope that occasionally they could get their way by acting "on the limited number of cultivated minds," [4] by appealing, as James Ford Rhodes put it, to men of "property and intelligence." "We want a government," said Carl Schurz in 1874, "which the best people of this country will be proud of." [5] What they were really asking for was leadership by an educated and civic-minded elite—in a country which had no use for elites of any kind, much less for an educated one. "The best people" were outsiders. Their social position seemed a liability; their education certainly was. In 1888 James Russell Lowell complained that "in the opinion of some of our leading politicians and many of our newspapers, men of scholarly minds are *ipso facto* debarred from forming any judgment on public affairs; or if they should be so unscrupulous as to do so . . . they must at least refrain from communicating it to their fellow-citizens." [6]

Aware that their public following was too small to admit of a frontal attack on any major citadel of politics or administration, the genteel reformers were driven to adopt a strategy of independency. The margin of strength between the two major parties was frequently so narrow that, by threatening to bolt, a strong faction of independents might win an influence out of proportion to their numbers.[7] For a short time, the reformers seemed to be poised tantalizingly on the fringes of real influence. At first, they thought they might have some say in the Grant administration, and when Grant disappointed them, most of them took part in the ill-fated bolt of the Liberal Republicans in 1872. Then they were courted so carefully by Hayes that their expectations were aroused, only to be disappointed again. For the most part, they had to content themselves with limited victories, like the reform of the post

[4] Adams to Gaskell, quoted in Ernest Samuels: *The Young Henry Adams* (Cambridge, Mass., 1948), p. 182. Cf. Putnam's view: "It was our hope that as the youngsters came out of college from year to year with the kind of knowledge of the history of economics that would be given to them by professors like William Graham Sumner of Yale, we should gradually secure a larger hold on public opinion, and through the influence of leaders bring the mass of the voters to an understanding of their own business interests." Putnam: op. cit., pp. 42–3.

[5] Quoted in Eric Goldman: *Rendezvous with Destiny* (New York, 1952), p. 24. One advocate of civil-service reform pointed out that in "the early days of the Republic" all public servants from cabinet officers down to subordinate members "were generally selected from well-known families," and argued that civil-service reform would reintroduce this practice. Julius Bing: "Civil Service of the United States," *North American Review,* Vol. CV (October, 1867), pp. 480–1.

[6] "The Place of the Independent in Politics," *Writings,* Vol. VI (Cambridge, Mass., 1890), p. 190.

[7] On the strategy of independency, see James Russell Lowell: "The Place of the Independent in Politics," pp. 190 ff.; and E. McClung Fleming: *R. R. Bowker, Militant Liberal* (New York, 1952), pp. 103–8.

office and the New York Customs House, or the occasional appointment of such men as Hamilton Fish, E. R. Hoar, William M. Evarts,
Carl Schurz, or Wayne MacVeagh, to Cabinet posts. Their happiest
moment came in the election of 1884, when they convinced themselves that the Mugwump bolt from the Republican Party had swung
the state of New York from Blaine to Cleveland, and with it the election. But their outstanding legislative success was in civil-service reform, with the passage of the Pendleton Act in 1883. This deserves
special attention, for civil-service reform, the class issue of the gentleman, was a touchstone of American political culture.

· 2 ·

The central idea of the reformers—the idea which they all agreed upon
and which excited their deepest concern—was the improvement of the
civil service, without which they believed no other reform could be
successfully carried out.[8] The ideal of civil-service reform brought into
direct opposition the credo of the professional politicians, who put their
faith in party organization and party rewards and the practice of rotation in office, and the ideals of the reformers, who wanted competence,
efficiency, and economy in the public service, open competition for
jobs on the basis of merit, and security of tenure. The reformers looked
to various models for their proposals—to the American military services, to bureaucratic systems in Prussia or even China; but principally
this English-oriented intellectual class looked for inspiration to England, where civil-service reorganization had been under way since the
publication of the Northcote-Trevelyan Report in 1854.

  The English civil-service reformers had designed their proposals in
full awareness of the organic relation of the civil service to the class
structure and to the educational system. They had planned a civil service which, as Gladstone observed, would give the gentlemanly classes
"command over all the higher posts" and allot to members of the lower
classes the positions that could be filled by persons with more practical
and less expensive training.[9] The scheme owed much to the influence
of Lord Macaulay, who conceived of "a public service confined in its
upper reaches to gentlemen of breeding and culture selected by a literary competition." The higher posts would be filled by gentlemen who

---

[8] On the centrality of this reform, see Paul P. Van Riper: op. cit., pp. 83–4.
[9] See J. Donald Kingsley: *Representative Bureaucracy: An Interpretation of the
British Civil Service* (Yellow Springs, Ohio, 1944), pp. 68–71 and *passim*.

had received a rigorous classical training at one of the ancient universities, the lower posts by candidates with a less exalted education—and within each category recruitment by competitive examination would guarantee the merit of those chosen. By 1877, Sir Charles Trevelyan, one of the leading reformers, reported to an American friend that the British changes had been not only successful but popular. "Large as the number of persons who profited by the former system of patronage were," he observed,

> those who were left out in the cold were still larger, and these included some of the best classes of our population—busy professional persons of every kind, lawyers, ministers of religion of every persuasion, schoolmasters, farmers, shopkeepers, etc. These rapidly took in the idea of the new institution, and they gladly accepted it as a valuable additional privilege.

Moreover, Sir Charles remarked, the same change that had increased the efficiency of the civil and military services "has given a marvellous stimulus to education." Formerly, upper-class boys who intended to go into public service had had no inducement to exert themselves because they were certain to get an appointment. Now they knew that their future depended in some good measure upon their own energies, and "a new spirit of activity has supervened. The opening of the civil and military services, in its influence upon national education, is equivalent to a hundred thousand scholarships and exhibitions of the most valuable kind. . . ."[1]

The appeal of the British reformers to their American counterparts is quite understandable. The concern of the leading American reformers was not, for the most part, self-interested, in so far as most jobs that would be opened in the American civil service, if competitive examinations were adopted, would not be of sufficient rank to attract them.[2] But it was humiliating to know that by the canons of the society in which they lived they were not preferred for office and could not

---

[1] Sir Charles Trevelyan to Dorman B. Eaton, August 20, 1877, in Dorman B. Eaton: *Civil Service in Great Britain: A History of Abuses and Reforms and Their Bearing upon American Politics* (New York, 1880), pp. 430–2.

[2] No doubt many reformers hoped wistfully that the kind of recognition Lincoln had given to literary men might be resumed, but such posts were above and outside the civil-service system. Characteristically, the reformers aspired to elective rather than appointive office. About half of the leading reformers held office at one time or another, but chiefly in elective positions. A few went to Congress, but most of their elected offices were in state legislatures. McLachlan: op. cit., p. 25.

help their friends.[3] What was mainly at issue for them was a cultural and political ideal, a projection of their own standards of purity and excellence into governmental practice. It was the "national character" which was at stake. The principles of freedom and competitive superiority which they had learned in their college courses in classical economics and had applied to the tariff question ought to be applied to public office: open competition on the basis of merit should be the civil-service analogue of fair competition in industry.[4] But to the professional politicians the means of determining merit—the competitive examination—seemed to have about it the aura of the school, and it instantly aroused their hostility to intellect, education, and training. It was, as they began to say, a "schoolmaster's test." Touching the professions directly on a sensitive nerve, the issue brought forth a violent reaction which opened the floodgates of anti-intellectualist demagogy. The professionals denounced the idea of a civil service based upon examinations and providing secure tenure as aristocratic and imitative of British, Prussian, and Chinese bureaucracies; as deferential to monarchical institutions, and a threat to republicanism; and as militaristic because it took as one of its models the examination requirements that had been instituted in the armed services. From the first, the distrust of trained intellect was invoked. When a bill calling for civil-service reform was introduced in 1868 by Representative Thomas A. Jenckes of Rhode Island, it was denounced in the House by John A. Logan of Illinois in these terms: [5]

> This bill is the opening wedge to an aristocracy in this country.
> . . . It will lead us to the point where there will be two national

[3] Consider the implications of Henry Adams's letter to Charles Francis Adams, Jr., April 29, 1869: "I can't get you an office. The only members of this Government that I have met are mere acquaintances, not friends, and I fancy no request of mine would be likely to call out a gush of sympathy. [David Ames] Wells has just about as much influence as I have. He can't even protect his own clerks. Judge Hoar has his hands full, and does not interfere with his colleagues. . . ."*Letters,* p. 157.

[4] There was an assumption on the part of some that social standing would count, however, in the competition for jobs. Carl Schurz once proposed that "mere inquiries concerning the character, antecedents, social standing, and general ability [of a candidate] may be substituted for formal examination." Hoogenboom: op. cit., p. 115.

[5] *Congressional Globe,* 40th Congress, 3rd session, p. 265 (January 8, 1869). It is suggestive that competitive civil service, so often criticized in the United States as undemocratic, was at times assailed in Britain as excessively democratic, and as throwing the aristocracy on the defensive in the competition for posts. Kingsley: op. cit., p. 62. Others felt that this would only raise the morale and tone of the class of gentlemen. Cf. Asa Briggs: *Victorian People* (London, 1954), pp. 116–21, 170–1.

schools in this country—one for the military and the other for civil education. These schools will monopolize all avenues of approach to the Government. Unless a man can pass one or another of these schools and be enrolled upon their lists he cannot receive employment under this Government, no matter how great may be his capacity, how indisputable may be his qualifications. When once he does pass his school and fixes himself for life his next care will be to get his children there also. In these schools the scholars will soon come to believe that they are the only persons qualified to administer the Government, and soon come to resolve that the Government shall be administered by them and by none others.

It became clear, as the debate over civil service developed, that the professionals feared the demand for competence and the requirements of literacy and intelligence as a threat to the principles upon which the machines were based, and with this threat before them, there was almost no limit to the demagogy they would exert in behalf of the spoils principle. A Congressman from Indiana held up the frightening prospect that a graduate of, say, Washington College in Virginia, of which Robert E. Lee was president, would do better on a competitive examination than a disabled soldier of some "common school or workshop of the West, who lost a limb at the battle of Chickamauga." The people, he said, "are not quite ready to permit the students of rebel colleges, upon competitive examinations and scholastic attainments, to supersede the disabled and patriotic soldiers of the Republic, who with fewer educational advantages but larger practical experience are much better fitted for the position." [6]

In similar terms, Senator Matthew H. Carpenter of Wisconsin declaimed that during the Civil War, [7]

---

[6] *Congressional Globe*, 42nd Congress, 2nd session, p. 1103 (February 17, 1872). This form of competition with college-trained men also troubled the veterans' organizations. See Wallace E. Davies: *Patriotism on Parade* (Cambridge, Mass., 1955), pp. 247, 285–6, 311.

[7] *Congressional Globe*, 42nd Congress, 2nd session, p. 458 (January 18, 1872). Many local bosses, of course, were as troubled as the Congressmen about the effect of competitive examinations on their procedures. "I suppose," objected the Boston boss, Patrick Macguire, apropos a Massachusetts civil-service law, "that if any one of my boys wants to have a position in any of the departments of Boston, to start with I shall have to send him to Harvard College. It is necessary that he should graduate with the highest honors, and I suppose that the youths who are now studying there can look forward to the brilliant career that waits for them in our metropolis when they shall have been educated up to the proper point where

when the fate of the nation was trembling in the balance, and our gallant youths were breasting the storm of war, the sons of less patriotic citizens were enjoying the advantages of a college course. And now, when our maimed soldiers have returned, and apply for a Federal office, the duties of which they are perfectly competent to discharge, they are to be rejected to give place to those who were cramming themselves with facts and principles from the books, while they were bleeding for their country, because they do not know the fluctuations of the tide at the Cape of Good Hope, how near the moon ever approaches the earth, or the names of the principal rivers emptying into the Caspian Sea.

Suggesting that "admission into the kingdom of heaven does not depend upon the result of a competitive examination," the senator rang the changes on the contrast between formal education and practical intelligence: "The dunce who has been crammed up to a diploma at Yale, and comes fresh from his cramming, will be preferred in all civil appointments to the ablest, most successful, and most upright business man of the country, who either did not enjoy the benefit of early education, or from whose mind, long engrossed in practical pursuits, the details and niceties of academic knowledge have faded away as the headlands disappear when the mariner bids his native land goodnight."

Such comments were not confined to Northerners who were waving the bloody shirt. Representative McKee of Mississippi objected that educational criteria would make it almost impossible for the less educated sections of the country to capitalize on their old privileges under the geographic criterion for appointment. His complaint, quite candidly put, was that if competence were to be required he would be unable to get jobs for his Mississippi constituents. "Suppose," he said, "some wild mustang girl from New Mexico comes here for a position, and it may be that she does not know whether the Gulf stream runs north or south, or perhaps she thinks it stands on end, and she may answer that the 'Japan current' is closely allied to the English gooseberry, yet although competent for the minor position she seeks, she is sent back home rejected, and the place is given to some spectacled school ma'am who probably has not half as much native sense as the New Mexican." [8] McKee complained:

---

they are able to handle the pick-axe and the shovel, and all others who don't have the good fortune to be well educated must stand aside and look for positions elsewhere." Quoted in Lucius B. Swift: *Civil Service Reform* (n.p., 1885), p. 10.

[8] *Congressional Globe,* 42nd Congress, 3rd session, p. 1631 (February 22, 1873).

I had a constituent here who knew more than your whole civil service board. He was brought up here from Mississippi and they found him incompetent for the lowest grade of clerkship; and yet he is now cashier or teller of one of the largest banks on the Pacific slope. And they gave the appointment to a spectacled pedagogue from Maine, who, as far as business capacity and common sense was concerned, was not fit to be clerk to a boot-black. [Laughter.] That is the way it has been all along.

For a long time the opponents of civil service succeeded in creating in the public mind a conception of civil-service reform which had very little to do with reality but which appealed formidably to egalitarian sentiments, machine cupidity, and anti-intellectualism. E. L. Godkin once remarked that when reform agitation first appeared, it was greeted as simply another of "the thousand visionary attempts to re-generate society with which a certain class of literary men is supposed to beguile its leisure." In the inner political circles, between 1868 and 1878, it was known, with much mingled disgust and amusement, as "snivel service reform." "The reformers were sometimes spoken of as a species of millennarians, and others as weak-minded people, who looked at political society as a sort of Sunday-school which could be managed by mild exhortation and cheap prizes, and whom it was the business of practical men to humor in so far as it could be done harm-lessly, but not to argue with." [9] The professional politicians succeeded in persuading themselves that civil-service reform meant favoritism to the college-educated; that it would restrict job-holding to a hereditary college-educated aristocracy; and that all kinds of unreasonable and esoteric questions would be asked on civil-service examinations. (R. R. Bowker protested that "a great deal of nonsense [is] talked and written about asking a man who had to clean streets questions about ancient history, astronomy, and Sanskrit.") The idea of a literate com-petitive examination filled the anti-reformers with horror, a horror doubtless shared by many potential job applicants. "Henceforth," de-clared one of the more articular opponents of reform, [1]

entrance into the civil service is to be through the narrow portal of competitive examination, practically limiting entry to the graduates of colleges, thus admitting a Pierce and excluding a

[9] E. L. Godkin: "The Civil Service Reform Controversy," *North American Review*, Vol. CXXXIV (April, 1882), pp. 382–3.
[1] William M. Dickson: "The New Political Machine," *North American Review*, Vol. CXXXIV (January 1, 1882), p. 42.

Lincoln; the favored few thus admitted remaining for life; exempt, likewise, from vicissitudes; advancing, likewise, in a regular grada- tion, higher and higher; a class separate from the rest of the community, and bound together by a common interest and a com- mon subordination to one man, he also the commander-in-chief of the Army—the President of the United States.

In vain did reformers protest that there was nothing undemocratic about tests open equally to all applicants, especially since the Ameri- can educational system itself was so democratic, even at the upper levels.[2] In vain did they reprint the texts of examinations which al- ready existed in order to show that potential clerks were not expected to be members of the American Philosophical Society or graduates of the Ivy League colleges. In vain did they produce statistics showing that, for instance, in the New York Customs House, where the com- petitive examination system had been used before 1881, only a very modest proportion of candidates examined or appointed were college graduates.[3] The grim specter of the educated civil servant haunted the professionals to the very end. Even after President Garfield's assassi- nation, when public sentiment for civil-service reform rapidly mounted, his successor, Chester A. Arthur, professed to Congress his anxiety that civil-service examinations would exalt "mere intellectual proficiency" above other qualities and that experienced men would be at a disadvantage in competing with immature college youths.[4] Sena- tor George H. Pendleton, steering the civil-service reform bill through Congress, found it necessary to reassure the Senate that the system of examinations did not present only "a scholastic test" unfairly favor- ing the college-bred.[5] Had it not been for the fortuitous shooting of Garfield, it is likely that the reforms embodied in the Pendleton Act would have been delayed for almost a generation.

· 3 ·

In the attacks made by the reformers on the professional politicians, one finds a few essential words recurring: *ignorant, vulgar, selfish,*

[2] Andrew D. White: "Do the Spoils Belong to the Victor?" *North American Review,* Vol. CXXXIV (February, 1882), p. 129–30.

[3] Godkin: "The Civil Service Reform Controversy," p. 393.

[4] J. R. Richardson: *Messages and Papers of the Presidents,* Vol. X, pp. 46, 48–9.

[5] *Congressional Record,* 47th Congress, 2nd session, pp. 207–8 (December 12, 1882).

corrupt. To counter such language, the politicians had to have an adequate and appealing answer. It was not merely the conduct of the public debate which was at stake but also their need to salve their own genuine feelings of outrage. Where rapport with the public was concerned, the politicians, of course, had a signal advantage. But if the debate itself were to be accepted in the terms set by the reformers, the politicians would suffer considerably. Like all men living at the fringes of politics, and thus freed of the burdens of decision and responsibility, the reformers found it much easier than the professionals to keep their boasted purity. Most of the reform leaders were men from established families, with at least moderate wealth and secure independent vocations of their own, and not directly dependent upon politics for their livelihood; it was easier for them than for the professionals to maintain the atmosphere of disinterestedness that they felt vital to the public service. Besides, they *were* in fact better educated and more cultivated men.

The politicians and bosses found their answer in crying down the superior education and culture of their critics as political liabilities, and in questioning their adequacy for the difficult and dirty work of day-to-day politics. As the politicians put it, they, the bosses and party workers, had to function in the bitter world of reality in which the common people also had to live and earn their living. This was not the sphere of morals and ideals, of education and culture: it was the hard, masculine sphere of business and politics. The reformers, they said, claimed to be unselfish; but if this was true at all, it was true only because they were alien commentators upon an area of life in which they did not have to work and for which in fact they were unfit. In the hard-driving, competitive, ruthless, materialistic world of the Gilded Age, to be unselfish suggested not purity but a lack of self, a lack of capacity for grappling with reality, a lack of assertion, of masculinity.

Invoking a well-established preconception of the American male, the politicians argued that culture is impractical and men of culture are ineffectual, that culture is feminine and cultivated men tend to be effeminate. Secretly hungry for office and power themselves, and yet lacking in the requisite understanding of practical necessities, the reformers took out their resentment upon those who had succeeded. They were no better than carping and hypocritical censors of office-holders and power-wielders. They were, as James G. Blaine once put it, "conceited, foolish, vain, without knowledge . . . of men. . . .

They are noisy but not numerous, pharisaical but not practical, ambitious but not wise, pretentious but not powerful." [6]

The clash between reformers and politicians created in the minds of the professionals a stereotype of the educated man in politics that has never died. It is charmingly illustrated in the sayings, recorded (and perhaps dressed up) by a reporter around the turn of the century, of a candid practitioner of metropolitan politics, George Washington Plunkitt of Tammany Hall. If Tammany leaders were "all bookworms and college professors," Plunkitt declared,[7]

> Tammany might win an election once in four thousand years. Most of the leaders are plain American citizens, of the people and near to the people, and they have all the education they need to whip the dudes who part their name in the middle. . . . As for the common people of the district, I am at home with them at all times. When I go among them, I don't try to show off my grammar, or talk about the Constitution, or how many volts there is in electricity or make it appear in any way that I am better educated than they are. They wouldn't stand for that sort of thing.

Again: [8]

> Some young men think they can learn how to be successful in politics from books, and they cram their heads with all sorts of college rot. They couldn't make a bigger mistake. Now, understand me, I ain't sayin' nothin' against colleges. I guess they have to exist as long as there's bookworms, and I suppose they do some good in certain ways, but they don't count in politics. In fact, a young man who has gone through the college course is handi-

---

[6] Gail Hamilton: *Biography of James G. Blaine* (Norwich, 1895), p. 491. For a testy attack on literary men and reformers in politics, and their patronizing attitude toward professionals, see Senator Joseph R. Hawley: *Congressional Record*, 47th Congress, 2nd session, p. 242 (December 13, 1882).

[7] William L. Riordon: *Plunkitt of Tammany Hall* (1905; ed. New York, 1948), pp. 60–1. One is reminded here of the techniques of the delightful Brooklyn Democratic leader Peter McGuiness. Challenged for the leadership of his district during the early 1920's by a college graduate who maintained that the community should have a man of culture and refinement as its leader, McGuiness dealt with the newcomer "with a line that is a favorite of connoisseurs of political strategy. At the next meeting McGuiness addressed, he stood silent for a moment, glaring down at the crowd of shirtsleeved laborers and housewives in Hoover aprons until he had their attention. Then he bellowed, 'All of yez that went to Yales or Cornells raise your right hands. . . . The Yales and Cornells can vote for him. The rest of yez vote for me.'" Richard Rovere: "The Big Hello," in *The American Establishment* (New York, 1962), p. 36.

[8] Ibid., p. 10.

capped at the outset. He may succeed in politics, but the chances
are 100 to 1 against him.

It was not enough for the politicians to say that the reformers were
hypocritical and impractical. Their cultivation and fastidious manners
were taken as evidence that these "namby-pamby, goody-goody gentlemen" who "sip cold tea" [9] were deficient in masculinity. They were on
occasion denounced as "political hermaphrodites" (an easy transition
from their uncertain location as to political party to an uncertain location as to sex). The waspish Senator Ingalls of Kansas, furious at their
lack of party loyalty, once denounced them as "the third sex"—"effeminate without being either masculine or feminine; unable either to
beget or bear; possessing neither fecundity nor virility; endowed with
the contempt of men and the derision of women, and doomed to
sterility, isolation, and extinction." [1]

From the moment the reformers appeared as an organized force in
the Liberal Republican movement of 1872, they were denounced by
Roscoe Conkling, one of the most flamboyant of the spoilsmen, as a
"convention of idealists and professors and sore-heads." [2] Conkling also
produced one of the classics of American invective, and spelled out
the implications of the charge of deficient masculinity. Conkling's victim was George William Curtis, once a student at the German universities, editor of *Harper's* and a prominent reformer, the friend of such
men as Bryant, Lowell, and Sumner, and one of the most prominent
advocates of a more aggressive role in politics for educated men. The
occasion was the New York State Republican Convention of 1877,
at which a battle between bosses and reformers over the party organization came to a head. When Conkling's moment came, he asked:
"Who are these men who, in newspapers and elsewhere, are cracking
their whips over Republicans and playing school-master to the Republican party and its conscience and convictions?" "Some of them are
the man-milliners, the dilettanti and carpet knights of politics," he

[9] A letter to *The New York Times*, June 17, 1880, quoted by R. R. Bowker:
Nation, Vol. XXXI (July 1, 1880), p. 10.
[1] *Congressional Record*, 49th Congress, 1st session, p. 2786 (March 26, 1886).
"They have two recognized functions," the senator said of the third sex. "They sing
falsetto, and they are usually selected as the guardians of the seraglios of Oriental
despots."
[2] Matthew Josephson: *The Politicos* (New York, 1938), p. 163. Conkling's words
are reminiscent of those of the businessman who objected to economic reformers as
"philanthropists, professors, and Lady Millionaires." Edward C. Kirkland: *Dream
and Thought in the Business Community* (Ithaca, 1956), p. 26.

went on—and the term man-milliners, a reference to the fashion articles that Curtis's magazine had recently started to publish, evoked howls of derisive laughter. After denouncing the reformers for parading "their own thin veneering of superior purity," and ridiculing their alleged treachery and hypocrisy, their "rancid, canting self-righteousness," he closed with the remark: "They forget that parties are not built by deportment, or by ladies' magazines, or by gush. . . ."[3]

What Plunkitt later suggested when he referred to "dudes that part their name in the middle" Conkling here made as clear as it was admissible to do. The cultivated character and precise manners of the reformers suggested that they were effeminate. Culture suggested feminity; and the editorship of a ladies' magazine proved it in Curtis's case. The more recent attacks by Senator McCarthy and others upon the Eastern and English-oriented prep-school personnel of the State Department, associated with charges of homosexuality, are not an altogether novel element in the history of American invective. That the term "man-milliners" was understood in this light by many contemporaries is suggested by the fact that though the New York *Tribune* reported Conkling's speech in full, with the offending word, Conkling's nephew dropped "man-milliners" from his account of this incident in the biography of his uncle and substituted asterisks as though he were omitting an unmistakable obscenity.[4]

What the politicians relied upon, as the basis for an unspoken agreement about the improper character of the reformers, was the feeling, then accepted by practically all men and by most women, that to be active in political life was a male prerogative, in the sense that women were excluded from it, and further, that capacity for an effective role in politics was practically a test of masculinity. To be active in politics was a man's business, whereas to be engaged in reform movements (at least in America) meant constant association with aggressive, reforming, moralizing women—witness the case of the abolitionists. The common male idea, so often heard in the debate over woman suffrage, was that women would soil and unsex themselves if they

[3] Alfred R. Conkling: *Life and Letters of Roscoe Conkling* (New York, 1889), pp. 540–1; for the full account of the incident, see pp. 538–49.
[4] See also the attack on Curtis in the Elmira *Advertiser*, October 6, 1877, as reported in Thomas Collier Platt's *Autobiography* (New York, 1910), pp. 93–5. Here "a smart boy named Curtis, who parted his hair in the middle like a girl" and lived in an exclusively feminine environment, ran afoul of a masculine redhead named Conkling, who beat him up, to the indignation of Curtis's maiden aunts and all the female neighbors.

entered the inevitably dirty male world of political activity, about which Senator Ingalls once said that its purification was "an iridescent dream."

If women invaded politics, they would become masculine, just as men became feminine when they espoused reform. Horace Bushnell suggested that if women got the vote and kept it for hundreds of years, "the very look and temperament of women will be altered." The appearance of women would be sharp, their bodies wiry, their voices shrill, their actions angular and abrupt, and full of self-assertion, will, boldness, and eagerness for place and power. It could also be expected that in this nightmare of female assertion women would actually "change type physiologically, they will become taller and more brawny, and get bigger hands and feet, and a heavier weight of brain," and would very likely become "thinner, sharp-featured, lank and dry, just as all disappointed, over-instigated natures always are." [5]

In compensation for their political disability, women were always conceded to embody a far greater moral purity than men (though this purity was held to be of a frailer variety); [6] and it was conventionally said that they would make it effective in the world through their role as wives and mothers. So long as they stayed out of politics, the realm of ideals and of purity belonged to them. By the same token, the realm of reality and of dirty dealings, in so far as it must exist, belonged to men; and the reformers who felt that they were bringing purer and more disinterested personal ideals into politics were accused by their opponents of trying to womanize politics, and to mix the spheres of the sexes. Just as women unsexed themselves by entering politics, so reformers unsexed themselves by introducing female standards—i.e., morality—into political life. The old byword for reformers—"long-haired men and short-haired women"—aptly expressed this popular feeling.

The notion that the demand for women's suffrage was perversely unsexing, even dehumanizing, was one of the central themes of Henry

[5] Horace Bushnell: *Women's Suffrage: the Reform against Nature* (New York, 1869), pp. 135–6. Cf. p. 56: "The claim of a beard would not be a more radical revolt against nature."

[6] Cf. Bushnell: "We also know that women often show a strange facility of debasement and moral abandonment, when they have once given way consentingly. Men go down by a descent—*facilis descencus*—women by a precipitation. Perhaps the reason is, in part, that more is expected of women and that again because there is more expectancy of truth and sacrifice in the semi-christly, subject state of women than is likely to be looked for in the forward, self-asserting headship of men." Ibid., p .142.

James's *The Bostonians*. Like Bushnell, James feared that the male world would be undone by the perverse aggressiveness of women and of feminine principles. His Southern hero, Basil Ransom, bursts out: [7]

> The whole generation is womanized; the masculine tone is pass-
> ing out of the world; it's a feminine, a nervous, hysterical, chatter-
> ing, canting age, an age of hollow phrases and false delicacy and
> exaggerated solicitudes and coddled sensibilities, which, if we
> don't soon look out, will usher in the reign of mediocrity, of the
> feeblest and flattest and the most pretentious that has ever been.
> The masculine character, the ability to dare and endure, to know
> and yet not fear reality, to look the world in the face and take it
> for what it is—a very queer and partly very base mixture—that is
> what I want to preserve, or rather, as I may say, recover. . . .

The world that James had in mind as having already been deprived of its masculine character was not, surely, the world of Jim Fisk, Carnegie, Rockefeller, or the railroad barons, nor the world of the Tweed Ring or Roscoe Conkling; rather it was the world of the cultivated man, whose learning had once been linked with masculine firmness to the life of action and assertion, the Eastern society, epitomized by Boston, which in all America James knew best. There seemed to be an almost painful need in this society for the kind of man who could join the sphere of ideas and moral scruples with the virile qualities of action and assertion.

· 4 ·

Whether or not the reformers fully realized it, the stigma of effeminacy and ineffectuality became a handicap to them, a token of their insulation from the main currents of American politics. One of the first to meet this challenge was Theodore Roosevelt. A recruit from the same social and educational strata as the reform leaders, he decided at an early age that the deficiencies charged against them were real, and that if reform was to get anywhere, their type must be replaced by a new and more vigorous kind of leader from the same class. In his *Autobiography*, he recalled that the reformers were [8]

> gentlemen who were very nice, very refined, who shook their
> heads over political corruption and discussed it in drawing-rooms

[7] *The Bostonians* (1886; ed. London, 1952), p. 289.
[8] *An Autobiography* (New York, 1920), pp. 86–7.

and parlors, but who were wholly unable to grapple with real men in real life. They were apt vociferously to demand "reform" as if it were some concrete substance, like cake, which could be handed out at will, in tangible masses, if only the demand were urgent enough. These parlor reformers made up for inefficiency in action by zeal in criticizing. . . .

When T. R. wrote this, he had long since been separated from reformers of Godkin's stripe by an intense and almost obsessive hatred, occasioned on his side by an irritating sense that they thought of him as a moral traitor, and on their side by an incomprehension that a man of his background could have made his moral compromises. But it was one of the major sources of his popularity in the country at large, toward the end of the century, that he could be portrayed as an Easterner, a writer, and a Harvard man from the well-to-do classes who nevertheless knew how to get along with cowboys and Rough Riders.

In spite of the disapproval of his family and friends, Roosevelt entered politics at the bottom in 1880 by joining the Jake Hess Republican Club near his home in New York City. He persisted in playing the political game despite his early distaste for the environment and the rebuffs of the ward heelers. The next year he had won enough support within the Republican machine to be sent to the legislature at Albany. When Roosevelt first entered the New York Assembly at twenty-three, he still suffered from the stigma of his fashionable background. As Henry F. Pringle has written: "In addition to his origin among New Yorkers of moderate wealth, he was a Harvard man. He wore eyeglasses on the end of a black silk cord, which was effeminate. In brief, he was a dude; that comic-supplement creation born of American inferiority toward Great Britain. Even Isaac L. Hunt, who was also a new member and who fought at Roosevelt's side in many a battle, was to recall him as 'a joke . . . a dude the way he combed his hair, the way he talked—the whole thing.' " Handicapped, as Pringle observes, by his manners, his grammatical English, and his feeling for clothes, and cursed with a comically high-pitched voice, which he used, as a contemporary said, to address the chairman "in the vernacular of the first families of New York," Roosevelt began his career inauspiciously.[9] His opponents were quick to

[9] Henry F. Pringle: *Theodore Roosevelt* (New York, 1931), pp. 65–7.

brand him as a college-bred sissy. Learning that four members of the national collegiate fraternity, Alpha Delta Phi, were on the Assembly Elections Committee, the New York *World* wrote: "Dear! Dear! Brother Roosevelt [is] a trader of positions on an Assembly Committee. Let the Alpha Delta veil the Mother symbol in crepe." "The horny-handed voters of the State will learn with surprise and disgust that some horny-headed legislators and lawyers are introducing 'college politics' into contested elections to the Legislature. The Alpha Delta Phi fraternity no doubt affords an innocent and agreeable recreation for undergraduates, but it is not exactly a safe guide for maturer statesmanship." [1]

In a short time, however, the strong personal image of himself that Roosevelt managed to create began to take hold in the newspapers. His vigor and sincerity began to win a hearty response, and he got favorable notices in spite of his education and background. An upstate editor found it "cheering to see an occasional young man of wealth and education who cares for something more than to be a butterfly of society—who is willing to bring the gifts of fortune to the public service." A Boston paper thought that even though he had "aesthetic leanings," he had delivered a "sagacious and level-headed Republican speech." Another decided that although he was "weighed down . . . with a good deal of theory taken aboard in the leading universities of the Old World and the New," he was none the less "really a very bright young man, with some practical ideas." The Springfield *Republican* was troubled about intellectual training that would hinder young men's understanding of the problems of the average citizen, but it conceded that Roosevelt's was "a culture that does not separate him from the cause of the people." By the time Roosevelt became a Civil Service Commissioner, an editor was able to say: "Reform with him will never become either a literary recreation or a hypocritical subterfuge to cover submission to party."

Roosevelt's familiarity with the West and his ranching experiences were a great help in establishing his virility. He was described as a "manly, athletic, vigorous person . . . fond of hunting big game in

---

[1] This and subsequent press comments on Roosevelt are taken from a mass of such quotations in two master's essays written at Columbia University in 1947 and based upon an examination of Roosevelt's scrapbooks—Anne de la Vergne: *The Public Reputation of Theodore Roosevelt, 1881–1897*, pp. 9–16, 45–6; and Richard D. Heffner: *The Public Reputation of Theodore Roosevelt: The New Nationalism, 1890–1901*, pp. 21–4, 41–5, 53–4.

the Far West [where] he is the owner of great ranches," and as "schooled in the art of self-protection during his early days of *roughing it* in the West." Heroic tales were retold of his experiences with Indians. His skill in hunting became a political asset: "He is capable of showing the same spirit of true sport in following the trail of the spoilsman, as in his pursuit of the grizzly-bear of the Rocky Mountains, and when he opens fire on civic corruption it is a good deal like the action of a magazine-rifle at close range." Roosevelt was the only reformer whose life could have suggested that civil-service reform was analogous to hunting dangerous game.

Against the urban, commercial, cynical, effeminate world, Roosevelt represented the West and the outdoors, the vigorous, energetic, manly style of life, and a "sincere" and idealistic outlook. T. R. himself was aware of his achievement in dramatizing the compatibility of education and reform with energy and virility, and he took it upon himself to bring this message to the rising generation. When he was invited to speak to Harvard undergraduates in 1894, he chose the subject, "The Merit System and Manliness in Politics," and urged his listeners that they be not only "good men but also manly men, that they should not let those who stand for evil have all the virile qualities." During the 1890's he was especially vociferous in exhorting American men to commit themselves to an active, hardy, practical, and yet idealistic engagement in political struggles. "The strenuous life," of which he often spoke, was not simply a matter of nationalism and imperial assertion but of domestic reform politics. The good American, he repeated, would not merely criticize; he would act. He would throw himself into "the rough hurly-burly of the caucus" and bear his part as a man should, not shrinking from association with "men who are sometimes rough and coarse, who sometimes have lower ideals than they should, but who are capable, masterful, and efficient." He should develop "the rougher, manlier virtues, and above all the virtue of personal courage, physical as well as moral," and must be "vigorous in mind and body," possessing the "hardy virtues" which are admired in the soldier, "the virile fighting qualities without which no nation . . . can ever amount to anything." It would be "unmanliness and cowardice to shrink from the contest because at first there is failure, or because the work is difficult or repulsive." The educated and cultivated class had a special obligation not to show "weak good-nature," not to "cease doing their share of the rough, hard work which must be done" or sink into the kind of "dilettanteism" which resembles the position not of the true artist but of the "cultivated, ineffective man with a taste for bric-a-brac." [2]

In the midst of the anxieties aggravated by the severe economic depression of the nineties, this attitude was widely welcomed. "The ardor and strength of prime manhood," wrote a California paper, "is a much needed quality in American government, especially at this time, when all things political and all things social are in the transition stage."

Roosevelt's preaching of militant nationalism and the strenuous life helped to round out the picture of his aggressiveness. Here was an intellectual-in-politics who had the Jacksonian qualities of militancy and decision, who could never be charged with cowardice, like Jefferson, or academicism like John Quincy Adams, or with the eunuchoid indecisiveness of a Curtis. He was unmistakably a "fighter." "He loves fighting, but all his fighting is for good government. Roosevelt is aggressiveness itself." In 1896, when American imperialism was being criticized by academics like Theodore Woolsey and Hermann von Holst, the Cleveland *World* found in Roosevelt a perfect antidote to timid scholarship. T. R.'s influence was like a "patriotic breeze. . . . Across the alkali plains of non-patriotism where the Woolseys . . . the von Holsts and other professors have been evaporating, comes this fresh welcome breath from a man as well equipped in scholarship as they." If there was anything missing from the picture of virile patriotism and pugnacity, it was supplied by Roosevelt's active and well-publicized services with the Rough Riders in the Spanish War, which made him, beyond question, the national hero. "His popularity comes from certain virile characteristics which most men like," asserted *Harper's Weekly* in 1899. "They are fond of the picture of the man on horseback—whether he is riding after Spaniards or grizzlies or steers, whether he is a soldier, hunter or ranchman." Describing an ovation given Roosevelt in 1900, the Detroit *News* said: "It was for the man who banded together a strangely contrasted crew—college men and cowboys—and swept with them across the page of current history, that men cheered themselves hoarse and women paid dainty tribute." "It is not to be expected," said the Chicago *Journal* the following year, "that anemic, town-bred, stage-door-haunting, dissipated

[2] *Harvard Crimson*, November 10, 1894; see especially "The Manly Virtues and Practical Politics" (1894) and "The College Graduate and Public Life" (1894), from which these quotations were taken, in *American Ideals* (New York, 1897), pp. 51–77.

youths can sympathize with a real man of Theodore Roosevelt's sort. But . . . live, vigorous Americans, with red blood coursing through their veins know how to appreciate him."

A citified, commercial civilization, bedeviled by serious depression and troubled for the first time by the fear of decadence, greeted Roosevelt as the harbinger of a new and more vigorous and masculine generation. Roosevelt paved the way for Progressivism by helping to restore prestige to educated patricians who were interested in reform, by reinvesting their type with the male virtues. American men, impelled to feel tough and hard, could respond to this kind of idealism and reform without fearing that they had unmanned themselves. In Roosevelt one finds the archetype of what has become a common American political image: the aspiring politician, suspected of having too gentle an upbringing, too much idealism, or too many intellectual interests, can pass muster if he can point to a record of active military service; if that is lacking, having made the football team may do.

But Roosevelt had accomplished more than the negative service of dispelling the image of the gentleman scholar as effeminate and ineffectual in politics. He had begun to show that this type of man had a useful part to play. In the generation he and his contemporaries were replacing, men of intellect had laid claim to leadership too much on the ground that their social standing and their mental and moral qualities entitled them to it. T. R. and his generation were more disposed to rest their claim on the ground that they performed a distinct and necessary function in the national scheme of things. For them, the role of the scholar in politics was founded upon his possession of certain serviceable skills that were becoming increasingly important to the positive functions of government. The era of the frustrated gentleman-reformer in politics was coming to a close. With the emergence of the Progressive generation, the era of the scholar as expert was about to begin.

CHAPTER VIII

The Rise of the Expert

❦

· 1 ·

I N THE Progressive era the estrangement between intellectuals and power which had been so frustrating to the reformers of the Gilded Age came rather abruptly to an end. America entered a new phase of economic and social development; the old concern with developing industry, occupying the continent, and making money was at last matched by a new concern with humanizing and controlling the large aggregates of power built up in the preceding decades. The country seems to have been affected by a sort of spiritual hunger, a yearning to apply to social problems the principles of Christian morality which had always characterized its creed but too rarely its behavior. It felt a greater need for self-criticism and self-analysis. The principles of good government that the gentlemen reformers had called for in vain seemed to be closer to realization.

But these principles, too, had begun to change: the civil-service reformers had had a constricted idea of what good government would actually do, and one reason for their small following had been their inability to say very appealingly what good government was good for. Now, in increasing numbers, intelligent Americans began to think they knew. To control and humanize and moralize the great powers that had accumulated in the hands of industrialists and political bosses, it would be necessary to purify politics and build up the administrative state to the point at which it could subject the American economy to a measure of control. Of necessity, the functions of government would become more complex; and as they did so, experts would be in greater demand. In the interests of democracy itself, the old Jacksonian suspicion of experts must be abated. The tension between democracy and the educated man now seemed to be disappearing—because the type of man who had always valued expertise was now learning to value democracy and because democracy was learning to value experts.

The new social order also required exploration and explanation: there was an all but universal awareness that America was standing at the threshold of a new era. The imperative business of national self-criticism stirred ideas into life. Partly as expert, partly as social critic, the intellectual now came back to a central position such as he had not held in American politics for a century. But the recognition of intellect in national affairs was not accorded on the terms anticipated by the gentlemen reformers of the previous decades. In their eyes, the claims of mind had been founded largely on social class and gentility: they had lamented the disuse of intellect partly because they felt it was entitled to greater deference; but their notion of how it ought to be used was altogether conservative. Now, however, the claims of intellect were not based on the social position of the men who exemplified it, but on their usefulness in mobilizing and directing the restless, critical, reforming energies of the country. Intellect was reinstalled not because of its supposed conservative influence but because of its service to change. In this respect, the changes of the Progressive era in social criticism and administrative organization did not look back to the conservative civil service envisaged in the days of Hayes and Garfield but forward to the New Deal welfare state and Franklin D. Roosevelt's brain trust.

Doubtless, the Progressives were more effective in creating a new moral atmosphere than in realizing a new administrative regime. It was the moral and intellectual requirements of the period which put its intellectuals in unprecedented rapport not only with the American public but with the country's political leaders. Some men of intellect were drawn toward politics from the outside: but others emerged directly within the political order, and found there a more secure and honored place than their predecessors. Political life offered prominent roles to men who were interested in ideas and scholarship—men like Theodore Roosevelt, Woodrow Wilson, Henry Cabot Lodge, Albert J. Beveridge, Robert M. La Follette. Among the outstanding political leaders of the Progressive movement, Bryan alone kept alive the anti-intellectualist strain in popular democracy.[1] La Follette enjoys a special

[1] For a revealing contemporary encounter, see the interview with Bryan reported by John Reed in *Collier's*, Vol. LVII (May 20, 1916), pp. 11 ff.

place; though less a scholar or an intellectual than some of his contemporaries, he must be credited with the origins of the brain-trust
idea, both because of the effective union he achieved, as governor
of Wisconsin, between the University of Wisconsin and the state
government, and because of the efficient, research-minded staff he
brought with him to Washington during his senatorial days. From the
very beginning of his political career, La Follette gave the lie to
George Washington Plunkitt's assertion that a college background was
of no use in practical politics, when he rallied his former classmates
for his first campaigns and made them the nucleus of a well-knit
political machine. If Roosevelt had shown that intellect was compatible with virility, La Follette showed that intellect could be politically effective.

· 2 ·

Progressivism moved from local and state levels to national politics.
It was in the state governments that the new agencies of regulation
first went into operation and that a substantial place for experts in
legislation was first created. The trial ground for the role of experts
in political life was not Washington but the state capitals, particularly
Madison, Wisconsin, which offered the first example of experts in the
service of "the people" and the state. In its successes and failures,
in the very antagonisms it aroused, the La Follette experiment in
Wisconsin was a bellwether for national Progressive politics and a
historical prototype for the New Deal brain trust. The Wisconsin
experience is particularly instructive because it prefigured an entire
cycle in the role of experts and intellectuals in politics which has by
now become familiar: first, there was an era of change and discontent
which brought a demand for such men; next, the intellectuals and
experts became identified with the reforms they formulated and
helped to administer; then, an increasing distaste for reforms arose,
often in direct response to their effectiveness. This distaste was felt
above all by business interests, which arraigned governmental meddling, complained of the costs of reform, and attempted to arouse the
public against reformers with a variety of appeals, among them anti-
intellectualism. Finally, the reformers were ousted, but not all their
reforms were undone.

The first impetus toward what came to be known as "the Wisconsin
idea" occurred in 1892, when the new School of Economics, Political

Science, and History was set up at the University of Wisconsin, under the direction of the young economist, Richard T. Ely. Frederick Jackson Turner and President Thomas C. Chamberlain, the leaders of this movement, hoped to make Wisconsin a pioneer among Midwestern states in promoting social science, which they felt had immense potentialities for providing practical guidance to the complex industrial world that had come into being within the past quarter century. As they planned it, the university would become a center of training in administration and citizenship, and would evolve into an efficient practical servant of the state.

The role of the university, it must be emphasized, was to be wholly nonpartisan; it would be impartial between the political parties, and, in a larger sense, it was expected to serve "the people" as a whole, not a particular class interest. It would not offer propaganda or ideologies, but information, statistics, advice, skill, and training. By the same token, it was hoped that the prestige of the university would grow with its usefulness. University leaders did not anticipate any profound challenge to vested interests. In an early letter Turner asked that Ely "briefly indicate to me the practical ways in which such a school, in your opinion, can be made serviceable to the people of Wisconsin. . . . The very novelty of these practical aspects of the School is what will win us support from these hard headed Wisconsin capitalists—if anything will." [2] Turner later expressed this notion of impartial science more clearly:

> By training in science, in law, politics, economics, and history the universities may supply from the ranks of democracy administrators, legislators, judges and experts for commissioners *who shall disinterestedly and intelligently mediate between contending interests.* When the word "capitalistic classes" and "the proletariate" can be used and understood in America, it is surely time to develop such men, with the ideal of service to the State, who may *help to break the force of these collisions,* to find common grounds between the contestants and to possess the respect and confidence of all parties which are genuinely loyal to the best American ideals. The signs of such a development are already plain in the expert commissions of some States; in the increasing proportion of university men in legislatures; in the university men's influence in

[2] Merle Curti and Vernon Carstensen: *The University of Wisconsin* (Madison, 1949), Vol. I, p. 632. This work has a full-bodied account of the role of the university in the "Wisconsin idea."

federal departments and commissions. It is hardly too much to say
that the best hope of intelligent and principled progress in economic and social legislation and administration lies in the increasing influence of American universities.

Turner went on to say that he could see the danger to the universities
in all this. "Pioneer democracy" had always had scant respect for the
expert, and the expert would have to go on contending against the
"inherited suspicion" of his kind; but he could overcome it with "creative imagination and personality." [3]

By the end of the century, the university had gathered some distinguished scholars, who were concentrating on social and economic
problems, notably on those of the state and the municipality; it had
produced a number of excellent monographs. With its extension system
it was helping to educate the people of the state. Through its farmers'
institutes it had drawn close to the agricultural interests and had done
much to raise the technical level of agriculture in Wisconsin. Its
program became truly controversial, however, after the election of
Robert M. La Follette as governor in 1900. A graduate of the university, fully in sympathy with the aspirations of its idealistic leaders, La
Follette was quick to make use of its experts, who were called upon
for advice in his program of tax reform, railroad control, and direct
primary legislation.

The efforts of the university were soon supplemented by those of
another independent agency, the Legislative Reference Service, organized under another recent Wisconsin graduate student, the energetic Charles McCarthy. McCarthy's aspirations for the reference library were like those of Turner for the university: it was to be an
impartial service organization. In the age of the railroad, the telephone,
the telegraph, and the insurance company, the problems of the state,
he remarked, were growing so various and complex that vast amounts
of information were necessary for legislators to deal with them intelligently. "The only sensible thing to do is to have experts gather this
material." It was not a question of commitment to one side or another
of a legislative debate: [4]

As to our department in Wisconsin, we are not trying to influence our legislators in any way, we are not upon one side or an-

---

[3] F. J. Turner: "Pioneer Ideals and the State University," a commencement
address delivered at the University of Indiana in 1910 and reprinted in *The
Frontier in American History* (New York, 1920), pp. 285–6; italics are mine.
[4] Charles McCarthy: *The Wisconsin Idea* (New York, 1912), pp. 228–9.

other of any question nor are we for or against anybody or any-thing; we are merely a business branch of the government. We are not dictating legislation but are merely servants of the able and honest legislators of our state, clerks to gather and index and put together the information that these busy men desire; it is a busi-ness proposition.

This ideal may now seem as naïve as it was sincere. La Follette's governorship was on "one side or another" of quite a few questions; it challenged the interests of the "hard headed Wisconsin capitalists" whose support Turner had hoped to win. Moreover, after 1903, when the president of the university was La Follette's friend, Charles P. Van Hise, who believed in making the university an integral arm of the state, the irritation of conservatives mounted. Matters were not eased by the publicity the "Wisconsin idea" got from journalists throughout the country (most of them sympathetic) who came to examine Wis-consin as a model Progressive state in action and went away to write in exaggerated terms about "the university that governs a state." [5]

The publicity inspired by the journalists may have caused progres-sives in other states to consider a closer imitation of the Wisconsin model, but within the state it contributed to the conviction of the conservatives that the university was part of a conspiracy against them. Actually, the university experts did not think of themselves as radicals, and did not even consider that they had brought a great deal of initia-tive into government. An examination of university personnel most active in state service shows that it was mainly technicians (engineers, geologists, scientists, and various kinds of agricultural experts) rather than policy advisers who served the state, and that the university of-fered far more technical information than ideology. John R. Commons, one of the most outstanding of the Wisconsin social scientists, con-sidered the university faculty itself overwhelmingly conservative, and recalled: "I was never called in except by Progressives, and only when they wanted me. I never initiated anything." [6]

Nevertheless, university men were consulted on taxation and rail-road regulation, and on other matters, and their influence was resented.

[5] On political tension in the Van Hise era, see Curti and Carstensen: op. cit., Vol. II, especially pp. 4, 10–11, 19–21, 26, 40–1, 87–90, 97, 100–7, 550–2, 587–92.

[6] John R. Commons: *Myself* (New York, 1934), p. 110. Cf. McCarthy: "As a general rule the professors wait until asked before venturing to give an opinion upon a public question." Op. cit., p. 137; for a list of university personnel in the service of the state, see pp. 313–17.

La Follette was proud that for the old-fashioned secret back-room conferences of bosses which prevailed in the days when Wisconsin was run in the interests of private corporations, he had substituted a Saturday lunch club at which he sat down with McCarthy and President Van Hise, with Commons, Edward A. Ross, Ely, and other university professors to discuss the problems of the state.[7] Business interests which suffered from the Progressive policies—and indeed many which suffered from nothing more than fear of further extension of regulation —became convinced that the university and the Legislative Reference Service must be counted among their enemies, along with the Railroad Commission, the Tax Commission, and the Industrial Commission.

In 1914, when the Wisconsin Progressive Republicans were hurt by the nation-wide split in the party, the conservatives saw their opportunity. They defeated La Follette's Progressive successor, and returned to power with Emanuel L. Philipp, a railroad and lumber man. In his campaign Philipp featured anti-intellectualist denunciations of university experts, and called for a reduction in taxes, retrenchment in the university, and an end to its political "meddling." There must be, he said, a thorough house-cleaning at the university; socialism was gaining ground there, and "many graduates are leaving with ideas that are un-American." The employment of experts, he said, would lead to the continuing encroachment of the university upon politics. To turn government over to experts was, in any case, a confession that the duly elected officials were incompetent. If the state reached the point of conceding that all political wisdom was locked up in the university, the rest of the people might as well confess "mental bankruptcy." Philipp's attack included a demand for the abolition of McCarthy's "bill factory," the Legislative Reference Library.

Once elected, Philipp proved more benign toward these institutions than his campaign had promised. Although he did ask the legislature for the abolition of McCarthy's library and for university retrenchment and consolidation, he became increasingly circumspect as time passed. The growth of the university was checked and its influence trimmed, but Philipp, confronted with a formidable and highly respectable opposition among the friends of the university throughout the country, made peace with Van Hise. Even McCarthy escaped: the governor discovered that his claim to impartiality had some foundation, when

<hr>

[7] *Autobiography* (Madison, Wisconsin, 1913), p. 32; on his use of university personnel, see pp. 26, 30–1, 310–11, 348–50.

draftsmen of conservative bills began to use the Legislative Reference Service.[8]

The commitment of the university to Progressivism had never been completely accepted within the institution itself. As Commons remarked, many of its staff were thoroughly conservative. But more than this, many felt that the practical involvement of the university, regardless of its precise political shading, was itself a betrayal of the old-fashioned ideals of pure, disinterested intellectualism. J. F. A. Pyre, writing about the university in 1920, took issue with Van Hise's view that the university should be conceived as "an asset of the state." This, he said, was an excessively materialistic view of its function and downgraded the tradition of disinterested and autonomous learning, to the ultimate cost of the university.[9] But most of the experts at the university would doubtless have accepted the pragmatism expressed by McCarthy in his book, *The Wisconsin Idea*. The older thinkers, in fields like economics, he contended, had been "men of doctrinaire theories who had never studied the actual problems of government at first hand." They were being replaced by common-sense experts who looked at economic questions at first hand and could test their theories "by the hard facts of actual events."[1] Hence, while the lay community debated whether it should accept or reject experts, the scholarly community debated whether the serviceable expert or the man of pure learning held the true key to the future of the university.

· 3 ·

Progressive achievement in the arena of power may have been limited, but the Progressive atmosphere seemed indefinitely expansive; this was immensely heartening to those who were concerned with the place of mind in American society. The horizons of intellect grew wider, it was free and exuberant, and it seemed now to have been

[8] See Robert S. Maxwell: *Emanuel L. Philipp: Wisconsin Stalwart* (Madison, Wisconsin, 1959), chapters 7 and 8, especially pp. 74, 76–9, 82, 91, 92, 96–104. The *Nation* saw a disheartening lesson on American anti-intellectualism in the attack on the university. "Between Demos and the professor," it lamented, "there is a gulf of misunderstanding and ignorance unbridged since the days of Aristophanes." "Demos and the Professor," Vol. C (May 27, 1915), p. 596.

[9] J. F. A. Pyre: *Wisconsin* (New York, 1920), pp. 347–51, 364–5.

[1] *The Wisconsin Idea*, pp. 188–9; cf. p. 138. McCarthy's point of view can best be understood against the background of the development of pragmatism and the rebellion against the older generation of scholars described in Morton G. White's *Social Thought in America: The Revolt against Formalism* (New York, 1949).

put in touch with the higher reaches of power, as well as with the national mood. What Mabel Dodge Luhan said, thinking mainly of arts and letters, was true of every area of American life: "Barriers went down and people reached each other who had never been in touch before; there were all sorts of new ways to communicate, as well as new communications." [2] In this age of the "Little Renaissance" the keynote for arts and letters was liberation; for scholarship it was the enlarged possibilities for influence. Everywhere there was the intoxicant of new interests and new freedom. There was nothing that could not be re-examined, from railway franchises and the misdeeds of the trusts to sexual life and the conduct of education. Muckrakers were in demand to tell the public just how wicked things were, publicists to interpret the meaning of events, ministers and editors to point the moral, scholars to work out a theoretical rationale for Progressivism in philosophy, law, history, and political science, and technicians of all kinds to emerge from the academies and make detailed factual studies of social and economic problems, even to staff the new regulatory commissions.

This ferment of ideas, however, brought no social revolution; the old masters of America emerged, at the end of the period, almost as fully in control as they had been before it began. But in matters of tone and style there was a powerful uplift, and tone and style are of first importance not only to scholars and men of letters, but to politicians as well. No one benefited more than the intellectuals, whether they were publicists like Walter Lippmann and Herbert Croly or academic scholars like John Dewey and Charles A. Beard. All their work was animated by the heartening sense that the gulf between the world of theory and the world of practice had been finally bridged. Lippmann captured the essence of this feeling in his book, *Drift and Mastery,* published in 1914, in which he found that the new capacity for control, for mastery, was the key to the promise of his generation. The most abstracted of scholars could derive a sense of importance from belonging to a learned community which the larger world was compelled to consult in its quest for adequate means of social control. It was no longer possible to dismiss ideas by calling them "academic," for no one any longer saw a clear boundary between the academy and society. "A newer type of college professor is . . . everywhere in evidence," wrote an observer,[3]

---

[2] *Movers and Shakers* (New York, 1936), p. 39.
[3] B.P.: "College Professors and the Public," *Atlantic Monthly,* Vol. LXXXIX (February, 1902), pp. 284–5.

the expert who knows all about railroads and bridges and sub-
ways; about gas commissions and electrical supplies; about currency and banking, Philippine tariffs, Venezuelan boundary
lines, the industries of Porto Rico, the classification of the civil
service, the control of trusts.

Perhaps most important of all, the skills of such academic experts
were not only needed but applauded. A few commentators might
worry about the relationship between the expert and democracy,[4] and
an occasional businessman, frightened by the costs of regulation, might
fulminate against the rising influence of theorists,[5] but on the whole the
new experts had a good press and were widely accepted by the public.
Brander Matthews thought in 1909 that it was "an evidence of the common sense of the American people that the prejudice against the College Professors, like that against the men of letters, is rapidly dying
down, and that there is beginning to be public recognition and public
appreciation of the service they are rendering to the Commonwealth.
. . . It is partly due to a growing understanding of the real value of
the expert and the theorist." [6]

There was a significant acceptance, moreover, among political leaders themselves. It was characteristic of the age that a journalist like
Isaac Marcosson should bring Theodore Roosevelt the proofs of a book
by a muckraking novelist like Upton Sinclair, and that his doing so
would speed the passage of a pure food bill. Quite aside from the presence in the Senate of men like Beveridge and Lodge who prided themselves on their "scholarship," this was the first time since the nation's
beginnings that presidents of the United States could be described as
intellectuals.

[4] See Joseph Lee: "Democracy and the Expert," *Atlantic Monthly,* Vol. CII
(November, 1908), pp. 611–20.

[5] For example, the Chicago packer, Thomas E. Wilson, who pleaded before a
Congressional committee in 1906: "What we are opposed to, and what we appeal to
you for protection against is a bill that will put our business in the hands of
theorists, chemists, sociologists, etc., and the management and control taken away
from the men who have devoted their lives to the upbuilding and perfecting of this
great American industry." Lest it be imagined that Wilson was fighting against a
proposal to nationalize the packing industry, it should be explained that he was ap-
pearing against a pure food and drug measure. House Committee on Agriculture,
59th Congress, 1st session, *Hearings on the So-Called "Beveridge Amendment,"*
(Washington, 1906), p. 5. On the actual role of experts in the fight for food and
drug control, see Oscar E. Anderson, Jr.'s biography of Harvey W. Wiley: *The
Health of a Nation* (Chicago, 1958).

[6] "Literary Men and Public Affairs," *North American Review,* Vol. CLXXXIX
(April, 1909), p. 536.

A closer look at both T.R. and Wilson will show that each in his own way provided a kind of living commentary on the limits of the relationship between intellect and power. Their presidencies encouraged the belief that ideas had a vital part in government; but at the same time, neither was entirely in sympathy with his intellectual contemporaries, and neither enjoyed their full confidence. T.R., it must be said, took a lively and wide-ranging interest in ideas, enjoyed the company of men like Croly, Lippmann, and Steffens, found a government job for Edwin Arlington Robinson, attracted into public service a vigorous and dedicated type of man not much seen in government for well over a generation—one thinks of Robert Bacon, Charles Bonaparte, Felix Frankfurter, James Garfield, Franklin K. Lane, and Gifford Pinchot— and called upon academic experts for advice on railroad control, immigration, meat inspection, and other issues. In this he did more to restore mind and talents to public affairs than any president since Lincoln, probably more indeed than any since Jefferson. Lord Bryce, commenting on Roosevelt's achievement, thought that he had "never in any country seen a more eager, high-minded and efficient set of public servants, men more useful and creditable to their country, than the men doing the work of the American Government in Washington and in the field." [7] It sounds exactly like the kind of regime the gentleman reformers of the Gilded Age had called for.

Yet Roosevelt was rather quick to turn on his intellectual friends for what might have been considered marginal differences of opinion, and to dress himself as a stuffed-shirt Americanist when confronted with heterodox ideas. He misgauged the significance of many a mild protest —he imagined, for example, that the muckrakers were a dangerous lot who were building up "revolutionary feeling." Although no twentieth-century president has a greater claim to be considered an intellectual, his feeling about the place of intellect in life was as ambivalent as that of the educated strata of the middle class which looked up to him. He admired intellectual ability, just as he admired business ability, and, if anything, his admiration for intellect was firmer.[8] But what he called

---

[7] Quoted by Paul P. Van Riper: *History of United States Civil Service*, p. 206; cf. pp. 189–207, and John Blum: "The Presidential Leadership of Theodore Roosevelt," *Michigan Alumnus Quarterly Review*, Vol. LXV (December, 1958), pp. 1–9.

[8] Cf. a famous letter of 1908: "I am simply unable to make myself take the attitude of respect toward the very wealthy men which such an enormous multitude of people evidently really feel. I am delighted to show any courtesy to Pierpont Morgan or Andrew Carnegie or James J. Hill; but as for regarding any one of them as, for instance, I regard Professor Bury, or Peary, the Arctic explorer, or Admiral

"character" he unceasingly placed above both. Indeed, he embodied the American preference for character over intellect in politics and life, and the all but universal tendency to assume that the two somehow stand in opposition to each other. His writings continually return to this contrast: "Character is far more important than intellect to the race as to the individual." "Exactly as strength comes before beauty, so character must stand above intellect, above genius." "Oh, how I wish I could warn all my countrymen . . . against that most degrading of processes, the deification of mere intellectual acuteness, wholly unaccompanied by moral responsibility. . . ." [9] What seems questionable about these repeated adjurations against intellect-without-character is not that they were wrong but that they were pointless unless he actually believed that there was a tendency in American life to exalt intellect at the expense of morals—a curious judgment in the high moral climate of the Progressive era.

Wilson has been said to have brought to the presidency the temper of the scholar, with its faults and virtues; and few students of the man believe that he had the personal qualities best suited to effective political leadership in the United States. The peculiar rigidity of his mind and his lack of bonhomie, however, seem to be more the result of his Presbyterianism than his scholarly vocation, and probably still more constituted distinctively personal qualities. As a scholar and a critical intellect, he was a creature of the past. His creative intellectual life had almost come to an end by the close of the 1880's, the decade in which he wrote his brilliant book on *Congressional Government* and his more compendious effort, *The State*. In his tastes, his ideas, and his reading he was a somewhat parochial Southern version of a Victorian gentleman, his mind pleasantly fixed in the era just before the United States became a complex modern society. He believed in small business, competitive economics, colonialism, Anglo-Saxon and white supremacy, and a suffrage restricted to men, long after such beliefs had become objects of mordant critical analysis. His first ideas had come from Bagehot and Burke, and he had just missed exposure to the remarkable *fin de siècle* sunburst of critical thought whose impact car-

Evans, or Rhodes the historian, or Selous, the big game hunter . . . why, I could not force myself to do it even if I wanted to, which I do not." Elting Morison, ed.: *The Letters of Theodore Roosevelt*, Vol. VI (Cambridge, 1952), p. 1002.

[9] *Works*, Memorial Ed., Vol. XIV, p. 128; *Outlook* (November 8, 1913), p. 527; *Works*, Vol. XVI, p. 484; cf. other statements to the same effect: *Outlook* (April 23, 1910), p. 880; Address, October 11, 1897, at the *Two Hundredth Anniversary of the Old Dutch Reformed Church of Sleepy Hollow* (New York, 1898); *Works*, Vol. XVII, p. 3; XII, p. 623.

ried over into the Progressive era. During the 1890's he was busy as a
kind of academic man of affairs, bridging the gap between the academic community and the lay world; and while many of his scholarly
contemporaries were ripping up the complacent assumptions of the
Gilded Age, Wilson was speaking to groups of laymen, dishing out the
kind of fare that bankers and industrialists like to have served by
university presidents. From the moment he took the presidency of
Princeton in 1902, he ceased trying to stay in touch with developments
in the world of ideas. In 1916 he candidly confessed: "I haven't read a
serious book through for fourteen years." [1] Understandably, then, his
style of thought during his active public career was not much affected
by the most creative side of American intellectual life, and his mind
was hardly the object of unstinted admiration by contemporary intellectuals.

It is true that when Wilson was elected in 1912 he was supported by
many intellectuals who were by then disillusioned by T.R. and who
responded to the unmistakable note of nobility in Wilson. But Wilson
was not disposed, before the war, to make the extensive use of intellectual advisers in politics that his academic background seemed to
promise. Moreover, he had a persistent distrust of what he called
"experts." Unlike T.R. and La Follette, he did not conceive of experts
as likely agents or administrators of reform, but rather as hirelings
available only to big business and special interests. Whereas most
Progressive thinkers contrasted government by big business with a
popular government that would employ experts to regulate unacceptable business practices, Wilson thought of big business, vested interests, and experts as a solid combine that could be beaten only by
returning government to "the people." As against T.R., he contended
that any experts engaged to regulate big business would be controlled
by big business. "What I fear," he said during his 1912 campaign,[2]

> is a government of experts. God forbid that in a democratic coun-
> try we should resign the task and give the government over to ex-
> perts. What are we for if we are to be scientifically taken care of

[1] Arthur Link: *Wilson: The New Freedom* (Princeton, 1956), p. 63; cf. Link's
discussion of Wilson's mind, pp. 62–70.
[2] *A Crossroads of Freedom: The 1912 Campaign Speeches of Woodrow Wilson*,
ed. by John W. Davidson (New Haven, 1956) pp. 83–4. Wilson's ideas about
experts seem to have been influenced to some extent by the part played by experts
in the tariff controversy and also by the fight over pure food practices in T.R.'s
administration. Ibid., pp. 113, 160–1; see also the comments on experts in *The
New Democracy: Presidential Messages, Addresses, and Other Papers*, ed. by
R. S. Baker and W. E. Dodd, Vol. I (New York, 1926), pp. 10, 16.

by a small number of gentlemen who are the only men who understand the job? Because if we don't understand the job, then we
are not a free people. We ought to resign our free institutions and
go to school to somebody and find out what it is we are about. I
want to say I have never heard more penetrating debate of public
questions than I have sometimes been privileged to hear in clubs
of workingmen; because the man who is down against the daily
problem of life doesn't talk about it in rhetoric; he talks about it in
facts. And the only thing I am interested in is facts.

The picture of Wilson frequenting workingmen's clubs and disdain-
ing rhetoric is refreshingly novel. But on the whole Wilson lived up to
the promise of these remarks when he formulated his domestic policies.
Inevitably, the role of experts in government grew considerably during his administration,[3] as it had for more than a decade. And the
president did, of course, solicit a great deal of advice on economic
policy from Louis D. Brandeis, whose ideas about business competition coincided with his own predilections. But Wilson bowed to the
animus of Back Bay and the business community in keeping Brandeis
out of his Cabinet, and in the main he sought advice from different
types—from men like his worshipful secretary, Joe Tumulty, who had a
good grasp of machine politics and press relations; or his son-in-law,
William Gibbs McAdoo, an amply progressive but not highly reflective
mind; and above all, from the subtle and intelligent Colonel House, not

[3] This was notably true of the Department of Agriculture under the Secretary-
ship of David F. Houston, the former chancellor of Washington University and
president of the University of Texas whom Wilson had appointed upon House's
suggestion. During Houston's tenure, the problems of marketing and distribution
received much greater attention than before and the Department of Agriculture
became a magnet for able agricultural economists.
   There is suggestive information on the growth of expertise in government during
the Progressive era in Leonard D. White: "Public Administration," *Recent Social
Trends in the United States* (New York, 1934), Vol. II, pp. 1414 ff.
   It should be added that Wilson adhered to the venerable tradition of making
diplomatic appointments from the ranks of scholars and men of letters. He offered
two appointments, both declined, to President Charles William Eliot of Harvard;
sent Professor Paul Reinsch, an expert on international affairs, to China, Walter
Hines Page (an unfortunate choice) to Great Britain, Thomas Nelson Page (a
politically opportune appointment) to Italy, the ineffable Henry Van Dyke of
Princeton to the Netherlands, and Brand Whitlock to Belgium. The level of
Wilson's ambassadorial appointments was generally considered satisfactory, but
they were offset by Bryan's raid upon the competent professional diplomatic corps
which had been built up by John Hay, Roosevelt, and Taft. Bryan's raid on
ministerial appointments in the interest of "deserving Democrats," to which
Wilson consented, has been described by Arthur Link as "the greatest debauchery
of the Foreign Service in the twentieth century." *Wilson: The New Freedom*,
p. 106.

the least of whose talents was the capacity to feed Wilson's vanity. House, who served among other things as a channel for the views of the wealthy and powerful, was a strong counterpoise to Progressive figures in the Wilson circle such as Brandeis, Bryan, and McAdoo.

Wilson's administration was not overwhelmingly popular among intellectuals in its first few years—especially among those who thought that the Progressive movement should go beyond the effort to realize the old competitive ideals of small businessmen and do something about child labor, the position of Negroes, the condition of working-men, and the demand for women's suffrage.[4] Intellectuals interested in reform were too skeptical about Wilson to welcome unreservedly even the music of his sonorous speeches, which seemed to them to have overtones of a moralistic but unprogressive past, and their skepticism seemed justified by the halting manner in which reforms were pursued. Herbert Croly, who observed that Wilson's mind "is fully convinced of the everlasting righteousness of its own performances and surrounds this conviction with a halo of shimmering rhetoric," complained also that the President's thinking made "even the most concrete things seem like abstractions. . . . His mind is like a light which destroys the outlines of what it plays upon; there is much illumination, but you see very little." [5]

Only by 1916, in response to the recent achievements of the New Freedom and Wilson's success in keeping out of war, did liberal intel-lectuals swing wholeheartedly to his support. The war itself, ironically, raised many of them to heights of influence as no domestic issue could. Historians and writers were mobilized for propaganda, and experts of all kinds were recruited as advisers. Military Intelligence, Chemical Warfare, the War Industries Board swarmed with academics, and Washington's Cosmos Club was reported to be "little better than a fac-ulty meeting of all the universities." [6] In September 1919 Colonel House

[4] Link: *Wilson: The New Freedom*, chapter 8. A classic statement of this view was made by Walter Lippmann in *Drift and Mastery*, especially chapter 7.

[5] "Presidential Complacency," *New Republic*, Vol. I (November 21, 1914), p. 7; "The Other-Worldliness of Wilson," *New Republic*, Vol. II (March 27, 1915), p. 195. Charles Forcey's *The Crossroads of Liberalism, Croly, Weyl, Lippmann and the Progressive Era, 1900–1925* (New York, 1961) is instructive about the relations of the *New Republic* group with Roosevelt and Wilson. On the impasse the New Freedom seemed to have reached by 1914 and the discouragement of liberal intellectuals, see Arthur Link: *Woodrow Wilson*, and his *The Progressive Era, 1910–1917* (New York, 1954), especially pp. 66–80.

[6] Gordon Hall Gerould: "The Professor and the Wide, Wide World," *Scribner's*, Vol. LXV (April, 1919), p. 466. Gerould thought it would no longer be possible to condescend to the professors after this experience. "The professor," wrote another, ". . . was reputed to be learned, and much to everyone's surprise

organized for Wilson the group of scholars known as The Inquiry
(which already had its counterparts in Great Britain and France). At
one time the expert personnel of The Inquiry numbered 150 persons
—historians, geographers, statisticians, ethnologists, economists, political scientists—and these, with their assistants and staffs, brought the
number of the whole organization to several hundred. Kept secret until
the Armistice, The Inquiry was then revamped as the Intelligence
Division of the American Commission to Negotiate Peace, and its staff
accompanied Wilson to Paris, where it played a part of no small importance. There was a certain amount of amused comment about this
group in the press, and a certain skepticism among old-school diplomats
about this tribe of political amateurs, with their three army truckloads
of documents.[7] On the whole, however, considering the passions
aroused by the war, the peace negotiations, and the debate over the
treaty and the League Covenant, what is most remarkable is the general
public acceptance of scholars in their advisory role. A politician like
Senator Lawrence Sherman of Illinois who launched a long and ferocious diatribe against the expansion of governmental powers during the
war, and particularly against "a government by professors and intellectuals," stood out as an exception for his rancorous anti-intellectualism.[8]

he has turned out to be *intelligent*." "The Demobilized Professor," *Atlantic
Monthly*, Vol. CXXIII (April, 1919), p. 539. Paul Van Dyke thought that the
college man had succeeded, during the war, in showing that he was virile and
practical, not soft or incompetent. "The College Man in Action," *Scribner's*, Vol.
LXV (May, 1919), pp. 560–3. It is instructive to compare the argument of this
piece with the earlier utterances of Theodore Roosevelt.
    [7] On The Inquiry and its personnel, see the article by its head, Sidney E.
Mezes, in E. M. House and Charles Seymour, eds.: *What Really Happened at
Paris* (New York, 1921); *Papers Relating to the Foreign Relations of the United
States*, 1919, Vol. I, *The Paris Peace Conference* (Washington, 1942); J. T. Shot-
well: *At the Paris Peace Conference*, pp. 15–16. On wartime mobilization of
science, see A. Hunter Dupree: *Science in the Federal Government*, chapter 16.
    [8] This remarkable speech is replete with the clichés of anti-intellectualism, and
though it can hardly be imagined to have had much influence at the time, it must
be taken as a landmark in anti-intellectualist oratory: ". . . a coterie of politicians
gilded and plated by a group of theorizing, intolerant intellectuals as wildly impractical as ever beat high heaven with their phrase-making jargon. . . . They
appeal to the iconoclast, the freak, the degenerate . . . essayists of incalculable
horsepower who have essayed everything under the sun . . . a fair sprinkle of
socialists. . . . Everything will be discovered. . . . Psychologists with X-ray
vision drop different colored handkerchiefs on a table, spill a half pint of navy
beans, ask you in a sepulchral tone what disease Walter Raleigh died of, and demand the number of legumes without counting. Your memory, perceptive faculties,
concentration, and other mental giblets are tagged and you are pigeonholed for
future reference. I have seen those psychologists in my time and have dealt with
them. If they were put out in a forest or in a potato patch, they have not sense
enough to kill a rabbit or dig a potato to save themselves from the pangs of
starvation. This is a government by professors and intellectuals. I repeat, intellec-

But he was prophetic of the future, for the reaction against the war liquidated the Progressive spirit.

The public mood changed with stunning abruptness. William Allen White, who in 1919 was still telling the chairman of the Republican National Committee that the party's "incrusted old reactionaries" were done for, was lamenting a year later that "the Pharisees are running the temple" and that the people were not even troubling to object. "What a God-damned world this is!" he wrote to Ray Stannard Baker in 1920. "If anyone had told me ten years ago that our country would be what it is today . . . I should have questioned his reason." [9] The consequences were fatal for the position of the intellectuals: having tied themselves to Wilson and the conduct of the war, they had made it certain that they would suffer from the public reaction against him and everything connected with him. But, more decisively, they had broken their own morale by the uncritical enthusiasm with which most of them had entered into the war spirit. With the exception of some socialists and a few thinkers like Randolph Bourne and the group behind the *Seven Arts* magazine, the intellectuals were either engaged in the war or supported it wholeheartedly, and they entertained the same fervid expectations of triumph and reform as a result of it that many of them had had with respect to the Progressive movement. The peace left them disappointed, ashamed, guilty. "If I had it to do all over again," said Walter Lippmann, "I would take the other side. . . . We supplied the Battalion of Death with too much ammunition." And Herbert Croly confessed that he had had no idea "what the psychology of the American people would be under the strain of fighting a world war." [1] The *rapprochement* between the intellectuals and the people dissolved even more quickly than it had been made. The public turned on the intellectuals as the prophets of false and needless reforms, as architects of the administrative state, as supporters of the war, even as ur-Bolsheviks; the intellectuals turned on America as a nation of boobs, Babbitts, and fanatics. Those who were young and free enough expatriated themselves; the others stayed home and read Mencken. It would take a depression and another era of reform to overcome this estrangement.

---

tuals are good enough in their places, but a country run by professors is ultimately destined to Bolshevism and an explosion." *Congressional Record,* 65th Congress, 2nd session, pp. 9875, 9877 (September 3, 1918).

[9] Walter Johnson, ed.: *Selected Letters of William Allen White* (New York, 1947), pp. 199–200, 208, 213.

[1] Forcey: op. cit., pp. 292, 301.

· 4 ·

During the New Deal the *rapprochement* between intellectuals and
the public was restored. Never had there been such complete harmony
between the popular cause in politics and the dominant mood of the
intellectuals. In the Progressive era, the intellectuals and the public
had, by and large, espoused the same causes. In the New Deal era, the
causes were still more engaging, and the need for intellectuals to play a
practical role was greater than anyone could have anticipated in the
days of Wilson and T.R. But the minority that opposed the New Deal
did so with a feverish hostility rarely seen in American politics. While
the intellectuals were riding high, a rancorous feeling was forming
against them that burst out spectacularly after World War II.

In the long run, the intellectuals were to suffer from this intransigent
minority almost as much as they profited in the short run from the patronage of the New Deal. But, in its first flush, what patronage it was!
Like everyone else, intellectuals had suffered from the depression,
sharing in its unemployment and in its shock to morale. The New
Deal gave thousands of jobs to young lawyers and economists, who
flocked to Washington to staff its newly created agencies of regulation;
the research, artistic, and theater projects of the WPA and NYA helped
unemployed artists, intellectuals, and college students. Even more important than this practical aid was a pervasive intangible: by making
use of theorists and professors as advisers and ideologists, the New
Deal brought the force of mind into closer relation with power than
it had been within the memory of any living man—closer than it had
been since the days of the Founding Fathers. To offer important work
to young men emerging from colleges and law schools was in itself an
arresting novelty. But to give to academic advisers such importance as
the New Deal gave was to aggrandize the role of every professor and
of every speculative or dissenting mind. Ideas, theories, criticisms took
on a new value, and the place to go for them was to men who were
intellectually trained.[2] The economic collapse had demonstrated that
such men were needed, but it was the New Deal that showed how
they could make themselves felt. Not surprisingly, the New Deal
aroused the enthusiasm of all but a small number of conservative intellectuals on one side and a small number of radicals at the other.

[2] As Paul P. Van Riper points out, this led to a certain privilege in influencing
new policies, which he describes as "ideological patronage." Op. cit., pp. 324–8.

(Even the Communists, who opposed the New Deal violently from 1933 to 1935, were able, as we now know, both to infiltrate its ranks and to exploit the public mood in which it flourished.)

The primary manifestation of the changed position of intellectuals was the creation of the brain trust, which was almost constantly in the news during the first few years of the New Deal. Conspicuous brain trusters like Raymond Moley, Rexford Guy Tugwell, and Adolph A. Berle, who were most often under attack, were symbols of the hundreds of obscurer men who staffed federal agencies, notably the protégés of Felix Frankfurter who came to Washington from Harvard. In the earliest days of the New Deal President Roosevelt himself enjoyed such prestige that it was psychologically more natural and strategically easier for his opponents to strike at him through those around him by suggesting that he was accepting ideas from sinister or irresponsible advisers. Among other things, the brain trust became useful to the President as a kind of lightning rod. Much invective that might otherwise have fallen directly upon him as the central figure of the New Deal fell instead upon those around him—and they could be shifted, if the going got rough, into more obscure positions.

After the early eclipse of Raymond Moley, Professor Rexford Guy Tugwell became the favorite target for conservative critics of the New Deal. It was Tugwell's misfortune to believe in some forms of planning and to have written several books expounding his ideas. His nomination as Undersecretary of Agriculture in June, 1934 brought a wave of protest against the exaltation of so sinister a theorist. "Cotton Ed" Smith of South Carolina, one of the most implacable mastodons of the Senate, was so insistent in establishing the point that Tugwell was "not a graduate of God's Great University" that the Columbia economist had to go to great lengths to prove himself a true dirt farmer who as a boy had had plenty of mud on his boots. ("Tell Rex," said F.D.R. to Henry A. Wallace, "that I was surprised to hear that he was so dirty.") The diploma needed for agriculture, Smith told the Senate, "is obtained by bitter experience, and no man can solve the problems of agriculture in America but the man who has trodden the wine press of experience in the field." (He was unable to name a single past Secretary of Agriculture who met this requirement.) Roosevelt could appease Smith only by appointing as United States Marshal one of Smith's favored constituents, who had a record of homicide and whom the President described to the Cabinet as Smith's "favorite murderer." On the strength of this trade—one professor for one murderer—Tugwell finally won Senate confirmation by a vote of fifty-three to twenty-four.

The bad press Tugwell got became worse when his ardent sponsorship of pure food and drug legislation caused such influential advertisers as the proprietary drug houses to mobilize the press against him. Even James A. Farley, neither a radical nor an intellectual, winced at publicity so "raw and uncalled for." The picture of Tugwell painted by his most ardent critics was two-faced: on one side he was a totally feckless, academic, impractical theorist (half an inferior pedagogue, Mencken said, and half a "kept idealist of the *New Republic*"); on the other he was an effective, insidious, subversive force, quite capable of wreaking major damage on the fabric of society. Tugwell's patience under fire suggests that the academic man recruited into politics need not necessarily be thin-skinned.[3]

If the brain trust was to serve the opposition as a suitable whipping boy, it was necessary that its significance as a center of power be greatly exaggerated. "The 'brain trust,'" said a writer in the Chicago *Tribune*, "completely overshadows the Cabinet. It is reputed to have more influence with the President. . . . It has taken the professors from various colleges to put the Cabinet members in their places at last—merely department heads, chief clerks. On a routine administrative matter you go to a Cabinet member, but on matters of policy and the higher statesmanship you consult the professoriat."[4] It is true that at the very beginning of the New Deal—during its first hundred days —a panicky Congress quickly and complaisantly passed a great mass of legislation that it did not have the time or the will to scrutinize with the customary care. This left an unusual amount of discretion in legal draftsmanship and even in policy-making to the inner planning circles of the New Deal, in which expert advisers, though never controlling,

[3] Tugwell's reputation and his role in the New Deal are amply accounted for by Bernard Sternsher's unpublished doctoral dissertation: *Rexford Guy Tugwell and the New Deal*, Boston University, 1957. The debate over his appointment is instructive: *Congressional Record*, 73rd Congress, 2nd session, pp. 11156–60, 11334–42, 11427–62 (June 12, 13, 14, 1934). See also Arthur Schlesinger, Jr.: *The Coming of the New Deal* (Boston, 1958), chapter 21; James A. Farley: *Behind the Ballots* (New York, 1938), pp. 219–20; H. L. Mencken: "Three Years of Dr. Roosevelt," *American Mercury* (March, 1936), p. 264. For further insight into the position of New Deal experts, see Richard S. Kirkendall's unpublished doctoral dissertation: *The New Deal Professors and the Politics of Agriculture*, University of Wisconsin, 1958.

[4] *Literary Digest*, Vol. CXV (June 3, 1933), p. 8. In fact, the brain trust, as an identifiable organization, was called into being for the 1932 campaign and ceased to exist when it was over. In speaking of it more loosely, I have followed the usage of contemporaries.

were decidedly influential. However, the structure of power in the United States makes it impossible for many vital decisions to be made for very long by a small portion of the professoriat without roots in any basic class interest or political constituency. As the mood of panic passed, the normal processes of Congressional scrutiny returned and limited the influence of the technical advisers. For the most part, the steps taken under the New Deal which pleased the intellectuals and the experimenters were taken not because the experts favored them but because some large constituency wanted them. The brain trusters served the public—often very well—but they did not govern it. With few exceptions, the more idealistic and experimental schemes of the liberal brain trusters were circumvented, circumscribed, or sabotaged. It is true that the New Deal tried some unsuccessful inflationary monetary experiments advocated by a few academic theorists. But these were backed by immensely powerful inflationist pressures in the Senate, and they were not dear to the hearts of most of Roosevelt's expert advisers. On vital issues, the liberal experts almost invariably lost. The liberal theorists, led by Jerome Frank, who tried to represent the interests of the consumers in the NRA and of sharecroppers in the AAA were soon driven out. Rexford Tugwell's imaginative ideas for rural resettlement were crippled beyond recognition, and Tugwell himself was eventually consigned to the outer regions. Raymond Moley, who fell into conflict with Secretary of State Cordell Hull over the London Economic Conference, lost out to the Cabinet member.[5]

None the less, the notion became widely current that the professors were running things, and a veritable brain-trust war began which reawakened and quickened the old traditions of anti-intellectualism. The professors were not running things—and yet there was some kernel of truth in the popular notion that they were: they did represent something new in the constellation of power in the United States. They did not wield a great deal of power themselves, in the sense that it did not rest with them to make the central decisions. But upon those who did wield power they exercised a pervasive and vital influence, for it had now become a prerogative of experts to set the very terms in which the issues were perceived, to define the contours of economic and social issues. The right wingers who denounced professors and brain trusters, however cranky their conceptions of the world of power, thus had a

[5] For detailed information on the manner in which the proposals of professors were blunted in one area by business power, see the work by Kirkendall already cited.

sound instinct. And if they did not have the ear of the majority of the public, they did at least have on their side some of the old weapons of popular prejudice, which they soon began to brandish. Moreover, the celebrity the professors enjoyed for a time enabled them to overshadow old-line politicians and businessmen, who found it particularly galling that a class of men hitherto so obscure and so little regarded should eclipse them in the public eye and make their role in society seem so much less significant. With his usual bald exaggeration, H. L. Mencken saw the irony of the transformation: "A few years ago all the New Deal Isaiahs were obscure and impotent fellows who flushed with pride when they got a nod from the cop at the corner; today they have the secular rank of princes of the blood, and the ghostly faculties of cardinal archbishops." The brain trusters, he continued, were so successful that they had begun to believe in their own panaceas. "What would *you* do," he asked,[6]

> if you were hauled suddenly out of a bare, smelly school-room, wherein the razzberries of sophomores had been your only music, and thrown into a place of power and glory almost befitting Caligula, Napoleon I, or J. Pierpont Morgan, with whole herds of Washington correspondents crowding up to take down your every wheeze, and the first pages of their newspapers thrown open to your complete metaphysic?

The critics of the New Deal exaggerated the power of the intellectuals and also portrayed them as impractical, irresponsible, conspiratorial experimentalists, grown arrogant and publicity-conscious because of their sudden rise from obscurity to prominence. Choosing comment almost at random from the *Saturday Evening Post*, an unimpeachable source of anti-intellectualism, one finds them characterized thus: [7]

> A bunch of professors hauled from their classrooms and thrust into the maelstrom of the New Deal. Very self-conscious; arrogant seekers after publicity for themselves now they have a chance to

[6] H. L. Mencken: "The New Deal Mentality," *American Mercury*, Vol. XXXVIII (May, 1936), p. 4.

[7] Samuel G. Blythe: "Kaleidoscope," *Saturday Evening Post*, Vol. CCVI (September 2, 1933), p. 7; Blythe: "Progress on the Potomac," *Saturday Evening Post*, December 2, 1933, p. 10; editorials, *Saturday Evening Post*, December 9, 1933, p. 22, and April 7, 1934, pp. 24–5; William V. Hodges: "Realities Are Coming," *Saturday Evening Post*, April 21, 1934, p. 5. See also Margaret Culkin Banning: "Amateur Year," *Saturday Evening Post*, April 28, 1934; Katherine Dayton: "Capitol Punishments," *Saturday Evening Post*, December 23, 1933.

get it; eager self-expressionists basking like cats before a fireplace in their new distinctions. . . . The men who rush about and ask excitedly: "What's the dollar going to do?" As if it makes the slightest difference to them what the dollar does—not one of them can muster a hundred dollars of any sort. . . . Out came the professorial law, modified of course, here and there by non-professorial meddlers in the halls of Congress, but with plenty of professorial ideas in them at that. . . . No thoughtful man can escape the conclusion that many of the brain trust ideas and plans are based on Russian ideology. . . . Somebody should tell these bright young intellectuals and professors the facts of business life. The stork does not bring profits and prosperity, and sound currency does not grow under cabbages. . . . In the end it must be the farmer and the industrialist, assisted by nature and wisely backed by Government, who cure their own ills. . . .

Are we so silly, so supine as to permit amateur, self-confessed experimentalists to take our social and business fabric apart to see if they cannot reconstruct it in a pattern that is more to their liking? . . . laboratory experiments on the life, liberty and industry of America. . . . There is a vast difference between an experiment made in a test tube and one made on a living nation. That smacks altogether too much of vivisection . . . men untainted with any practical experience . . . government by amateurs—college boys, irrespective of their age—who have drunk deep, perhaps of the Pierian spring, have recently taken some hearty swigs of Russian vodka . . . the theorist, the dreamer of political dreams, rainmakers and prestidigitators. . . . Realistic senators and representatives have no haven but the seclusion of the locker room. . . .

Defenders of the intellectuals tried to arrive at a more reasonable estimate of their actual power, and to point out that they could hardly do worse than the "practical" men they had displaced. Oswald Garrison Villard, writing in the *Nation*, welcomed the "complete rout of the practical men," and pointed out that all over the world "the practical men are utterly at a loss." [8] Jonathan Mitchell, then a liberal journalist and a former New Deal adviser, in one of the most thoughtful analyses of the subject, tried to show that Roosevelt's use of academic experts

[8] "Issues and Men, the Idealist Comes to the Front," *Nation*, Vol. CXXXVII (October 4, 1933), p. 371. Cf. the same view in the *New Republic*: "The Brain Trust" (June 7, 1933), pp. 85–6.

was a natural consequence of the crisis and of the peculiarities of American administrative life. The professors were not in fact setting major policies, he wrote, but simply advising about instrumentalities. In the absence of a class of civil servants trained for such a purpose, the President's sudden resort to men from outside political or administrative circles was almost inevitable.[9] On this count Mitchell was entirely right. Politicians could not handle the issues raised by the depression; civil servants of the right type did not exist to cope with them; and most business leaders seemed worse than useless. As Samuel I. Rosenman advised the President: "Usually in a situation like this a candidate gathers around him a group composed of some successful industrialists, some big financiers, and some national political leaders. I think we ought to steer clear of all those. They all seem to have failed to produce anything constructive to solve the mess we're in today. . . . Why not go to the universities of the country?"[1]

But Mitchell's analysis might well have been taken by foes of the New Deal as inflammatory:

What Mr. Roosevelt needed was a neutral, someone who didn't smell of Wall Street but who, on the other hand, wouldn't too greatly scare the wealthy. Moreover, he needed someone who would have the brains, competence, and willingness to carry through whatever policies he determined upon. Mr. Roosevelt chose college professors; there is no other group in the country which these specifications fit. . . .

We have in America no hereditary land-owning class from which to recruit our New Deal civil service. Our nearest equivalents are the college professors, and the neutral professor in Washington is the element which will decide the New Deal's success or failure. . . . There was once a time in this country when we did have a class set apart, to whom others submitted their disputes without question. That class was the colonial ministers, particularly of New England. They were generally unconcerned with worldly things; they regulated their communities with a sterner hand than Mr. Roosevelt's New Deal is ever likely to employ, and they gave judgment according to the light they had. . . . The New England ministers have long since departed, but the college professors are their collateral heirs. . . . In the future, we shall

[9] Jonathan Mitchell: "Don't Shoot the Professors! Why the Government Needs Them," *Harper's*, Vol. CLXVIII (May, 1934), pp. 743, 749.
[1] Samuel I. Rosenman: *Working with Roosevelt* (New York, 1952), p. 57.

succeed in building for ourselves a professional American civil service, supported by its own loyalties and tradition.

None of this could have been expected to appease or reassure the businessmen, displaced politicians, and other members of the conservative classes, who felt little need for a professional civil service, who understandably could not believe that the professors were "neutral," who thought that professors did indeed scare the wealthy, and who could only have been alarmed at the thought of having any class to which disputes would be submitted "without question." No answer, not even an answer couched more moderately than Mitchell's, could assuage their basic fear, which was not a fear of the brain trust or the expert, but of the collapse of the world in which they had put their faith. Among such enemies, the prerogatives offered by the New Deal to intellectuals and experts only served to confirm old traditions of anti-intellectualism, and to strengthen them with new suspicions and resentments.

The Second World War, like the first, increased the need for experts, not only the sort the New Deal employed but also men from previously untapped fields of scholarship—even classicists and archaeologists were suddenly thought important because of their knowledge of the Mediterranean area. But when the war ended, the long-delayed revulsion from the New Deal experience and the war itself swept over the country. For this reaction the battle against the brain trust had laid the groundwork. With it, the *rapprochement* between the intellectuals and the popular democracy once more came to an end.

· 5 ·

In 1952 Adlai Stevenson became the victim of the accumulated grievances against intellectuals and brain trusters which had festered in the American right wing since 1933. Unfortunately, his political fate was taken as a yardstick by which liberal intellectuals measured the position of intellect in American political life. It was a natural mistake to make: Stevenson had the dimensions and the appeal of a major tragic hero, and intellectuals identified his cause with their own. After the embarrassments of the Truman administration, it was refreshing to listen to his literate style. But more decisive were the overwhelming differences between Stevenson's manner and the Eisenhower–Nixon campaign. Strong as the contrast was between Stevenson's flair for the apt phrase (and his evident ability to work with campaign advisers who shared it) and the fumbling inarticulateness of Eisenhower's early political manner, it was heightened by Nixon, with his egregious "Checkers" speech, his sure touch for the philistine cliché, and his crass eulogies of his senior partner. Finally, there was the ugly image of McCarthy, whose contributions to the campaign were all too plainly welcomed by his party. One does not expect American presidential campaigns to set a high tone, but the tone of the Republican campaign of 1952, which by comparison seemed to endow even Truman's shameless baiting of Wall Street with a touch of old-fashioned dignity, was such as to throw into high relief every one of Stevenson's attractive qualities.

Intellectuals embraced Stevenson with a readiness and a unanimity that seems without parallel in American history. Theodore Roosevelt, after all, had had to earn such popularity as he enjoyed among the intellectuals of his day during a long public career; when he took the presidency there were many intellectuals who regarded him with a mixture of suspicion and amusement; his closest rapport with them was indeed achieved only after he left the White House; it was climaxed by the Bull Moose campaign of 1912 and then eclipsed by his wartime jingoism. Woodrow Wilson, for all his style and his academic origins, was treated by a substantial segment of the intellectual community with a cold reserve that matched his own manner; many intellectuals agreed with Walter Lippmann's contemporary diagnosis of the New Freedom as an ill-conceived, backward-looking movement designed mainly for small business interests; and finally, Wilson's reputation suffered badly from the reaction against the mob-mindedness of the war years from which the President himself had not been immune. Franklin D. Roosevelt, for all the publicity given his brain trust, disappointed most intellectuals during his first presidential campaign, and remained an object of distrust and sharp left-wing criticism during the early years of the New Deal. The intellectuals did not greatly warm to him until the very eve of the 1936 campaign, and even then seemed to love him mainly for the enemies he had made. With Stevenson it was different: men who had hardly heard of him as Governor of Illinois, and for whom he was a new star in the firmament at the time of his nomination in 1952, took him to their hearts at once upon hearing his acceptance speech. He seemed too good to be true.

At a time when the McCarthyist pack was in full cry, it was hard to resist the conclusion that Stevenson's smashing defeat was also a repudiation by plebiscite of American intellectuals and of intellect it-self. Those intellectuals who drew this conclusion were confirmed by their critics, among whom there was a great deal of solemn head-shaking: American intellectuals, it was said, did not feel for or under-stand their country; they had grown irresponsible and arrogant; their chastening was very much in order. That many intellectuals were hurt there can be no doubt; but the notion that Stevenson was repudiated by the public because of his reputation for wit and intellect will not bear analysis, and the implications of his defeat on this count have been vastly exaggerated. In 1952, he was hopelessly overmatched. It was a year in which any appealing Republican could have beaten any Demo-crat, and Eisenhower was more than appealing: he was a national hero of irresistible magnetism whose popularity overshadowed not only Stevenson but every other man on the political scene. After twenty years of Democratic rule, the time for a change in the parties was over-due, if the two-party system was to have any meaning. The Korean War and its discontents alone provided a sufficient issue for the Repub-licans; and they were able to capitalize on lesser issues like the Hiss case and other revelations of Communist infiltration into the federal government, and the discovery of trifling but titillating corruption in the Truman administration. Stevenson's hopeless position might more readily have been accepted as such if the Republican campaign, in which Nixon and McCarthy seemed more conspicuous than Eisen-hower, had not struck such a low note as to stir the will to believe that such men must be rejected by the public.

In retrospect, however, there seems no reason to believe that Steven-son's style and wit and integrity were anything but assets in his cam-paign, and that if he had not won a reputation for himself on these counts his defeat would have been still more complete. The notion that the greater part of the public was totally immune to the value of his qualities will not bear even a casual examination. If his personal qualities had been so unattractive as some admirers and detractors alike believed, it is hard to understand how he could have won the governorship of Illinois in 1948 by the largest plurality in the state's history, or why the Democratic convention should have drafted him four years later, in spite of his well-publicized reluctance to be nomi-nated, after the merest brief exposure to his eloquent welcoming speech. (It was the first draft since Hughes's in 1916, and perhaps the only draft of a thoroughly reluctant candidate in our political history.)

Even the dimensions of Stevenson's defeat were magnified by the dramatic contrast between his campaign and that of the Republicans. Twelve years earlier, Wendell Willkie, also running against the great political hero of the moment, received almost exactly the same per cent of the popular vote as Stevenson—44.4 to 44.3—and Willkie was considered a leader of exceptionally dynamic qualities. The truth seems to be that both candidates in 1952 were personally strong, and with political excitements running high, both drew the voters to the polls in large numbers. Stevenson in defeat had a larger popular vote than Truman in his victory of 1948 or Roosevelt in 1944 and 1940. And after the election his mail was full of letters from people who had voted for Eisenhower but who expressed their admiration for his campaign and their wish that circumstances had been different enough to justify their supporting him.

This is not to deny that something was missing from the "image"—in the now fashionable jargon—that Stevenson projected. He knew all too well the difficulty of taking over the leadership of the Democratic Party after its twenty years in power. But his reluctance to assume power—though in a certain light it may be taken as creditable—was all too real, and it aroused misgivings. "I accept your nomination—and your program," he said to the Democratic convention. "I should have preferred to hear these words uttered by a stronger, a wiser, a better man than myself." It was not the right note for the times; it made for uneasiness, and many found it less attractive than Eisenhower's bland confidence. Stevenson's humility seemed genuine, but he proffered it all too proudly. One could recognize his ability to analyze public questions with integrity and without deference to the conventional hokum, and yet remain in doubt as to whether he had that imaginative grasp of the uses and possibilities of power which, in recent times, the two Roosevelts had conveyed with the most effective force. (One cannot, however, refrain from commenting on the delusive character of the contrasting impressions given by Eisenhower and Stevenson: Eisenhower's regime had its merits, but the General, in power, failed to unite or elevate his party, whereas Stevenson out of power did a great deal to renew and invigorate his.)

We would be deluded, then, if we attributed Stevenson's defeat to his reputation for intellectuality, or even if we assumed that this reputation was a liability instead of an asset. But for a substantial segment of the public this quality was indeed a liability; and without any desire to exaggerate the size or influence of this group, we must examine it, for these people are of primary interest to any study of anti-intellectual imagery.

The quality in Stevenson that excited most frequent attack was not his intellect as such, but his wit.[2] In this country wit has never been popular in political leaders. The public enjoys and accepts humor— Lincoln, T.R., and F.D.R. used it to some effect—but humor is folkish, usually quite simple, and readily accessible. Wit is humor intellectualized; it is sharper; it has associations with style and sophistication, overtones of aristocracy. Repeatedly Stevenson was referred to as a "comedian" or a "clown" and portrayed in cartoons as a jester with fool's cap and bells. Against the somber, angry, frustrating background of the Korean War, his wit seemed to his detractors altogether out of place; Eisenhower's dull but solid sobriety of utterance seemed more in keeping with the hour. It did Stevenson's supporters little good to point out that he did not jest about the Korean War itself or about other matters of solemn moment to the voters. Far from overcoming other handicaps in his public image, his wit seemed to widen the distance between himself and a significant part of the electorate. ("His fluent command of the English language is far above the heads of the ordinary American.") One of the revealing comments of the campaign was made by a woman who wrote to the Detroit *News* that "we should have something in common with a candidate for President, and that's why I'm voting for General Eisenhower."

Stevenson had been a character witness for Alger Hiss and on this account was especially vulnerable to the common tandem association between intellect and radicalism, radicalism and disloyalty. His intellectual supporters were easily tarred with the same brush, and the fact that so many of them came from the East, particularly from Harvard, was significant in the minds of many critics. HARVARD TELLS INDIANA HOW TO VOTE, ran a headline in a Chicago *Tribune* editorial whose argument was that Stevenson was in the hands of the Schlesingers, father and son, and Archibald MacLeish, all of whom were held to have had the most sinister associations. Westbrook Pegler, who had not forgotten Felix Frankfurter's influence on the New Deal,

[2] For information and for the quoted matter in the following paragraphs, which is taken from editorials and letters to newspapers, I have drawn on George A. Hage's illuminating unpublished study: *Anti-intellectualism in Newspaper Comment on the Elections of 1828 and 1952*, University of Minnesota doctoral dissertation, 1958; see the same writer's "Anti-intellectualism in Press Comment—1828 and 1952," *Journalism Quarterly*, Vol. XXXVI (Fall, 1959), pp. 439–46.

took pains to remind readers that Stevenson, like F.D.R., had had Harvard associations. He had spent a few years at Harvard Law School, where it seemed to Pegler that he must surely have succumbed to Frankfurter's wiles; Stevenson had been, Pegler thought, "a New Deal bureaucrat of the most dangerous type intermittently ever since 1933." Pegler imagined he had noticed an attempt by Stevenson's supporters and biographers to play down his Harvard connections and his supposed left-wing associations; but none of this could conceal from the vigilant Pegler the fact that "the Springfield wonder boy is serving a warmed-over version of the leftist political line." As a consequence of Stevenson's malign Harvard associations, Frankfurter, Hiss, the Schlesingers, and Stevenson all merged into a single ominous image in right-wing fantasies.

Other university associations were no better. When a large number of Columbia University faculty members published a manifesto praising Stevenson and criticizing Eisenhower, then the university's president, the New York *Daily News* countered with an exposure of alleged "pinko professors" among the signers. A Midwestern newspaper more calmly remarked that the opposition of Columbia students and faculty would work in Eisenhower's favor because everyone knew that university people "have had their minds infiltrated with strong leftist Socialistic ideas, as well as with definite Communistic loyalties." Such support only damned Stevenson. "Stevenson, the intellectual, must share the views of his advisers or he would not have selected them. A vote for Eisenhower, the plain American, is a vote for democracy." Old resentments against the New Deal were everywhere in evidence among writers to whom this argument of disloyalty was significant: "We have strayed far afield from the good old American ways which made this country great. Our colleges are full of leftists, and these 'bright young boys' want to make this country over into a 'bright new world.' May we be protected from another four years of New Deal-Fair Deal."

The association of intellectuality and style with effeminacy which I have remarked on in connection with the reformers of the Gilded Age reappeared in the 1952 campaign. Here Stevenson was sadly handicapped. Since his service in both world wars had been in a civilian capacity, he had nothing to counter Eisenhower's record as a general. Had he been a boxer, hunter, or soldier like T.R., or a football player (Eisenhower had this too to his credit), or an artilleryman like Harry Truman, or a war hero like Kennedy, the impression that he was removed from the hard masculine world of affairs might have been mitigated. But he was only a gentleman with an Ivy League back-ground, and there was nothing in his career to spare him from the reverberations this history set up in the darker corners of the American mind. The New York *Daily News* descended to calling him Adelaide and charged that he "trilled" his speeches in a "fruity" voice. His voice and diction were converted into objects of suspicion—"teacup words," it was said, reminiscent of "a genteel spinster who can never forget that she got an A in elocution at Miss Smith's Finishing School." His supporters? They were "typical Harvard lace-cuff liberals," "lace-panty diplomats," "pompadoured lap dogs," who wailed "in perfumed anguish" at McCarthy's accusations and on occasions "giggled" about their own anti-Communism. Politics, Stevenson's critics were disposed to say, is a rough game for men. The governor and his followers ought to be prepared to slug it out. They would do well to take a lesson from Richard Nixon's "manly explanation of his financial affairs."

Even in quarters where rancor and vulgarity were absent, there was a frequently stated preference for the "proven ability" of Eisen-hower as compared with Stevenson, who smacked of the "ivory tower." "On the basis of past performance, I feel we need Eisenhower, the man of outstanding achievement, rather than Stevenson, the thinker and orator." Jefferson and John Quincy Adams might well have found a familiar note in this remark of a partisan: "Eisenhower knows more about world conditions than any other two men in the country, and he didn't obtain his knowledge through newspapers and books either." The theme is unlikely to lose its usefulness. Eight years later, cam-paigning for Nixon and Lodge, Eisenhower himself said of them: "These men didn't learn their lessons merely out of books—and not even by writing books. They learned these lessons by meeting the day-in, day-out problems of our changing world." [3]

But in the same campaign John F. Kennedy proved what perhaps should not have had to be proved again—that the reading of books, even the writing of books, is hardly a fatal impediment for a presi-dential aspirant who combines a reputation for mind with the other necessary qualities. Kennedy seems to have brought back to presidential politics the combination of intellect and character shown at the be-ginning of the century by T.R.—a combination in which a respect for intellectual and cultural distinction and a passion for intelligence and expertise in public service are united with the aggressive and practical virtues. Stevenson as a campaigner had seemed all sensitivity and

[3] *The New York Times,* November 3, 1960.

diffidence and had appealed to the intellectuals' fond obsession with
their own alienation and rejection; Kennedy, on the other hand, was
all authority and confidence, and he appealed to their desire that intellect and culture be associated with power and responsibility. He had
all of Eisenhower's confidence without his passivity; and his victory
over Nixon, despite his religion, his youth, and his relative obscurity
at the time of his nomination, was in good part attributable to his
visibly superior aggressiveness and self-assurance in their television
debates—to his show, as T.R. might have said, of the manly virtues.

To most intellectuals, even to many with an ingrained suspicion of
the manifestations of power, the mind of the new President seemed
to be, if hardly profound, at least alert and capacious, sophisticated and
skeptical, and he was quick to convey his belief that in the national
concert of interests the claims of intellect and culture ought to have a
place. Some highly intelligent Presidents before Kennedy—Hoover,
for example—had been utterly impatient with the ceremonial functions
of the presidency, which seemed to them only a waste of precious
time on trivialities. The Founding Fathers had conceived the office
differently. Many of them understood that the chief of state, above all
in a republican political order, ought to be a *personage*, and that the
communion between this personage and the public is an important
thread in the fabric of government. Washington himself, whose very
presence contributed to the success of the new government, was a
perfect example of the performance of this function. In the twentieth
century, the American mania for publicity and the development of the
mass media have put a great strain upon the ceremonial and public
side of the presidential office. Franklin D. Roosevelt, through skillful
use of the radio and the press conference, was the first President to
turn the demands of modern publicity into a major asset. Kennedy has
been the first to see that intellectuals and artists are now a sufficiently
important segment of the public to warrant not simply inclusion in the
ceremonial aspects of state but some special effort to command their
loyalty by awarding them a kind of official recognition. The President's
mansion has thus been restored as a symbol: to the great audience its
renovation has been displayed on television; for a smaller but strategic
audience it has become once again a center of receptivity to culture
—Robert Frost, e. e. cummings, and Pablo Casals have been welcomed
there. And the idea that power may owe some deference to intellect
has been reaffirmed many times—perhaps most impressively by a
memorable dinner for Nobel laureates given in the spring of 1962, at

which the President characteristically remarked that there were now more brains at the White House table than at any time since the days when Thomas Jefferson dined alone.

Of course, all this was merely a ceremonial means of recognizing the legitimacy of a special interest—the kind of ceremonial whose function had long been understood, for example, by Irish politicians who attended Italian festivals or Jewish politicians who went to Irish wakes. Like the ethnic minorities, the intellectuals were to have their place in the scheme of public acknowledgment. The interest and pleasure of the new administration in the ceremonial recognition of culture was less important than its sustained search for talent, which brought the place of expertise in American government to a new high. From time to time the reputation and recognition of intellect in politics may vary, but the demand for expertise seems constantly to rise. The Eisenhower regime, for example, despite its expressed disdain for eggheads and its pique at their opposition, made considerable strategic use of experts; and Republican leaders also showed interest in what they called the "utilization" of friendly academics. The larger question, to which I shall return in my final chapter, concerns the relations between experts who are also intellectuals, of whom there are many, and the rest of the intellectual community; and touches upon the condition of intellectuals when they find themselves on the fringes of power. One of the difficulties in the relation of intellect to power is that certain primary functions of intellect are widely felt to be threatened almost as much by being associated with power as by being relegated to a position of impotence. An acute and paradoxical problem of intellect as a force in modern society stems from the fact that it cannot lightly reconcile itself either to its association with power or to its exclusion from an important political role.

PART 4

The Practical Culture

CHAPTER IX

Business and Intellect

❦

· 1 ·

For at least three quarters of a century business has been stigmatized by most American intellectuals as the classic enemy of intellect;
businessmen themselves have so long accepted this role that by now
their enmity seems to be a fact of nature. No doubt there is a certain
measure of inherent dissonance between business enterprise and intellectual enterprise: being dedicated to different sets of values, they are
bound to conflict; and intellect is always potentially threatening to
any institutional apparatus or to fixed centers of power. But this enmity, being qualified by a certain mutual dependence, need not take
the form of constant open warfare. Quite as important as the general
grounds that make for enmity are the historical circumstances that
have muted or accentuated it. The circumstances of the industrial
era in America gave the businessman a position among the foes of
mind and culture so central and so powerful that other antagonists
were crowded out of the picture.

Some years ago the business journalist, John Chamberlain, complained in *Fortune* that American novelists have consistently done
rank injustice to American businessmen. In the entire body of modern
American fiction, he pointed out, the businessman is almost always
depicted as crass, philistine, corrupt, predatory, domineering, reactionary, and amoral. In a long list of business novels, from Dreiser's
Cowperwood trilogy to the present, Chamberlain could find only
three books in which the businessman was favorably portrayed:
one was by a popular novelist of no consequence; the others were
William Dean Howells's *The Rise of Silas Lapham* and Sinclair Lewis's

Dodsworth.[1] But the very transiency of these two exceptions confirms Chamberlain's complaint. *Silas Lapham* was written in 1885, before novelists and businessmen had become solidly alienated; five years later, Howells published *A Hazard of New Fortunes,* in which one of the characteristically saurian businessmen of fiction appears, and he later wrote some vaguely socialist social criticism. And it was Sinclair Lewis, after all, who in *Babbitt* gave the world its archetype of the small-town, small-business American philistine.

In the main, Chamberlain remarked, the novelists' portrait of the businessman is drawn out of doctrine ("a dry and doctrinaire attitude," he called it) and not out of direct observation of business or out of an intimate knowledge of businessmen. The perverse intent suggested by this charge may be largely a creation of Chamberlain's fancy. Our society has no unitary elites in which writers and businessmen associate on easy terms; and if real live businessmen fail to appear in the American novel, it is partly because the American writer rarely appears in the society of businessmen: chances for close observation are minimal. The hostility is not one-sided but mutual; and it would be an unenviable task to try to show that the businessman lacks the instruments of self-defense or retaliation, or that he has not used them.

But Chamberlain's main point stands: the portrait of the businessman offered in the social novel in this country conveys the general attitude of the intellectual community, which has been at various times populistic, progressive, or Marxist, or often some compound of the three. Since the development of industrialism after the Civil War, the estrangement between businessmen and men of letters has been both profound and continuous; and since the rise of Progressivism and the New Deal, the tension between businessmen and liberal intellectuals in the social sciences has also been acute. In times of prosperity, when the intellectual community has not been deeply engaged with political conflict, it is content to portray businessmen as philistines. In times of political or economic discontent, the conflict deepens, and the businessmen become ruthless exploiters as well. The values of business and intellect are seen as eternally and inevitably at odds: on the one side, there is the money-centered or power-centered man, who cares only about bigness and the dollar, about boosting and hollow optimism; on the other side, there are the men of critical intellect, who distrust American civilization and concern themselves with quality and moral

[1] "The Businessman in Fiction," *Fortune,* Vol. XXXVIII (November, 1948), pp. 134–48.

values. The intellectual is well aware of the elaborate apparatus which the businessman uses to mold our civilization to his purposes and adapt it to his standards. The businessman is everywhere; he fills the coffers of the political parties; he owns or controls the influential press and the agencies of mass culture; he sits on university boards of trustees and on local school boards; he mobilizes and finances cultural vigilantes; his voice dominates the rooms in which the real decisions are made.

The contemporary businessman, who is disposed to think of himself as a man of practical achievement and a national benefactor, shouldering enormous responsibilities and suffering from the hostility of flighty men who have never met a payroll, finds it hard to take seriously the notion that he always gets his way. He sees himself enmeshed in the bureaucratic regulations of a welfare state that is certainly no creation of *his;* he feels he is checkmated by powerful unions and regarded suspiciously by a public constantly piqued by intellectuals. He may also be aware that in former days—in the times, say, of Andrew Carnegie—the great business leader, despite some hostility, was a culture-hero. In those days businessmen were prominent national figures in their own right, sages to be consulted on almost every aspect of life. But since the times of Henry Ford—the last of his kind—this heroic image has gone into eclipse. Businessmen figure in the headlines only when they enter politics or public administration. A man like Charles E. Wilson, for example, had ten times as many notices in *The New York Times* when he was Secretary of Defense in 1953 as he had three years earlier as president of General Motors.[2] Rich men may still be acceptable in politics—John F. Kennedy, Nelson Rockefeller, Averell Harriman, Herbert Lehman, G. Mennen Williams—but these are not truly businessmen: they are men of inherited wealth, often conspicuous for their liberal political views.

At times the businessman may think of himself as having been stripped of his prestige by the intellectual and his allies, in a hostile environment created by intellectuals. If so, he overestimates the power of the intellectuals. In fact, the prestige of the businessman has been destroyed largely by his own achievements: it was he who created the giant corporation, an impersonal agency that overshadows his reputation as it disciplines his career; it was his own incessant propaganda about the American Way of Life and Free Enterprise that made these

[2] Mabel Newcomer: *The Big Business Executive* (New York, 1955), p. 7; on the declining prestige of executives, see p. 131.

spongy abstractions into public generalities which soak up and assimilate the reputations of individual enterprisers. Once great men created fortunes; today a great system creates fortunate men.

The tension between intellect and business has about it, however, a kind of ungainly intimacy, symbolized in the fact that so many intellectuals are rebelling against the business families in which they were reared. An uneasy symbiosis has actually developed between business and intellect. In the United States, where government has done far less for the arts and learning than in Europe, culture has always been dependent upon private patronage; it has not been any less dependent in recent decades, when the criticism of business has been so dominant a concern of intellectuals. The position of the critical intellectual is thus a singularly uncomfortable one: in the interests of his work and his livelihood he extends one hand for the institutional largesse of dead businessmen, the Guggenheims, Carnegies, Rockefellers, Fords, and lesser benefactors; but in his concern for high principles and values his other hand is often doubled into a fist. The freedom of intellect and art is inevitably the freedom to criticize and disparage, to destroy and re-create; but the daily necessity of the intellectual and the artist is to be an employee, a protégé, a beneficiary—or a man of business. This ambiguous relationship affects businessmen as well. Sensitive of their reputation, fearful and resentful of criticism, often arrogant in their power, they can hardly help but be aware that the patronage of learning and art will add to their repute. To speak less cynically, they are also the heirs of traditional moral canons of stewardship; they often feel a responsibility to do good with their money. And they are not without a certain respect for mind; under modern technological conditions, they must, in any case, more or less regularly call upon mind for practical counsel. Finally, being rather more human than otherwise, they too have a natural craving for unbought esteem.

The anti-intellectualism of businessmen, interpreted narrowly as hostility to intellectuals, is mainly a political phenomenon. But interpreted more broadly as a suspicion of intellect itself, it is part of the extensive American devotion to practicality and direct experience which ramifies through almost every area of American life. With some variations of details suitable to social classes and historical circumstances, the excessive practical bias so often attributed only to business is found almost everywhere in America. In itself, a certain wholesome regard for the practical needs no defense and deserves no disparagement, so long as it does not aspire to exclusiveness, so long as other aspects of human experience are not denigrated and ridiculed. Practical vigor is a virtue; what has been spiritually crippling in our history is the tendency to make a mystique of practicality.

· 2 ·

If I put business in the vanguard of anti-intellectualism in our culture, it is not out of a desire to overstate its role. Certainly the debt of American culture to a small number of wealthy men, patrons of learning and art, is great enough to be thrown immediately into the balance as a counterpoise. The main reason for stressing anti-intellectualism in business is not that business is demonstrably more anti-intellectual or more philistine than other major sections of American society, but simply that business is the most powerful and pervasive interest in American life. This is true both in the sense that the claims of practicality have been an overweening force in American life and in the sense that, since the mid-nineteenth century, businessmen have brought to anti-intellectual movements more strength than any other force in society. "This is essentially a business country," said Warren G. Harding in 1920, and his words were echoed by the famous remark of Calvin Coolidge: "The business of America is business." [3] It is this social preponderance of business, at least before 1929, that gives it a claim to special attention.

One reason for the success of the argument of American business against intellect is that it coincides at so many points with the conventional folk wisdom. For example, the feeling about intellect expressed in the businessman's statements about higher education and vocationalism was also the popular feeling, as Edward Kirkland has suggested: the people constantly voted on the educational system by taking their children out of school or by not sending them to college. We need not be surprised to find a "radical" labor reformer like Henry George advising his son that since college would fill his head with things which would have to be unlearned, he should go directly into newspaper work to put himself in touch with the practical world; the same advice might have come from a business tycoon. [4]

[3] Warren G. Harding: "Business Sense in Government," *Nation's Business*, Vol. VIII (November, 1920), p. 13. Coolidge is quoted, from an address at the December, 1923 meeting of the American Society of Newspaper Editors, by William Allen White: *A Puritan in Babylon* (New York, 1938), p. 253.

[4] Edward Kirkland: *Dream and Thought in the Business Community, 1860–1900* (Ithaca, New York, 1956), pp. 81–2, 87.

The fear of mind and the disdain for culture, so quickly evident wherever the prior claims of practicality are urged in the literature of business, are ubiquitous themes. They rest upon two pervasive American attitudes toward civilization and personal religion—first, a widely shared contempt for the past; and second, an ethos of self-help and personal advancement in which even religious faith becomes merely an agency of practicality.

Let us look first at the American attitude toward the past, which has been so greatly shaped by our technological culture. America, as it is commonly said, has been a country without monuments or ruins—that is, without those inescapable traces of the ancestral human spirit with which all Europeans live and whose meanings, at least in their broadest outlines, can hardly be evaded by even the simplest peasant or workman. America has been the country of those who fled from the past. Its population was selected by migration from among those most determined to excise history from their lives.[5] With their minds fixed on the future, Americans found themselves surrounded with ample land and resources and beset by a shortage of labor and skills. They set a premium upon technical knowledge and inventiveness which would unlock the riches of the country and open the door to the opulent future. Technology, skill—everything that is suggested by the significant Americanism, "know-how"—was in demand. The past was seen as despicably impractical and uninventive, simply and solely as something to be surmounted. It should be acknowledged that the American disdain for the past, as it emerged toward the end of the eighteenth and the beginning of the nineteenth centuries, had some aspects which were at the very least defensible and at best distinctly praiseworthy. What was at stake was not entirely a technological or materialistic barbarianism which aimed merely to slough off all the baggage of history. Among other things, the American attitude represented a republican and egalitarian protest against monarchy and aristocracy and the callous exploitation of the people; it represented a rationalistic protest against superstition; an energetic and forward-looking protest against the passivity and pessimism of the Old World; it revealed a dynamic, vital, and originative mentality.

[5] "It is not indiscriminate masses of Europe," Emerson thought, "that are shipped hitherward, but the Atlantic is a sieve through which only or chiefly the liberal, adventurous, sensitive, *America-loving* part of each city, clan, family are brought. It is the light complexion, the blue eyes of Europe that come: the black eyes, the black drop, the Europe of Europe, is left." *Journals* (1851; Boston, Riverside ed., 1912), Vol. VIII, p. 226.

But certainly in its consequences, if not in its intentions, this attitude was anti-cultural. It stimulated the development of an intellectual style in which the past was too often regarded simply as a museum of confusion, corruption, and exploitation; it led to disdain for all contemplation which could not be transformed into practical intelligence and for all passion which could not be mobilized for some forward step in progress. This view of human affairs lent itself too readily to the proposition that the sum and substance of life lies in the business of practical improvement; it encouraged the complacent notion that there is only one defensible way of life, the American way, and that this way had been willfully spurned or abandoned by peoples elsewhere.[6] Many Americans found the true secret of civilization in the Patent Office. An orator at Yale in 1844 told the undergraduates that they could read the future there: [7]

> The age of *philosophy* has passed, and left few memorials of its existence. That of *glory* has vanished, and nothing but a painful tradition of human suffering remains. That of *utility* has commenced, and it requires little warmth of imagination to anticipate for it a reign lasting as time, and radiant with the wonders of unveiled nature.

Everywhere, as machine industry arose, it drew a line of demarcation between the utilitarian and the traditional. In the main, America took its stand with utility, with improvement and invention, money and comfort. It was clearly understood that the advance of the machine was destroying old inertias, discomforts, and brutalities, but it was not so commonly understood that the machine was creating new discomforts and brutalities, undermining traditions and ideals, sentiments and loyalties, esthetic sensitivities. Perhaps the signal difference between Europe and America on this count is that in Europe there always existed a strong counter-tradition, both romantic and moralistic, against the ugliness of industrialism—a tradition carried on by figures as di-

---

[6] Cf. Thomas Paine in *The Rights of Man:* "From the rapid progress which America makes in every species of improvement, it is rational to conclude that, if the governments of Asia, Africa, and Europe had begun on a principle similar to that of America, or had not been very early corrupted therefrom, those countries must by this time have been in a far superior condition to what they are." *Writings*, ed. by Moncure D. Conway (New York, 1894), Vol. II, p. 402.

[7] Arthur A. Ekirch: *The Idea of Progress in America, 1815–1860* (New York, 1944), p. 126. I am indebted to chapter 4 for its documentation of the American faith in technology, though I feel that the author is slightly amiss in speaking of it simply as faith in science, for it is largely *applied* science which is involved. The whole work is illuminating on the American mentality before the Civil War.

verse as Goethe and Blake, Morris and Carlyle, Hugo and Chateau-
briand, Ruskin and Scott. Such men counterposed to the machine a
passion for language and locality, for antiquities and monuments, for
natural beauty; they sustained a tradition of resistance to capitalist
industrialism, of skepticism about the human consequences of industrial progress, of moral, esthetic, and humane revolt.

I do not mean to suggest that there were no American counterparts.
Some writers did protest against complacent faith in improvement,
though one senses among them a poignant awareness of their futility
and isolation, of their opposition to the main stream. Nathaniel Hawthorne might complain, as he did in the preface to *The Marble Faun*,
of the difficulties of writing in a country "where there is no shadow,
no antiquity, no mystery, no picturesque and gloomy wrong, nor anything but a commonplace prosperity, in broad and simple daylight";
Herman Melville might warn, as he did in *Clarel*, of

> Man disennobled—brutalized
> By popular science

and answer scientific progressivism with: "You are but drilling the new
Hun"; Henry Adams might later view the American scene with ironic
detachment and detached resignation—but none of these men
imagined himself to be a representative spokesman. Thoreau's *Walden*
was, among other things, a statement of humane protest, a vision of the
dead men, the lost life, buried under the ties of the railroads. He was
immune to the American passion for the future; he was against the
national preference for movement, expansion, technology, and utility.
"The whole enterprise of this nation," he wrote in 1853,[8]

> which is not an upward, but a westward one, toward Oregon,
> California, Japan, etc., is totally devoid of interest to me, whether
> performed on foot, or by a Pacific railroad. It is not illustrated by a
> thought, it is not warmed by a sentiment; there is nothing in it
> which one should lay down his life for, nor even his gloves—
> hardly which one should take up a newspaper for. It is perfectly
> heathenish—a filibustering *toward* heaven by the great western
> route. No; they may go their way to their manifest destiny, which
> I trust is not mine.

In a somewhat similar spirit, the conservative classicist and Orientalist,
Tayler Lewis, objected that America boasted of its individualism while

[8] *Writings,* (Boston, 1906), Vol. VI, p. 210 (February 27, 1853).

encouraging "mediocre sameness" in its utilitarian education. "When
may we look for less of true originality," he asked, "than at a time
when every child is taught to repeat this inane self-laudation, and
all distinction of individual thought is lost, because no man has room for
anything else than a barren idea of progress, a contempt for the past,
and a blinding reverence for an unknown future?" [9] But only a vociferous minority concurred with these protests. Andrew Carnegie, who
spoke of "an ignorant past whose chief province is to teach us not
what to adopt, but what to avoid"; the oil magnate who saw no value
in having students "poring over musty dead languages, learning the
disgusting stories of the mythical gods, and all the barbarous stuff of
the dead past"; James A. Garfield, who did not want to encourage
American youth to "feed their spirits on the life of dead ages, instead of
the inspiring life and vigor of our own times"; Henry Ford, who told
an interviewer that "history is more or less bunk. It's tradition"—
such men were in the main stream.[1]

When a representative American voice is raised, there is a good
chance that sooner or later this feeling of condescension toward the ma-
chineless past, this note of hope in technological progress will assert
itself. Mark Twain, whose voice is one of the most authentic of all, is
a case in point. Many years ago, in a memorable passage in his brilliant
book, *The Ordeal of Mark Twain,* Van Wyck Brooks reproached
Mark Twain because "his enthusiasm for literature was as nothing
beside his enthusiasm for machinery: he had fully accepted the illusion
of his contemporaries that the progress of machinery was identical
with the progress of humanity." Quoting Twain's raptures on the
Paige typesetting machine, which the writer considered superior to
anything else produced by the human brain, Brooks went on to cite
the perversity of Twain's letter to Whitman on the poet's seventieth
birthday, in which the author congratulated Whitman for having lived
in an age of manifold material benefactions, including "the amazing,
infinitely varied and innumerable products of coal-tar," but neglected
to recognize that the age was remarkable also for having produced
Walt Whitman.[2]

In this, as in so many of his other perceptions about Mark Twain,

[9] Ekirch: op. cit., p. 175.
[1] Kirkland: op. cit., pp. 86, 106; Irvin G. Wyllie: *The Self-Made Man in
America* (New Brunswick, New Jersey, 1954), p. 104. Ford's explanation of his
remark was an illuminating one: "I did not say it was bunk. It was bunk to me. . . .
I did not need it very bad." Allan Nevins: *Ford: Expansion and Challenge, 1915–
1933* (New York, 1957), p. 138.
[2] *The Ordeal of Mark Twain* (New York, 1920), pp. 146–7.

Brooks seems essentially right. But the letter would not have seemed so exceptionable to Whitman himself. More than thirty years earlier, Whitman had written, in very much the same vein: [3]

> Think of the numberless contrivances and inventions for our comfort and luxury which the last half dozen years have brought forth—of our baths and ice houses and ice coolers—of our fly traps and mosquito nets—of house bells and marble mantels and sliding tables—of patent ink-stands and baby jumpers—of serving machines and street-sweeping machines—in a word give but a passing glance at the fat volumes of Patent Office Reports and bless your star that fate has cast your lot in the year of our Lord 1857.

Mark Twain is especially interesting in this because he refracted with extraordinary fidelity the concerns of the technocratic mind. I say refracted, not embodied, because he was too much a moralist and a pessimist to imagine that mechanical progress was an all-sufficient end. He was a man of contradictions, and few men have more passionately embraced the values of business industrialism and at the same time more contemptuously rejected them. His most extended commentary on technical progress, *A Connecticut Yankee in King Arthur's Court*, juxtaposes a nineteenth-century technical Yankee mind with a sixth-century society to satirize both civilizations. The moral burden of this tale is that human rascality and credulity will prevail even over mechanical progress; but within the dialectic of the story all the advantages lie with the Connecticut Yankee, who establishes a benevolent dictatorship on the strength of his command of steam power and electricity. "The very first official thing I did, in my administration—and it was on the very first day of it, too—was to start a patent office; for I knew that a country without a patent office and good patent laws was just a crab, and couldn't travel any way but sideways or backwards." [4] Of course, Twain was somewhat ambivalent about his Yankee hero; although he may have been, as Henry James tartly remarked, a writer for rudimentary minds, he was not so rudimentary as to be unaware of at least some of the limitations of the industrial tinkerer.[5] None the less, it is the Connecticut Yankee who

[3] Emory Holloway and Vernolian Schwarz, eds.: *I Sit and Look Out: Editorials from the Brooklyn Daily Times* (New York, 1932), p. 133.

[4] *A Connecticut Yankee* (1889; Pocket Book ed., 1948), p. 56.

[5] Speaking to Dan Beard about the illustrations for the book, he said: "You know, this Yankee of mine has neither the refinement nor the weakness of a college education; he is a perfect ignoramus; he is boss of a machine shop; he can build a locomo-

enjoys mental and moral superiority and with whom we are expected
to sympathize. Mark Twain's national *amour-propre* was engaged in
the book—he wrote his British publisher that the work was written
not for America but for England; that it was an answer to English
criticisms of America (particularly, though he did not say so, to those
of Matthew Arnold), an attempt to "pry up the English nation to a
little higher level of manhood." Such intentions as he may have had
to satirize mankind in general and, more particularly, Yankee industrialism were in effect swallowed up in this impulse to justify what
later came to be called the American way of life. Despite a few side-
swipes at modern American abuses, the book is mainly a response to
Europe and the past, to a society characterized entirely by squalor,
superstition, cruelty, ignorance, and exploitation. If it was Mark
Twain's intention to be equally satirical about sixth-century and nineteenth-century society, his execution was at fault. But it is easier to
believe that his animus ran mostly in one direction; this interpretation
accords better with his raptures over the Paige machine, which he
hoped would make millions but on which he lost thousands. It accords
better with the tone of *The Innocents Abroad,* in which the author
confessed that he cared more for the railroads, depots, and turnpikes
of Europe than for all the art in Italy, "because I can understand the
one and am not competent to appreciate the other." [6] It may help,
too, to illuminate one aspect of the long, anticlimactic sequence near
the end of *Huckleberry Finn,* in which Tom Sawyer, enamored of the
outworn heroics of European romances, insists that Nigger Jim be
rescued from captivity by what he conceives to be the only proper
method, with all its cumbersome rituals, and overrules Huck Finn's
untutored common-sense proposals. This extravagant burlesque has
been much condemned as a distraction from the fundamental moral
drama of the book, but for Mark Twain it had a vital importance. Tom
Sawyer represents the impracticality of traditional culture, and Huck
stands for the native American gift for coming to grips with reality.

· 3 ·

Mark Twain gave voice to what was undoubtedly a widespread American ambivalence. Its main tenet was a robust faith in the patent

---

tive or a Colt's revolver, he can put up and run a telegraph line, but he's an ignoramus, nevertheless." Gladys Carmen Bellamy: *Mark Twain as a Literary Artist*
(Norman, Oklahoma, 1950), p. 314.
   [6] *The Innocents Abroad* (1869; New York ed., 1906), pp. 325–6.

office and the future; but a great many Americans, along with Mark Twain, also felt a certain respectful and wistful regard for the genteel culture that flourished largely in the East. (Clemens's own desire to "make good" with this culture and yet somehow to flout it led to one of the most painful confrontations in all our history—the terrible fiasco of his Whittier birthday speech.) This culture had its limitations, but during the greater part of Mark Twain's life, it was the only high culture the country knew. To a considerable degree, it leaned upon the support of a commercial class.

In the absence of either a strong hereditary aristocracy or state patronage, the condition of art and learning in America was dependent upon commercial wealth, and on this account the personal culture of the American business class was always a matter of special importance to intellectual life. From the beginning, America was, of necessity, a work-bound society, but even in the middle of the eighteenth century a material basis for art and learning had been created in the seaboard towns, and foundations had been laid for a kind of mercantile society with an interest in culture. As early as 1743 Benjamin Franklin, outlining a plan for intercolonial co-operation in promoting science, observed: "The first drudgery of settling new colonies which confines the attention of people to mere necessaries is now pretty well over; and there are many in every province in circumstances that set them at ease, and afford leisure to cultivate the finer arts and improve the common stock of knowledge." [7] In the coastal towns, which were even then among the largest in the British empire, the mercantile and professional class was seriously interested in the advancement of learning, science, and the arts, and it was this class that established a model for patronage in the New World.

The backbone of this class was mercantile wealth—wealth, it is important to say, in the hands of men who did not invariably consider the pursuit of business and the accumulation of money an all-sufficient end in life. By some businessmen business is considered to be a way of life; by others, a way *to* life, a single side of a many-sided existence, possibly only a means to such an existence. Among the latter, retirement after the accumulation of a substantial fortune is at least a conceivable goal. Andrew Carnegie, an exceptional man among his generation of millionaires, gave lip service to this ideal, even though he did

[7] Smyth, ed.: *Writings* (New York, 1905–07), Vol. II, p. 228.

not quite live up to it. At thirty-three, when he was making $50,000 a year, he wrote: [8]

> To continue much longer overwhelmed by business cares and with most of my thoughts wholly upon the way to make more money in the shortest time, must degrade me beyond the hope of permanent recovery. I will resign business at thirty-five.

Severely business-minded men, to whom this would have made no sense, have always existed in America. But the ideal that Carnegie was expressing did have considerable power. The old-fashioned merchant in Boston, New York, Philadelphia, or Charleston was a versatile and often a cosmopolitan man. Mercantile contacts with Europe and the Orient led his mind outward. The slow pace of business transactions in the days of the sailing ship, which was so soon speeded up by the increasing rapidity of mid-nineteenth century communication, made the successful pursuit of business consistent with a life of dignified leisure. In the relatively stratified society of the late eighteenth century a significant proportion of the upper business classes were men of inherited wealth and position, who brought to their mercantile roles the advantages of breeding, leisure, and education. Moreover, eighteenth-century merchants were often actively involved in politics; their concerns with officeholding, legislating, and administering, as well as business, made for versatility in action and a reflective turn in thought.

The early nineteenth century inherited this ideal of the man of business as a civilized man and a civilizing agent. Spokesmen of this ideal did not feel any inconsistency in preaching at the same time the Puritan values of dedication to work, frugality, and sobriety, and the gentlemanly ideals of leisure, culture, and versatility. This view of life is expressed in the columns of the leading mercantile journal, *Hunt's Merchants' Magazine*.[9] Its publisher and editor, Freeman Hunt, the

---

[8] Burton J. Hendrick: *The Life of Andrew Carnegie* (New York, 1932), Vol. I, pp. 146–7. Compare with this the surprise frequently expressed by American businessmen at their European counterparts who hope to accumulate enough to retire as soon as possible. Francis X. Sutton, et al.: *The American Business Creed* (Cambridge, Mass., 1956), p. 102.

[9] On examining the sketches of businessmen collected in Freeman Hunt's *Worth and Wealth: A Collection of Maxims, Morals, and Miscellanies for Merchants and Men of Business* (New York, 1856), I have been struck by the breadth of qualities sought for in the good merchant, and by the coexistence of three constellations of virtues. The first are the classic Puritan virtues, having to do with the development and discipline of the individual, and expressed in such terms as *ambitious, frugal, economical, industrious, persevering, disciplined, provident, diligent, simple*. The

son of a Massachusetts shipbuilder, had come to his business, like so
many other nineteenth-century publishers, from the printer's trade.
He combined in his person the intellectualism and mercantile inheritance of New England with the practical experience of the self-
made man; his father's death when Hunt was still a child had made it
necessary for him to find his own way. The opening issue of Hunt's
monthly journal in 1839 portrayed commerce as a high vocation that
elevates the mind, enlarges the understanding, and adds "to the store
house of general knowledge." "One of our prominent objects," he
wrote, "will be, to raise and elevate the commercial character." He
stressed the importance of "probity, and that high sense of honor,
wanting which, however abounding in everything else, a man may
assume the name, and be totally deficient in all that forms the high
and honorable merchant." Commerce, too, was "a profession embracing
and requiring more varied knowledge, and general information of the
soil, climate, production, and consumption of other countries—of
the history, political complexion, laws, languages, and customs of the
world—than is necessary in any other. . . ." He took upon himself
the duty of maintaining the intellectual and moral level of the trade.
"Wherever the minds of the young are to be formed [to take the places
of the old merchants] they will find us . . . doing all in our power to
aid the incipient merchant in his high and honorable avocation." [1]
One of his books was significantly entitled *Wealth and Worth*. Later
writers frequently reiterated the idea that "commerce and civilization
go hand in hand." For many years Hunt's magazine ran an extensive
"literary department" in which books of general intellectual interest

---

second are the mercantile-aristocratic virtues, having to do with the elevation of
business and society, and expressed in such terms as *upright, generous, noble,
civilizing, humane, benevolent, veracious, responsible, liberal, suave, gentlemanly,
moderate*. The third might be considered categorically good attributes for almost
any undertaking: *clear, explicit, decisive, careful, attentive, lively, firm*.

[1] *The Merchants' Magazine and Commercial Review*, Vol. I (July, 1839), pp.
1–3; between 1850 and 1860 the title of the periodical was changed to *Hunt's
Merchants' Magazine*. For further passages of interest, see Vol. I, pp. 200–2,
289–302, 303–14, 399–413. Jerome Thomases, writing on "Freeman Hunt's America," *Mississippi Valley Historical Review*, Vol. XXX (December, 1943), pp. 395–
407, attempts to assess the influence of the magazine, which was considerable. He
touches on the theme I have emphasized, but also points out how much the magazine preached the principles of work, practicality, and self-reliance. It seems a
significant token of the extent to which the image of the merchant had established
itself as an ideal among businessmen that in New York, by 1850, "bankers, capitalists, brokers, commercial lawyers, railroad speculators, and manufacturers referred to themselves as merchants." Philip S. Foner: *Business and Slavery* (Chapel
Hill, 1941), p. vii.

were discussed. Lectures delivered under the auspices of the New York Mercantile Library Association were reported. A clergyman's article on "Leisure—Its Uses and Abuses" was considered important enough to publish. An article on "Advantages and Benefits of Commerce" pointed out that "in every nation whose commerce has been cultivated upon great and enlightened principles, a considerable proficiency has been made in liberal studies and pursuits." What is essential here is that the role of the merchant was justified not solely on the ground that he is materially useful, nor even on the honor and probity with which he pursues his vocation, but also because he is an agent of a more general culture that lies outside business itself.[2]

The old mercantile ideal, with its imposing set of practical, moral, and cultural obligations, may seem to have been difficult to live up to, but enough men, especially in the large seaboard towns, were capable of living up to it to keep it alive and real. One thinks, for example, of the immensely wealthy and powerful Appleton brothers of Boston, Samuel (1776–1853) and Nathan (1779–1861). Samuel, who was active in politics as well as business, chose to retire from business at sixty, and to devote the rest of his life to philanthropy. He patronized colleges and academies, learned societies, hospitals, and museums with an open hand. His brother Nathan, who was actively interested in science, politics, and theology, was helpful to the Boston Athenaeum, the Massachusetts Historical Society, and other cultural organizations; he once said that the $200,000 he had made in trade would have satisfied him had he not gone into the cotton industry by chance. The grandfather of Henry and Brooks Adams, Peter Chardon Brooks (1767–1849), whose three daughters married Edward Everett, Nathaniel Frothingham, and the elder Charles Francis Adams, was sufficiently detached from trade to retire at thirty-six (he returned to it for a few years later on) and devote his time to public offices, philanthropy, and the political careers of two of his sons-in-law. Men like these, though assiduous in business, were capable of detaching themselves from it. The ideal of civilized accomplishment never ceased to glimmer in their minds. Emerson's eloquent tribute to John Murray

---

[2] Sigmund Diamond has observed that the early nineteenth-century entrepreneur was commonly judged by society on the basis of the personal *use* he made of his wealth, whether philanthropic or economic. In the twentieth century it became more common to look at business enterprise *as a system,* and not to judge it by its philanthropic by-products. *The Reputation of the American Businessman* (Cambridge, Mass., 1955), pp. 178–9.

Forbes (1813–1898), the versatile and cultivated merchant and railroad entrepreneur, is a token of the *rapprochement* that was possible between intellectuals and the best representatives of the mercantile ideal: [3]

> Wherever he moved he was the benefactor. It is of course that he should ride well, shoot well, sail well, keep house well, administer affairs well; but he was the best talker, also, in the company. . . . Yet I said to myself, How little this man suspects, with his sympathy for men and his respect for lettered and scientific people, that he is not likely, in any company, to meet a man superior to himself. And I think this is a good country, that can bear such a creature as he is.

In New York the pre-eminent example of the mercantile ideal was the famous diarist, Philip Hone (1780–1851). Hone's experience shows how capable a well-knit local aristocracy was of absorbing a gifted newcomer, for no one lived more fully the life of the civilized merchant than this parvenu, who began life as the son of a joiner of limited means. At nineteen Hone went into an importing business with an older brother. At forty he retired with a fortune of half a million and went off upon a grand tour of Europe. Hone had had no schooling beyond the age of sixteen, but unlike the typical self-made man he did not make a virtue of the circumstance. "I am sensible of my deficiency," he wrote in 1832, "and would give half I possess in the world to enjoy the advantages of a classical education." [4] But in his case the lack of formal education was balanced by an enormous appetite for experience. Over the years he collected an extensive library and read widely and intelligently, acquired a small but good collection of works of art, became a patron of the opera and the theater, a preceptor of New York society, a trustee of Columbia, and a sponsor of innumerable philanthropies. His home became a meeting-place for writers, actors, and diplomats, as well as leading politicians. He was active in politics; he served as assistant alderman and for one brief term as mayor of New York, and played a significant role as the host and counselor of Whigs like Webster, Clay, and Seward. His culture, like that of many men of his kind, may have been rather derivative and genteel; but, without

[3] *Letters and Social Aims* (Riverside ed.), p. 201. There are many interesting sidelights on Forbes in Thomas C. Cochran: *Railroad Leaders, 1845–1890* (Cambridge, Mass., 1953).

[4] Quoted by Allan Nevins in the Introduction to *The Diary of Philip Hone* (New York, 1936), p. x.

the patronage and interest of such men, American cultural and intellectual life would have been considerably impoverished.

• 4 •

The lives of merchants like Forbes and Hone may be taken to discount the statement of Tocqueville that "there is no class . . . in America in which the taste for intellectual pleasures is transmitted with hereditary fortune and leisure, and by which the labors of the intellect are held in honor." [5] But for Tocqueville the word "hereditary" was no doubt vital; and it was a matter of consequence that the Hones and the Forbeses were in the main unable to propagate their social type. This had begun to be evident even by the third decade of the nineteenth century, when Tocqueville visited the United States and wrote his great commentary; it became increasingly evident in the subsequent decades. With the relative decline in the importance of commerce and the rise in manufacturing, a smaller part of the business community was exposed to the enlarging, cosmopolitan effects of overseas trade. The American economy and the American mind began to face inward and to become more self-contained. With the rapid inland spread of business into the trans-Allegheny region and the Middle West, cultural institutions and leisured habits of mind were left behind. Men and materials could move faster than institutions and culture. The breakdown of class barriers and the opening of new business opportunities for the common man meant that the ranks of business and society were filling with parvenus, whose tastes and habits tended increasingly to dominate society. In earlier days, especially in the seaboard cities, established local aristocracies had been strong enough to absorb and mold and train parvenus like Hone. In the new cities of the interior, which had been wilderness when thriving cultures were centered in Boston, New York, and Philadelphia, the new men and the descendants of aristocracy mingled on even terms; and in many of them it was the parvenus who leveled the gentlemen down. Of course, some of the inland towns, such as Cincinnati and Lexington, managed in their own way to become cultural centers, but their efforts were relatively feeble. In inland society the newly successful businessmen had less need or opportunity to temper themselves and to elevate their children through marriage into an established professional and business aristocracy such as one found in Boston. Everything was new and raw.

[5] *Democracy in America,* (1835; New York, 1898), Vol. I, p. 66.

It was not only new and raw, but increasingly unstable and hazardous. Even such a man as Hone was hurt by the instability of the times. In the 1830's he lost perhaps as much as two-thirds of his fortune, and after his reverses drove him back into business, he was unable to repeat his earlier successes. Fortunes were easily made and unmade in the uncommonly speculative ethos of American business. The pace of transactions was stepped up; business became increasingly specialized. The between-times leisure often possible in the past for importers whose business was attuned to the pace of Atlantic crossings did not exist for men faced with new threats or new opportunities at almost every turning. Business needed more tending. Men of business withdrew, to some degree, from their previous direct involvement in politics as officeholders, and to a much greater degree from cultural life. In 1859 Thomas Colley Grattan, a British traveler, observed of young American businessmen: [6]

> They follow business like drudges, and politics with fierce ardour. They marry. They renounce party-going. They give up all pretension in dress. They cannot force wrinkles and crow's feet on their faces, but they assume and soon acquire a pursed-up, keen, and haggard look. Their air, manners, and conversation are alike contracted. They have no breadth, either of shoulders, information, or ambition. Their physical powers are subdued, and their mental capability cribbed into narrow limits. There is constant activity going on in one small portion of the brain; all the rest is stagnant. The money-making faculty is alone cultivated. They are incapable of acquiring general knowledge on a broad or liberal scale. All is confined to trade, finance, law, and small, local provincial information. Art, science, literature, are nearly dead letters to them.

At the same time, the cultural tone of business publications fell off. Hunt's magazine, whose literary department had been fairly conspicuous and serious, allowed this feature to dwindle. During and after 1849, the book reviews that had once taken about eight pages in each issue shrank to four or five, then to two and a half pages of perfunctory notices, and finally disappeared altogether from the penultimate volume in 1870. At the end of that year the magazine itself was merged with the *Commercial and Financial Chronicle. Hunt's Merchants' Magazine* had been a monthly; its successor was a weekly.

[6] *Civilized America* (London, 1859), Vol. II, p. 320; see, however, the writer's misgivings, expressed in the same passage.

The increasing speed of business communication, the publishers explained in the last issue of the older journal, had made that kind of business monthly out of date.[7] Its successor was also intelligently edited, but such nods as it gave to literature were few and far between.

The more thoroughly business dominated American society, the less it felt the need to justify its existence by reference to values outside its own domain. In earlier days it had looked for sanction in the claim that the vigorous pursuit of trade served God, and later that it served character and culture. Although this argument did not disappear, it grew less conspicuous in the business rationale. As business became the dominant motif in American life and as a vast material empire rose in the New World, business increasingly looked for legitimation in a purely material and internal criterion—the wealth it produced. American business, once defended on the ground that it produced a high standard of culture, was now defended mainly on the ground that it produced a high standard of living.[8] Few businessmen would have hesitated to say that the advancement of material prosperity, if not

[7] *Hunt's Merchants' Magazine,* Vol. LXIII, pp. 401–3. A cultural history of the business magazines might be illuminating. The first article in the first issue of *Hunt's Merchants' Magazine* was entitled "Commerce as Connected with the Progress of Civilization," Vol. I (July, 1839), pp. 3–20; it was written by Daniel D. Barnard, an Albany lawyer and politician who also wrote historical brochures and who later became minister to Prussia. Barnard's essay dwelt on "the humanizing advantages of a growing and extended commerce." Cf. Philip Hone: "Commerce and Commercial Character," Vol. IV (February, 1841), pp. 129–46. Another writer in the opening volume, to be sure, made note of "an opinion [that] very generally prevails among the mercantile classes of the present day, that commerce and literature are at war with each other; that he who is engaged in the pursuit of the one must entirely abandon the pursuit of the other." This writer announced his intention to confute this view and his confidence that "more liberal views . . . are fast growing upon the public mind." "Commerce and Literature," Vol. I (December, 1839), p. 537. This confidence seems hardly justified by the trend in the cultural fare of *Hunt's* itself, which grew thinner during the 1850's. One must, no doubt, be careful not to assume too readily from such evidence that the cultural interests of businessmen were declining. What does seem to be true, however, is that for these men, *in their character as businessmen,* cultural interests no longer seemed so vital; nor did it seem any longer so important to vindicate business by reference to its civilizing influence.

[8] Francis X. Sutton, et al., in their study of *The American Business Creed* find material productivity a dominant theme; see chapter 2 and pp. 255–6. In so far as non-material values are advanced by business, they are the values of "service," personal opportunity, and political and economic freedom. Some businessmen are disposed to argue that success is sufficient justification for more or less complete neglect of "self-improvement." Ibid., p. 276. Small businessmen, though expressing a special proprietorship in freedom and democracy, along with a resentment of big business, seem to have absorbed the general business emphasis on material productivity as a central vindication. See John H. Bunzel: *The American Small Businessman* (New York, 1962), chapter 3.

itself a kind of moral ideal, was at least the presupposition of all other moral ideals. In 1888 the railroad executive, Charles Elliott Perkins, asked: [9]

> Have not great merchants, great manufacturers, great inventors, done more for the world than preachers and philanthropists? . . . Can there be any doubt that cheapening the cost of necessaries and conveniences of life is the most powerful agent of civilization and progress? Does not the fact that well-fed and well-warmed men make better citizens, other things being equal, than those who are cold and hungry, answer the question? Poverty is the cause of most of the crime and misery in the world—cheapening the cost of the necessaries and conveniences of life is lessening poverty, and there is no other way to lessen it, absolutely none. History and experience demonstrate that as wealth has accumulated and things have cheapened, men have improved . . . in their habits of thought, their sympathy for others, their ideas of justice as well as of mercy. . . . Material progress must come first and . . . upon it is founded all other progress.

Almost a century and a half after Franklin had considered the material foundations of cultural progress to have been established, the necessity of the material prerequisites was thus being asserted with greater confidence than ever.

[9] Edward C. Kirkland: *Dream and Thought in the Business Community, 1860–1900,* p. 164–5. This conservative economic materialism has its curious parallel today in the thought of radical apologists for dictatorships in backward countries. Let poverty, misery, and illiteracy be conquered, it is held, and the goods of political freedom and cultural development will follow soon enough. This argument was commonly invoked in defense of the Soviet Union in the Stalinist period, and one hears it again today from apologists for Fidel Castro and others.

CHAPTER X

Self-Help
and Spiritual Technology

❦

· 1 ·

As the mercantile ideal declined, it was replaced by the ideal of the self-made man, an ideal which reflected the experiences and aspirations of countless village boys who had become, if not millionaires, at least substantial men of business. Modern students of social mobility have made it incontestably clear that the legendary American rags-to-riches story, despite the spectacular instances that adorn our business annals, was more important as a myth and a symbol than as a statistical actuality.[1] The topmost positions in American industry, even in the most hectic days of nineteenth-century expansion, were held for the most part by men who had begun life with decided advantages. But there were enough self-made men, and their rise was dramatic and appealing enough, to give substance to the myth. And, quite aside from the topmost positions, there were intermediate positions, representing success of a substantial kind; only a few could realistically hope to be a Vanderbilt or a Rockefeller, but many could in a smaller way imitate their success. If life was not a movement from rags to riches, it could at least be from rags to respectability; and the horizons of experience were scanned eagerly for clues as to how this transformation could be accomplished.

---

[1] For a summary and evaluation of the now considerable literature on social mobility in American history, see Bernard Barber: *Social Stratification* (New York, 1957), chapter 16; Joseph A. Kahl: *The American Class Structure* (New York, 1957), chapter 9; Seymour M. Lipset and Reinhard Bendix: *Social Mobility in Industrial Society* (Berkeley, 1959), chapter 3.

Moreover, if the self-made men of America were not self-made in the sense that most of them had started in poverty, they were largely self-made in that their business successes were achieved without the benefits of formal learning or careful breeding. Ideally, the self-made man is one whose success does not depend on formal education and for whom personal culture, other than in his business character, is unimportant. By mid-century, men of this sort had come so clearly to dominate the American scene that their way of life cried out for spokesmen. Timothy Shay Arthur, the Philadelphia scribbler who is best known to history as the author of *Ten Nights in a Barroom and What I Saw There,* but who was also well known in his day as a moralist and self-help writer, pointed out in 1856 that "in this country, the most prominent and efficient men are not those who were born to wealth and eminent social positions, but those who have won both by the force of untiring personal energy." To them, Arthur insisted, the country was indebted for its prosperity.[2]

Invaluable, therefore, are the lives of such men to the rising generation. . . . Hitherto, American Biography has confined itself too closely to men who have won political or literary distinction. . . . Limited to the perusal of such biographies, our youth must, of necessity, receive erroneous impressions of the true construction of our society, and fail to perceive wherein the progressive vigor of the nation lies. . . . We want the histories of our self-made man spread out before us, that we may know the ways by which they came up from the ranks of the people.

The idea of the self-made man was not new. It was a historical outgrowth of Puritan preachings and of the Protestant doctrine of the calling. Benjamin Franklin had preached it, but it is significant that his own later life was not lived in accordance with his catchpenny maxims. After making a modest fortune, he was absorbed into the intellectual and social life of Philadelphia, London, and Paris, and interested himself more in politics, diplomacy, and science than in business. The self-made man as a characteristic American type became a conspicuous figure early in the nineteenth century. Apparently the

---

[2] Quoted in Freeman Hunt: *Worth and Wealth* (New York, 1856), pp. 350–1. Only a few years earlier the London *Daily News* remarked: "It is time that the *millionaire* should cease to be ashamed of having made his own fortune. It is time that *parvenu* should be looked on as a word of honor." Sigmund Diamond: *The Reputation of the American Businessman* (Cambridge, Mass., 1955), p. 2.

term was first used by Henry Clay in 1832, in a Senate speech on a protective tariff. Denying that the tariff would give rise to a hereditary industrial aristocracy, he maintained, to the contrary, that nothing could be more democratic; it would give further opportunities for men to rise from obscurity to affluence. "In Kentucky, almost every manufactory known to me is in the hands of enterprising and self-made men, who have acquired whatever wealth they possess by patient and diligent labor."[3] By the time of Clay's death thirty years later, the type was more than recognizable, it was spiritually dominant.

I say spiritually without ironic intent. Irvin G. Wyllie, in his illuminating study, *The Self-Made Man in America,* points out that the literature of self-help was not a literature of business methods or techniques; it did not deal with production, accounting, engineering, advertising, or investments; it dealt with the development of character, and nowhere were its Protestant origins more manifest. Not surprisingly, clergymen were prominent among the self-help writers, and especially Congregational clergymen.[4] Self-help was discipline in character. The self-help literature told how to marshal the resources of the *will*—how to cultivate the habits of frugality and hard work and the virtues of perseverance and sobriety. The writers of self-help books imagined that poverty in early life was actually a kind of asset, because its discipline helped to produce the type of character that would succeed.

The conception of character advocated by the self-help writers and the self-made men explicitly excluded what they loosely called genius. No doubt there was a certain underlying ambivalence in this—who does not desire or envy "genius"? But the prevailing assumption in the self-help literature was that character was necessary and remarkable talents were not; still more, that those who began by having such talents would lack the incentive or the ability to develop character. The average man, by intensifying his good qualities, by applying common sense to a high degree, could have the equivalent of genius, or something much better. "There is no genius required," said one New York merchant. "And if there were, some great men have said that genius is no more than common-sense intensified." Reliance on outstanding gifts would lead to laziness and lack of discipline or responsibility. "Genius" was vain and frivolous. Speaking on this subject

[3] Daniel Mallory, ed.: *The Life and Speeches of the Hon. Henry Clay* (New York, 1844), Vol. II, p. 31.

[4] Wyllie: *The Self-Made Man in America* (New Brunswick, New Jersey, 1954), chapters 3 and 4.

to an audience of young men in 1844, Henry Ward Beecher re-marked: [5]

> So far as my observations have ascertained the species, they abound in academies, colleges, and Thespian societies; in village debating clubs; in coteries of young artists and young professional aspirants. They are to be known by a reserved air, excessive sensitiveness, and utter indolence; by very long hair, and very open shirt collars; by the reading of much wretched poetry, and the writing of much, yet more wretched; by being very conceited, very affected, very disagreeable, and very useless:—beings whom no man wants for friend, pupil, or companion.

Through the decades, this suspicion of genius or brilliance rooted itself into the canons of business. Eighty years after Beecher's characterization of genius, an article appeared in the *American Magazine* under the title, "Why I Never Hire Brilliant Men." The writer identified brilliance in business with mercurial temperament, neuroticism, and irresponsibility; his experience as an entrepreneur with men of this type had been disastrous. "Even fine material, carelessly put together, will not make a fine shoe," he remarked. "But if material which is of just average quality is fashioned with special care and attention, it will result in a quite superior article." "So I took most of my raw material from our delivery wagons, or other places right at hand. Out of this hard-muscled, hard-headed stuff I have built a business that has made me rich according to the standards of our locality." Somewhat defensively, the writer anticipated that he might be considered simply a mediocre man without the capacity to appreciate anyone better than himself. This judgment might well be justified, he said candidly,[6]

> for I *am* mediocre. But . . . business and life are built upon successful mediocrity; and victory comes to companies not through the employment of brilliant men, but through knowing how to get the most out of ordinary folks. . . .
>
> I am sorry to forego the company of [brilliant] men in my rather dingy building here in the wholesale grocery district. But I comfort myself with the thought that Cromwell built the finest army in Europe out of dull but enthusiastic yeomen; and that the greatest

[5] Ibid., pp. 35–6.
[6] Anon.: "Why I Never Hire Brilliant Men," *American Magazine*, Vol. XCVII (February, 1924), pp. 12, 118, 122.

organization in human history was twelve humble men, picked up along the shores of an inland lake.

With all this there went a persistent hostility to formal education and a countervailing cult of experience. The canons of the cult of experience required that the ambitious young man be exposed at the earliest possible moment to what one writer called "the discipline of daily life that comes with drudgery." Formal schooling, especially if prolonged, would only delay such exposure. The lumber magnate, Frederick Weyerhaeuser, concluded that the college man was "apt to think that because he is a college graduate he ought not be obliged to commence at the bottom of the ladder and work up, as the office boy does who enters the office when he is fourteen years of age." [7] It must be said that here the writers of self-help books disagreed with the businessmen: they usually advised more formal schooling, but this part of their prescription was not convincing to the self-made man of business. In the ranks of business, opinion on free common schools was divided between those who felt that such schools would create a more efficient and disciplined working class and those who balked at taxes or believed that education would only make workers discontented.[8]

On two matters there was almost no disagreement: education should be more "practical"; and higher education, as least as it was conceived in the old-time American classical college, was useless as a background for business. Business waged a long, and on the whole successful, campaign for vocational and trade education at the high-school level and did much to undermine the high school as a center of liberal education. The position of the Massachusetts wool manufacturer who said that he preferred workers with only a common-school education, since he considered that the more learned were only preparing themselves for Congress, and who rejected educated workmen on the ground that he could not run his mill with algebra, was in no way unusual or extreme; nor was the argument of the industrial publicist Henry Carey Baird, the founder of the first publishing firm in America specializing in technical and industrial books. "Too much education of a certain sort," he protested in 1885,[9]

[7] Charles F. Thwing: "College Training and the Business Man," *North American Review,* Vol. CLXVII (October, 1903), p. 599.

[8] On attitudes toward education, see Wyllie: op. cit., chapter 6; Kirkland: *Dream and Thought in the Business Community, 1860–1900* (Ithaca, New York, 1956), chapters 3 and 4; Merle Curti: *The Social Ideas of American Educators* (New York, 1935), chapter 6.

[9] Kirkland: op. cit., pp. 69–70.

such as Greek, Latin, French, German, and especially bookkeeping, to a person of humble antecedents, is utterly demoralizing in nine cases out of ten, and is productive of an army of mean-spirited "gentlemen" who are above what is called a "trade" and who are only content to follow some such occupation as that of standing behind a counter, and selling silks, gloves, bobbins, or laces, or to "keep books." . . . Our system of education, as furnished by law, when it goes beyond what in Pennsylvania is called a grammar school, is vicious in the extreme—productive of more evil than good. Were the power lodged with me, no boy or girl should be educated at the public expense beyond what he or she could obtain at a grammar school, except for some useful occupation. "The high school" of today must, as I believe, under an enlightened system, be supplanted by *the technical school,* with possibly "shops" connected with it. . . . We are manufacturing too many "gentlemen" and "ladies," so called, and demoralization is the result.

The extension of classical and liberal studies through the college years was often considered even worse than academic schooling at the high-school level, because it prolonged the youth's exposure to futile studies and heightened his appetite for elegant leisure. One businessman rejoiced that his son's failure in college-entrance examinations had spared the boy all this. "Whenever I find a rich man dying and leaving a large amount of money to found a college, I say to myself, 'It is a pity he had not died while he was poor.' " [1]

Fortunately, many influential businessmen did not wholly share this attitude. Old Cornelius Vanderbilt was often considered the acme of self-satisfied ignorance, and the story is told that when a friend reported to him Lord Palmerston's remark that it was too bad that a man of his ability had not had the advantages of formal education, Vanderbilt replied: "You tell Lord Palmerston from me that if I had learned education I would not have had time to learn anything else." None the less, Vanderbilt's wealth had brought him into a society in which his lack of culture was a staggering handicap (he is reported to have read one book in his life, *Pilgrim's Progress,* and that at an advanced age). "Folks may say that I don't care about education," he confessed to his clergyman, "but I do. I've been to England, and seen them lords and other fellows, and knew that I had twice as much

[1] *Ibid.,* p. 101.

brains as they had maybe, and yet I had to keep still, and couldn't say anything through fear of exposing myself." When his son-in-law entered the room in time to catch this remark, and chided the Commodore for having at last made such an admission, Vanderbilt beat a retreat: "I seem to get along better than half of your educated men." Still, he had said to his minister: "I'd give a million dollars today, Doctor, if I had your education"; and in the end precisely this magnificent sum was extracted from him for the support of what became Vanderbilt University.[2]

Andrew Carnegie, it is reported, once saw the older and much richer Vanderbilt on the opposite side of Fifth Avenue, and mumbled to his companion: "I would not exchange his millions for my knowledge of Shakespeare." [3] But Carnegie shared, at a higher level, the mixture of feelings about education that Vanderbilt had shown. "Liberal education," he once wrote, "gives a man who really absorbs it higher tastes and aims than the acquisition of wealth, and a world to enjoy, into which the mere millionaire cannot enter; to find therefore that it is not the best training for business is to prove its claim to a higher domain." [4] Carnegie's munificent gifts to education and his evident pleasure in the company of intellectuals protect him from the charge that such utterances were hypocritical. And yet he took delight in demonstrating how useless higher education was in business; much as he praised "liberal education," he had nothing but contempt for the prevailing liberal education in American colleges. He enjoyed reciting the names of other successful men who had gone through a tough apprenticeship like his own, and in recording the evidences of the superiority of non-college men to college men in business. "College education as it exists seems almost fatal to success in that domain," he wrote.[5] On the classical college curriculum he was unsparing. It was a thing on which men "wasted their precious years trying to extract education from an ignorant past whose chief province is to teach us, not what to adopt, but what to avoid." Men had sent their sons to colleges "to waste their energies upon obtaining a knowledge of such languages as Greek and Latin, which are of no more practical use to them than Choctaw" and where they were "crammed with the details

[2] W. A. Croffut: *The Vanderbilts and the Story of Their Fortune* (Chicago and New York, 1886), pp. 137–8.

[3] Burton J. Hendrick: *The Life of Andrew Carnegie* (New York, 1932), Vol. I, p. 60.

[4] *The Empire of Business* (New York, 1902), p. 113.

[5] Wyllie: op. cit., pp. 96–104.

of petty and insignificant skirmishes between savages." Their education
only imbued them with false ideas and gave them "a distaste for
practical life." "Had they gone into active work during the years spent
at college they would have been better educated men in every true
sense of that term." [6] Leland Stanford was another educational philan-
thropist who had no faith in existing education. Of all the applicants
for jobs who came to him from the East, the most helpless, he said,
were college men. Asked what they could do, they would say "anything," while in fact they had "no definite technical knowledge of
anything," and no clear aim or purpose. He hoped that the university
he endowed would overcome this by offering "a practical, not a
theoretical education." [7]

One must, of course, be careful about the conclusions one draws
from anyone's dislike of the classical curriculum as it was taught in the
old college; many men of high intellectual distinction shared this feeling. The old college tried to preserve the Western cultural heritage
and to inculcate a respectable form of mental discipline, but it was
hardly dedicated to the vigorous advancement of critical intellect.
The rapid advancement of scientific knowledge, the inflexibility of the
old curriculum in the hands of its most determined custodians, and the
dismal pedagogy that all too often prevailed in the classical college,
did more to undermine the teaching of classics than the disdain of
businessmen. To the credit of men like Carnegie, Rockefeller, Stanford, Vanderbilt, Johns Hopkins, and other millionaires, it must be
added that their support made possible the revamping of the old-time
college and the creation of universities in the United States. But if one
looks closely into business pronouncements on education, one finds a
rhetoric which reveals a contempt for the reflective mind, for culture,
and for the past.

· 2 ·

Around the turn of the century the attitudes of businessmen toward
formal education as a background for business success underwent a
conspicuous change. The rapid development of large-scale business in
the last two decades of the nineteenth century had made the characteristic big-business career a bureaucratic career. By their very success the self-made men rapidly made their own type obsolete. How-

[6] *The Empire of Business*, pp. 79–81; cf. pp. 145–7.
[7] Kirkland: op. cit., pp. 93–4.

ever reluctantly, men began to see that the ideal of the uneducated self-made man, especially in the most desirable business positions, was coming to have less and less reality. Formal education, it had to be admitted, was a distinct asset for the more stable careers now being followed in bureaucratic businesses: the need for engineering, accountancy, economics, and law grew from the changes in business organization itself. Hence, although the "school of experience" and the "college of hard knocks" still kept their nostalgic appeal for business spokesmen, the need for formally inculcated skills had to be recognized. "The day has quite gone by," the *Commercial and Financial Chronicle* recognized in 1916, "when it is sufficient for a young man to begin at the bottom and, without more training than he can gather in the daily routine, to grow up to be something more than a manager of an existing concern, or to acquire that breadth of knowledge and completeness of training which are necessary if he is to be fitted to compete with the expert young business men produced in other countries." The steel magnate, Elbert H. Gary, considered that the more the businessman knew "of that which is taught in schools, colleges and universities of a general character, the better it will be for him in commencing business." [8]

This new acceptance of education was reflected in the background of men who stood at the helm of the great corporations. The generation of corporation executives that flourished from 1900 to 1910 was only slightly better educated than the generation of the 1870's.[9] But the rising young executives of the first decade of the new century were being recruited out of the colleges. In Mabel Newcomer's sample of top business executives, 39.4 per cent of those chosen from 1900 had some college education; but in 1925 this figure rose to 51.4 per cent and in 1950 to 75.6 per cent.[1] In 1950, about one of every five execu-

[8] Wyllie: op. cit., p. 113; see pp. 107–15 for a good brief account of changing business attitudes toward education after 1890.

[9] See Frances W. Gregory and Irene D. Neu: "The American Industrial Elite in the 1870's: Their Social Origins," in William Miller, ed.: *Men in Business* (Cambridge, Mass., 1952), p. 203, comparing the generation of the 1870's with that of 1901–1910 encompassed by William Miller in "American Historians and the Business Elite," *The Journal of Economic History*, Vol. IX (November, 1949), pp. 184–208. In the 1870's, 37 per cent of the executives had some college training; in 1901–1910, 41 per cent had. On the emergence of the bureaucratic business career, see Miller's essay: "The Business Elite in Business Bureaucracies," in *Men in Business*, pp. 286–305.

[1] Mabel Newcomer: *The Big Business Executive* (New York, 1955), p. 69. In 1950, the author concludes (p. 77), "it is accepted that the college degree is the ticket of admission to a successful career with the large corporation, even though the initial employment for the college graduate may be manual labor." Joseph A.

tives had also had some training in a graduate school (mainly in law or engineering).

Although these figures show that the once cherished model of the self-made man was being relinquished, they cannot be taken as showing a rise in esteem for the liberal arts. The colleges themselves, under the elective system, became more vocational. In the nineteenth century, when the well-to-do sent their sons to college, it was a fair assumption that they were sending them not for vocational training but out of a regard both for intellectual discipline and for social advantages (the two are not always easily distinguishable). In the twentieth century, they may send them, rather, for the gains measurable in cold cash which are supposedly attainable through vocational training. (Among male college graduates in 1954–55, the largest single group was majoring in business and commerce; they outnumbered the men in the basic sciences and the liberal arts put together.) [2]

A sign of the increasing vocational character of American higher education was the emergence of both undergraduate and graduate schools of business. The first of these was the Wharton School at the University of Pennsylvania, founded in 1881; the second was founded at the University of Chicago eighteen years later. There followed an efflorescence of such schools between 1900 and 1914. The early business schools were caught between the hostility of the academic faculties and the lingering suspicion of businessmen, who were sometimes still inclined to doubt that any kind of academic training, even that acquired in a business school, could be of practical use. Like almost every other kind of educational institution in America, the business schools quickly became heterogeneous in the quality of their faculties and students and in the degree to which they included the liberal arts in their curriculums. Thorstein Veblen dealt scathingly with these "keepers of the higher business animus," suggesting mischievously that they were on a par with the divinity schools in that both were equally extraneous to the intellectual enterprise which is the true end of the

Kahl has suggestively remarked in his study of *The American Class Structure*, p. 93, that "if one should demand a single oversimplified distinction underlying class differences in contemporary America to replace the outworn one of Marx, the answer would be this: the possession of a college degree."

Employers sometimes still show a certain ceremonial loyalty to the ideal of the self-made man by putting a new employee, clearly destined for an executive position, through a quick ascending series of minor posts. This is called learning the business from the bottom up, and is especially recommended for the sons or sons-in-law of high executives.

[2] William H. Whyte, Jr.: *The Organization Man* (Anchor ed., 1956), p. 88.

university. Abraham Flexner, acknowledging in his famous survey of the universities that business-school faculties sometimes recruited distinguished men, considered their heavily vocational curriculums to be in the main beneath the dignity of the academic enterprise.[3] Within the universities, business schools were often non-intellectual and at times anti-intellectual centers dedicated to a rigidly conservative set of ideas. When Dean Wallace Donham of the Harvard Graduate School of Business suggested to one such school in the Middle West that it offer a course on the problems of trade unionism, he was told: "We don't want our students to pay any attention to anything that might raise questions about management or business policy in their minds." [4]

The condition of American business today, as it is reflected in William H. Whyte's celebrated study of the social and cultural aspects of large business organization, displays a pattern recognizably similar to that of the past. Gone is the self-made man, of course. He may be cherished as a mythological figure useful in the primitive propaganda battles of politics, but every sensible businessman knows that in the actual recruitment and training of big business personnel it is the bureaucratic career that matters. Yet in this recruitment and training the tradition of business anti-intellectualism, quickened by the self-made ideal, remains very much alive. It no longer takes the form of ridiculing the value of college or other formal education in preparation for business, but of selective recruiting governed by narrow vocational principles. Here it is important to note, as Whyte does, that top business executives do not characteristically defend these vocational principles. When they make pronouncements on the subject, at commencement exercises or elsewhere, they usually speak of the importance of liberal education, broad training, and imaginative statecraft in the business world. There is little reason to doubt their sincerity. Most of them, although they are enormously hard-working and too preoccupied to keep their own general culture very much alive, are better educated than their subordinates, and they are disposed to lament mildly their own intellectual stagnation. They have begun to organize arts courses for their junior executives and to sponsor meetings be-

[3] Thorstein Veblen: *The Higher Learning in America* (New York, 1918), p. 204; Abraham Flexner: *Universities: American, English, German* (New York, 1930), pp. 162–72.

[4] Peter F. Drucker: "The Graduate Business School," *Fortune*, Vol. XLII (August, 1950), p. 116. For a general account of these schools and their problems, see L. C. Marshall, ed.: *The Collegiate School of Business* (Chicago, 1928); and Frank C. Pierson et. al.: *The Education of American Businessmen: A Study of University-College Programs in Business Administration* (New York, 1959).

tween intellectuals and businessmen. In this way, the old mercantile regard for culture as a sanction for business life is beginning to be revived. However, the news about their concern for the liberally educated man does not seem to filter down to the ranks of the personnel men who turn up each year on the college campuses to recruit talent. At this point of leverage, the overwhelming pressure of business on American higher education is severely vocational.

The preference for vocationalism is linked to a preference for character—or personality—over mind, and for conformity and manipulative facility over individuality and talent. "We used to look primarily for brilliance," said one president, who must have been speaking of the past history of an idiosyncratic firm. "Now that much-abused word 'character' has become very important. We don't care if you're a Phi Beta Kappa or a Tau Beta Phi. We want a well-rounded person who can handle well-rounded people." A personnel manager reports that "any progressive employer would look askance at the individualist and would be reluctant to instill such thinking in the minds of trainees." A trainee agrees: "I would sacrifice brilliance for human understanding every time." Mr. Whyte tells us, in a chapter entitled "The Fight against Genius," that even in the field of industrial science this code prevails; that industrial scientists are shackled by the commitment to applied knowledge; that a famous chemical company's documentary film, made to recruit scientists for the firm, shows three of its research men conferring in a laboratory while the narrator announces: "No geniuses here; just a bunch of average Americans working together"; that the creativity of industrial scientists is pathetically low as compared with that of the men in the universities; and that when the word *brilliant* appears, it is commonly coupled with such words as *erratic, eccentric, introvert,* and *screwball.*[5]

· 3 ·

As late nineteenth-century America became more secular, traditional religion became infused with, and in the end to some degree displaced by, a curious cult of religious practicality. If we are to accept the evidence of a long history of best-selling handbooks, from Russell H. Conwell's "Acres of Diamonds" to the works of Norman Vincent Peale, this cult has had millions of devotees. It has become, by all internal evidence and everything we know about its readership, one

[5] Ibid., pp. 150, 152, 227–8, 233, 235, and chapter 16 *passim.*

of the leading faiths of the American middle class. It is, as I hope to show, a rather drastically altered descendant of the older self-help literature, but it affords, in any case, striking evidence of the broad diffusion in American society of the practical motif. Modern inspirational literature takes its stand firmly with the world: what it has to offer is practical. *"Christianity,"* writes Norman Vincent Peale, *"is entirely practical.* It is astounding how defeated persons can be changed into victorious individuals when they actually utilize their religious faith as a workable instrument." [6]

The literature of inspiration is of course by no means confined to America; it flourishes wherever the passion for personal advancement has become so intense that the difference between this motive and religious faith has been obscured. There has always been in Christian civilization a conviction that the world of business and that of religion must somehow be related, if only through their hostility or tension, since both have to do with morals, character, and discipline. At first, the negative relation was most clear: medieval prohibitions or limitations on usury expressed the conviction that it was a part of the task of the Church in the world to restrain economic exploitation. Later, the Puritan doctrine of the calling suggested another more positive relationship: diligence in business was one of the ways of serving God. Success or failure in business might then be a clue as to an individual's spiritual condition. But over the years this relationship gradually became reversed. The distinction between service to God and service to self broke down. Whereas business had been an instrument in religious discipline, one of the various means of serving God, religious discipline now became an instrument in business, a way of using God to a worldly end. And whereas men had once been able to take heart from business success as a sign that they had been saved, they now took salvation as a thing to be achieved in this life by an effort of will, as something that would bring with it success in the pursuit of worldly goals. Religion is something to be *used.* Mr. Peale tells his readers that his work demonstrates "a simple, workable technique of thinking and acting." It "emphasizes scientific spiritual principles which have been demonstrated in the laboratory of personal experience." "The best place to get a new and workable idea for your business is in the type of church service described in this chapter." "If you will practice faith, you can be healed of ill-will, inferiority, fear, guilt, or any other block which impedes the flow of recreative energy.

[6] *A Guide to Confident Living* (New York, 1948), p. 55.

Power and efficiency are available to you if you will believe." [7] As H. Richard Niebuhr has remarked, there is a strain in modern American theology which "tends to define religion in terms of adjustment to divine reality for the sake of gaining power rather than in terms of revelation which subjects the recipient to the criticism of that which is revealed." The consequence is that "man remains the center of religion and God is his aid rather than his judge and redeemer." [8]

The older self-help literature, whatever its faults, had some organic relation both to the world of affairs and to the religious life. It assumed that business success is to a very large degree the result of character, and that character is formed by piety. It was in this way a natural, if intellectually simple, response to the historical convergence of Protestant moral imperatives, the doctrines of classical economics, and a fluid, open society. American society, as most modern studies of the subject show, is still fluid; but the conditions of success have changed: success now seems more intimately related to the ability to seize upon formal training than it does to the peculiar constellation of character traits that figured so prominently in the old self-help books. An early nineteenth-century businessman, queried as to what "discipline" made for success, might well have answered: "The discipline of poverty and the school of hard knocks," or "The discipline of frugality and industriousness." The modern businessman, faced with the same query, is likely to answer: "Well, law is excellent, but engineering is pretty good too."

Modern inspirational literature builds upon the old self-help tradition and bears a general resemblance to it, but it also has major differences. In the old self-help system, faith led to character and character to a successful manipulation of the world; in the new system, faith leads directly to a capacity for self-manipulation, which is believed to be the key to health, wealth, popularity, or peace of mind. On the surface, this may seem to indicate a turning away from the secular goals of the older self-help books, but it actually represents a turning away from their grasp of reality, for it embodies a blurring of the distinction between the realms of the world and the spirit. In the old literature these realms interacted; in the new they become vaguely fused. The process represents, I believe, not a victory for religion but a fundamental, if largely unconscious, secularization of the American

[7] Ibid., pp. viii, 14, 108, 148, 165.
[8] "Religious Realism in the Twentieth Century," in D. C. Macintosh, ed.: *Religious Realism* (New York, 1931), pp. 425-6.

middle-class mind. Religion has been supplanted, not, to be sure, by a consciously secular philosophy, but by mental self-manipulation, by a kind of faith in magic. Both religion and the sense of worldly reality suffer. It is easy to believe that rising young businessmen actually turned to the old self-help literature for a kind of rough guidance to the requisites of the business world, however little actual help they may have got. Today the inspirational literature seems to be read mainly by "defeated persons," to use Peale's words, and not as much by men as by women, who, though affected by the practical code of business, do not actually enter business life.

It is what Raymond Fosdick calls "power for daily living" that the success writers purport to give. In the nineteenth century the primary promise of success writers was that religion would bring wealth. Since the early 1930's there has been a growing emphasis on the promise of of mental or physical health; inspirational writing has been infused with safe borrowings from psychiatry and has taken on a faint coloration from the existential anxieties of the past twenty years. Although success literature has given way to a literature of inspiration, its goals largely remain everyday practical goals. For more than a generation, the metaphorical language of this writing has been infiltrated and coarsened by terms taken from business, technology, and advertising; one often gets the sense that the spiritual life can be promoted by good copy and achieved like technological progress by systematic progressive means. Louis Schneider and Sanford M. Dornbusch, in their illuminating study of the themes of inspirational books, have spoken of this as "spiritual technology." [9] One success writer tells us that "God is a twenty-four-hour station. All you need to do is to plug in." Another that "religious practice is an exact science that . . . follows spiritual laws as truly as radio follows its laws." Another that "high octane thinking means Power and Performance" and that readers should "plug into the Power House." Another that "the body is . . . a receiving set for the catching of messages from the Broadcasting Station of God" and that "the greatest of Engineers . . . is your silent partner." Another that the railroad "saves money by having a Christian hand on the throttle." Another exhorts readers to "open every pore of your being to the health of God." Another relates that a Sinclair gasoline ad provided "the idea for a sermon about the unused power in our souls." Bruce

[9] *Popular Religion: Inspirational Books in America* (Chicago, 1958), pp. 16–4; the quotations in this paragraph may be found on pp. 1, 6, 7, 44, 51n., 58, 61n., 63, 90, 91n., 106, 107.

Barton, in his ineffable book, *The Man Nobody Knows,* remarked that Jesus "picked up twelve men from the bottom ranks of business and forged them into an organization that conquered the world." "Conduct the affairs of your soul in a businesslike way," exhorts Emmet Fox. Prayer is conceived as a usable instrument. "A man," says Glenn Clark, "who learns and practices the laws of prayer correctly should be able to play golf better, do business better, work better, love better, serve better." "Learn to pray correctly, scientifically," commands Norman Vincent Peale. "Employ tested and proven methods. Avoid slipshod praying."

One of the striking things that has occurred in the inspirational literature is that the voluntaristic and subjective impulses which I noted in commenting on the development of American Protestantism seem to have come into complete possession and to have run wild. There has been a progressive attenuation of the components of religion. Protestantism at an early point got rid of the bulk of religious ritual, and in the course of its development in the nineteenth and twentieth centuries went very far to minimize doctrine. The inspirational cult has completed this process, for it has largely eliminated doctrine—at least it has eliminated most doctrine that could be called Christian. Nothing, then, is left but the subjective experience of the individual, and even this is reduced in the main to an assertion of his will. What the inspirational writers mean when they say you can accomplish whatever you wish by taking thought is that you can will your goals and mobilize God to help you release fabulous energies. Fabulous indeed they are: "There is enough power in *you,*" says Norman Vincent Peale in an alarming passage, "to blow the city of New York to rubble. That, and nothing less, is what advanced physics tells us." Faith can release these forces, and then one can overcome any obstacle. Faith is not a way of reconciling man to his fate: it "puts fight into a man so that he develops a terrific resistance to defeat." [1]

Horatio W. Dresser, discussing one of the earlier manifestations of inspirational thinking, the New Thought movement, once remarked that "the tendency of the New Thought . . . has been to make light of the intellect and of 'the objective mind,' as if it were undesirable to become intellectual and as if one could have whatever one wishes by 'sending out a requisition into the great subconscious.' " [2] In the main, however, the anti-intellectualism of the inspirational cults has been

[1] *A Guide to Confident Living,* pp. 46, 55.
[2] *Handbook of the New Thought* (New York, 1917), pp. 122–3.

indirect: they represent a withdrawal from reality, a repudiation of all philosophies whose business is an engagement with real problems. At the same time, they manifest a paradoxical secularization. Although professing Christians and ministers of the gospel are proud of having written successful inspirational books, the books themselves are likely to strike even secular intellectuals as blasphemous. The religious inheritance of the West seems more in the custody of such intellectuals than in the custody of these hearty advocates of the "utilization" of religion.

The confusion between religion and self-advancement is perhaps most aptly embodied in the title of Henry C. Link's remarkable book, *The Return to Religion,* a best-seller from 1936 to 1941. I do not think that this singular work could be regarded as entirely representative of inspirational literature, but it deserves special notice here, for it is possibly the most consummate manual of philistinism and conformity ever written in America. Despite its title, it is in no sense a religious or devotional work. Written by a consulting psychologist and personnel adviser to large business corporations, who reports that he found his way back to religion by way of science, this book views religion as "an aggressive mode of life by which the individual becomes the master of his environment, not its complacent victim." [3] The author feels obliged to wage a running battle against both individuality and mind in the interests of the will to conformity.

The issue is not put quite this way. Link's basic polar terms are introversion and extroversion (used in the popular, not the Jungian sense). Introversion, which involves withdrawal, self-examination, individuality, and reflection, is bad. It is in fact merely selfish. For the Socratic maxim, "Know thyself," Link would substitute the injunction, "Behave yourself," because "a good personality or character is achieved by practice, not by introspection." On the other hand, extroversion, which involves sociability, amiability, and service to others, is unselfish and good. Jesus was a great extrovert. One of the functions of religion —and it would appear that Link considers it the main function—is to discipline the personality by developing extroversion. Link goes to church, he reports, "because I hate to go and because I know that it will do me good." Church attendance builds better personalities. So do bridge-playing and dancing and salesmanship—they bring the individ-

---

[3] Quotations in this and the following paragraphs are in *The Return to Religion* (1936; Pocket Book ed., 1943), pp. 9, 12, 14, 17, 19, 35, 44–5, 54–61, 67, 69, 71, 73, 78–9, 115–16, 147–9, 157.

ual into contact with others whom he must please. The important thing for the individual is to get away from self-analysis and do work which will give him power over things. This, in turn, will lead to power over people, which will heighten self-confidence.

For all these purposes, the critical mind is a liability. In college it is the intellectuals, the analytical students, who lose their religion; in later life it is thoughtful men who become excessively withdrawn. In a chapter entitled "Fools of Reason," Link argues that intellect and rationality are commonly overvalued.

> Reason is not an end in itself but a tool for the individual to use in adjusting himself to the values and purposes of living which are beyond reason. *Just as the teeth are intended to chew with, not to chew themselves, so the mind is intended to think with, not to worry about. The mind is an instrument to live with, not to live for.*

To believe and act on faith is central. Although religion has been called the refuge of weak minds, the real weakness "lies rather in the failure of minds to recognize the weakness of all minds." "Agnosticism is an intellectual disease, and faith in fallacies is better than no faith at all . . . foolish beliefs are better than no beliefs at all." Even palmistry leads to holding other people's hands, phrenology to studying their heads—and "all such beliefs take the individual out of himself and propel him into a world of greater interests." Anyway, "the idolatry of reason and the intellectual scorn of religion" has left men prey to quackery and pseudo-science and political panaceas. In America there is an unfortunate national tendency to introversion, which, among other things, causes people to shirk their responsibility for the unemployed and to imagine that the federal government should do something about them.

Mind is also a threat to marriage, because introversion undermines marital happiness. Divorced people turn out to have more intellectual interests than the happily married. A liking for philosophy, psychology, radical politics, and for reading the *New Republic* are much less auspicious for marital bliss than a liking for Y.M.C.A. work, Bible study, and the *American Magazine*. In a chapter entitled "The Vice of Education," Link attacks "the creation of a liberal mind" as "probably the most damaging single aspect of education"—a dogma of education as mystical and irrational, he finds, as any dogma of the church ever was. Such education produces "ruthless iconoclasm" and creates a culture for its own sake and a demand for knowledge for its own sake. Liberalism releases a person from the traditions and restraints of the past and substitutes nothing for them. The liberally educated young are disposed to regard parents as old-fashioned, to spend freely, show intellectual scorn for the pieties of their elders, seek intellectual vocations rather than the occupations of their fathers, and deprecate business as a career. A better insight into the abundant life can be found in army and navy barracks, where people face real values and are certain to become more extroverted.

CHAPTER XI

Variations on a Theme

❧

• 1 •

THE REFRAIN about the prior virtues of practicality to which businessmen give expression is a refrain they can easily pick up from the folklore of American life, and it is not always certain who is echoing whom. Expressions of the refrain have differed from time to time and from class to class, but its melody has always been distinguishable, as it resounds through a wide range of occupations and in the most disparate political camps. The evidence is abundant, and it is nearly unanimous in its testimony to a popular culture that has been proudly convinced of its ability to get along—indeed, to get along better—without the benefits of formal knowledge, even without applied science. The possession and use of such knowledge was always considered to be of doubtful value; and in any case it was regarded as the prerogative of specialized segments of the population that were resented for their privileges and refinements.

We can begin with the peculiar accents given to the common theme by farmers, simply because the United States was for a long time primarily a nation of farmers. At the end of the eighteenth century, about nine out of ten Americans made their living directly from farming; in 1820, seven out of ten; not until 1880 did persons otherwise employed equal farmers in numbers. In many ways the American farmer was primarily a businessman. He may often have thought of farming as a way of life, but this way of life soon became astonishingly businesslike in its aspirations if not always in its mode of conduct. The vast extent of the American land, the mobile and non-traditional character of American rural life, and the Protestant dynamism of American society made for a commercially minded and speculative style in farming. The farmer was constantly tempted to engross more land than he could economically cultivate, to hold it speculatively for a rise in values, to go in for extensive and careless rather than intensive and careful cultivation, to concentrate on raising a single big commercial crop, to mine and deplete the soil, then to sell out and move. As early as 1813 John Taylor of Caroline, in his *Arator,* found that Virginia was "nearly ruined" for lack of careful cultivation, and begged his countrymen: "Forbear, oh forbear matricide, not for futurity, not for God's sake, but for your own sake." In the 1830's Tocqueville concluded: "The Americans carry their businesslike qualities into agriculture, and their trading passions are displayed in that as in their other pursuits." [1]

Farmers had their own notion of what was practical, most simply expressed in their attitude toward scientific improvement in agriculture and toward agricultural education. Among a busy and hard-working farm community that was seldom very affluent one could hardly expect to find patrons of art and learning; but a receptive state of mind at least toward applied science would have been immensely useful to the farmers themselves. Even this was considered useless. There was, of course, a deviant minority; but the preponderant attitude of dirt farmers toward improvement in their own industry was a crass, self-defeating kind of pragmatism.

Like almost everything else in American life, the farm industry was large and heterogeneous. But there was one basic class division within it that coincided with a cleavage in philosophical outlook—and that was the early nineteenth-century division between the dirt farmers and a small stratum of gentlemen farmers. The gentlemen farmers were large farmers, professional men, college or university scientists, businessmen, or agricultural editors who commonly had incomes from sources outside farming, who were interested in agricultural experimentation, read and on occasion wrote books on the subject, hoped to use scientific knowledge to improve agriculture, formed agricultural societies, and joined or led movements to uplift agricultural education. Distinguished names, recognizable for their achievements in other areas, can be found among the gentleman farmers. They include such men as the Connecticut preacher Jared Eliot, who wrote his classic *Essay on Field Husbandry in New England* between 1748 and 1759, and Eliot's sometime correspondent, Benjamin Franklin, who main-

[1] John Taylor: *Arator* (Georgetown, 1813), pp. 76–7; Alexis de Tocqueville: *Democracy in America* (New York, 1945), Vol. II, p. 157; I have tried to assess the commercial element in American agriculture in *The Age of Reform* (New York, 1955), chapter 2.

tained a farm near Burlington, New Jersey, from which he hoped to reap a profit but which he also used as a terrain on which to pursue his scientific curiosity. Washington, Jefferson, Madison, and John Taylor of Caroline, who belonged to the tradition of the enlightened agriculturists, attempted to import into the practices of Virginia agriculture the benefits of the revolution in eighteenth-century English farming. They were followed by Edmund Ruffin, famous for his experiments with calcareous fertilizers, editor of the *Farmer's Register,* and later a militant sectionalist who fired the first shot at Fort Sumter. Outside Virginia, the most active and impressive center of agitation for agricultural improvement was not in a notable farming community but at Yale College, where an understanding of the needs of agriculture was linked to the study of advanced chemistry. There, academic scientists, beginning with the younger Benjamin Silliman, concerned themselves with soil chemistry, crops, and scientific agriculture; Silliman was followed by John P. Norton, John Addison Porter, and Samuel W. Johnson. Among other things, these men attempted to popularize the work of Justus Liebig in soil chemistry. Jonathan B. Turner of Illinois, also educated at Yale, was one of the leading agitators for improved agricultural education; the inspiration of the Morrill Act has been rather uncertainly credited to him. In New York the self-educated farm editor Jesse Buel preached consistently for higher standards in agriculture. In Pennsylvania Evan Pugh, a brilliant student of plant growth and plant chemistry, became president of the Agricultural College of Pennsylvania and helped promote the Morrill Act before his premature death at thirty-six.

In that they combined scientific curiosity with agricultural practice and a sense of civic responsibility with the pursuit of agricultural profits, such men provided an example of the admirable union of the intellectual and the practical. And they were not altogether without a public. Their work reached a fairly broad class of gentleman farmers— men who were the backbone of agricultural societies and farm fairs, readers of farm periodicals, proponents of agricultural schools and colleges. A good practical book on agriculture, if successful, might sell from ten to twenty thousand copies. Perhaps one farmer in ten subscribed to an agricultural journal, and on the eve of the Civil War there were more than fifty such journals, in various stages of prosperity or poverty.[2]

[2] On the number of farm journals, see Albert L. Demaree: *The American Agricultural Press, 1819–1860* (New York, 1941), pp. 17–19; on books and journals,

But the advocates of agricultural improvement and the gentlemen
farmers were resented by dirt farmers. This resentment had in it an
element of class feeling: the gentlemen organized and promoted the
agricultural activities, and overshadowed the small farmers. At the
county fairs, they were likely to turn up with the prize specimens,
produced experimentally and without regard to cost; the common
farmer could not compete with these.[3] Their preachments also ran up
against a state of mind that was conservative, unreceptive, suspicious
of innovation, and often superstitious. The American farmer, untraditional though he was about land speculation, about moving from place
to place, or about adopting new machinery, was ultra-conservative
about agricultural education or the application of science to farming.
As a consequence, the professional agriculturists and farm editors felt
that they were working in a skeptical, if not hostile, environment. "If
the farmers in your neighborhood," wrote Benjamin Franklin to Jared
Eliot, "are as unwilling to leave the beaten road of their ancestors as
they are near me, it will be difficult to persuade them to attempt any
improvement." George Washington wrote apologetically to Arthur
Young that American farmers were more eager to take advantage
of cheap land than to expend dear labor, and that, as a consequence,
"much ground has been *scratched* over and none cultivated or improved as it ought to have been." Edmund Ruffin, who conducted his
early experiments under the eyes of mocking neighbors, concluded:
"Most farmers are determined *not* to understand anything, however
simple it may be, which relates to chemistry." "Our farmers," complained Jesse Buel, "seem generally indifferent or spiritless in regard to
the general improvement of our agriculture, either because they mistake their duty and true interest or that, under the influence of a
strange fatuity, they fear they shall sink as others rise." The farmers,
said the editor of the *American Farmer* in 1831, "will neither take an
agricultural paper, read it when given them, nor believe in its contents
if by chance they hear it read." Twenty years later the eminent British
agricultural scientist, James F. W. Johnston, reported after a lecture
tour in America that the farmers were "averse to change, and more
averse still to the opinion that they are not already wise enough for all

---

Paul W. Gates: *The Farmer's Age: Agriculture, 1815–1860* (New York, 1960), pp.
343, 356.
   [3] On this aspect of the fairs, see Gates: op. cit., pp. 312–15; cf. W. C. Neely:
The Agricultural Fair (New York, 1935), pp. 30, 35, 42–5, 71, 183; and P. W. Bidwell and J. I. Falconer: *History of Agriculture in the Northern United States*
(Washington, 1925), pp. 186–93.

they have to do." In New York they were opposed to an agricultural college, he found, "on the ground that the knowledge to be given in the school is not required, and that its application to the soil would be of doubtful benefit." [4]

In fact, the farmer had a good deal to learn from the agricultural reformers. Even the open-minded farmer was likely to be ignorant of the principles of plant and animal breeding, of plant nutrition, of sound tillage, of soil chemistry. Many farmers were sunk in the super-stitions of moon-farming—sowing, reaping, and mowing in accordance with the phases of the moon. Their practices were wasteful and deple-tive.[5] For the educative efforts of the reformers they had the disdain of the "practical" man for the theorist expressed in the contemptuous term *book farming*. "The men who are farmers by book are no farmers for me," said one. "Give me the man who prefers his hands to books . . . let those who follow husbandry for amusement try experiments. . . . Let learned men attend to cases, genders, moods and tenses: you and I will see to our flocks, dairies, fields and fences." [6] Against this overwhelming prejudice the reformers and farm editors manfully waged a difficult struggle. Jesse Buel complained that in every other sphere—in war and navigation, law and medicine—Americans had thought of formal education as a meaningful aid, indeed as a neces-sity: [7]

> And yet, in Agriculture, by which, under the blessing of Provi-dence, we virtually "live, and move, and have our being," and which truly embraces a wider range of useful science than either law, medicine, war, or navigation, we have no schools, we give no instruction, we bestow no governmental patronage. Scientific knowledge is deemed indispensable in many minor employments of life; but in this great business, in which its influence would be most potent and useful, we consider it, judging from our practice,

[4] Carl Van Doren: *Benjamin Franklin* (New York, 1938), p. 178; Bidwell and Falconer: op. cit., p. 119; Avery O. Craven: *Edmund Ruffin, Southerner* (New York, 1932), p. 58; Harry J. Carman, ed.: *Jesse Buel: Agricultural Reformer* (New York, 1947), p. 10; Demaree: op. cit., p. 38; James F. W. Johnston: *Notes on North America: Agricultural, Economic, and Social* (Edinburgh, 1851), Vol. II, p. 281.

[5] Demaree: op. cit., pp. 4–6, 10, 48–9. On wasteful cultivation, see Gates: op. cit., who makes the necessary regional and ethnic qualifications.

[6] Richard Bardolph: *Agricultural Literature and the Early Illinois Farmer* (Urbana, Illinois, 1948), p. 14; cf. pp. 13, 103.

[7] Carman: op. cit., pp. 249–50. See the instructive essay in which these remarks appeared, pp. 234–54, and Buel's remarks "On the Necessity and Means of Improv-ing Our Husbandry," pp. 8–21.

of less consequence than the fictions of the novelist. We regard mind as the efficient power in most other pursuits; while we forget that in Agriculture it is the Archimedean lever, which, though it does not *move*, tends to *fill* a world with plenty, with moral health, and human happiness. Can it excite surprise that, under these circumstances of gross neglect, Agriculture should have become among us, in popular estimation, a clownish and ignoble employment?

But "the great bar to agricultural improvement," Buel thought, "is the degrading idea, which too many entertain, that everything denominated science is either useless in husbandry or beyond the reach of the farmer." [8] The continuous exhortations of the farm editors, their constant efforts to overcome the feeling against book farming, seem to bear out his words. Not all the farm journals were impeccable; some of them had their own quackeries to peddle. But, in any case, they found it constantly necessary to explain apologetically that they were not advocating anything ultra-theoretical, that most of their copy was written by practicing farmers. When Liebig's great work on soil chemistry was brought out in an American edition in 1841—this, it must be said, found a receptive and eager public among agricultural reformers and even among a few dirt farmers—his discoveries were described in the *Southern Planter* as "new fine-spun theories." [9]

Mr. Justus Liebig is no doubt a very clever gentleman and a most profound chemist, but in our opinion he knows about as much of agriculture as the horse that ploughs the ground, and there is not an old man that stands between the stilts of a plough in Virginia that cannot tell him of facts totally at variance with his finest spun theories.

• 2 •

In the light of what has been said about opposition to science and book farming, it will hardly be surprising that there was great reluctance

---

[8] Carman: op. cit., p. 53. For a temperate answer by another editor to the ultra-practical bias of the working farmer, see: "An Apology for 'Book Farmers,'" *Farmer's Register*, Vol. II. (June, 1834), pp. 16–19; cf. "Book Farming," *Farmer's Register*, Vol. I (May, 1834), p. 743.

[9] Demaree: op. cit., p. 67. On the dirt farmers and the farm press, see pp. 113–16; cf. Sidney L. Jackson: *America's Struggle for Free Schools* (Washington, 1940), pp. 111–14, 142–4. The farmer's favorite secular reading seems to have been his almanac, and the old farmer's almanac at times catered to his anti-intellectual sentiments with racy anecdotes or poems about the impracticality and foolishness of the learned. Jackson: op. cit., pp. 12–13.

among farmers to accept the idea that education (other than a highly practical on-the-farm training) could do much for their children. Such hopes as the farmers may have had for agricultural education seems to have been overweighed by their fear that more schools would only mean more taxes. An advocate of agricultural schools in the *American Farmer* in 1827 found that farmers themselves had offered "the warmest opposition to them." [1] A correspondent writing to the *New England Farmer* in 1852, himself an opponent of a proposed Massachusetts agricultural college, thought that nine tenths of the practical farmers of the state agreed with him. In any case, he set forth articulately enough the arguments of the opposition to the school: farmers would not make use of it; they would consider it "a grand and expensive experiment" that did not promise a corresponding return; it would only give "a few men a rich and lucrative office" that they had no experience to qualify for; the advocates of the scheme hoped to give the sons of rich men and those in genteel pursuits a knowledge of farming. As to that, *"the art cannot be taught to any advantage, except by practice."* [2]

This was only a facet of a more general rural reluctance to support educational enterprises. Sidney L. Jackson, in his analysis of attitudes toward the common-school movement, reports that the farmer "was more a hindrance than a help in the struggle for better schools." [3] The various experiments in agricultural colleges that were made in the United States before the passage of the Morrill Act in 1862 were chiefly the work of small, dedicated groups of agricultural reformers— which no doubt accounts in some part for the fact that in a nation overwhelmingly agricultural and desperately in need of agricultural skills [4] so little was done until the federal government intervened.

---

[1] Gates: op. cit., pp. 358–60.

[2] "Agricultural Colleges," reprinted from the *New England Farmer*, n.s. Vol. IV (June, 1852), pp. 267–8, in Demaree; *op. cit.*, pp. 250–2.

[3] Jackson: op. cit., p. 172; cf. pp. 113, 127, *passim.*

[4] Professor John P. Norton of Yale wrote in 1852: "If any six states of the Union were within the present year to make provision for the establishment of state agricultural schools, or colleges, within their respective borders—were to endow them largely in every department, to furnish them with libraries, implements, museums, apparatus, buildings, and lands, they could not find on this continent the proper corps of professors and teachers to fill them." He doubted, in fact, that a single institution in New York could find a faculty of "thoroughly competent men." Demaree: op. cit., p. 245.

For a brief history of efforts to improve education in farming, see A. C. True: *A History of Agricultural Education in the United States, 1785–1925* (Washington, 1929). In 1851 Edward Hitchcock made a survey of agricultural education in Europe for the Massachusetts legislature; in it the work of the American states appeared to great disadvantage when compared with the continental countries, especially Germany and France.

The passage in 1862 of the Morrill Act owed little to popular enthusi-asm; once again, it was the achievement of a group of determined lobbyists. Earle D. Ross, in his excellent study of the land-grant move-ment, observes that "there was no indication of spontaneous public interest." The Morrill Act was hardly noticed, amid the war news, by the general press; the agricultural papers themselves failed to show much enthusiasm, and some did not even take cognizance of its exist-ence.[5]

The law itself, at first, was hardly more than a well-intentioned promise; and the reformers were to find out in the next thirty years how difficult it was to execute meaningfully a reform so far in advance of public opinion. Senator Morrill's notions were sensible enough. The American soil, he recognized, was badly and wastefully cultivated; other countries were doing far more than the United States in the way of agricultural and mechanical education; experiments and surveys were needed; the farmer had to have instruction in new scientific find-ings; the creation of sound agricultural and mechanical schools, sup-ported by the revenues from the public lands, would be in line with earlier American precedents for aid to education; it would not interfere with the autonomy of the states or with the kind of education then be-ing offered by the classical colleges. For a time, Morrill's proposals ran afoul of sectional politics, and the idea of agricultural land-grant col-leges was vetoed by Buchanan in 1859. But Lincoln signed a similar bill three years later. Congress seems to have been more persuaded of the need for reform than the majority of farmers.[6] Unfortunately, however, as Ross remarks, the measure was never discussed on its educational merits. Objections to it were based largely on its alleged unconstitutionality and on trivia—with the consequence that the law, as it emerged from Congress, was inadequate to realize the intentions of its framers.

Once established, the land-grant colleges were beset by all kinds of difficulties, not least among them the jealousy of the existing colleges and the American preference for educational diffusion and dispersion

[5] Earle D. Ross: *Democracy's College* (Ames, Iowa, 1942), p. 66.

[6] Rather exceptional in the Congressional debates over the land-grant college principles were such echoes of the feeling about book-farming as were uttered by Senator Rice of Minnesota: "If you wish to establish agricultural colleges, give to each man a college of his own in the shape of one hundred and sixty acres of land . . . but do not give lands to the states to enable them to educate the sons of the wealthy at the expense of the public. We want no fancy farmers; we want no fancy mechanics. . . ." I. L. Kandel: *Federal Aid for Vocational Education* (New York, 1917), p. 10.

as against concentration of effort. It was inordinately difficult to recruit competent staffs. Old-line educators, reared on the traditions of the classical colleges, often could not really accept the legitimacy of agricultural and mechanical education, and on occasion they sabotaged the new colleges from within. On the opposite side, there was the traditional small-minded opposition from farmers and folk leaders, who persisted in believing that science had nothing "practical" to offer farmers. As Ross points out, "the farmers themselves were the hardest to convince of the need and possibility of occupational training." When they did not resist the idea of such education, they resisted proposals that it have any university connections or any relation to experimental science. Separate farm colleges, severely utilitarian in purpose, would do. The Wisconsin Grange argued that each profession should be taught by its practitioners. "Ecclesiastics should teach ecclesiastics, lawyers teach lawyers, mechanics teach mechanics, and farmers teach farmers." Some governors wanted to get as far away as possible from the tradition of liberal education represented by the classical colleges. The governor of Ohio wanted the instruction to be "plain and practical, not theoretically and artistically scientific in character"; the governor of Texas imagined that an agricultural college was "for the purpose of training and educating farm laborers"; the governor of Indiana thought that any kind of higher education would be a deterrent to honest labor.[7]

More decisive than any argument was the fact that not many farmers sent their sons; and when they did, the sons took advantage of their educational opportunities to get out of farming—usually to go into engineering. For years the agricultural colleges had relatively few students, and among these the students of "mechanic arts"—i.e., engineering—outnumbered the students of agriculture from year to year by ratios of two, three, four, or five to one. An improvement in the situation of agricultural science came with the Hatch Act of 1887, which created the system of federal experiment stations working in close cooperation with the agricultural colleges and also made available expanding research facilities. By the 1890's the colleges of agriculture

[7] Ross: op. cit., chapters 5 ,6, 7, and pp. 66, 72, 80, 87, 89–90, 96–7, 108–9. One paper called the agricultural colleges "asylums for classical idiots and political professors," and another suggested that the necessary task was "to clean out the smug D.D.'s and the pimply-faced 'Professors,' and put in their places men who have a lively sense of the lacks in learning among men and women who have to grapple daily with the world's work in this busy age." Ibid., pp. 119–20. Cf. James B. Angell: *Reminiscences* (New York, 1912), p. 123: "The farmers . . . were the hardest class to convince that we could be of any help to them."

finally had something of considerable value to offer in the way of scientific training.

Another flaw in the land-grant system was that it had been built from the top down. No provision had been made by Congress to develop a system of rural secondary schools good enough to equip graduates for admission to agricultural colleges. This defect was remedied in 1917 in the Smith-Hughes Act, which made federal subsidies available to secondary vocational education in agriculture. The return of agricultural prosperity after the long deflationary period from 1873 to 1897 also brought a turn in the fortunes of agricultural education. Better profits encouraged farmers to think about business management, animal breeding, soil science, and agricultural economics. The advance of mechanization made it easier for them to spare their sons from the farms. The number of agricultural students rose consistently and rapidly after 1905, and on the eve of the First World War it almost equalled the number of engineers. As M. L. Wilson, Undersecretary of Agriculture under Franklin D. Roosevelt, recalled, the contempt for book farming, almost universal in his Iowa community down to the turn of the century, was overcome only during the years of his youth: [8]

> Shortly after the twentieth century began, science began to work a revolution among the mass of farmers. When I went to Ames to study agriculture in 1902, I was not the first boy in my Iowa neighborhood to go to college, but I was the first boy from that neighborhood to go to an *agricultural* college. Ten or fifteen years later it was becoming an accepted thing for all who could afford it.

I. L. Kandel, surveying the subject in 1917, remarked with ample justification that the land-grant colleges, "intended by Senator Morrill and his supporters for the function primarily of scientific preparation for agricultural pursuits, are only just now, more than fifty years after their foundation, beginning to fulfil the function for which they were established." [9]

The reader, who will be unlikely to think of the agricultural and mechanical colleges as pre-eminently centers of intellectualism, may question what was accomplished and what is being asserted here. I have no intention of misstating the character of the agricultural colleges

[8] Milburn L. Wilson, in O. E. Baker, R. Borsodi, and M. L. Wilson: *Agriculture in Modern Life* (New York, 1939), pp. 223–4.

[9] Kandel: op. cit., p. 103; cf. p. 106. On the number of students in agricultural and mechanical courses in these colleges, see p. 102.

in this respect: they were meant only to bring vocational education and applied science into some kind of fruitful union, which I take to be a useful objective. The essential point here is that this much-needed fusion was achieved only after a century of agitation by agricultural reformers in the teeth of a widespread and extremely obstinate conviction among working farmers that theory has nothing to offer to practice.

· 3 ·

Farming could be plausibly portrayed as a "natural" way of living, whose practitioners might lose far more than they would gain by attending to sophisticated critics and adopting bookish or scientific ideas. It was quite otherwise with the industrial working class, whose way of life was considered unnatural, and who needed to be brought to some level of self-awareness and organization before they could give expression to any attitude toward their fate. From the outset, the relationship of intellectual criticism and the labor movement took on a more complex character than it had among farmers. In his brilliant inquiry into *The Psychology of Socialism*, Henri de Man remarked: "The labor movement, uninfluenced by the intelligentsia and its concerns [Intelligenzlermotives], would be nothing more than a representation of interests intended to turn the proletariat into a new bourgeoisie."[1] There is in this observation a certain ironic appropriateness for the American labor movement, which more than any other has aimed at making the proletariat into a new bourgeoisie. In the United States, as elsewhere, the labor movement was in a very real sense the creation of intellectuals. But it was a child that turned upon its own father in order to forge its distinctive character. It was not possible to develop labor leadership of the type that could finally succeed in creating permanent organizations in America until a curious dialectic had been gone through: first, the influence of intellectuals and their systematic critique of capitalism created an awareness of the necessity for and the possibilities of a labor movement; but then, in successive stages, this influence had to be thrown off before the labor movement could shed distractions and excrescences, devote itself to organizing job-conscious trade unions, and establish itself on a durable and successful footing.

Historically, the American labor movement did not begin with that narrow concentration on the job, the wage bargain, and the strike which

[1] Henri de Man: *Zur Psychologie des Sozialismus* (Jena, 1926), p. 307.

eventually became the essence of its character. It was always heavily infiltrated with bourgeois leadership, affected by the aims of reform theorists, and colored by the interest of its members either in achieving a solid place in bourgeois society or in entirely reforming that society. Its early history consists of association with one sweeping reform panacea or another—land reform, anti-monopoly, Greenbackism, producers' co-operatives, Marxism, Henry George's single tax. Not until more than three quarters of a century of such experimentation had left the American labor movement with next to nothing to show in the way of solid permanent organization did it develop any effectiveness, and this only when it was taken over by pragmatic leaders of the order of Samuel Gompers and Adolph Strasser, who brought it to a focus on the job and the wage bargain and on the organization of skilled trades strong enough to hope to monopolize the labor market in their own crafts.

Both Adolph Strasser, who had been a socialist, and Samuel Gompers, the guiding spirit of the A. F. of L. during its first generation of existence, undoubtedly owed a good deal to their own youthful dialogues with the socialists. Gompers paid what was perhaps a reluctant tribute to this early intellectual training in his autobiography, when he pointed out:

> Many of those who helped to lay the foundations of the trade union movement were men who had been through the experience of Socialism and found their way to sounder policies. . . . They were always men of vision. . . . Experiences in Socialism served a constructive purpose if the individual was able to develop beyond the formulas of Socialism, for such carried to their practical duties a quickened insight and an understanding that tangible objectives are merely instrumentalities for reaching a higher spiritual goal.

However, whereas socialism may have taught such men the possibilities of a labor movement, the labor movement itself, once established, taught them the impossibility of socialism in America. From his earliest days in the labor movement, Gompers had to battle with "faddists, reformers, and sensation-loving spirits"—his terms for the ideologues who hovered around the labor movement; and there were times when these ideologues were among his most formidable enemies. It was the socialists who were instrumental in defeating him for the presidency of the A. F. of L. in 1894, the only year when he was not re-elected. He was convinced that leadership could be entrusted "only to those into whose hearts and minds had been woven the experiences of earning their bread by daily labor." "I saw the danger of entangling alliances with intellectuals who did not understand that to experiment with the labor movement was to experiment with human life." [2]

Intellectuals were estranged from labor leaders like Gompers because their expectations from the labor movement were altogether different. The intellectuals tended to look upon the labor movement as a means to a larger end—to socialism or some other kind of social reconstruction. They came from outside the labor movement, and were rarely recruited from the working class itself. As a rule, they disdained the middle-class respectability to which most labor leaders, and in fact most rank and file skilled workers, aspired. A bread-and-butter organization like the A. F. of L. never appealed to their idealism, and they persistently looked down upon its leadership. The labor leaders themselves may best be understood, I believe, as a group of self-made men, in this respect not profoundly different from hundreds of such men in industrial corporations. As Strasser said, in a classic encounter: "We are all practical men." [3] They came from the ranks of the working class, for the most part, and never quite ceased to hope that labor and its leaders would achieve a respectability comparable to that enjoyed by businessmen. They had been exposed to anti-capitalist and anti-monopoly thought, but unlike the intellectuals they were unfamiliar with the thoroughgoing indictments of bourgeois civilization that pervaded avant-garde thought in politics and esthetics. They were good patriots, good family men, in time good Republicans or Democrats. [4] Their early contacts with intellectuals—or what they took to be intellectuals—were of the sort to arouse their suspicion. At first there were the battles with the socialist doctrinaires within the labor movement

[2] Samuel Gompers: Seventy Years of Life and Labor (1925; ed. New York, 1943), Vol. I, pp. 55, 57, 97–8, 180, 382. This distrust of intellectuals in the labor movement was shared by one of the early labor intellectuals, John R. Commons, who felt that the labor movement attracted a type of intellectual who made a poor leader. See John R. Commons: Myself (New York, 1934), pp. 86–9; see also his Industrial Goodwill (New York, 1919), pp. 176–9.

[3] Senate Committee on Education and Labor, Relations between Labor and Capital, Vol. I (Washington, 1885), p. 460. Cf. the equally classic remark of Gompers in 1896: "The trade unions are the business organizations of the wage earners." Report of the Sixteenth Annual Convention of the American Federation of Labor, 1896, p. 12.

[4] My remarks here have been shaped in part by Selig Perlman's A Theory of the Labor Movement (1928; ed. New York, 1949), pp. viii–ix, 154, 176, 182, and chapter 5, passim. See C. Wright Mills's provocative remarks about labor leaders as self-made men, in The New Men of Power (New York, 1948), chapter 5.

itself. The labor leaders constantly smarted from the criticism of academic economists,[5] who were for a long time an almost united phalanx against labor—"the professoriate," as Gompers labeled them, "the open and covert enemies of the workers," and "faddists, theorists and effeminate men." Finally, around the turn of the century, the movement for "scientific management" was regarded by labor as a grave menace; Gompers saw its leaders as "academic observers" and "intellectuals" who merely wanted to get the most out of the energies of workers before sending them to the junkpile. These were not experiences to encourage confidence.[6] The labor movement was in fact struggling to

[5] Although the American labor movement was always favorable to the development of the common-school system, it was chronically suspicious of the higher culture and of institutions of higher learning. From time to time labor journals made acid comments about the gifts of millionaires to museums, libraries, and universities, pointing out that these had been wrung out of the wages of the workers—"millions taken from the earnings of the toilers, given to institutions which the workmen and their children can never enter and enjoy." A particular hostility was expressed toward universities and colleges, as places where poor men's sons could never go and where "millions are annually expended in teaching the sons of the wealthy some new brutality in football." Quite understandably the labor editors feared that the universities would be bound by their endowments to teach that the status quo was beyond criticism, and that colleges and universities would become "incubators" for scabs and strikebreakers. What could be expected to be taught at a university endowed by Rockefeller? Would it be the rights of man or the superiority of the wealthy? One writer even suggested in 1905 that the new "theoretical college men" who were replacing the old practical men in the leadership of industry would be more remote from the workers because they had not risen from the ranks. College men "have nothing in common with plain workingmen upon whom they look down with disdain as did the patricians of old upon the plebians, or the slave owners of the South upon the Negroes." In 1914 the *American Federationist* suggested that private endowments were unsuited to the pursuit of the truth, and were "a menace to free institutions." If they could not be better devoted to the truth, "then they must give way to state institutions supported by public funds." *American Federationist*, Vol. XXI (February, 1914), pp. 120–1. See *Rail Road Conductor* (November, 1895), p. 613; *Typographical Journal* (June 15, 1896), p. 484; *Boilermakers' Journal* (March, 1899), p. 71; *Railway Conductor* (August, 1901), pp. 639–40; *American Federationist* Vol. X (October, 1903), p. 1033; *The Electrical Worker* (May, 1905), p. 40; *Railroad Trainmen's Journal*, Vol. XXIV (1907), pp. 264–5; (April, 1907), p. 368; *Locomotive Firemen's Magazine*, Vol. XLIV (January, 1908), pp. 86–7.

No doubt the growing social sympathies of American academics did something to overcome this feeling. The *American Federationist* thought in 1913 that colleges and universities were in fact "helping to establish a more sympathetic, democratic understanding of social and industrial problems." Vol. XX (February, 1913), p. 129. Gompers found himself much sought after by the universities as a speaker, and spent considerable time cultivating good relations there. *Seventy Years of Life and Labor*, Vol. I, pp. 437 ff.

[6] See Gompers: *Organized Labor: Its Struggles, Its Enemies and Fool Friends* (Washington, 1901), pp. 3, 4; Gompers: "Machinery to Perfect the Living Machine," *Federationist*, Vol. XVIII (February, 1911), pp. 116–17; cf. Milton J. Nadworny: *Scientific Management and the Unions* (Cambridge, Mass., 1955), especially chapter 4.

establish itself in an unfriendly environment, and before 1900 the official intellectuals, on balance, contributed to that unfriendliness. Those who were not unfriendly were in any case regarded as unwise and unwelcome allies. It was not until the advent of the Progressive movement that middle-class intellectuals in any great number were notably friendly to the cause of labor, and not until the New Deal era that a strong, if not altogether durable, alliance was forged.[7]

Over the years since the time of Gompers, the growth, success, and stabilization of the trade unions has made it increasingly necessary for these big bureaucratic hierarchies to hire experts for legal, actuarial, and economic advice, for research and journalism, for publicity and lobbying, for their own large educational divisions. In this way, the men who lead the country's eighteen million organized workers have become the employers of substantial staffs of intellectuals. But intellectuals in union headquarters have not found a more comfortable home than those in other areas of organized society—they have, in fact, a relationship to the union leaders not altogether unlike that of business intellectuals to corporation heads.

Three pressures, in the main, seem to alienate the intellectual from the union milieu. The first, operative only for some, is a passion for reform, an ideological commitment that may have made the intellectual want to work for a union in the first place. Sooner or later he will come to see that he has not made the labor movement radical—but rather that he himself has been absorbed into the machinery that buttresses the power and prestige of the leaders. Inevitably, the idealism of the union expert is blunted, as he finds himself caught up in a going concern that is ready to use him but unwilling to be bent by his will. (Union experts who come to the job with missionary enthusiasm tend to be paid somewhat less than more self-centered careerists.) The second source of alienation is his professional feeling for research, his disinterested desire for the truth, which on occasion runs up against the necessities of the union as a militant organization or the personal imperatives of a leader. "They're sloppy in their use of data," complains one expert about his union associates.[8]

[7] On the recent partial dissolution of this alliance, see James R. Schlesinger: "Organized Labor and the Intellectuals," *Virginia Quarterly Review*, Vol. XXXVI (Winter, 1960), pp. 36–45.

[8] For my argument here, as well as the quotations from labor leaders and labor experts, I am indebted to Harold L. Wilensky: *Intellectuals in Labor Unions* (Glencoe, Illinois, 1956), *passim*, and especially pp. 55, 57, 68, 88–90, 93, 106, 116–20, 132, 260–5, 266n., 267, 273–6. On the limitations of the power of the labor intellectual, see also C. Wright Mills: op. cit., pp. 281–7.

They don't give a damn. They're philosophical relativists with no real belief in truth or in scientific objectivity; or at least they think the search for truth is too difficult, so they abandon it and excuse themselves from it by saying, "Who's interested in the truth, anyway—management?" Basically, it's because they have a Marxist or a social reform attitude. Everything becomes a matter of partisan advantage. . . . All they want to do is build up the prejudices of the leader. . . . I sometimes wish I'd gone into university teaching.

From time to time, experts seek unwelcome truths or become the medium through which union leaders are brought face to face with some unwelcome reality, say in the legal or economic world. In this capacity they are resented, much as they are needed. The labor editor may aspire to run an intelligent organ of critical opinion; his union leader may be far more concerned that the union's journal take the right side in factional disputes. The union educational director may wish to offer something akin to a liberal education for workers; the leader may seek only simple indoctrination and ideological safety.

Finally, there is a type of alienation which is simply personal, which arises from the education and in some cases the personal culture of the expert. He is out of place, he is not the right kind of man, he would not be sought after as a companion if his services weren't needed. Mumbled complaints pursue him in the union offices, just as though he were actually on the assembly line—or for that matter at a Rotary Club meeting: "Prima donna types . . . you can't work together with them. . . . They aren't liked. . . . They're not the same Joes. They don't like the same kind of women. . . ."

The attitude of labor leaders toward labor intellectuals displays an ambivalence somewhat similar to that found in the business community and in society at large. Harold Wilensky has found in his study of labor experts that the labor leader is sometimes intimidated or overawed by the specialized knowledge of the intellectual, and often admires it. But he reassures himself with disdainful remarks about the impracticality of the expert, if not about his oddities. One high-ranking union officer who boasted: "I was educated in the school of hard knocks," voiced these mixed feelings when he said with equal pride: "I've told my son to take up labor law in college!" In some areas the non-intellectual is afflicted by a nagging envy of the expert's job: "Why, that S.O.B., he's got the soft job. . . . I knock myself out taking crap from the rank and file, I gotta go out to local meetings night after night while he sits behind a desk and writes up all that stuff." Like the businessman, the union leader loudly praises practical experience—first-hand acquaintance with the workbench or with union organizing activity. "You can't learn it from books. There's no substitute for experience." *He* was in the struggle from the beginning; the expert is an outsider and a Johnny-come-lately who cannot understand the labor struggle or the psychology of the worker because he has not dealt with it at first hand. "Your whole thinking on this matter . . . is fantastic. You are a legal mind; you are from Harvard, or Yale, or some other place like the rest of the guys up there, and you don't understand the thinking of the workers." Under the circumstances, it is not surprising that the experts at times give way to a feeling of self-distrust and adopt a quietistic pose or attempt to camouflage themselves. The atmosphere in which they work may be in many ways stimulating and benign, but, according to a student of experts in the labor bureaucracy, one of its components is a "pervasive anti-intellectualism." [9]

· 4 ·

It is hardly surprising that the organized labor movement in America, directed as it is toward "bourgeois" goals, has provided intellectuals with an environment that is not thoroughly congenial. It is somewhat more surprising to find similar problems arising in the non-Communist left, and especially in the Socialist Party, whose debt to intellectuals was heavy indeed. It would be altogether misleading to suggest that the Socialist Party in its day was an anti-intellectual force, or that it was inhospitable to intellectuals. From 1900 to 1914, the American Socialist Party attracted a large number of intellectuals whose support was invaluable and whose writings brought it cachet and greatly widened its influence. Among them were not only muckrakers like Upton Sinclair and John Spargo but the authors of stimulating critical books about socialism and various aspects of American life which are still worth reading—men like Louis B. Boudin, W. J. Ghent, Robert Hunter, Algie M. Simons, and William English Walling. Unlike the later Communist Party, the Socialist Party maintained an intellectual atmosphere that was far from monolithic, and produced a theoretical literature not entirely cramped by Marxian scholasticism. American socialism, pluralistic in its social recruitment, was still free and even adventurous in

[9] Wilensky: op. cit., pp. 269, 276.

thought, and some of its supporters brought to it a light-spirited Bohe-mian touch. "The *Masses*," one of its periodicals advertised, "has a Sense of Humor. . . . Enjoy the Revolution."

But in some quarters even the Socialist Party suffered from the cult of proletarianism. In the party's frequent factional fights, intellectual spokesmen were often branded as middle-class academics and were compared invidiously with the true proletarians who were the bulwark of the movement. (When revolutionary fervor was in question, the intellectuals were found in the left-wing faction much more often than in the right.) Inevitably, the attempt of socialist intellectuals, often from solid middle-class and sometimes from wealthy backgrounds,[1] to declass themselves spiritually and to accommodate to the proletarian ideals of Marxism led to a certain self-depreciation and self-alienation. Hence, the anti-intellectual wing of the party was not without its intellectual spokesmen.[2] One of them, W. J. Ghent, thought that the *Masses*, with its latitudinarian enthusiasms, was far too frivolous to contribute seriously to the fundamental business of converting workers to socialism:

> It has found no trouble in mixing Socialism, Anarchism, Com-munism, Sinn Feinism, Cubism, sexism, direct action, and sabotage into a more or less harmonious mess. It is peculiarly the product of the restless metropolitan coteries who devote themselves to the cult of Something Else; who are ever seeking the bubble Novelty even at the door of Bedlam.

Another intellectual, Robert Rives La Monte, felt that although the party needed brains in abundance, brains should not be identified with the possession of "a conventional bourgeois education," and con-cluded that the existence of "a reasonable degree of suspicion of

[1] Finley Peter Dunne was much amused by the interest of a few of the rich in socialism. "Mrs. Vanderhankerbilk," said Mr. Dooley, "Give a musical soree f'r th' ladies iv th' Female Billyonaires Arbeiter Verein. . . . Th' meetin' was addhressed be th' well-known Socialist leader, J. Clarence Lumley, heir to th' Lumley millyons. This well-known prolytariat said he had become a Socialist through studyin' his father. He cud not believe that a system was right which allowed such a man to ac-cumylate three hundherd millyon dollars. . . . Th' ladies prisint cud appreciate how foolish th' captains iv industhree are, because they were marrid to thim an' knew what they looked like in th' mornin'. . . . Th' meetin' thin adjourned afther passin' a resolution callin' on th' husband iv th' hostess to go an' jump in th' river." Finley Peter Dunne: *Mr. Dooley: Now and Forever* (Stanford, California, 1954), pp. 252–3.
[2] Charles Dobbs, writing on "Brains" in the *International Socialist Review*, Vol. VIII (March, 1908), p. 533, noticed that "it is the 'intellectuals' who are attacking the 'intellectuals' and the 'leaders' who are delivering the mightiest blows at 'leader-ship.'"

Intellectuals and Parlor Socialists" was a "most reassuring sign that the proletariat are approaching maturity as a class." [3] With this a right-wing party wheelhorse like George H. Goebel could agree. When it came to a choice between the intellectual, preacher, or professor and the working man, "that man who is fresh from the ranks of the working class and who in his every day life is in actual contact with the work and the struggle," Goebel said, he was always with the representative of the working class.[4]

The most extreme anti-intellectual position in the party—a veritable proletarian mucker pose—was taken not by the right-wingers nor by the self-alienated intellectuals but by Western party members affected by the I.W.W. spirit. The Oregon wing of the party, one of its strong Western segments, was a good example of this spirit. The story is told that at the party's 1912 convention in Indianapolis the Oregon delegates refused to have dinner in a restaurant that had tablecloths. Thomas Sladden, their state secretary, once removed the cuspidors from the Oregon headquarters because he felt that hardboiled tobacco-chewing proletarians would have no use for such genteel devices. It was Sladden, too, who in the *International Socialist Review* wrote an implacable challenge to the intellectuals. As he saw it, the movement belonged to the worker and to no one else. The Socialist Party and the labor unions "must either give way to, or take up arms against 'the man that thinks through his stomach.'" Sladden delineated the true socialist proletarian in these terms: [5]

> He has a language of his own, different from the accepted language of civilization, he is uncultured and uncouth in appearance, he has a code of morals and ethics as yet unrecognized

[3] David Shannon: *The Socialist Party of America* (New York, 1955), p. 57; Robert R. La Monte: "Efficient Brains versus Bastard Culture," *International Socialist Review*, Vol. VIII (April, 1908), pp. 634, 636. On intellectuals in the socialist movement, see Shannon: op. cit., pp. 8, 12, 19, 53–8, 281–2; Daniel Bell: "The Background and Development of Marxian Socialism in the United States," in Donald Drew Egbert and Stow Persons, eds.: *Socialism and American Life* (Princeton, 1952), Vol. I, pp. 294–8; Ira Kipnis: *The American Socialist Movement, 1897–1912* (New York, 1952), pp. 307–11, and Bell's review of this work in *The New Leader*, December 7, 1953.

[4] Bell: "Background and Development," p. 294. Cf. the attack by the right-wing leader, Max Hayes, on parlor socialists and theorists in the party convention of 1912. Socialist Party of America, *Convention Proceedings, 1912* (Chicago, 1912), p. 124.

[5] "The Revolutionist," *International Socialist Review*, Vol. IX (December, 1908), pp. 429–30. On Sladden, see Shannon: op. cit., p. 40; for an answer to Sladden by a socialist who considered that the proletariat embraced the intellectuals, see Carl D. Thompson: "Who Constitute the Proletariat?" *International Socialist Review*, Vol. IX (February, 1909), pp. 603–12.

by society, he has a religion unpreached in orthodox and un-
orthodox churches, a religion of hate. . . . He has an intelligence
which passes the understanding of the intellectuals who are born,
reared and living outside his sphere.

Like the instinct of the brute in the forest, his vision is clear and
he is ever on the alert, his hearing is keen, his nature suspicious,
his spirit is unconquerable. . . . With one swoop he will tear
away your puny intellectuality, your bogus respectability and as
master of all he surveys he will determine what is right and what
wrong.

This is the proletarian. . . . He has little education, no manners, and little care for what people think of him. His school has
been the hard school of human experience.

Here the cult of proletarianism seems blended with a variety of
primitivism of the sort another Westerner, Jack London, tried unsuc-
cessfully to graft onto the socialist movement. More typical of the
feelings of non-intellectuals in the Socialist Party was the moderate
position of its leader, Eugene V. Debs. Observing that there were
many socialists "who sneer at a man of intellect as if he were an inter-
loper and out of place among Socialists," Debs remonstrated that
intellectual ought not be a term of reproach. The movement needed
brains; the party should seek to attract them. What was important to
Debs was that normally "officials and representatives, and candidates
for public office, should be chosen from the ranks of the workers. The
intellectuals in office should be the exceptions, as they are in the rank
and file." Organizations of workers should not be run by intellectuals,
just as organizations of intellectuals should not be run by workers. Debs
considered that workers had ample ability to fill the official positions
themselves. His fear of intellectuals in official posts was consistent
with his fear of stratification and bureaucracy within the socialist
movement. Like a good Jacksonian, he acknowledged his belief in
"rotation in office." "I confess," he said, "to a prejudice against official-
ism and a dread of bureaucracy." [6]

· 5 ·

Whereas the Socialist Party had admitted some measure of diversity,
the Communist Party was monolithic: it wanted no writers who would

[6] "Sound Socialist Tactics," *International Socialist Review*, Vol. XII (February,
1912), pp. 483–4. Three years after these remarks Robert Michels published his
Political Parties, an analysis of oligarchical tendencies in European left-wing parties.

not subject themselves to its characteristic rigid discipline. Moreover, the intellectuals who were drawn to the Socialist Party during its most vital period, before the First World War, were mainly thinkers independently acquainted with Marxism, who took over leadership in the party ranks as theorists. The Communist Party attracted a far higher proportion of creative writers and literary critics, who knew little or nothing of Marxism or of the formal social disciplines and were willing, at least for a time, to submit themselves to the tutelage and discipline of the party apparatus. Within the Communist Party, as its intellectual influence widened during the 1930's, certain anti-intellectual tendencies, notably the cult of proletarianism, which had been hardly more than visible in the Socialist Party, became actually dominant. The change in the balance of moral power was dramatic: in Socialist Party circles one senses the discomfort of true proletarians at the thought that the intellectuals among them wielded so much influence; in Communist Party circles one is aware of the anguish of party or fellow-traveling intellectuals because they are not, by occupation or birth, workers themselves.

Earlier American radicals, like Edward Bellamy and Henry Demarest Lloyd, had sometimes taken a slightly condescending and custodial attitude toward the working class; but in the 1930's a number of American writers gave way to the fatally maudlin notion that the sufferings and the "historic mission" of the working class endow it with an immense inherent moral superiority over middle-class intellectuals. To atone for their tainted class origins and their middle-class character, many such intellectuals felt they must immolate themselves on the altar of the working class by service of one kind or another to the party. The Communist Party itself, keenly aware of the usefulness of its intellectual converts and at the same time of the danger that might be posed to its discipline by an influx of independent minds, adopted the strategy of exploiting the guilt and self-hatred of intellectuals as a means of keeping them in line. On one hand, it provided them with a creed and gave them a small but growing audience; on the other, it attempted to play upon their psychological vulnerability to prevent them from straying. This policy had mixed results; the most distinguished writers, whose prestige the party particularly coveted—Dreiser, Sinclair, Steinbeck, Hemingway, MacLeish, Dos Passos—proved to be the most refractory, the most unwilling to follow tamely the decrees of obscure party hacks. Lesser writers, less self-confident and more dependent upon the public the party could give them, were more submissive, though not always submissive enough for the party's purposes. Paul Rosenfeld had writers like these in mind when he complained in 1933 that they had renounced their responsibilities as artists and were competing "as to which could most quickly reconcile himself with the philistinism which the Communist party shares with every other party." [7]

If the true spirit of Bolshevik discipline was to be instilled in radical American writers, the Bohemianism that had flowered in the days of the *Masses* had to be destroyed. Writers must be made to feel that Bohemianism and all forms of merely personal revolt were unserious, trivial, neurotic. John Reed, once a Bohemian himself, led the way. "This class struggle," he said, "plays hell with your poetry"; and if it did, no doubt poetry would have to go. "Bolshevism," he declared on another occasion, "is not for the intellectuals; it is for the people." "You fellows," he remarked to a Menshevik theorist, "are not living beings; at best you are bookworms always thinking about what Marx said or meant to say. What we want is a revolution, and we are going to make it—not with books, but with rifles." Reed did not live long enough to demonstrate how far he would have carried the implications of this creed. After his death, the role of goad to the intellectuals was assumed by Michael Gold, for many years the party's critical hatchetman. Gold had succeeded more fully than most left intellectuals in declassing and deintellectualizing himself.[8] Floyd Dell, a party sympathizer but an incurable Bohemian, perceived that Gold, as a literary man, "is for some obscure reason ashamed of not being a workingman. . . . And so he is in awe of the workingman when he meets him, and says extravagant things in praise of him." To a generation of writers younger than Dell, the reasons for this shame and awe were not so obscure.

The Communist view of the intellectual's function brought forth certain ironic variations on the themes of practicality, masculinity, and primitivism that run through the national code at large; and it is amusing to see how, with a few changes in terms, the party code is similar

[7] Quoted in Daniel Aaron: *Writers on the Left* (New York, 1961), pp. 254–5. I have drawn heavily for my argument and illustrations on this thorough and perceptive study, and the quotations and incidents in the following paragraphs are from pp. 25, 41, 65, 93–4, 132*n.*, 162, 163–4, 168, 209, 210–12, 216, 227, 240–2, 254, 308, 337–8, 346, 409, 410, 417, 425. The attitude of the Communist Party toward intellectuals was far more rigid before 1935, when it adopted the "united front" line, than afterwards.

[8] Gold, who was as impeccably anti-Harvard as any McCarthyite of the 1950's, was impelled to deny his brief attendance there. "Certain enemies have spread the slander that I once attended Harvard College. This is a lie. I worked on a garbage dump in Boston, city of Harvard. But that is all."

to certain attitudes expressed by businessmen. The important task was a ruggedly practical one—to make a revolution. Everything else was subordinate; art and intellect were useless if they could not be put to work. Writers who failed to serve the revolution were accused, in the party's characteristic imagery, of being literary prostitutes to the bourgeoisie: they were "the most ancient and venerable of prostitutes," and (in the language of a young writer of impeccable proletarian origins) "literary vermin . . . who play the scented whore, and for thirty pieces of silver, will do the hootchi-kootchi dance, or wriggle their abdomens in imitation of legendary oriental ladies."

The making of revolutions was a task that called not only for greater moral purity but for a kind of heavy masculinity that too many writers lacked. Again, the practical and masculine demands of politics were contrasted with the futility of estheticism. One writer was taken aback when a party leader referred to his poetry and short stories as his "hobby" for after-hours activity—a revealing illustration of the party's conception of letters as fundamentally unserious. Worst of all was the failure of masculinity in writers who would not deal with the hard realities of the class struggle. Party intellectuals differed over the matter, but the most rugged of them were unsparing in their denunciation of what they called, in their crusade against the literary Humanists, "fairy literature." Michael Gold once told Sinclair Lewis that writers of this sort were nursing a "mad jealousy" because they had been "deprived of masculine experiences." In the course of a famous literary vendetta against Thornton Wilder, Gold accused the novelist of propagating a "pastel, pastiche, dilettante religion, without the true neurotic blood and fire, a daydream of homosexual figures in graceful gowns moving archaically among the lilies."

In their most extreme moments, those who tried to formulate a Communist canon for literature called for working-class writers who would supply the "Proletarian Realism" (Gold's phrase) that bourgeois writers allegedly failed to produce. Let the *New Masses*, the party organ, be written and read by "lumberjacks, hoboes, miners, clerks, sectionhands, machinists, harvesthands, waiters—the people who should count more to us than paid scribblers," urged one of these working-class writers. "It might be crude stuff—but we're just about done primping before a mirror and powdering our shiny noses. Who are we afraid of? Of the critics? Afraid that they will say the *New Masses* prints terribly ungrammatical stuff? Hell, brother, the newsstands abound with neat packages of grammatical offal." Such utterances tended to drive writers away from the movement. They were alienated by what one of them called "the affectation of idealized proletarianism, the monotonous strumming on the hard-boiled string, the hostility to ideas on other levels than one, the contempt for modulated writing and criticism, the evasion of discussion."

These differences were indicative of a major problem faced by the party in dealing with writers and other intellectuals: the conflict between its urgent desire to use them and its inability to sustain a tone that would hold them. Even Michael Gold, whose polemical extravagances did as much as anything to keep otherwise sympathetic intellectuals at arm's length from the party, at times grew restless with the attitude of party leaders toward writers. He once admitted that intellectuals were too commonly made to feel that they were outsiders: "The word 'intellectual' became a synonym for the word 'bastard,' and in the American Communist movement there is some of this feeling." Members of the party were not above exploiting this feeling about intellectuals as a weapon in internal struggles: during a factional fight in the twenties, Joseph Freeman has recalled, the Foster group attacked the Lovestone group in a word-of-mouth campaign on the ground, among others, that they were college men, bourgeois, and Jews. The feeling had astonishing consequences. Malcolm Cowley, writing during the Moscow trials from his post as a fellow-traveling editor of a major metropolitan non-party weekly, said of Trotsky in all seriousness: "I have never liked the big-city intellectuals of his type, with their reduction of every human question to a bald syllogism in which they are always right at every point. . . ."

For a time, if only a brief time in the life of most radical writers, the canons of the party were accepted, and with them the corollary that the intellectuals, and the institutions that had reared them, were no good. "I think we are all of us a pretty milky lot," John Dos Passos wrote during the First World War, "with our tea-table convictions and our radicalism that keeps so consistently within the bounds of decorum. . . . I'd like to annihilate these stupid colleges of ours, and all the nice young men therein, instillers of stodginess—every form of bastard culture, middle class snobism." Genevieve Taggard, deferring to the urgent "practical" task of revolution, felt that writers were useless:

Practical men run revolutions, and there's nothing more irritating than a person with a long vague look in his eye to have around, when you're trying to bang an army into shape, or put over a N.E.P. If I were in charge of a revolution, I'd get rid of every single artist immediately; and trust to luck that the fecundity of the earth would produce another crop when I had got some of the hard work done. Being an artist, I have the sense that a small child has when its mother is in the middle of house-work. I don't intend to get in the way, and I hope that there'll be an unmolested spot for me when things have quieted down.

Many writers had entered the movement in the belief that the revolt against the bourgeois world would be, for them at least, a revolt against its disrespect for culture. But whichever world one might choose, there was always a prior practical job to be done—bourgeois industrialization or a New Economic Policy, the quest for individual success or the need to "bang" an army into shape.

PART 5

Education in a Democracy

CHAPTER XII

The School and the Teacher

• 1 •

Anyone who speaks of anti-intellectualism as a quality in American life must reckon with one of the signal facts of our national experience—our persistent, intense, and sometimes touching faith in the efficacy of popular education. Few observers, past or present, have doubted the pervasiveness or sincerity of this faith. Henry Steele Commager, assessing the primary characteristics of the nineteenth-century American, remarks that "education was his religion"—though he is quick to add that Americans expected of education what they expected of religion, that it "be practical and pay dividends." [1] The Americans were the first other people in modern history to follow the Prussian example in establishing free common-school systems. Among their earliest statutes were land ordinances setting aside a portion of the public domain to support school systems. Their rapidly proliferating schoolhouses and libraries testified to their concern for the diffusion of knowledge, and their lyceums and Chautauquas showed that this concern, far from ending with the school years, extended to the education of adults.

From the beginning, American statesmen had insisted upon the necessity of education to a republic. George Washington, in his Farewell Address, urged the people to promote "institutions for the general diffusion of knowledge." To the degree that the form of government gave force to public opinion, Washington argued, "it is essential that

[1] Henry Steele Commager: *The American Mind* (New Haven, 1950), p. 10; cf. pp. 37–8. Rush Welter: *Popular Education and Democratic Thought in America* (New York, 1962), is an informative study of what Americans expected from education.

public opinion should be enlightened." The aging Jefferson warned in 1816: "If a nation expects to be ignorant and free in a state of civilization, it expects what never was and never will be." The young Lincoln, making his first appeal to a constituency, told the voters of Sangamon County in 1832 that education was "the most important subject which we as a people can be engaged in." [2] The image of the youthful Lincoln lying before a log fire and reading a book by its flickering light has been fixed as an ideal in the minds of millions of school children (who are not, I believe, pressed to consider what he may have been reading). In popular rhetoric it was always good practice for an editor or orator who wanted to take off on an extended flight of idealism to pay tribute to education. "If the time shall ever come," wrote a small-town Midwestern editor in 1836,[3]

> when this mighty fabric shall totter; when the beacon of joy that now rises in pillar of fire . . . shall wax dim, the cause will be found in the ignorance of the people. If our union is still to continue . . . ; if your fields are to be untrod by the hirelings of despotism; if long days of blessedness are to attend our country in her career of glory; if you would have the sun continue to shed his unclouded rays upon the face of freemen, then EDUCATE ALL THE CHILDREN OF THE LAND. This alone startles the tyrant in his dreams of power, and rouses the slumbering energies of an oppressed people. It was intelligence that reared up the majestic columns of national glory; and this and sound morality alone can prevent their crumbling to ashes.

But if we turn from the rhetoric of the past to the realities of the present, we are most struck by the volume of criticism suggesting that something very important has been missing from the American passion for education. A host of educational problems has arisen from indifference—underpaid teachers, overcrowded classrooms, double-schedule schools, broken-down school buildings, inadequate facilities and a number of other failings that come from something else—the cult of athleticism, marching bands, high-school drum majorettes, ethnic

[2] Washington, in Richardson, ed.: *Messages and Papers of the Presidents,* Vol. I, p. 220; Jefferson: *Writings,* P. L. Ford, ed., Vol. X (New York, 1899), p. 4; Lincoln: *Collected Works,* Roy P. Basler, ed., Vol. I (New Brunswick, New Jersey, 1953), p. 8.
[3] R. Carlyle Buley: *The Old Northwest Pioneer Period, 1815–1840* (Indianapolis, 1950), Vol. II, p. 416.

ghetto schools, de-intellectualized curricula, the failure to educate in serious subjects, the neglect of academically gifted children. At times the schools of the country seem to be dominated by athletics, commercialism, and the standards of the mass media, and these extend upwards to a system of higher education whose worst failings were underlined by the bold president of the University of Oklahoma who hoped to develop a university of which the football team could be proud.[4] Certainly some ultimate educational values seem forever to be eluding the Americans. At great effort and expense they send an extraordinary proportion of their young to colleges and universities; but their young, when they get there, do not seem to care even to *read.*[5]

· 2 ·

That something has always been seriously missing in our educational performance, despite the high promise of our rhetoric, has been evident to the educators who have taken our hopes most seriously. The history of our educational writing poses a formidable challenge to those modern educational critics who yield too readily to nostalgia for good old days that apparently were never too good. The educational writing that has been left to us by men whose names command our respect is to a remarkable degree a literature of acid criticism and bitter complaint. Americans would create a common-school system, but would balk at giving it adequate support. They would stand close to the vanguard among the countries of the world in the attempt to diffuse knowledge among the people, and then engage drifters and misfits as teachers and offer them the wages of draymen.

The history of American educational reformers often seems to be the history of men fighting against an uncongenial environment. The educational jeremiad is as much a feature of our literature as the jeremiad in the Puritan sermons. That this literature should have been one of complaint is not in itself surprising, for complaint is the burden of anyone who aims at improvement; but there is a constant undercurrent of something close to despair. Moreover, one finds it not only on the

---

[4] An impressive brief critique of these failings may be found in Robert M. Hutchins: *Some Observations on American Education* (Cambridge, 1956).

[5] On American reading, in and out of college, see Lester Asheim: "A Survey of Recent Research," in Jacob M. Price, ed.: *Reading for Life* (Ann Arbor, Michigan, 1959); Gordon Dupee: "Can Johnny's Parents Read?" *Saturday Review,* June 2, 1956.

educational frontiers of the West, or in darkest Mississippi, but in Massachusetts, the state that stood first in the development of the common-school system and has never lost her place among the leading states in education. Yet, in this state, the educational reformer James Gordon Carter warned in 1826 that if the legislature did not change its policies the common schools would be extinct within twenty years.[6]

The criticisms made by Horace Mann about one of the nation's best school systems during his years as secretary of the Massachusetts Board of Education after 1837 are illuminating. Schoolhouses, he said, were too small, and ill-situated; school committees, to save money, had neglected to insure uniformity in the textbooks, with the consequence that a single class might be using as many as eight or ten manuals in a given subject; school committees were neither well paid nor accorded social recognition; one portion of the community was so apathetic about education that it would do nothing for the school system, but the wealthier portion had given up on the common schools and were sending their children to private institutions; many towns neglected to comply with the state's school requirements; there was an "extensive want of competent teachers for the Common Schools," but the existing teachers, however ill-equipped, were "as good as public opinion has demanded"; there was "an obvious want of intelligence in the reading-classes"; "the schools have retrograded within the last generation or half generation in regard to orthography"; "more than eleven-twelfths of all the children in the reading-classes in our schools do not understand the meaning of the words they read." He was afraid that "neglectful school committees, incompetent teachers, and an indifferent public, may go on degrading each other" until the whole idea of free schools would be abandoned.[7]

[6] *Essays upon Popular Education* (Boston, 1826), p. 41.

[7] Horace Mann: *Lectures and Annual Reports on Education*, Vol. I (Cambridge, 1867), pp. 396, 403–4, 408, 413, 422, 506–7, 532, 539. Of considerable interest is Mann's report of 1843, in which he made extensive comparisons with Prussian education. There, he remarked, "the teacher's profession holds such a high rank in public estimation, that none who have failed in other employments or departments of business are encouraged to look upon school-keeping as an ultimate resource." *Life and Works*, Vol. III (Boston, 1891), pp. 266 ff. and especially pp. 346–8. Francis Bowen, Harvard's professor of moral philosophy, concurred with Mann's views; the New England school system, he said, looking backward in 1857, "had degenerated into routine, it was starved by parsimony. Any hovel would answer for a school-house, any primer would do for a text-book, any farmer's apprentice was competent to 'teach school.'" *American Journal of Education*, Vol. IV (September, 1857), p. 14.

The complaints continued, and the plaintive note spread from New England to the country at large. In 1870, when the country was on the eve of a great forward surge in secondary education, William Franklin Phelps, then head of a normal school in Winona, Minnesota, and later a president of the National Education Association, declared: [8]

> They [the elementary schools] are mainly in the hands of ignorant, unskilled teachers. The children are fed upon the mere husks of knowledge. They leave school for the broad theater of life without discipline; without mental power or moral stamina. . . . Poor schools and poor teachers are in a majority throughout the country. Multitudes of the schools are so poor that it would be as well for the country if they were closed. . . . They afford the sad spectacle of ignorance engaged in the stupendous fraud of self-perpetuation at the public expense. . . . Hundreds of our American schools are little less than undisciplined juvenile mobs.

In 1892 Joseph M. Rice toured the country to examine its school systems and reported the same depressing picture in city after city, with only a few welcome exceptions: education was a creature of ward politics; ignorant politicians hired ignorant teachers; teaching was an uninspired thing of repetitive drill.[9] Ten years later, when the Progressive movement was barely under way, the New York *Sun* had a different kind of complaint: [1]

> When we were boys, boys had to do a little work in school. They were not coaxed; they were hammered. Spelling, writing, and arithmetic were not electives, and you had to learn. In these more fortunate times, elementary education has become in many places a vaudeville show. The child must be kept amused, and learns what he pleases. Many sage teachers scorn the old-fashioned rudiments, and it seems to be regarded as between a misfortune and a crime for a child to learn to read.

[8] NEA *Proceedings*, 1870, pp. 13, 17. For a series of complaints similar to these, and ranging from 1865 to 1915, see Edgar B. Wesley: *N.E.A.: The First Hundred Years* (New York, 1957), pp. 138–43.

[9] *The Public School System of the United States* (New York, 1893).

[1] Marian G. Valentine: "William H. Maxwell and Progressive Education," *School and Society*, LXXV (June 7, 1952), p. 354. Complaints of this order began to emerge at this time as a response to the new education. See the remarks of Lys D'Aimee as quoted in R. Freeman Butts and Lawrence Cremin: *A History of Education in American Culture* (New York, 1953), pp. 385–6.

A generation later, after the nation had developed its great mass system of secondary education, and education itself had become highly professionalized, Thomas H. Briggs of Teachers College, delivering his Inglis Lecture at Harvard, assessed the nation's "great investment" in secondary education and concluded that it had gone sadly awry. "There has been no respectable achievement," he observed, "even in the subjects offered in the secondary school curricula." Performance in mathematics, he thought, was of the sort which, applied in business, would lead to bankruptcy or the penitentiary. Only half the students could find the area of a circle, when given the value of *pi* and all necessary data. Students of foreign languages acquired neither the ability to read nor the ability to communicate. Only half the students who had completed a year's study of high-school French could translate *Je n'ai parlé à personne;* and only one fifth of the pupils who elected French took more than two years of the language. In Latin, the results were as bad. A year's study of ancient history yielded students who could not tell who Solon was; and after a year of American history, students were unable to define the Monroe Doctrine—even though both subjects were stressed in these courses. Courses in English failed to produce in the majority any "permanent taste for what is called standard literature" and brought results in written English that were "in a large fraction of the cases shocking in their evidence of inadequate achievement." [2]

Today we live in the age of systematic surveys, and the evidences of our various educational failures have accumulated to the point at which documentation is futile. [3] The widest range of difference exists with regard to the practical meaning of this evidence. Many professional educationists welcome it as further proof of their contention that the traditional course of studies is unsuited to vast numbers of children in a system of mass education. Critics of the educational system argue that these findings simply show the need to return to higher standards and to improve our educational morale. Concerning the central fact of educational failure there is relatively slight dispute; and the failure itself underlines one of the paradoxes of American life: that in a society

---

[2] Thomas H. Briggs: *The Great Investment: Secondary Education in a Democracy* (Cambridge, Mass., 1930), pp. 124–8.

[3] My favorite among such surveys is one Los Angeles made of 30,000 of its school children in 1951. Among other things, it showed that almost one of every seven eighth graders could not find the Atlantic Ocean on a map, and that approximately the same proportion of eleventh graders (aged sixteen to eighteen), could not calculate 50 per cent of 36. *Time,* December 10, 1951, pp. 93–4.

so passionately intent upon education, the yield of our educational system has been such a constant disappointment.

· 3 ·

We may, of course, nourish the suspicion that there is something misleading about these findings and criticisms. Is not the history of constant complaint by school authorities and educational reformers simply a sign of healthy self-criticism? Were not many of these complaints followed by reforms? If the American public educational system is measured not by some abstract standards of perfection but by the goals for which it was originally established, must it not be considered a success? On this count there is undoubtedly much to be said. The American system of common schools was meant to take a vast, heterogeneous, and mobile population, recruited from manifold sources and busy with manifold tasks, and forge it into a nation, make it literate, and give it at least the minimal civic competence necessary to the operation of republican institutions. This much it did; and if in the greater part of the nineteenth century the United States did not astound the world with its achievements in high culture, its schools at least helped to create a common level of opinion and capacity that was repeatedly noticed with admiration by foreign observers.

Here no doubt the American educational creed itself needs further scrutiny. The belief in mass education was not founded primarily upon a passion for the development of mind, or upon pride in learning and culture for their own sakes, but rather upon the supposed political and economic benefits of education. No doubt leading scholars and educational reformers like Horace Mann did care for the intrinsic values of mind. But in trying to persuade influential men or the general public of the importance of education, they were careful in the main to point out the possible contributions of education to public order, political democracy, or economic improvement. They understood that the most irresistible way to "sell" education was to stress its role not in achieving a high culture but in forging an acceptable form of democratic society. They adopted and fixed upon the American mind the idea that under popular government popular education is an absolute necessity. To the rich, who were often wary of its cost, they presented popular education as the only alternative to public disorder, to an unskilled and ignorant labor force, to misgovernment, crime, and radicalism. To the people of middle and lower classes they presented it as the foundation of popular power, the door to opportunity, the great equalizer in the race for success.[4]

As to the vast, inarticulate body of the American public, it is impossible to be certain exactly what it expected from the school system, other than an opportunity for the advancement of its children. That the development of intellectual power was not a central concern seems clear, but there is also some evidence that the anti-intellectualism I have already characterized in religion, politics, and business found its way into school practice. There seems to have been a prevailing concern that children should not form too high an estimate of the uses of mind. Ruth Miller Elson's recent researches in the content of nineteenth-century schoolbooks indicate that the compilers of school readers tried to inculcate in the children attitudes toward intellect, art, and learning which, we have already seen, were widely prevalent in adult society.[5] The old school readers contained a considerable proportion of good literature, but even at their best the selections were hardly chosen because they would inculcate the values of creative intellect.

As Mrs. Elson remarks, the primary intellectual value these books embodied was utility. As an early reader said: "We are all scholars of useful knowledge." Jedidiah Morse's famous geography boasted: "While many other nations are wasting the brilliant efforts of genius in monuments of ingenious folly, to perpetuate their pride, the Americans, according to the true spirit of republicanism, are employed almost entirely in works of public and private utility." Authors of schoolbooks were proud of the democratic diffusion of knowledge in America and were quite content to pay the price of not having so many advanced or profound scholars. "There are none of those splendid establishments such as Oxford and Cambridge in which immense salaries maintain the professors of literature in monastic idleness. . . . The People of this country have not yet been inclined to make much

[4] The arguments used by educational reformers are discussed by Lawrence Cremin: *The American Common School* (New York, 1951); Merle Curti: *The Social Ideas of American Educators* (New York, 1935); and Sidney L. Jackson: *America's Struggle for Free Schools* (Washington, 1940). One of the most illuminating documents of American social history is Robert Carlton [Baynard Rush Hall]: *The New Purchase, or Seven and a Half Years in the Far West* (1843; Indiana Centennial ed., Princeton, 1916); it is full of information about folk attitudes toward education in the old Midwest.

[5] I am much enlightened by Mrs. Elson's article, "American Schoolbooks and 'Culture' in the Nineteenth Century," *Mississippi Valley Historical Review*, Vol. XLVI (December, 1959), pp. 411–34; the quotations in the following paragraphs are taken from this essay, pp. 413, 414, 417, 419, 421, 422, 425, 434.

literary display—they have rather aimed at works of general utility." A similar pride was expressed that American colleges and universities, unlike those of Europe, were not devoted simply to the acquisition of knowledge but to the moral cultivation of their students. The American college was complacently portrayed as a place designed to form character and inculcate sound principle rather than to lead to the pursuit of truth.

The common school was thought to have been designed for a similar purpose. "Little children," said Alice Cary in a selection used in a third reader of 1882, "you must seek rather to be good than wise." "Man's intellect," said another writer, "is not man's sole nor best adorning." The virtues of the heart were consistently exalted over those of the head, and this preference found its way into the hero literature of the school readers. European heroes might be haughty aristocrats, soldiers destructive on the battlefield, or "great scholars who were pensioned flatterers of power, and poets, who profaned the high gift of genius to pamper the vices of a corrupted court." But American heroes were notable as simple, sincere men of high character. Washington, a central figure in this literature, was portrayed in some of the books as an example both of the self-made man and of the practical man with little use for the intellectual life. "He was more solid than brilliant, and had more judgment than genius. He had great dread of public life, cared little for books, and possessed no library," said a history book of the 1880's and 1890's. Even Franklin was not depicted as one of the intellectual leaders of the eighteenth century, or as a distinguished scientist at home in the capitals of the world and among its aristocracies, but rather as an exemplar of the self-made man and the author of catchpenny maxims about thrift and industry.

The highbrow sources anthologized in the readers consisted of materials that would confirm these sentiments. Anti-intellectual quotations from Wordsworth were prominent in the first half of the century, and from Emerson in the second half. A fifth reader of 1884 quoted Emerson's *Goodbye:*

> I laugh at the lore and the pride of man,
> At the sophists' schools, and the learned clan;
> For what are they all in their high conceit,
> When man in the bush with God may meet.

There was a certain bias, too, against the idea of intellectual pleasure; the standard injunctions against novel-reading were repeated; and the notion was on occasion set forth that reading for pleasure is an altogether bad business: "A book which is torn and mutilated is abused, but one which is merely read for enjoyment is misused." Mrs. Elson concludes, from an intensive analysis of these readers, that "anti-intellectualism is not only not new in American civilization, but that it is thoroughly imbedded in the school books that have been read by generations of pupils since the beginning of the republic."

This downgrading of intellect was not compensated by any high regard for the arts. Music and the fine arts appeared primarily in connection with discussions of the self-made artist or of national monuments or with exaltation of American art. What seemed to be important to the compilers of school readers was not the aesthetic content of an artist's work but his career as evidence of the virtues of assiduous application. Benjamin West was portrayed as having been too poor as a boy to buy paint brushes and as having plucked hairs from his cat's tail to enable himself to paint: "Thus we see that, by industry, ingenuity, and perseverance, a little American boy became the most distinguished painter of his day in England." But if a career in art could be a means of disciplining character, it also had its dangers. An excerpt from the eighteenth-century English moralist, Hannah More, was exhumed to suggest "that in all polished countries an entire devotedness to the fine arts has been one grand source of the corruption of women . . . and while corruption brought on by an excessive cultivation of the arts has contributed its full share to the decline of states, it has always furnished an infallible symptom of their impending fall." The Italians were commonly held up as an example of a people whose distinguished achievements in the arts went hand in hand with an unsound national character. As time went on, it should be said, the school readers showed an increasing disposition to point to the development of American art and letters as an answer to European critics of American culture. Art, linked to national pride and conceived as an instrument, was at least acceptable.

We cannot know, of course, how much impact the content of school readers had on the minds of children. But any child who accepted the attitudes prevalent in these books would have come to think of scholarship and the fine arts as embellishments identified with the inferior society of Europe, would have thought of art primarily with regard to its services to nationality, and would have judged it almost entirely by its contributions to character. As Mrs. Elson puts it, he would grow up "to be honest, industrious, religious, and moral. He would be a useful citizen untouched by the effeminate and perhaps even dangerous influence of the arts or scholarship." The concept of culture presented in his readers had prepared him for "a life devoted to the pursuit of material success and a perfected character, but a life in which intellectual and artistic achievements would seem important only when they could be made to subserve some useful purpose."

These gleanings from the school readers suggest a clearer definition of the American faith in education as it was manifested during the nineteenth century. Perhaps the most touching aspect of this faith was the benevolent determination that education should not be exclusive, that it should be universally accessible. With impressive success this determination was executed: the schools were made into powerful agencies for the diffusion of social and economic opportunities. Americans were somewhat less certain about what the internal, qualitative standards of education should be and, in so far as they could define these standards, had difficulty in implementing them on the large scale on which their educational efforts were conceived. The function of education in inculcating usable skills and in broadening social opportunities was always clear. The value of developing the mind for intellectual or imaginative achievement or even contemplative enjoyment was considerably less clear and less subject to common agreement. Many Americans were troubled by the suspicion that an education of this kind was suitable only to the leisured classes, to aristocracies, to the European past; that its usefulness was less evident than its possible dangers; that an undue concern with the development of mind was a form of arrogance or narcissism which one would expect to find mainly in the morally corrupt.

· 4 ·

American reluctance to accept intellectual values in the educational process could hardly have been overcome by a strong, respected teaching profession, since such a profession did not exist. Popular attitudes did not call for the development of such a profession, but even if they had, the conditions of American life made it difficult to recruit and train a first-rate professional corps.

The figure of the schoolteacher may well be taken as a central symbol in any modern society. The teacher is, or at least can be, the first more or less full-time, professional representative of the life of the mind who enters into the experience of most children; and the feeling the child entertains toward the teacher, his awareness of the community's regard for the teacher, are focal points in the formation of his early, rudimentary notions about learning. This is, of course, somewhat less important in the primary school, where the essential work is the inculcation of elementary skills, than it is in the secondary school, where the rapidly awakening mind of the child begins to be engaged with the world of ideas. At any level, however, from the primary grades to the university, the teacher is not merely an instructor but a potential personal model for his (or her) pupils and a living clue to the attitudes that prevail in the adult world. From teachers children derive much of their sense of the way in which the mind is cultivated; from observing how their teachers are esteemed and rewarded they quickly sense how society looks upon the teacher's role.

In countries where the intellectual functions of education are highly valued, like France, Germany, and the Scandinavian countries, the teacher, especially the secondary-school teacher, is likely to be an important local figure representing a personal and vocational ideal worthy of emulation. There it seems worth becoming a teacher because what the teacher does is worth doing and is handsomely recognized. The intellectually alert and cultivated teacher may have a particular importance for intelligent children whose home environment is not highly cultivated; such children have no alternative source of mental stimulation. All too often, however, in the history of the United States, the schoolteacher has been in no position to serve as a model for an introduction to the intellectual life. Too often he has not only no claims to an intellectual life of his own, but not even an adequate workmanlike competence in the skills he is supposed to impart. Regardless of his own quality, his low pay and common lack of personal freedom have caused the teacher's role to be associated with exploitation and intimidation.

That American teachers are not well rewarded or esteemed is almost universally recognized in contemporary comment. A few years ago Marion Folsom, then Secretary of Health, Education, and Welfare, observed that the "national disgrace" of our teachers' salaries reflected "the lack of respect accorded to teaching by the public." [6] Reminders of this situation constantly appear in the press. One day the public learns that a city in Michigan pays its teachers $400 a year less than its garbage collectors; another that a group of teachers in Florida, finding that the governor pays his cook $3,600 a year, have written to

[6] *The New York Times*, November 3, 1957.

point out that the cook is paid more than many of the state's college-educated teachers.[7] Like other Americans, teachers live better in absolute terms than their European counterparts, but their annual salaries, relative to the per capita income of their country, have been lower than those of teachers in every country of the Western world, except Canada. The American teacher's average annual salary in 1949 stood in a ratio of 1.9 to the per capita income; the comparable figure was 2.5 in England, 5.1 in France, 4.7 in the West German Republic, 3.1 in Italy, 3.2 in Denmark, and 3.6 in Sweden.[8]

The status of schoolteaching as an occupation is lower in this country than elsewhere, and it is far lower than that of the professions in the United States. Characteristically, as Myron Lieberman remarks, teachers are recruited "from the top of the lower half of the population." Upper and upper-middle class persons almost universally reject teaching as a vocation. Teachers frequently resort, during the school year or their summer "vacations," to low-status jobs to supplement their teaching incomes; they work as waitresses, bartenders, housekeepers, janitors, farm hands, checkroom attendants, milkmen, common laborers, and the like. They come from culturally constricted lower- or middle-class homes, where the *Saturday Evening Post* or the *Reader's Digest* is likely to be the characteristic reading matter.[9] For most teachers, their jobs, inadequate though they are, represent some improvement over the economic position of their parents, and they will, in turn, do still better by their children, who will be better educated than they are.

There is reason to believe, despite the sensationalism of *The Blackboard Jungle* and the obviously chaotic conditions of many urban slum schools, that the personal rapport between teachers and pupils in American secondary schools is good; it is particularly good among middle- and upper-class children, who are responsive to the educational goals of the schools and who tend to be favored by the teachers

[7] Ibid., March 24, 1957.

[8] Myron Lieberman: *Education as a Profession* (New York, 1956), p. 383; chapter 12 of this work is informative on the economic position of American teachers. The comparative disadvantage of American teachers registered in these figures does not take into account a variety of valuable non-salaried forms of compensation available elsewhere, like retirement allowances and free medical treatment.

[9] The best brief discussion of the occupational status of teachers is that of Lieberman: op. cit., chapter 14. There are studies indicating that teachers enjoy a higher social status than I have indicated, but they are based upon opinion polling, a technique which in my opinion yields very poor results on matters of status. On the position of teachers, see also the excellent and rather neglected book by Willard Waller: *The Sociology of Teaching* (New York, 1932).

over lower-class children even when the latter show equal ability. But the important fact is that American adolescents have more sympathy than admiration for their teachers. They know that their teachers are ill-paid and they are quick to agree that teachers should be better paid. The more ambitious and able among them also conclude that school-teaching is not for them.[1] In this way, the mediocrity of the teaching profession tends to perpetuate itself. In so far as the teacher stands before his pupils as a surrogate of the intellectual life and its rewards, he unwittingly makes this life appear altogether unattractive.

The unenviable situation of the teacher can be traced back to the earliest days of our history. The educational enthusiasm of the American people was never keen enough to dispose them to support their teachers very well. In part this seems to have reflected a common Anglo-American attitude toward the teaching function, which was sharply different from that prevailing on the European Continent.[2] In any case, the market in qualified labor was always a problem here, and early American communities had intense difficulties in finding and keeping suitable schoolmasters. In colonial times there was a limited supply of educated men, and they were blessed with too many opportunities to be content to settle for what the average community was willing to pay a schoolmaster. Various solutions were tried. Some elementary education was conducted by women in "dame schools," usually private but sometimes partly or largely paid for out of public funds; though it was not until well on in the nineteenth century that American communities generally turned to women for their supply of

---

[1] On the attitude of teen-agers toward their teachers, see H. H. Remmers and D. H. Radler: *The American Teenager* (Indianapolis, 1957); on class factors in the relations between teachers and pupils, see August B. Hollingshead: *Elmtown's Youth* (New York, 1949); and W. Lloyd Warner, Robert J. Havighurst, and Martin B. Loeb: *Who Shall Be Educated?* (New York, 1944).

[2] Presumably the labor market was somewhat different in England in the early nineteenth century, but the social and economic conditions of teachers in public education seem less enviable than that of Americans. See Asher Tropp: *The School Teachers* (London, 1957). Somewhat revealing in this connection was the remark of one of Her Majesty's Inspectors, H. S. Tremenheere, on a visit to the United States in the 1850's. He wrote: "Any one from England visiting those schools would be also greatly struck with the very high social position, *considering the nature of their employment,* of the teachers, male and female. . . ." *Notes on Public Subjects Made during a Tour in the United States and Canada* (London, 1852), pp. 57–8. I believe the phrase I have italicized here would have been intelligible to English and American readers and quite mystifying to most readers on the Continent. For another English observer, who found the status of American teachers high, though their pay was equally bad as in England, see Francis Adams: *The Free School System of the United States* (London, 1875), especially pp. 176–8, 181–2, 194–5, 197–8, 238.

schoolteachers. In some towns the minister doubled as a schoolmaster; or the schoolmaster doubled as a local man of all work, with a variety of civic and church duties ranging from ringing the church bells to serving as the local scribe, the town crier, or the town clerk. Others accepted the fact that a permanent schoolmaster was all but an impossibility and employed briefly a series of ambitious young men who were on the way to other careers, perhaps in the ministry or the law. Thus, many communities were able temporarily to secure able teachers of good character, but the very transience of their role seemed to establish the point that teaching was no better than a way station in life for a man of real ability and character.

Men permanently fixed in the role of schoolmaster seem often to have been of indifferent quality and extraordinarily ill-suited for the job. Perhaps it is because only the pathological aspects of a situation usually make historical news that Willard S. Elsbree, writing about the character of the colonial schoolmaster, in his history, *The American Teacher,* tells us mainly about drunkenness, slander, profanity, lawsuits, and seductions.[3] But it is also suggestive that colonial communities sometimes had to resort to indentured servants for teachers. A Delaware minister observed, around 1725, that "when a ship arrives in the river, it is a common expression with those who stand in need of an instructor for their children, *let us go and buy a school master.*" In 1776 the *Maryland Journal* advertised that a ship had just arrived at Baltimore from Belfast and Cork, and enumerated among its products for sale "various Irish commodities, among which are school masters, beef, pork, and potatoes." It was about the same time that the Connecticut press printed an advertisement offering a reward for a runaway described as "a school-master, of a pale complexion, with short hair. He has the itch very bad, and sore legs." Disabled men were frequently turned into schoolteachers for lack of anything better to do with them. The town of Albany in 1673 added a local baker to its existing staff of three teachers because, it said, "he was impotent in his hand."[4] Although such choices may have been motivated by a misplaced philanthropy, they also reflected a persistent difficulty in finding qualified men. Massachusetts alone stood out as having enough educated men so that a significant proportion of college graduates were schoolmasters.

[3] *The American Teacher* (New York, 1939), chapter 2.
[4] Howard K. Beale: *A History of Freedom of Teaching in American Schools* (New York, 1941), pp. 11–12; Elsbree: op. cit., pp. 26–7, 34.

Although competent and dedicated schoolmasters could be found from time to time, the misfits seem to have been so conspicuous that they set an unflattering image of the teaching profession. "The truth is," an observer wrote in 1725, "the office and character of such a person is generally very mean and contemptible here, and it cannot be other ways 'til the public takes the Education of Children into their mature consideration."[5] The tradition seems to have persisted well on into the nineteenth century, when we find this sad confession: "The man who was disabled to such an extent that he could not engage in manual labor—who was lame, too fat, too feeble, had the phthisic or had fits or was too lazy to work—well, they usually made schoolmasters out of these, and thus got what work they could out of them." There was a train of stereotypes of this order: the one-eyed or one-legged teacher, the teacher who had been driven out of the ministry by his weakness for drink, the lame teacher, the misplaced fiddler, and "the teacher who got drunk on Saturday and whipped the entire school on Monday."[6]

The concern of serious educators with the caliber of teachers was general and knew no bounds of geography. James Gordon Carter, describing the Massachusetts schools as they were in 1824, declared that[7] the men teachers could be divided into three classes: (1) Those who thought teaching easier and possibly more remunerative than common labor. (2) Those who were acquiring a good education, and who took up teaching as a temporary employment, either to earn money for necessities or to give themselves time to choose a regular profession. (3) Those who, conscious of weakness, despaired of distinction or even the means of subsistence by other employments: "If a young man be moral enough to keep out of State prison, he will find no difficulty in getting approbation for a schoolmaster."

Some years later President Joseph Caldwell of the University of North Carolina waxed indignant about the recruitment of the schoolteachers of his state:[8]

---

[5] Beale: op. cit., p. 13.

[6] R. Carlyle Buley: op. cit., Vol. II, pp. 370–1.

[7] James G. Carter: *The Schools of Massachusetts in 1824*, Old South Leaflets No. 135, pp. 15–16, 19, 21.

[8] Beale: op. cit., p. 93; cf. the early treatise on teaching, Samuel Hall's *Lectures on School-Keeping* (Boston, 1829), especially pp. 26–8. On the condition of the teaching profession in the Southwest ("The great mass of our teachers are mere adventurers"), see Philip Lindsley in Richard Hofstadter and Wilson Smith, eds.: *American Higher Education: A Documentary History* (Chicago, 1961), Vol. I, pp. 332–3.

Is a man constitutionally and habitually indolent, a burden upon all from whom he can extract support? Then there is one way of shaking him off, let us make him a schoolmaster. To teach school is, in the opinion of many, little else than sitting still and doing nothing. Has any man wasted all his property, or ended in debt by indiscretion and misconduct? The business of school-keeping stands wide open for his reception, and here he sinks to the bottom, for want of capacity to support himself. Has any one ruined himself, and done all he could to corrupt others, by dissipation, drinking, seduction, and a course of irregularities? Nay, has he returned from prison after an ignominious atonement for some violation of the laws? He is destitute of character and cannot be trusted, but presently he opens a school and the children are seen flocking into it, for if he is willing to act in that capacity, we shall all admit that as he can read and write, and cypher to the square root, he will make an excellent schoolmaster.

And what, after all, was the dominant stereotype of the schoolmaster in American literature if not Washington Irving's Ichabod Crane?

The cognomen of Crane was not inapplicable to his person. He was tall, but exceedingly lank, with narrow shoulders, long arms and legs, hands that dangled a mile out of his sleeves, feet that might have served for shovels, and his whole frame most loosely hung together. His head was small, and flat at the top, with huge ears, large, green, glassy eyes, and a long, snip nose, so that it looked like a weather-cock perched upon his spindle neck to tell which way the wind blew. To see him striding along the profile of a hill on a windy day, with his clothes bagging and fluttering about him, one might have mistaken him for the genius of Famine descending upon the earth or some scarecrow eloped from a cornfield.

As Irving portrayed him, Ichabod Crane was not altogether a bad fellow. In the course of boarding around, he did what he could to make himself agreeable to the families of the farmers, undertook a wide variety of chores and dandled and petted the young children. Among the women of the community he cut a figure of some importance, being somewhat more cultivated than the bumpkins they ordinarily met. But this "odd mixture of small shrewdness and simple credulity" was no hero to the men, and when Brom Bones in his ghastly masquerade frightened Ichabod out of town and smashed a pumpkin on his credulous head, he was passing the symbolic judgment of the American male community on the old-time schoolmaster.

· 5 ·

Complaints such as those of Caldwell and Carter, men who hoped to work some educational reform, probably exaggerated the case; but if they did, they only reflected a stereotype of the teacher that had fixed itself in the mind of the country. A vicious circle had been drawn. American communities had found it hard to find, train, or pay for good teachers. They settled for what they could get, and what they got was a high proportion of misfits and incompetents. They tended to conclude that teaching was a trade which attracted rascals, and, having so concluded, they were reluctant to pay the rascals more than they were worth. To be sure, there is evidence that the competent schoolteacher of good character was eagerly welcomed when he could be found, and soon earned a status in the community higher than that of his colleagues elsewhere; but it was a long time before any considerable effort could be made to improve the caliber of teachers generally.

What helped American education to break out of the vicious circle was the development of the graded primary school and the emergence of the woman teacher. The graded school, a response to the educational problems of the largest cities, began to develop in the 1820's and had become prevalent by 1860. In the latter year most cities had such schools, which pupils entered at about six and could leave at fourteen. The graded school, modeled largely on the German system, made possible smaller classrooms holding more homogeneous groups of pupils and did much to put American teaching on a respectable basis. It also increased the need for teachers and opened the trade to women. Until 1830, most teachers had been men, and women had dealt mainly with very small children and summer classes. The notion prevailed that women were inadequate to the disciplinary problems of the schoolroom, especially in large classes and more advanced age groups. The emergence of the graded school provided a partial answer to these objections. Opponents of women teachers were still to be heard in many communities, but they were often easily silenced when it was pointed out that women teachers could be paid one third or one half as much as men. Here was one answer to the great American quest to educate everybody but to do it cheaply. By 1860 women teachers outnumbered men in some states, and the Civil War accelerated the replacement of men. By 1870 it is estimated that women constituted almost sixty per cent of the teaching force, and their numbers were increasing rapidly. By 1900 over seventy per cent of teachers were women, and in another quarter of a century the figure reached a peak of over eighty-three per cent.[9]

Acceptance of the woman teacher solved the problem of character as well as that of cost, since it was possible to find a fair supply of admirable young girls to work at low pay and to keep them at work as teachers only so long as their personal conduct met the rigid and sometimes puritanical standards set by school boards. But it did not altogether solve the problem of competence. The new teachers were characteristically very young and poorly prepared. For a long time there were practically no public facilities to give them specialized training, and private seminaries for the purpose were not numerous. European countries experimented with the training of teachers for more than a century before the United States gave much thought to it. Horace Mann was instrumental in establishing the first public normal school in Massachusetts in 1839; but at the beginning of the Civil War there were only a dozen such institutions. They proliferated rapidly after 1862; yet at the end of the century they were still unable to keep pace with the rapidly growing demand for teachers. In 1898 only a small proportion of new teachers—perhaps about one fifth— was taken from public or private schools of this order.

Moreover, the training these schools offered was not very exalted. Their admissions standards were haphazard, and even as late as 1900 a high-school diploma was seldom considered a prerequisite of entrance. Two years of high-school work, or the equivalent, was usually the prelude to two or three years of normal school. The four-year normal school became prevalent only after 1920, by which time it was beginning to be superseded by the teachers' college. Even in 1930, a survey by the United States Office of Education showed that only eighteen per cent of the country's current graduates of teachers' colleges and normal schools had had four-year courses. Two thirds of them were products of one-year or two-year curricula.[1]

In spite of the considerable effort made by American communities

---

[9] Elsbree: op. cit., pp. 194–208, 553–4. By 1956 the figure had fallen to seventy-three per cent. Women school teachers received about two thirds the salaries of men in rural areas. In the cities, where pay was higher for both, they tended at first to get only a little more than one third of the salaries of men.

[1] Elsbree: op. cit., pp. 311–34.

to meet the demand for competent teachers around the turn of the century and afterwards, they were engaged in a taxing race with the explosive growth of the school population; and the excess of demand over supply in the market for teachers militated against efforts to raise standards of preparation. The best estimates for 1919–20 indicate that half of America's schoolteachers were under twenty-five, half served in the schools for not more than four or five years, and half had had no more than four years of education beyond the eighth grade. A period of rapid improvement at least in the quantitative dimension of teacher education ensued in the next several years. But in 1933, when the United States Office of Education published its *National Survey of the Education of Teachers*, it found that only ten per cent of the elementary teachers of the country, and only fifty-six per cent of the junior high-school teachers and eighty-five per cent of the senior high-school teachers, had B.A. degrees. Education beyond the B.A. degree was almost negligible except among senior high-school teachers, of whom a little more than one sixth had taken their M.A.'s. A comparison of teacher education in America and in selected countries of Western Europe showed the United States to be at some considerable disadvantage, significantly behind England and far behind France, Germany, and Sweden. "What inspires grave concern," wrote the authors of the survey, "is the fact that students in general and important groups of teachers in particular were not much more intelligent than a cross-section of the population at large." [2]

To what extent able students stayed out of teaching because of its poor rewards and to what extent because of the nonsense that figured so prominently in teacher education, it is difficult to say. That teachers did not have enough training in the subjects they intended to teach was clear enough; but even more striking was the fact that, however prepared they might be in the field of their major interest, their chances of teaching in that field were no better than fair. The survey's collation of existing studies showed that a high-school teacher with a good preparation in an academic subject had hardly better than a fifty per cent chance of being assigned to teach it. In part this may have been a consequence of administrative negligence, but mainly it

---

[2] E. S. Evenden: "Summary and Interpretation," *National Survey of the Education of Teachers*, Vol. VI (Washington, 1935), pp. 32, 49, 89. For later information on the caliber of persons entering education, see Henry Chauncey: "The Use of Selective Service College Qualification Test in the Deferment of College Students," *Science*, Vol. CXVI (July 25, 1952), pp. 73–9. See also Lieberman: op. cit., pp. 227–31.

was attributable to the large number of uneconomically small high schools about which James Bryant Conant was still complaining in 1959.[3]

As one looks at the history of teacher training in the United States, one can hardly escape Elsbree's conclusion that "in our efforts to supply enough teachers for the public schools we have sacrificed quality for quantity." [4] The prevailing assumption was that everyone should get a common-school education, and on the whole this was realized, outside the South. But the country could not or would not make the massive effort that would have been necessary to supply highly trained teachers for this attempt to educate everybody. The search for cheap teachers was perennial. Schoolteachers were considered to be public officers, and it was part of the American egalitarian philosophy that the salaries of public officers should not be too high. In colonial times salaries of schoolmasters, which varied widely, seem on the whole to have been roughly on a par with or below the wages of skilled laborers and distinctly below those of professional men. In 1843 Horace Mann, after making a survey of wages of various occupational groups in a Massachusetts community, reported that skilled workers were getting from fifty to a hundred per cent more than was being paid to any of the district schoolteachers of the same town. He found women teachers getting less than women factory workers. A New Jersey school administrator in 1855 believed that although teachers were generally "miserably qualified for their duties," they were "even better prepared than they can afford to be." It was absurd, he pointed out, to expect men of ability and promise to work for a teacher's pay, and chiefly for this reason "the very name of teacher has been, and is yet to some extent, a term of reproach." Many a farmer would pay a better price for shoeing his horse than he would "to obtain a suitable individual to mould and form the character of his child." [5]

Certainly what was lacking in salary was not made up in dignity or

[3] On the strength of his observations, Conant concluded that "unless a graduating class contains at least one hundred students, classes in advanced subjects and separate sections within all classes become impossible except with extravagantly high costs." His survey showed that 73.9 per cent of the country's high schools had twelfth-grade enrollments of less than a hundred, and that 31.8 per cent of the twelfth-grade pupils were in such schools. *The American High School Today* (New York, 1959), pp. 37–8, 77–85, 132–3. Of course, an important reason for the failure to make good use of the academic specialities of teachers was the practice of specifying requirements in education courses for teachers' certificates but paying insufficient attention to academic requirements.

[4] Op. cit., p. 334.

[5] Ibid., p. 273; for Mann, see pp. 279–80.

status. Moreover, the growing numerical preponderance of the woman teacher, which did so much to cure the teaching profession of the taint of bad character, created a new and serious problem. Elsewhere in the world the ideal prevails—and the actual recruitment of teachers by and large conforms to it—that men should play a vital role in education generally, and a preponderant role in secondary education. The United States is the only country in the Westernized world that has put its elementary education almost exclusively in the hands of women and its secondary education largely so. In 1953 this country stood almost alone among the nations of the world in the feminization of its teaching: women constituted ninety-three per cent of its primary teachers and sixty per cent of its secondary teachers. Only one country in Western Europe (Italy, with fifty-two per cent) employed women for more than half of its secondary-school personnel.[6]

The point is not, of course, that women are inferior to men as teachers (in fact, at some levels, and particularly in the lower grades of the elementary school, there is reason to think that women teachers are preferable). But in America, where teaching has been identified as a feminine profession, it does not offer men the stature of a fully legitimate male role. The American masculine conviction that education and culture are feminine concerns is thus confirmed, and no doubt partly shaped, by the experiences of boys in school. There are often not enough male models or idols among their teachers whose performance will convey the sense that the world of mind is legitimately male, who can give them masculine examples of intellectual inquiry or cultural life, and who can be regarded as sufficiently successful and important in the world to make it conceivable for vigorous boys to enter teaching themselves for a livelihood. The boys grow up thinking of men teachers as somewhat effeminate and treat them with a curious mixture of genteel deference (of the sort due to women) and hearty male condescension.[7] In a certain constricted sense, the male teacher may be respected, but he is not "one of the boys."

[6] Lieberman: op. cit., p. 244, gives figures for twenty-five countries. Four Western countries, the United Kingdom, France, West Germany, and Canada, ranged from thirty-four per cent female secondary teachers to forty-five per cent—the average being forty-one per cent. In the U.S.S.R., sixty per cent of primary and forty-five per cent of secondary school teachers are women. See ibid., pp. 241–55, for a discussion of this problem.

[7] See, for example, the incident recounted by Waller: op. cit., pp. 49–50. "It has been said," Waller remarks, "that no woman and no Negro is ever fully admitted to the white man's world. Perhaps we should add men teachers to the list of the excluded." The problem is somewhat complicated by the aura of sexlessness that hangs over the public image of the teaching profession, and by the long-prevailing

But this question of the maleness of the teacher's role is only a small part of a large problem. In the nineteenth century men had all too often entered schoolteaching either transiently—as a step on the way to becoming lawyers, ministers, politicians, or college professors—or as a final confession of failure in more worthwhile occupations. Even today, surveys show, the ablest men tend to enter teaching in the expectation that they will become educational administrators or leave the field entirely. In recent decades a new area has opened up which may drain able men, and women as well, out of the public secondary school: the emergence of large numbers of heavily attended junior or community colleges has made it possible for enterprising teachers with an extra increment of ability and training to step up from the high school, or sidestep it altogether, in favor of an institution which offers an easier way of life as well as better pay and more prestige. There, however, some of the instruction they offer will be of a kind which could as well be offered in an efficient, first-rate secondary school. Giving the thirteenth and fourteenth years of public education a separate institutional setting may have a variety of advantages, but it does not in itself add to the total store of the country's teaching talents. In its pursuit of an adequate supply of well-trained teachers, the nation is caught in a kind of academic treadmill. The more adequate the rewards become in the upper echelons of education—in the colleges

---

prejudice against the married woman teacher. Nineteenth-century America was dominated by a curious conviction, probably somewhat dissipated in the more recent past, that teachers ought to be oddities in their personal lives—a conviction that was easy to enforce in small towns. No doubt the conviction had been quickened by unhappy experiences with the schoolmaster-scamp, but it seems also to have been shaped by the desire to have children schooled by sexual ciphers. This desire lingered to torment many a perfectly innocent girl even in our own time, and where imposed put hopeless restrictions on the lives of well-intentioned schoolmasters. See the touching letter of protest written in 1852 by a schoolmaster against efforts to prevent him from walking to and from school with his female assistant. Elsbree: op. cit., pp. 300–2. Howard Beale's *Are American Teachers Free?* has ample information on the personal restrictions imposed on teachers. I particularly like a pledge forced on all teachers in a Southern community in 1927, in which one of a number of promises was: "I promise not to fall in love, to become engaged or secretly married." Waller: op. cit., p. 43. Even today, Martin Mayer observes: "It is an interesting fact that most European schools are for boys or girls, but the teachers mingle freely, regardless of sex; most American schools are co-educational, but the teachers are rigidly segregated by sex during their time off." *The Schools* (New York, 1961), p. 4. Finally, the prevailing old-time prejudice against the married woman teacher, commonly carried to the point of compulsory job severance for teachers who marry, used to confine the female side of the profession in many places to spinsters and very young girls. For the reasons usually invoked for barring married women, see D. W. Peters: *The Status of the Married Woman Teacher* (New York, 1934).

and junior colleges—and the higher the proportion of the young population that attends such institutions, the greater their capacity becomes to pull talent out of the lower levels of the system. It remains difficult to find enough trained talent to educate large masses in a society that does not make teaching attractive.

CHAPTER XIII

The Road
to Life Adjustment

❦

• 1 •

THE appearance within professional education of an influential
anti-intellectualist movement is one of the striking features of American thought. To understand this movement, which has its most significant consequences in the education of adolescents, one must look at
the main changes in public education since 1870. It was in the 1870's
that this country began to develop free public secondary education on
a large scale, and only in the twentieth century that the public high
school became a mass institution.

Here certain peculiarities of American education are of the first
importance—above all, its democratic assumptions and the universality
of its aims. Outside the United States it is not assumed that all children
should be schooled for so many years or so uniformly. The educational
systems of most European countries were frankly tailored to their class
systems, although they have become less so in our time. In Europe
children are generally schooled together only until the age of ten or
eleven; after that they go separate ways in specialized schools, or at
least in specialized curricula. After fourteen, about eighty per cent
are finished with their formal education and the rest enter academic
pre-university schools. In the United States children must be in school
until the age of sixteen or more, and a larger portion of them are sent
to college than in European countries are sent to academic secondary
schools. Americans also prefer to keep their secondary-school children

in school under a single roof, usually the comprehensive community high school, and on a single educational track (though not in a uniform curriculum). They are not, ideally, meant to be separated, either socially or academically, according to their social class; though the relentless social realities of poverty and ethnic prejudice intervene to preserve most of the class selectivity that our democratic educational philosophy repudiates. In any case, the decision as to a child's ultimate vocational destiny does not have to be made so early in this country as elsewhere, if only because it is not institutionalized by the demands of early educational classification. In the United States specialized preparation even for the professions is postponed to graduate education or at best to the last two years of college. American education serves larger numbers for a longer period of time. It is more universal, more democratic, more leisurely in pace, less rigorous. It is also more wasteful: class-oriented systems are prodigal of the talents of the underprivileged; American education tends to be prodigal of talent generally.

The difference in structure was not always so great, especially in secondary schooling. Before the mass public high school emerged, American practice in secondary education was less in keeping with our democratic theory than with the selective European idea. During the nineteenth century, public education for most Americans ended with the last years of the graded primary school, if not earlier. Free education beyond the primary-school years was established only in the three decades after 1870. Before 1870, the class system, here as well as in Europe, was a primary determinant of the schooling children would get after the age of about thirteen or fourteen. Well-to-do parents, who could afford tuition and who had intellectual or professional aspirations for their children, could send them to private academies, which were often boarding schools. Since the days of Franklin these academies had offered a mixture of the traditional and the "practical": there was a liberal, classical course, founded upon Latin, Greek, and mathematics, commonly supplemented by science and history; but in many schools the students had an option between the "Latin course" and the "English course," the latter being a more "practical" and modern curriculum stressing subjects supposedly useful in business. Academies varied widely in quality, duplicating, in their lowest ranges, some of the work of the common schools and, at their peak, some of the work of the colleges. The best of them were so good that graduates who went on to college were likely to be bored by repetition in the first and even the second college year.[1]

The disparity between the country's moral commitment to educational democracy and its heavy reliance upon private schools for secondary education did not escape the attention of educational critics. On one side there were the generally available public primary schools; on the other, the rapidly proliferating colleges and universities—not free, of course, but cheap and undiscriminating. In between there was an extensive gap, filled by a few pioneering public high schools, but mainly by the private academies, of which it is estimated there were in 1850 about six thousand. As early as the 1830's the academies were denounced as exclusive, aristocratic, and un-American. For a nation already committed to the free common-school system, the extension of this system into the years of secondary education seemed a logical and necessary step. Industry was growing; vocational life was becoming more complex. Skills were more in demand, and it seemed that both utility and equality would be well served by free public education in the secondary years.

Advocates of the public high school had strong moral and vocational arguments, and the legal basis for their proposals already existed in the common-school system. Shortsightedness and mean-spirited tax-consciousness stood in their way, but not for long. The number of public high schools began to rise with great and increasing rapidity after 1860. From 1890 (when usable enrollment figures begin) to 1940, the total enrollment of the high schools nearly doubled every decade. By 1910, thirty-five per cent of the seventeen-year-olds were in school; today the figure has reached over seventy per cent. At this tempo the high school has become an institution which nearly all American youth enter, and from which about two thirds graduate.

Whatever may be said about the qualitative performance of the American high school, which varies widely from place to place, no one is likely to deny that the free secondary education of youth was a

---

[1] It was not necessary to go to an academy to prepare for college; one could also enroll in the "preparatory departments" many colleges maintained to give prospective applicants enough grounding in classics, mathematics, and English to enter upon the college course proper. The existence of a large number of such preparatory departments—as late as 1889, 335 of 400 colleges still had them—is testimony of the inadequacy of the secondary schools to prepare for college requirements those who wanted to go to college. Edgar B. Wesley: *N.E.A.: The First Hundred Years* (New York, 1957), p. 95. On the academies, see E. E. Brown: *The Making of Our Middle Schools* (New York, 1903).

signal accomplishment in the history of education, a remarkable token of our desire to make schooling an instrument of mass opportunity and social mobility. Since I shall have much to say about the high school's curricular problems, it seems important here to stress the positive value of this achievement, and to note that, in its democratic features, if not in its educational standards, the American high school has been to some degree emulated by European school systems in the last generation.

The development of the high school into a mass institution drastically altered its character. At the turn of the century the relatively small clientele of the high school was still highly selective. Its pupils were there, in the main, because they wanted to be, because they and their parents had seized upon the unusual opportunity the high school offered. It is often said, but mistakenly, that the high school, sixty or seventy years ago, was primarily attended by those preparing for college. This was less true than it has come to be in the past fifteen years. Today approximately half the high-school graduates enter college—an astonishing proportion. I do not know what proportion of the high-school graduates actually entered college at the turn of the century, but there is information as to how many of them were so *prepared*. In 1891, twenty-nine per cent of the graduates were. By 1910 the portion of those prepared for college and other advanced institutions was forty-nine per cent. The figure has fluctuated since.[2]

The great change which has affected the high school is that, whereas once it was altogether voluntary, and for this reason quite selective, it is now, at least for those sixteen and under, compulsory and unselective. During the very years when the high school began its most phenomenal growth, the Progressives and trade unionists were assailing the old industrial evil of child labor. One of the most effective devices to counteract this practice was raising the terminal age for compulsory schooling. In 1890, twenty-seven states required compulsory attendance; by 1918 all states had such laws. Legislators also became more exigent in fixing the legal age for leaving school. In 1900 it was set at a mean age of fourteen years and five months in those states which then had such laws. By the 1920's it was close to the figure it has reached today—a mean age of sixteen years and three months. The welfare

[2] See John F. Latimer: *What's Happened to Our High Schools?* (Washington, 1958), pp. 75–8. For a penetrating brief account of the place of secondary education in American society since 1870, see Martin Trow: "The Second Transformation of American Secondary Education," *International Journal of Comparative Sociology*, Vol. II (September, 1961), pp. 144–66.

state and the powerful trade union, moreover, saw to it that these laws were increasingly enforced. The young had to be protected from exploitation; and their elders had to be protected by keeping the young out of the labor market.

Now, in an increasing measure, secondary-school pupils were not merely unselected but also unwilling; they were in high school not because they wanted further study but because the law forced them to go. The burden of obligation was shifted accordingly: whereas once the free high school offered a priceless opportunity to those who chose to take it, the high school now held a large captive audience that its administrators felt obliged to satisfy. As an educational committee of the American Youth Commission wrote in 1940: "Even where a pupil is of low ability it is to be remembered that his attendance at secondary school is due to causes which are not of his making, and proper provision for him is a right which he is justified in claiming from society." [3]

As the years went by, the schools filled with a growing proportion of doubtful, reluctant, or actually hostile pupils. It is a plausible conjecture that the average level of ability, as well as interest, declined. It became clear that the old academic curriculum could no longer be administered to a high-school population of millions in the same proportion as it had been to the 359,000 pupils of 1890. So long as public education had meant, largely, schooling in the primary grades, the American conviction that everyone can and should be educated was relatively easy to put into practice. But as soon as public education included secondary education, it began to be more doubtful that everyone could be educated, and quite certain that not everyone could be educated in the same way. Beyond a doubt, change was in order.

The situation of school administrators can hardly fail to command our sympathies. Even in the 1920's, to a very large degree, they had been entrusted by the fiat of society with the management of quasi-custodial institutions. For custodial institutions the schools were, to the extent that they had to hold pupils uninterested in study but bound to the school by the laws. Moreover, the schools were under pressure not merely to fulfill the laws, but to become attractive enough to hold the voluntary allegiance of as large a proportion of the young for as long as they could.[4] Manfully settling down to their assignment,

---

[3] *What the High Schools Ought to Teach* (Washington, 1940), pp. 11–12.
[4] This was, of course, accentuated by the effects of the great depression and the growing power of the trade unions. But even in 1918 the N.E.A. was advocating

educators began to search for more and more courses which, however
dubious their merits by traditional educational standards, might interest and attract the young. In time they became far less concerned with
the type of mind the high school should produce or with the academic
side of the curriculum. (Boys and girls who wanted to go to college
would hang on in any case; it was the others they had to please.)
Discussions of secondary education became more frequently inter-
larded with references to a new, decisive criterion of performance—
"the holding power of the school."

The need to accept large numbers with varying goals and capacities
and to exercise for many pupils a custodial function made it necessary
for the schools to introduce variety into their curricula. The curriculum
of the secondary school could hardly have been fixed at what it
was in 1890 or 1910. But the issue posed for those who would guide
public education was whether the academic content and intellectual
standards of the school should be made as high as possible for each
child, according to his will and his capacities, or whether there was
good ground for abandoning any such end. To have striven seriously
to keep up the intellectual content of the curriculum would have
required a public and an educational profession committed to intellectual values; it would have demanded much administrative ingenuity; and in many communities it would have called for much more
generous financial support than the schools actually had.

But all this is rather in the nature of an imaginative exercise. The
problem of numbers had hardly made its appearance before a movement began in professional education to exalt numbers over quality
and the alleged demands of utility over intellectual development. Far
from conceiving the mediocre, reluctant, or incapable student as an
obstacle or a special problem in a school system devoted to educating
the interested, the capable, and the gifted, American educators
entered upon a crusade to exalt the academically uninterested or un-
gifted child into a kind of culture-hero. They were not content to say
that the realities of American social life had made it necessary to compromise with the ideal of education as the development of formal
learning and intellectual capacity. Instead, they militantly proclaimed
that such education was archaic and futile and that the noblest end of a
truly democratic system of education was to meet the child's immediate
interests by offering him a series of immediate utilities. The history of

---

that normal children be educated to the age of eighteen. *Cardinal Principles of
Secondary Education* (Washington, 1918), p. 30.

this crusade, which culminated in the ill-fated life-adjustment movement of the 1940's and 1950's, demands our attention; for it illustrates in action certain widespread attitudes toward childhood and schooling, character and ambition, and the place of intellect in life.

· 2 ·

The rise of the new interpretation of secondary education may be traced through a few examples of quasi-official statements by committees of the National Education Association and the United States Office of Education. These statements were, of course, not obligatory upon local school boards or superintendents. They represent the drift of educational thought without purporting to reflect exactly the changes actually being made in curricular policy.

Toward the close of the nineteenth century, two contrasting views of the purposes of the public high schools were already competing for dominance.[5] The original view, which remained in the ascendant until 1910 and continued to have much influence for at least another decade, might be dubbed old-fashioned or intellectually serious, depending upon one's sympathy for it. The high school, it was believed by those who held this view, should above all discipline and develop the minds of its pupils through the study of academic subject matter. Its well-informed advocates were quite aware that a majority of pupils were not being educated beyond high school; but they argued that the same education which was good preparation for college was good preparation for life. Therefore, the goal of secondary education, even when college was not the child's end-in-view, should be "mind culture," as it was called by William T. Harris, one of the leading advocates of the academic curriculum. Spokesmen of this school were intensely concerned that the pupil, whatever the precise content of his curriculum, should pursue every subject that he studied long enough to gain some serious mastery of its content. (In the continuing debate over education the ideal of "mastery" of subject matter dominates the thinking of the intellectualists, whereas the ideal of meeting the "needs" of children becomes the central conception of their opponents.)

The most memorable document expressing academic views on secondary education was the famous report of the National Education

---

[5] The general outlines of this controversy are sketched in Wesley: *N.E.A.: The First Hundred Years,* pp. 66–77.

Association's Committee of Ten in 1893. This committee was created to consider the chaos in the relations between colleges and secondary schools and to make recommendations about the high-school curriculum. Its personnel, which reflected the dominance of college educators, compares interestingly with that of later committees set up for similar purposes. The chairman was President Charles William Eliot of Harvard, and the members were William T. Harris, the Commissioner of Education, four other college or university presidents, the headmasters of two outstanding private secondary schools, a college professor, and only one public high-school principal. A series of subsidiary conferences set up by the committee to consider the place of the major academic disciplines in high-school programs also showed college authorities in full control. Although many principals and headmasters took part, there were also university professors whose names are recognizable in American intellectual history—Benjamin I. Wheeler, George Lyman Kittredge, Florian Cajori, Simon Newcomb, Ira Remsen, Charles K. Adams, Edward G. Bourne, Albert B. Hart, James Harvey Robinson, and Woodrow Wilson.

The Committee of Ten recommended to the secondary schools a set of four alternative courses—a classical course, a Latin-scientific course, a modern languages course, and an English course. These curricula varied chiefly in accordance with their relative emphasis on the classics, modern languages, and English. But all demanded, as a minimum, four years of English, four years of a foreign language, three years of history, three years of mathematics, and three years of science. In this respect, the contemporary reader will notice the close similarity between this program and that recently recommended by James Bryant Conant, in his survey of the high schools, as a minimum for "academically talented boys and girls." [6]

The curricula designed by the Committee of Ten show that they thought of the secondary school as an agency for academic training. But they did not make the mistake of thinking that these schools were simply college-preparatory institutions. Quite the contrary, the committee almost exaggerated the opposite point of view when it said that

---

[6] Conant recommended four years of mathematics, four years of a foreign language, three years of science, four years of English, and three years of history and social studies. In addition, he thought many academically talented pupils might wish to take a second foreign language or an additional course in social studies. *The American High School Today* (New York, 1959), p. 57. Conant felt that minimum requirements for graduation for *all* students should include at least one year of science, four years of English, and three or four years of social studies.

"only an insignificant percentage" of high-school graduates went on to colleges or scientific schools. The main function of high schools, said the committee, was "to prepare for the duties of life," not for college, but if the main subjects were all "taught consecutively and thoroughly, and . . . all carried on in the same spirit . . . all used for training the powers of observation, memory, expression, and reasoning," the pupil would receive an intellectual training that was good for college preparation or for life: "Every subject which is taught at all in a secondary school should be taught in the same way and to the same extent to every pupil so long as he pursues it, no matter what the probable destination of the pupil may be or at what point his education is to cease." [7]

The committee recognized that it would be desirable to find a larger place for music and art in the high schools, but it apparently found these of secondary importance and proposed to leave decisions about them to local initiative. Its members proposed, among other things, that language instruction should be begun in the last four years of the elementary schools, a suggestion that was lamentably ignored. They realized that an improvement in the caliber of secondary-school teachers was necessary to execute their recommendations effectively; they urged that the low standards of the normal schools be raised and suggested that universities might interest themselves more deeply in the adequate training of teachers.

In fact, the high schools had not developed entirely in accordance with the committee's conservative ideal. Even in the 1880's there had been a considerable efflorescence of programs of practical and vocational training—manual training, shop work, and other such studies. Increasingly, those primarily concerned with the management and curricula of high schools became restive about the continuing dominance of the academic ideal, which they considered arose from the high schools' "slavery" and "subjugation" to the colleges. The high schools, they insisted, were meant to educate citizens in their public

[7] For relevant passages, see *Report of the Committee on Secondary School Studies Appointed at the Meeting of the National Education Association, July 9, 1892* (Washington, 1893), pp. 8–11, 16–17, 34–47, 51–5. The committee believed that what pupils learned in high school should permit them to go to college if they should later make that decision. Colleges and scientific schools should be able to admit any graduate of a good secondary course, regardless of his program. At the present time, the committee found, this was impossible because the pupil might have gone through a high-school course "of a very feeble and scrappy nature— studying a little of many subjects and not much of any one, getting, perhaps, a little information in a variety of fields, but nothing which can be called a thorough training."

responsibilities and to train workers for industry, not to supply the colleges with freshmen. The high schools should be looked upon as "people's colleges" and not as the colleges' preparatory schools. Democratic principles, they thought, demanded much greater consideration for the needs of the children who did not go to college. Regard for these needs and a due respect for the principles of child development demanded that the ideal of "mastery" be dropped, and that youth should be free to test and sample and select among subjects, deriving from some what they could retain and use, and passing on to others. To hold children rigorously to the pursuit of particular subjects would only increase the danger of their dropping out of school.

A number of historical forces were working in favor of the new educators. Business, when it was favorably disposed to education, tended to applaud and encourage what they were doing. The sheer weight of growing student numbers increased the appeal of their arguments. Their invocation of democratic principles, which were undergoing a resurgence after 1890, struck a responsive chord in the public. The colleges themselves were so numerous, so competitive, so heterogeneous in quality that in their hunger for more students they were far from vigilant in upholding the admissions standards of the past. They were, moreover, still uncertain about the value of their own inherited classical curriculum, and had been experimenting since about 1870 with the elective system and a broader program of studies. College and university educators were no longer vitally interested in the problems of secondary education, and reformers in that field were left with little authoritative criticism or opposition. The staffs of high schools were increasingly supplied by the new state teachers colleges; and high-school textbooks, once written by college authorities in their fields, were now written by public-school superintendents, high-school principals and supervisors, or by students of educational methods.

· 3 ·

The slight concession made by the Committee of Ten to new schools of thought was hardly enough to allay discontent. It had not been able to foresee the extraordinary growth of the high-school population which would soon occur or the increasing heterogeneity of the student body. It quickly became evident that the curricular views of the Committee of Ten were losing ground. By 1908, when the N.E.A. was fast growing in size and influence, it adopted a resolution repudiating the notion that public high schools should be chiefly "fitting schools" for colleges (which, to be sure, had not been the contention of the Committee of Ten), urging that the high schools "be adapted to the general needs, both intellectual and industrial, of their students," and suggesting that colleges and universities too should adapt their courses to such needs.[8] The balance was tipping: the high schools were no longer to be expected to suit the colleges; instead, the colleges ought to try to resemble or accommodate the high schools.

In 1911, a new committee of the N.E.A., the Committee of Nine on the Articulation of High School and College, submitted another report, which shows that a revolution in educational thought was well on its way. The change in personnel was itself revealing. Gone were the eminent college presidents and distinguished professors of the 1893 report; gone, too, were the headmasters of elite secondary schools. The chairman of the Committee of Nine was a teacher at the Manual Training High School of Brooklyn, and no authority on any basic academic subject matter was on his committee, which consisted of school superintendents, commissioners, and principals, together with one professor of education and one dean of college faculties. Whereas the Committee of Ten had been a group of university men attempting to design curricula for the secondary schools, the new Committee of Nine was a group of men from public secondary schools, putting pressure through the N.E.A. on the colleges: "The requirement of four years of work in any particular subject, as a condition of admission to a higher institution, unless that subject be one that may properly be required of all high-school students, is illogical and should, in the judgment of this committee, be immediately discontinued."

The task of the high school, the Committee of Nine argued, "was to lay the foundations of good citizenship and to help in the wise choice of a vocation," but it should also develop unique and special individual gifts, which was "quite as important as the development of the common elements of culture." The schools were urged to exploit the dominant interests "that each boy and girl has at the time." The committee questioned the notion that liberal education should precede the vocational: "An organic conception of education demands the early introduction of training for individual usefulness, thereby blending the liberal and the vocational. . . ." It urged much greater attention to the

[8] N.E.A. *Proceedings*, 1908, p. 39.

role of mechanic arts, agriculture, and "household science" as rational elements in the education of all boys and girls. Because of the traditional conception of college preparation, the public high schools were [9]

> responsible for leading tens of thousands of boys and girls away from the pursuits for which they are adapted and in which they are needed, to other pursuits for which they are not adapted and in which they are not needed. By means of exclusively bookish curricula false ideals of culture are developed. A chasm is created between the producers of material wealth and the distributors and consumers thereof.

By 1918 the "liberation" of secondary education from college ideals and university control seems to have been consummated, at least on the level of theory, even if not yet in the nation's high-school curricula. In that year the N.E.A.'s Commission on the Reorganization of Secondary Education formulated the goals of American schools in a document about which Professor Edgar B. Wesley has remarked that "probably no publication in the history of education ever surpassed this little five cent thirty-two page booklet in importance." [1] This statement, *Cardinal Principles of Secondary Education,* was given a kind of official endorsement by the United States Bureau of Education, which printed and distributed an edition of 130,000 copies. It became the occasion of a nation-wide discussion of educational policy, and some teacher-training institutions regarded it so highly that they required their pupils to memorize essential portions (thus violating a central canon of the new educational doctrines).

The new commission pointed out that more than two thirds of those who entered the four-year high school did not graduate and that, among those who did, a very large proportion did not go to college. The needs of these pupils must not be neglected. The old concept of general intellectual discipline as an aim of education must be re-examined. Individual differences in capacities and attitudes needed more attention. New laws of learning must be brought to bear to test subject matter and teaching methods; these could no longer be judged "primarily in terms of the demands of any subject as a logically organized

[9] "Report of the Committee of Nine on the Articulation of High School and College," N.E.A. *Proceedings,* 1911, pp. 559–61.
[1] Wesley: op. cit., p. 75.

science." [2] In short, the inner structure of various disciplines was to be demoted as an educational criterion and supplanted by greater deference to the laws of learning, then presumably being discovered.

Moreover, the child was now conceived not as a mind to be developed but as a citizen to be trained by the schools. The new educators believed that one should not be content to expect good citizenship as a result of having more informed and intellectually competent citizens but that one must directly teach citizenship and democracy and civic virtues. The commission drew up a set of educational objectives in which neither the development of intellectual capacity nor the mastery of secondary academic subject matter was even mentioned. It was the business of the schools, the commission said, to serve democracy by developing in each pupil the powers that would enable him to act as a citizen. "It follows, therefore, that worthy home-membership, vocation, and citizenship demand attention as three of the leading objectives." The commission went on: "This Commission, therefore, regards the following as the main objectives of education: 1. Health. 2. Command of fundamental processes. [It became clear in context that this meant elementary skills in the three R's, in which the commission, no doubt quite rightly, felt that continued instruction was now needed at the secondary level.] 3. Worthy home-membership. 4. Vocation. 5. Citizenship. 6. Worthy use of leisure. 7. Ethical character."

With justice, the commission argued that the traditional high school had done too little to encourage interests in music, art, and the drama—but instead of presenting these as a desirable supplement to an intellectually ordered curriculum, it offered them as an alternative. The high school, it said, "has so exclusively sought intellectual discipline that it has seldom treated literature, art, and music so as to evoke right emotional response and produce positive enjoyment." Moreover, the high school placed too much emphasis on intensive pursuit of most subjects. Studies should be reorganized so that a single year of work in a subject would be "of definite value to those who go no further." This would make the courses "better adapted to the needs both of those who continue and of those who drop out of school."

The commission further argued that the colleges and universities should follow the example of the secondary schools in considering themselves obliged to become mass institutions and to arrange their

[2] Quotations in this and the following paragraph are from *Cardinal Principles of Secondary Education, passim.*

offerings accordingly. "The conception that higher education should be limited to the few is destined to disappear in the interests of democracy," it said prophetically. This meant, among other things, that high-school graduates should be able to go on to college not only with liberal but with vocational interests, and that, once in college, they should still be able to take whatever form of education they can which affords "profit to themselves and to society." In order to accommodate larger numbers, colleges and universities should supplant academic studies to some degree with advanced vocational education. The commission urged that all normal children should be encouraged to stay in school, on full time if possible, to the age of eighteen.

The commission quite reasonably urged that the high-school curriculum should be differentiated to offer a wide range of alternatives; but its way of expressing this objective was revealing:

> The basis of differentiation should be, in the broad sense of the term, vocational, thus justifying the names commonly given, such as agricultural, business, clerical, industrial, fine-arts, and household-arts curriculums. Provision should be made also for those having distinctively academic interests and needs.

Provision should be made also. This reference to the academic side of the high school as being hardly more than incidental to its main purposes captures in a phrase how far the dominant thinking on the subject had gone in the quarter century since the report of the Committee of Ten.

The rhetoric of the commission's report made it clear that the members thought of themselves as recommending not an educational retreat but rather an advance toward the realization of democratic ideals. The report is breathless with the idealism of the Progressive era and the war—with the hope of making the educational world safe for democracy and bringing a full measure of opportunity to every child. Our secondary education, the commission argued, "must aim at nothing less than complete and worthy living for all youth"—thus far had education gone beyond such a limited objective as developing the powers of the mind. Secondary-school teachers were urged to "strive to explore the inner meaning of the great democratic movement now struggling for supremacy." While trying to develop the distinctive excellences of individuals and various groups, the high school "must be equally zealous to develop those common ideas, common ideals, and common modes of thought, feeling, and action, whereby America, through a rich, unified, common life, may render her truest service to a world seeking for democracy among men and nations."

· 4 ·

The Cardinal Principles of Secondary Education, which set the tone and expressed the ideas current in all subsequent quasi-official statements on secondary-educational policy down to the life-adjustment movement, appeared in the midst of a focal change in the dimensions of the high-school population. Standing at 1.1 million in 1910, it rose swiftly to 4.8 million in 1930. When the document itself was published, all states had adopted compulsory education laws—Mississippi, in 1918, being the last to straggle into line.

The schools, moreover, had been coping for some years, and were to continue to cope for many years more, with the task of educating the children of that vast tidal wave of immigration that had come into the country between 1880 and the First World War. By 1911, for example, 57.5 per cent of the children in the public schools of thirty-seven of the largest cities were of foreign-born parentage.[3] The immigrant children, now entering secondary schools, brought the same problems of class, of language, of Americanization that they had brought to the primary schools. Giving such children cues to American life, and often to elementary hygiene, seemed more important to many school superintendents than developing their minds along the lines of the older education; and it is not difficult to understand the belief that a thorough grounding in Latin was not a primary need, say, of a Polish immigrant's child in Buffalo. Immigrant parents, unfamiliar with American ways, were inadequate guides to what their children needed to know, and the schools were now thrust into the parental role. Moreover, the children, exposed to Yankee schoolmarms in the morning, were expected to become instruments of Americanization by bringing home in the afternoon instructions in conduct and hygiene that their parents would take to heart. Against this background one may better understand the emphasis of the *Cardinal Principles* on "worthy home-membership," "health," and "citizenship." The common complaint that the modern school tries to assume too many of the functions of other social agencies,

[3] See, on this general subject, Alan M. Thomas, Jr.: "American Education and the Immigrant," *Teachers College Record,* Vol. LV (October, 1953–May, 1954), pp. 253–67.

including the family, derives in good measure from the response of educators to this problem.

Changes in professional education also favored new views of secondary education. The normal schools, which had been at best a kind of stop-gap in teacher education, were now being replaced by teachers' colleges and schools of education. Both the business of training teachers and the study of the educational process were becoming specialized and professional. Unfortunately, as Lawrence Cremin has observed, the schools of education and the teachers' colleges grew up with a high degree of autonomy.[4] Increasingly, the mental world of the professional educationist became separated from that of the academic scholar. The cleavage between Teachers College and the rest of Columbia University—which led to the quip that 120th Street is the widest street in the world—became symbolic of a larger cleavage in the structure of American education. Professional educators were left to develop their ideas without being subjected to the intellectual discipline that might have come out of a dialogue with university scholars. In sharp contrast to the days of Eliot, academicians scornfully turned away from the problems of primary and secondary education, which they now saw as the preoccupation of dullards; too many educationists were happy to see them withdraw, leaving the educationists free to realize their own credos in making plans for the middle and lower schools.

At the time the ideas of the *Cardinal Principles* were supplanting those of the Committee of Ten, a new kind of educational orthodoxy was taking form, founded in good part upon appeals to "democracy" and "science." John Dewey was the master of those for whom educational democracy was the central issue; Edward Lee Thorndike of those for whom it was the application to education of "what science tells us." It was not commonly believed that there was any problem in this union of democracy and science, for a widespread conviction existed (not shared, it must be said, by Thorndike) that there must be a kind of pre-established harmony between them—that since both are good, both must serve the same ends and lead to the same conclusions; that there exists, in fact, a kind of science of democracy.[5]

Concerning the use, or misuse, as it may be, of Dewey's ideas, I

[4] *The Transformation of the School* (New York, 1961), p. 176.
[5] For a witty analysis of the same blend of science and democracy in recent American political thought, see Bernard Crick: *The American Science of Politics* (London, 1959).

shall have something to say in the next chapter. Here it is important, however, to say a word about the use of the techniques of testing and the various kinds of psychological and educational research. Much of this research was, of course, valuable, though of necessity tentative. The difficulty was that what should have been simply a continuous inquiry had a way, in the fervent atmosphere of professional education, of being exalted into a faith—not so much by those who were actually doing research as by those who were hungry to find its practical applications and eager to invoke the authority of science on behalf of their various crusades. The American mind seems extremely vulnerable to the belief that any alleged knowledge which can be expressed in figures is in fact as final and exact as the figures in which it is expressed. Army testing in the First World War is a case in point. It was very quickly and very widely believed that the Army Alpha tests had actually measured intelligence; that they made it possible to assign mental ages; that mental ages, or intelligence as reported by tests, are fixed; that vast numbers of Americans had a mental age of only fourteen; and that therefore the educational system must be coping with hordes of more or less backward children.[6] Although such overconfident interpretations of these tests were never without sharp critics—among them John Dewey—the misuse of tests seems to be a recurrent factor in American education. Of course, the credence given to the low view of human intelligence that some people derived from the tests could lead to quite different conclusions. To those not enchanted by the American democratic credo—and Edward Lee Thorndike himself was among them—the effect of mental testing was to encourage elitist views.[7] But for those whose commitment to "democratic" values was imperturbable, the supposed discovery of the mental limitations of the masses only encouraged a search for methods and content in education that would suit the needs of the intellectually mediocre or unmotivated. Paraphrasing Lincoln, the educators-for-democracy might have said that God must love the slow learners because he made so many of them. Elitists might coldly turn their backs on these large numbers, but democratic educators, embracing them as a fond mother embraces her handicapped child, would attempt to build the curriculum upon their supposed needs.

[6] See the good brief account of the early impact of testing in Cremin: *The Transformation of the School*, pp. 185–92.

[7] See, for example, Merle Curti's discussion of the views of Thorndike in *The Social Ideas of American Educators* (New York, 1935), chapter 14.

It is impossible here to stress too much the impetus given to the new educational creed by the moral atmosphere of Progressivism, for this creed was developed in an atmosphere of warm philanthropy and breathless idealism in which the needs of the less gifted and the underprivileged commanded a generous response. Educators had spent many years discovering a canon and a creed, whose validity seemed now more certain than ever because it seemed to be vindicated morally by the needs of democracy and intellectually by the findings of science. More frequently than ever, the rallying cries of this creed were heard in the land: education for democracy, education for citizenship, the needs and interests of the child, education for all youth. There is an element of moral overstrain and a curious lack of humor among American educationists which will perhaps always remain a mystery to those more worldly minds that are locked out of their mental universe. The more humdrum the task the educationists have to undertake, the nobler and more exalted their music grows. When they see a chance to introduce a new course in family living or home economics, they begin to tune the fiddles of their idealism. When they feel they are about to establish the school janitor's right to be treated with respect, they grow starry-eyed and increase their tempo. And when they are trying to assure that the location of the school toilets will be so clearly marked that the dullest child can find them, they grow dizzy with exaltation and launch into wild cadenzas about democracy and self-realization.

The silly season in educational writing had now opened. The professionalization of education put a premium upon the sober treatment of every mundane problem, and the educators began to indulge in solemn and pathetic parodies of the pedantry of academic scholarship. Not liking to think of themselves as mere advocates of low-grade utilities, they began to develop the art of clothing every proposal, no matter how simple, common-sense, and sound, in the raiments of the most noble social or educational objectives. Was it desirable, for example, for the schools to teach children something about safety? If so, a school principal could read a pretentious paper to the N.E.A., not on the important but perhaps routine business of teaching children to be careful, but on the exalted theme, "The Value of Instruction in Accident Prevention as a Factor in Unifying the Curriculum." It had now become possible to pretend that the vital thing was not to keep youngsters from getting burnt or hit by vehicles but that teaching them about such things infused all learning with higher values—although in this case, at least, the speaker conceded, in closing: "Let me say that instruction in accident prevention serves not only to unify the curriculum but also to reduce accidents." [8]

· 5 ·

A traveler from a foreign country whose knowledge of American education was confined to the writings of educational reformers might well have envisaged a rigid, unchanging secondary-school system chained to the demands of colleges and universities, fixed upon old ideas of academic study, and unreceptive to the wide variety of pupils it had in charge. The speaker at the N.E.A. meeting of 1920 who lamented that the high schools were still "saturated with college requirement rules and standards" and filled with principals and teachers "trained in academic lore and possessing only the academic viewpoint" [9] sounded a note of complaint that has never ceased to echo in the writings of the new educationists. In fact, the innovators had very considerable success in dismantling the old academic curriculum of the high school. It is hard for an amateur, and perhaps even a professional in education, to know how much of this was justified. But two things it does seem possible to assert: first, that curricular change after 1910 was little short of revolutionary; and second, that by the 1940's and 1950's the demands of the life-adjustment educators for the destruction of the academic curriculum had become practically insatiable.

The old academic curriculum, as endorsed by the Committee of Ten, reached its apogee around 1910. In that year more pupils were studying foreign languages or mathematics or science or English—any one of these—than *all* non-academic subjects combined. During the following forty-year span the academic subjects offered in the high-school curricula fell from about three fourths to about one fifth. Latin, taken in 1910 by 49 per cent of public high-school pupils in grades 9 to 12, fell by 1949 to 7.8 per cent. All modern-language enrollments fell from 84.1 per cent to 22 per cent. Algebra fell from 56.9 per cent to 26.8 per cent, and geometry from 30.9 per cent to 12.8 per cent; total mathematics enrollments from 89.7 per cent to 55 per cent. Total science enrollments, if one omits a new catch-all course entitled "general science," fell from 81.7 per cent to 33.3 per cent; or to 54.1 per cent if general science is included. English, though it almost held its own in

[8] N.E.A. *Proceedings*, 1920, pp. 204–5.
[9] Ibid., 1920, pp. 73–5.

purely quantitative terms, was much diluted in many school systems. The picture in history and social studies is too complex to render in figures, but changing enrollments made it more parochial both in space and in time—that is, it put greater stress on recent and American history, less on the remoter past and on European history.[1]

When the Committee of Ten examined the high-school curricula in 1893, it found that forty subjects were taught, but since of these thirteen were offered in very few schools, the basic curriculum was founded on twenty-seven subjects. By 1941 no less than 274 subjects were offered, and only 59 of these could be classified as academic studies. What is perhaps most extraordinary is not this ten-fold multiplication of subjects, nor the fact that academic studies had fallen to about one fifth the number, but the response of educational theorists: they were convinced that academic studies were still cramping secondary education. In the life-adjustment movement, which flourished in the late 1940's and the 1950's with the encouragement of the United States Office of Education, there occurred an effort to mobilize the public secondary-school energies of the country to gear the educational system more closely to the needs of children who were held to be in some sense uneducable.[2]

[1] John F. Latimer, in *What's Happened to Our High Schools?*, has made a useful compilation of Office of Education statistics, and I have followed his presentation of the data; see especially chapters 4 and 7. It is important to note that enrollments thus put in percentages are not meant to conceal the fact that, with the immense growth in the high-school population, a larger number of the *nation's* youth could be studying some of these academic subjects even though a smaller portion of the *high-school* population was pursuing them. However, from 1933 to 1939 there occurred for the first time a drop not merely in the percentages of students studying certain subjects but in the *absolute* enrollments as well.

The consequences in one field, which happens to have been well surveyed, might be examined. During the Second World War the problems of secondary-school education in mathematics became a matter of some official concern. In 1941 the Naval Officers Training Corps reported that, of 4,200 candidates who were college freshmen, sixty-two per cent failed the arithmetic reasoning test. Only twenty-three per cent had had more than one and a half years of mathematics in high school. Later, a 1954 survey reported that sixty-two per cent of the nation's colleges had found it necessary to teach high-school algebra to entering freshmen. See I. L. Kandel: *American Education in the Twentieth Century* (Cambridge, Mass., 1957), p. 62; and H. S. Dyer, R. Kalin, and F. M. Lord: *Problems in Mathematical Education* (Princeton, 1956), p. 23. Many high schools appear to have been approaching the view, widespread among life-adjustment theorists, that foreign languages, algebra, geometry, and trigonometry have "relatively little value except as college preparation or except for a few college curricula," and that "therefore most of the instruction in those fields should be postponed until college." Harl R. Douglass: *Secondary Education for Life Adjustment of American Youth* (New York, 1952), p. 598.

[2] The term "uneducable" is, of course, not used by life-adjustment educators. It is my translation of what one is asserting about a youth in secondary school when

To some degree the life-adjustment movement was a consequence of the crisis in the morale of American youth which has been observable since the Second World War. But it was more than this: it was an attempt on the part of educational leaders and the United States Office of Education to make completely dominant the values of the crusade against intellectualism that had been going on since 1910. Looking at the country's secondary education shortly after the end of the Second World War, John W. Studebaker, then Commissioner of Education, observed that only about seven youths out of ten were entering senior high school (grades 10 to 12), and that fewer than four remained to graduate.[3] Despite the efforts made in the preceding forty years to increase the "holding power" of the schools, large numbers of youngsters were still uninterested in completing their secondary education. The effort to enrich the academic curriculum seemed to have failed in one of its main purposes; the suggestion was now made that the curriculum had not been enriched enough.

The life-adjustment movement proposed to remedy the situation by stimulating "the development of programs of education more in harmony with life-adjustment needs of all youth." This would be done by devising an education "which better equips all American youth to live democratically with satisfaction to themselves and profit to society as home members, workers, and citizens." At a national conference held in Chicago in May, 1947, the conferees adopted a resolution drafted by Dr. Charles A. Prosser, the director of Dunwoody Institute of Minneapolis, an agency of industrial education. In its original form (it was later slightly reworded in order "to avoid misinterpretation and misunderstanding"), this resolution expressed the belief of the members

_____

one says that he can neither absorb an academic education nor learn a desirable trade.

[3] *Life Adjustment Education for Every Youth* (Washington, n.d. [1948?]), p. iii. This publication was issued by the Office of Education of the Federal Security Agency and was prepared in the Division of Secondary Education and the Division of Vocational Education. For the Prosser resolution and other statements of purpose in this repetitive document, cited in the following paragraphs, see pp. 2–5, 15n., 18n., 22, 48–52 ,88–90, and *passim.*

At the same time that the Office of Education was sponsoring life adjustment, the President's Commission on Higher Education was advocating, in its report of 1947, that the colleges themselves should no longer select "as their special clientele persons possessing verbal aptitudes and a capacity for grasping abstractions," and that they should give more attention to cultivating other aptitudes—"such as social sensitivity and versatility, artistic ability, motor skill and dexterity, and mechanical aptitude and ingenuity." *Higher Education for American Democracy: A Report of the President's Commission on Higher Education,* Vol. I (Washington, 1947), p. 32.

of the conference that the needs of the great majority of American youth were not being adequately served by secondary schools. Twenty per cent of them, it was said, were being prepared for college; another twenty per cent for skilled occupations. But the remaining sixty per cent, according to spokesmen for the crusade, were unfit for either of these programs and should be given education for life adjustment. The life-adjustment theorists were explicit about the qualities they attributed to the neglected sixty per cent who needed life-adjustment education. These were mainly children from unskilled and semi-skilled families who had low incomes and provided a poor cultural environment. They began school later than others, continued to be retarded in school, made low grades, scored lower on intelligence and achievement tests, lacked interest in school work, and were "less emotionally mature—nervous, feel less secure."

After having compiled this depressing list of the traits of their clientele, the authors of the Office of Education's first manual on Life Adjustment went on to say that "these characteristics are not intended to brand the group as in any sense inferior." The peculiar self-defeating version of "democracy" entertained by these educators somehow made it possible for them to assert that immature, insecure, nervous, retarded slow learners from poor cultural environments were "in no sense inferior" to more mature, secure, confident, gifted children from better cultural environments.[4] This verbal genuflection before "democracy" seems to have enabled them to conceal from themselves that they were, with breathtaking certainty, writing off the majority of the nation's children as being more or less uneducable—that is, in the terms of the Prosser resolution, unfit not just for the academic studies that prepare for college but even for programs of vocational education leading to "desirable skilled occupations." What kind of education would be suitable for this unfortunate majority? Certainly not intellectual development nor cumulative knowledge, but practical training in being family members, consumers, and citizens. They must be taught—the

[4] That the capacities of such a large proportion of American youth should be so written off in the name of "democracy" is one of the more perplexing features of the movement. At least one of its supporters, however, faced up to its implications when he said that this neglected group lacks "aroused interests or pronounced aptitudes," but that this fact is "probably fortunate for a society having a large number of jobs to be done requiring no unusual aptitudes or interests." Edward K. Hankin: "The Crux of Life Adjustment Education," *Bulletin* of the National Association of Secondary-School Principals (November, 1953), p. 72. This is a possible point of view and a more realistic assessment of the implications of life-adjustment education. But it is hardly "democratic."

terms would have been familiar to any reader of the *Cardinal Principles*—"ethical and moral living"; home and family life; citizenship; the uses of leisure; how to take care of their health; "occupational adjustment." Here, as the authors of *Life Adjustment Education for Every Youth* put it, was "a philosophy of education which places life values above acquisition of knowledge." The conception, implicit in this observation, that knowledge has little or nothing to do with "life values," was an essential premise of the whole movement. Repeatedly, life adjustment educators were to insist that intellectual training is of no use in solving the "real life problems" of ordinary youth.

· 6 ·

The thinking behind the life-adjustment movement is difficult to exhume from the repetitive bulletins on the subject compiled by the Office of Education in Washington. But before the movement had been so named, its fundamental notions had been set forth by Dr. Prosser himself, an experienced administrator in vocational education, when he delivered his Inglis Lecture at Harvard University in 1939.[5] Although there are in the published lecture occasional traces of the influence of John Dewey's passion for educational democracy, Prosser relied mainly upon psychological research, and he expressed a more fundamental piety for the findings of "science." (Life-adjustment educators would do anything in the name of science except encourage children to study it.) Thorndike and his followers had shown, Prosser imagined, that there is no such thing as intellectual discipline whose benefits can be transferred from one study, situation, or problem to another. "Nothing could be more certain than that science has proven false the doctrine of general education and its fundamental theory that memory or imagination or the reason or the will can be trained as a power." When this archaic notion is abandoned, as it must be, all that is left is education in various specifics. There is no such thing as general mechanical skill; there are only specific skills developed by practice and use. It is likewise with the mind. There is, for example, no such thing as the memory; there are only specific facts and ideas which have become available for recall because we have found use for them.

Contrary, then, to what had been believed by exponents of the older

[5] *Secondary Education and Life* (Cambridge, Mass., 1939). The argument summarized in this and the following pages is largely in pp. 1–49; especially pp. 7–10, 15–16, 19–21, 31–5, 47–9.

concept of education as the development of intellectual discipline, there are no general mental qualities to be developed; there are only specific things to be known. The usability and teachability of these things go hand in hand; the more immediately usable an item of knowledge is, the more readily it can be taught. The value of a school subject can be measured by the number of immediate, actual life situations to which it directly applies. The important thing, then, is not to teach pupils how to generalize, but to supply them directly with the information they need for daily living—for example, to teach them, not physiology, but how to keep physically fit. The traditional curriculum consists simply of studies that once were useful in this way but have ceased to be so. "The general rule seems to be that the younger any school study, the greater is its utilitarian value in affairs outside the schoolroom, and the older the study, the less the usefulness of its content in meeting the real demands of living." Students learn more readily and retain more of what they learn when the transfer of content from school to life is immediate and direct. It is, in fact, the very usefulness of a subject that determines its disciplinary value to the mind. "On all these counts business arithmetic is superior to plane or solid geometry; learning ways of keeping physically fit, to the study of French; learning the technique of selecting an occupation, to the study of algebra; simple science of everyday life, to geology; simple business English, to Elizabethan Classics."

It was an irresistible conclusion drawn from scientific research, said Prosser, that the best teaching material is "the life-adjustment and not the education-for-more education studies." Why, then, had the colleges and universities persisted in fastening unusable and unteachable traditional subjects on the secondary schools? Quite aside from the vested interests of teachers of these subjects, the main reason, he thought, was that the higher institutions had needed some device for selecting the abler pupils and eliminating the others. (The teaching of such subjects as languages and algebra had the function, one must believe, not of educating anyone, but simply of acting as hurdles that would trip up weaker pupils before they got to college.) This outmoded technique required four wasteful and expensive years of futile study in supposedly "disciplinary" subjects. The selection of pupils suited to college, Prosser thought, could now be made with infinitely more economy and accuracy in a few hours of mental testing. Perhaps, then, traditionalists, "as a sporting proposition," could be persuaded to drop at least half the academic curriculum for all students and keep only a few of the older studies in proportion to their surviving usefulness. On this criterion, "all foreign languages and all mathematics should be dropped from the list of required college-preparatory studies" in favor of the more usable subjects—physical science, English, and social studies.

Many new studies of direct-use value should be added to the curriculum: English of a severely practical kind, offering "communication skills"; literature dealing with modern life; science (only "qualitative" science) courses that would give youth "the simple science of everyday life," tell "how science increases our comfort . . . promotes our enjoyment of life . . . helps men get their work done . . . increases wealth"; practical business guidance and "simple economics for youth," supplemented perhaps by material on the "economic history of youth in the United States"; civics, focusing on "civic problems of youth" and on the local community; mathematics, consisting only of varieties of applied arithmetic; social studies, giving attention to "wholesome recreation in the community," amenities and manners, uses of leisure, social and family problems of youth, and the "social history of youth in the United States"; finally, of course, "experiences in the fine arts," and "experiences in the practical arts," and vocational education. In this way, the curriculum could be made to conform to the laws of learning discovered by modern psychological science, and all children would benefit to a much greater degree from their secondary schooling.[6]

In a rather crude form Prosser had here given expression to the conclusion drawn by many educationists from experimental psychology, that "science," by destroying the validity of the idea of mental discipline, had destroyed the basic assumption upon which the ideal of a liberal education was based. Prosser had this in mind when he asserted with such confidence that *"nothing could be more certain"* than that science had proven false the assumptions of general education. Behind this remarkable dogmatism there lies an interesting chapter in the history of ideas. The older ideal of a classical liberal education, as expressed in nineteenth-century America and elsewhere, had been based upon two assumptions. The first was the so-called faculty psychology. In this psychology, the mind was believed to be a substantive entity composed of a number of parts or "faculties" such as reason, imagination, memory, and the like. It was assumed that these faculties, like physical faculties, could be strengthened by exercise; and

---

[6] For a later, full-scale, authoritative statement of the views of this school on the content of the curriculum, see Harold Alberty: *Reorganizing the High School Curriculum* (New York, 1953).

in a liberal education, through constant mental discipline, they were gradually so strengthened. It was also generally believed that certain subjects had an established superiority as agents of mental discipline— above all, Latin, Greek, and mathematics. The purpose of developing competence in these subjects was not merely to lay the foundation for learning more Latin, Greek, or mathematics, but, far more important, to train the powers of the mind so that they would be more adequate for whatever task they might confront.[7]

In good time it was found that the faculty psychology did not hold up under philosophic analysis or the scientific study of the functions of mind. Moreover, with the immense growth in the body of knowledge and the corresponding expansion of the curriculum, the old confidence that the classical languages and mathematics had an exclusive place of honor in mental discipline seemed more and more a quaint parochial conceit.[8]

But most modern psychologists and educational theorists were aware that the decline of the faculty psychology and the classical-mathematical curriculum did not in itself put an end to the question whether such a thing as mental discipline is a realizable end of educa-tion. If mental discipline were, after all, meaningless, everything that had been done in the name of liberal education for centuries seemed to have been based on a miscalculation. The question whether the mind can be disciplined, or generally trained, survived the faculty psychology and took on a new, more specific form: can training exer-cised and developed in one mental operation develop a mental facility that can be transferred to another? This general question could, of course, be broken down into endless specific ones: can acts of memori-zation (as William James asked in an early rudimentary experiment conducted on himself) facilitate other memorization? Can training in one form of sensory discrimination enhance other discriminations? Can

[7] The classic statement in America of this view of mental discipline was the Yale Report of 1828, which originally appeared in *The American Journal of Science and Arts*, Vol. XV (January, 1829), pp. 297–351. It is largely reprinted in Hofstad-ter and Smith, eds.: *American Higher Education: A Documentary History*, Vol. I, pp. 275–91.

[8] It was also a conceit that served to justify a good deal of inferior pedagogy. There is overwhelming evidence, for example, that the classical languages were taught in the old-time college in a narrow grammarian's spirit, and not as a means of introducing students to the cultural life of classical antiquity. See Richard Hofstad-ter and Walter P. Metzger: *The Development of Academic Freedom in the United States* (New York, 1955), pp. 226–30; Richard Hofstadter and C. DeWitt Hardy: *The Development and Scope of Higher Education in the United States* (New York, 1952), chapter 1 and pp. 53–6.

the study of Latin facilitate the subsequent study of French? If a transfer of training did occur, a cumulation of such transfers over several years of a rigorous liberal education might produce a mind which was better trained *in general*. But if transfer of training did not take place, most of the cumulative academic studies were quite pointless outside the items of knowledge contained in these studies themselves.

At any rate, in the confidence that they could throw light on a question of central importance, experimental psychologists, spurred by Thorndike, began early in the twentieth century to seek experimental evidence on the transfer of training. Anyone who reads an account of these experiments might well conclude that they were focused on such limited aspects of the problem that they were pathetically inadequate; individually and collectively, they did not shed very much light on the grand question to which they were ultimately directed. However, as a consequence of a great many ingenious and often interesting experiments, evidence of a kind did begin to accumulate. Some of it, notably in two papers published by Thorndike in 1901 and 1924, was taken by educational thinkers to be decisive evidence against transfer of training in any degree considerable enough to vindicate the idea of mental discipline. This and similar evidence from other researchers was, in any case, seized upon by some educational theorists. As W. C. Bagley once remarked: "It was inevitable that any theory which justified or rationalized the loosening of standards should be received with favor," by those who, without deliberate intent, distorted experimental findings in the interest of their mission to reorganize the high schools to accommodate the masses.[9]

Actually the accumulating experimental evidence proved contradictory and confusing, and those educators who insisted that its lessons were altogether clear and that nothing was so certain as what it yielded were simply ignoring all findings that did not substantiate their views. Their misuse of experimental evidence, in fact, constitutes a major scandal in the history of educational thought. If a quantitative survey of the experiments means anything, these educators ignored the bulk of the material, for four of five of the experimental studies showed the presence of transfer under certain conditions. There seems to have been no point at which the preponderant opinion of outstanding experimental psychologists favored the anti-transfer views that were drawn upon by educationists like Prosser as conclusive on what

[9] W. C. Bagley: "The Significance of the Essentialist Movement in Educational Theory," *Classical Journal*, Vol. XXXIV (1939), p. 336.

"science has proven." Today, experimental psychology offers them no comfort. As Jerome Bruner summarizes it in his remarkable little book, *The Process of Education:* "Virtually all of the evidence of the last two decades on the nature of learning and transfer has indicated that . . . it is indeed a fact that massive general transfer can be achieved by appropriate learning, even to the degree that learning properly under optimum conditions leads one to 'learn how to learn.'"[1] Presumably, the ideal of a liberal education is still better vindicated by the educational experience of the human race than by experimental psychology; but in so far as such scientific inquiry is taken as a court of resort, its verdict is vastly more favorable to the views of those who believe in the possibility of mental discipline than it was represented to be by the educational prophets of life adjustment.

· 7 ·

The life-adjustment movement stated, in an extreme form, the proposition toward which professional education had been moving for well over four decades: that in a system of mass secondary education, an academically serious training is an impossibility for more than a modest fraction of the student population. In setting the portion of uneducables with dogmatic certainty at sixty per cent, the spokesmen of this movement were taking such a strong position that some of their critics assumed the figure to be altogether arbitrary. Its source appears again to have been a touching faith in "science." In 1940, when Dr. Prosser, as a member of the National Youth Administration, was in close touch with Washington's view of the problems of youth, the psychologist, Lewis M. Terman, well known for his work in intelligence testing, estimated in a publication of the American Youth Commission, *How Fare American Youth?*, that an IQ of 110 is needed for success in traditional, classical, high-school curricula, and that sixty per cent of American youth rank below this IQ level. There is, in any case, a great discrepancy between this figure and the arithmetic of the life-adjustment educators.[2] But more important is the irresponsibility of trying to base the educational

---

[1] Jerome S. Bruner: *The Process of Education* (Cambridge, Mass., 1960), p. 6. The important consideration, as Bruner points out, is that the learner have a structural grasp of the matter which is learned. For the modern discussion of mental discipline and a brief review of the history of the experimental evidence, see Walter B. Kolesnik: *Mental Discipline in Modern Education* (Madison, 1958), especially chapter 3.

[2] That is, if Terman's findings are accepted, sixty per cent of American youth might be unfit for an academic high-school curriculum; but of these surely some

policy of an entire nation on any such finding. Psychologists do not agree (and were still heatedly debating in 1939) whether an individual's IQ is a permanently fixed genetic attribute; and there is now impressive experimental evidence that an individual IQ, given appropriate attention and pedagogy, can often be raised by 15 to 20 points or more. (Results can be particularly impressive when special attention is given to underprivileged children. In New York City's "Higher Horizons" program, many slum children with slightly subnormal or nearly retarded IQ's at the junior high-school level had both their IQ's and their academic performance raised so that they were acceptable in college and some even earned scholarships.) Moreover, the IQ alone would, in no case, be an infallible index to the ceiling of anyone's potential educational achievement; there are other variables, amenable to change, which it does not take into account, such as the caliber of teaching, the amount of schoolwork, and the pupil's morale and motivation. Psychologists and educators are far from being in precise agreement as to the proportion of the students in our high schools who, even with today's teaching and low educational morale, can profit from an academic curriculum.[3]

Finally, the plausibility of the life-adjustment movement's view of the educability of the country's youth hinged upon ignoring secondary-educational accomplishments in other countries. It had become a commonplace argument of the new educationists that secondary curricula of the countries of Western Europe, being "aristocratic," class-bound, selective, and traditional, had no exemplary value for the democratic, universal, and forward-looking secondary education of the United States. American educators, therefore, preferred to ignore European educational history as a source of clues to educational policy and looked to "modern science" for practical guidance and to "democracy" for their moral inspiration. European education pointed to the outmoded past; science and democracy looked to the future. This

considerable portion would be fit for the desirable trades mentioned in the Prosser resolution.

[3] For differing estimates of the distribution of academic ability and its implications for educational policy, see the Report of the President's Commission on Higher Education: *Higher Education for American Democracy*, Vol. I, p. 41; Byron S. Hollinshead: *Who Should Go to College* (New York, 1952), especially pp. 39–40; Dael Wolfle: *America's Resources of Specialized Talent* (New York, 1954); and Charles C. Cole, Jr.: *Encouraging Scientific Talent* (New York, 1956). "I am confident," writes one educational psychologist, "that with better teaching . . . half, or more, of the students in our high schools . . . can profit from it [the classical curriculum]." Paul Woodring: *A Fourth of a Nation* (New York, 1957), p. 49.

way of thought has been jolted by scientific competition with the Soviet Union. Russian secondary education is neither so universal nor so egalitarian as our own. But it offers the example of an educational system which cannot quite be dismissed as aristocratic or traditional and which is none the less modeled largely upon the secondary systems of Western Europe; it demonstrates in a way that can no longer be conveniently ignored the availability of a demanding academic curriculum to large numbers.

By no means should it be imagined that the life-adjustment educators were content to stop with the assertion that their educational aims should be applied only to the neglected sixty per cent of youth at the bottom of the ladder. Here it would be a mistake to underestimate the crusading idealism of this movement, which is nowhere so well illustrated as in Dr. Prosser's closing remarks to the 1947 Conference on Life Adjustment. "Never in all the history of education," he said, "has there been such a meeting as this . . . a meeting where people were so sincere in their belief that this was the golden opportunity to do something that would give to *all* American youth their educational heritage so long denied. What you have planned," Prosser assured the members, "is worth fighting for—it is worth dying for. . . . God Bless You All."

Accordingly, life-adjustment educators soon became convinced that their high educational ideals should be applied not merely to the neglected sixty per cent: what was good for them would be good for *all* American youth, however gifted. They were designing, as the authors of one life-adjustment pamphlet quite candidly admitted, nothing less than "a blueprint for a Utopian Secondary School"—a school which, they added, "could be operated only by teachers of rare genius." [4] As I. L. Kandel has sardonically remarked, the conviction of life adjustment was "that what is good for sixty per cent of the pupils attending high schools, and, according to reports, deriving no benefit from this stay, is also good for all pupils." [5] These crusaders had thus succeeded in standing on its head the assumption of universality once made by exponents of the classical curriculum. Formerly, it had been held that a liberal academic education was good for all pupils. Now it was argued

[4] *A Look Ahead in Secondary Education,* U.S. Office of Education (Washington, 1954), p. 76.
[5] *American Education in the Twentieth Century,* p. 156; cf. pp. 173–81. On the universalistic aspirations of the life-adjustment movement, see Mortimer Smith: *The Diminished Mind* (Chicago, 1954), p. 46.

that all pupils should in large measure get the kind of training originally conceived for the slow learner. American utility and American democracy would now be realized in the education of *all* youth. The life-adjustment movement would establish once and for all the idea that the slow learner is "in no sense" the inferior of the gifted, and the principle that all curricular subjects, like all children, are equal. "There is no aristocracy of 'subjects,'" said the Educational Policies Commission of the N.E.A. in 1952, describing the ideal rural school. "Mathematics and mechanics, art and agriculture, history and homemaking are all peers." [6]

In the name of utility, democracy, and science, many educators had come to embrace the supposedly uneducable or less educable child as the center of the secondary-school universe, relegating the talented child to the sidelines. One group of educationists, looking forward to the day when "the aristocratic, cultural tradition of education [will be] completely and finally abandoned," had this to say of pupils who showed unusual intellectual curiosity: "Any help we can give them should be theirs, but such favored people learn directly from their surroundings. Our efforts to teach them are quite incidental in their development. It is therefore unnecessary and futile for the schools to attempt to gear their programs to the needs of unusual people." [7] In this atmosphere, as Jerome Bruner puts it, "the top quarter of public school students, from which we must draw intellectual leadership in the next generation, is perhaps the group most neglected by our schools in the recent past." [8] This group has indeed been neglected by

[6] *Education for All American Youth, A Further Look* (Washington, 1952), p. 140.

[7] Charles M. MacConnell, Ernest O. Melby, Christian O. Arndt, and Leslee J. Bishop: *New Schools for a New Culture* (New York, 1953), pp. 154–5. In partial justification of this curious remark, it should be said that our secondary schools, *as they are now constituted,* often find it relatively difficult to do very much for talented and intellectually curious pupils.

[8] Bruner: op. cit., p. 10. Cf. James B. Conant: "In particular, we tend to overlook the especially gifted youth. We neither find him early enough, nor guide him properly, nor educate him adequately in our high schools." *Education in a Divided World* (Cambridge, Mass., 1948), p. 65; cf. p. 228. On the problems of educating the talented, see Frank O. Copley: *The American High School and the Talented Student* (Ann Arbor, 1961).

In the mid-1950's, about five per cent of the gifted were receiving special, formal attention in American schools. An earlier survey (1948) revealed that about 20,000 pupils were enrolled in special schools or classes for the gifted, about 87,000 in special schools or classes for the mentally deficient. For these and other figures on programs for the gifted, see Cole: *Encouraging Scientific Talent*, pp. 116–19.

many educators and looked upon by some not as the hope or the challenge or the standard of aspiration for the educational system, but as a deviant, a side issue, a special problem, at times even a kind of pathology. Possibly I exaggerate; but otherwise it is hard to understand how an official of the Office of Education could have written this insensitive passage: [9]

> A considerable number of children, estimated at about four million, deviate sufficiently from mental, physical, and behavioral norms to require special educational provision. Among them are the blind and the partially seeing, the deaf and the hard of hearing, the speech-defective, the crippled, the delicate, the epileptic, the mentally deficient, the socially maladjusted, *and the extraordinarily gifted.*

· 8 ·

To ideas such as these, and especially to the claims of their advocates for universality, there has always been a good deal of resistance from parents, school boards, and teachers in many parts of the country. Nevertheless, to fit the views of the new education the curriculum of many a junior and senior high school has been "enriched" with new courses in band, chorus, driver education, human relations, home and family living, "homemaking," and consumer education. It has been possible for an American child to reach his majority in some communities without having had an opportunity to understand that the curricula available in his public high school are not everywhere regarded as an education, and may be wholly unsuited to his own aspirations. A few years ago President A. Whitney Griswold of Yale reported a case of a type altogether familiar to college-admissions officers. An apparently able and otherwise promising youth from a Midwestern city applied for admission to Yale but could not be considered because the academic part of his last two years of high school consisted only of two years of English and one of American history; the rest was made up of two years of chorus, two years of speech, and one year each of typing,

---

[9] Lloyd E. Blauch, Assistant Commissioner for Higher Education, United States Office of Education, writing in Mary Irwin, ed.: *American Universities and Colleges,* published by the American Council on Education (Washington, 1956), p. 8; italics added. It has been pointed out that the author was, after all, proposing special programs for the gifted, among others, but this consideration does not seem to me to mitigate the implications of this bizarre list of categories.

physical education, journalism, marriage and family, and personality problems.[1]

If one examines the character and content of the new courses introduced into the public high school and the rhetoric of the debate between older and newer schools of education, it becomes clear that what was at issue in the argument over life adjustment was in fact the educational aspect of the much more widely debated issue of mass culture. For certainly one of the things at issue in the schools was what kind of character and culture the large masses of high-school children could and should be prepared for. Traditional education had been founded upon a primary conviction about the value of the various subject-matter disciplines and on the assumption that the child, through some degree of mastery of academic subjects, would enlarge his mind for the general ends of life and establish his preparation for the professions or business or other desirable occupations. (It was assumed that vocational education could serve those who could not or would not enter into such competition.) Contrary to the allegations of the new educators, traditional education was not altogether unmindful of the child, but it assumed, on the whole, that he would find some pleasure in the mental activity which was offered him in an academically disciplined education and that he would gain satisfaction from his sense of accomplishment as he moved from stage to stage. In so far as the learning process was irksome to him, it assumed that the self-discipline that came from overcoming irksomeness would at least be a net gain. (No doubt some even went so far as to suggest that there was a high intrinsic value in irksomeness, on the assumption satirized in the remark that it does not matter what a boy studies so long as he doesn't like it; extreme statements of this point of view helped the new educators to draw an unattractive caricature of traditional education.) Politically the older education was conservative, in that it accepted the existing order of society and called upon the child to assert himself within its framework—which was largely that of nineteenth-century individualism. But it was also democratic in that it did not commonly assume, much less rejoice in the idea, that large numbers, from any class in society, were necessarily incapable by native endowment of entering with some degree of hope into the world of academic competition, mastery of subject matter, and discipline of mind and character.

[1] *Liberal Education and the Democratic Ideal* (New Haven, 1959), p. 29; the case was first reported by Griswold in 1954.

The new education was also at bottom politically conservative, but its warm rhetoric about democracy, its philanthropic approach to the child (not to speak of its having become the object of much harassment by right-wing cranks) made it seem, at least to its advocates, "progressive" or even radical. It prided itself on the realism of recognizing and accepting the intellectual limitations of the masses, and yet on the idealism of accepting, encouraging, and providing for the least able members of the student body. It was founded upon a primary regard for the child, and avoided making large claims upon his abilities. It made no hopeful assumptions about the child's pleasure in intellectual activity, at least where such activity was difficult, or about his satisfaction in achievement. On the contrary, it assumed that the child's pleasure in schooling, which was a primary goal, came from having his needs and interests met; and it was content to posit these interests as the foundation of the educational process. Its spokesmen did not believe that they were neglecting to teach the child to think, but they took an altogether different view from traditional educators as to what he should be encouraged to think about and how much cumulative knowledge and effort might be prerequisite to his thinking effectively. They accepted his world as being, in the first instance, largely definitive for them, and were content to guide his thinking within its terms, however parochial in place and time, and however flat in depth. They did not concede that they were abandoning the task of developing character—but they insisted that they were encouraging a more amply social, sociable, and democratic character.

As one examines the range and content of the new courses the new educators demand—which they have in some measure actually succeeded in installing—one realizes that the new education is indeed trying to educate "the whole child," in that it is trying to shape the character and the personality of its charges; and that what it aims to do is not primarily to fit them to become a disciplined part of the world of production and competition, ambition and vocation, creativity, and analytical thought, but rather to help them learn the ways of the world of consumption and hobbies, of enjoyment and social complaisance— in short, to adapt gracefully to the passive and hedonistic style summed up in the significant term *adjustment*. For this world it is deemed important that the pupil learn, not chemistry, but the testing of detergents; not physics, but how to drive and service a car; not history, but the operation of the local gas works; not biology, but the way to the zoo; not Shakespeare or Dickens, but how to write a business letter.

The new education, instead of leaving matters of consumption and personal style to the family and other agencies, converts the family and the home themselves into objects of elaborate study and sometimes offensive re-evaluation ("How can my home be made democratic?"). One life-adjustment educator explained that he wanted children to learn to inquire in school (against, as he put it, the die-hard resistance of some teachers with "a very definite academic slant"): "How can I keep well? How can I look my best? How can I get along better with others? How can hobbies contribute to my social growth?" [2] The aspirations inculcated by the school are intended to conform with adolescent interests, including those inculcated in mass-media advertising. Witness the case of the course in "Home and Family Living" required repetitively in one New York State community in *all* grades from seven to ten. Among the topics covered were: "Developing school spirit," "My duties as a baby sitter," "Clicking with the crowd," "How to be liked," "What can be done about acne?" "Learning to care for my bedroom," "Making my room more attractive." Eighth-grade pupils were given these questions on a true-false test: "Just girls need to use deodorants." "Cake soap can be used for shampooing." [3]

Today life adjustment as a force in American education has passed its moment of strength and has gone into retreat. In part this may be attributed to certain long-range changes in the function of secondary education in the American social system. As Martin Trow has observed, our secondary education "began as an elite preparatory system; during its great years of growth it became a mass terminal system; and it is now having to make a second painful transition on its way to becoming a mass preparatory system." [4] The situation for which the new educators originally designed their programs no longer exists, and there is no longer such a large receptive audience for their views. From 1900 to the 1930's, most of the parents of high-school children had not gone to high school themselves, and many of them were new to the country and its language. They tended to accept rather passively the findings and the programmatic arrangements of the newly emerging educational

[2] Richard A. Mumma: "The Real Barrier to a More Realistic Curriculum: The Teacher," *Educational Administration and Supervision,* Vol. XXXVI (January, 1950), pp. 41–2.

[3] *Bulletin* of the Council for Basic Education (April, 1957), p. 11. The actual exploration of such subjects in the schools is unusual, but their place among the plans of core-curriculum educators is not. See, for instance, the lists of student interests recommended as bases for curricula in Alberty: *Reorganizing the High School Curriculum,* chapter 15.

[4] "The Second Transformation," p. 154.

specialists. Today the parents of high-school children are very commonly at least high-school graduates, and they have been joined by a large college-educated middle-class generation quite alert to educational problems. This public, which has its own ideas about what a high-school education might be, and which has cultural interests of its own, is less willing to accept as final the doctrines of the new education and has provided a large audience for the growing literature of counterattack against the ideas of the new education represented by the books of Arthur Bestor and Mortimer Smith. Moreover, the high school is no longer the terminal institution that it was for the earlier generation. The philosophy and program of the high school have to be adapted to the fact that half of its graduates are now going on to some kind of higher education, and that they are being trained for skills and specialities more complex than the ordinary white-collar jobs for which the old high school typically prepared. Parents are increasingly aware of the danger that inadequate local schools will jeopardize the chances of their children for privileged positions in college and university education, and they have become increasingly disposed to put pressure upon school authorities to raise educational standards. Finally, the post-Sputnik educational atmosphere has quickened the activities of those who demand more educational rigor, who can now argue that we are engaged in mortal educational combat with the Soviet Union. In recent years these counter-pressures have begun to take effect. But the attitudes that gave rise to life adjustment have not by any means disappeared from the educational profession or the public. Professional education is still largely staffed, at the administrative levels and in its centers of training, by people who are far from enthusiastic about the new demand for academic excellence. American education is in a position somewhat like that of a new political regime which must depend for the execution of its mandates upon a civil service honeycombed with determined opponents.

CHAPTER XIV

The Child and the World

❦

· 1 ·

THE NEW education rested on two intellectual pillars: its use, or misuse, of science, and its appeal to the educational philosophy of John Dewey. Of the two, Dewey's philosophy was much more important, for it embraced within it the belief in the power of science to illuminate educational thought, and yet went beyond this to give educators an inclusive and generous view of the world that satisfied their philanthropic sentiments and their urge to make education useful to democracy. Dewey's contribution was to take certain views of the child which were gaining force around the end of the nineteenth century, and to link them to pragmatic philosophy and the growing demand for social reform. He thus established a satisfying connection between new views of the child and new views of the world.

Anyone concerned with the new education must reckon with its use of Dewey's ideas. To consider this in a study of anti-intellectualism may unfortunately be taken as an attempt to characterize Dewey simply as an anti-intellectual—which hardly seems just toward a man who was so intent on teaching children how to think. It may also be taken as an attempt to locate the "blame" for the failings of American education—and will inevitably take on something of this color—but my purpose is quite otherwise: it is to examine the tendency and consequences of certain ideas to which Dewey gave by far the most influential expression.

An attempt to take account of the limitations and the misuse of these ideas should not be read as a blanket condemnation of progressive education, which, as Lawrence Cremin's discriminating history has shown, contained several streams of thought and a variety of tendencies. Although its reputation suffered unwarranted damage from extremists on its periphery, progressivism had at its core something sound and important. Today, partly because many "conservative" schools have borrowed discriminatingly from progressive innovations, we may easily forget how dismal and self-satisfied the older conservative pedagogy often was, how it accepted, or even exploited, the child's classroom passivity, how much scope it afforded to excessively domineering teachers, how heavily it depended on rote learning. The main strength of progressivism came from its freshness in method. It tried to mobilize the interests of the child, to make good use of his need for activity, to concern the minds of teachers and educators with a more adequate sense of his nature, to set up pedagogical rules that would put the burden on the teacher not to be arbitrarily authoritative, and to develop the child's capacity for expression as well as his ability to learn. It had the great merit of being experimental in a field in which too many people thought that all the truths had been established. In an experimental school, where one can find picked pupils and teachers and instill in them a special ethos of dedication and excitement, one is likely to get extraordinary results, as many progressive schools did and still do.[1] Unfortunately, one cannot expect to make universally applicable the results, however illuminating, which have been achieved in a special experimental situation.

The value of progressivism rested on its experimentalism and its work with younger children; its weakness lay in its efforts to promulgate doctrine, to generalize, in its inability to assess the practical limits of its own program, above all in its tendency to dissolve the curriculum. This tendency became most serious in the education of older children, and especially at the secondary level, where, as the need arises to pursue a complex, organized program of studies, the question of the curriculum becomes acute. Hitherto I have intentionally spoken not of progressivism in education, but of something still broader and more inclusive which I prefer to call "the new education." The new education represented the elaboration of certain progressive principles into a creed, the attempt to make inclusive claims for their applicability in a system of mass education, their extension from experimental work

[1] In this respect, the situation of an experimental school may be likened to the famous Hawthorne experiments in the field of industrial sociology, in which an attempt to find what working conditions would lead to increased productivity ended in the discovery that the psychological conditions of the experiment itself, and not any particular device, was what stimulated a continuing series of advances in productivity.

largely with very young children into a schematism for public education at all ages, and finally the development of an attack upon the organized curriculum and liberal education under the rubric of "progressivism." For all this, early and late, Dewey's thought was constantly invoked. His vocabulary and ideas, which were clearly evident in the *Cardinal Principles* of 1918, seem to appear in every subsequent document of the new education. He has been praised, paraphrased, repeated, discussed, apotheosized, even on occasions read.

It is commonly said that Dewey was misunderstood, and it is repeatedly pointed out that in time he had to protest against some of the educational practices carried on in his name. Perhaps his intent was widely, even regularly violated, but Dewey was hard to read and interpret. He wrote a prose of terrible vagueness and plasticity, which William James once characterized as "damnable; you might even say God-damnable." His style is suggestive of the cannonading of distant armies: one concludes that something portentous is going on at a remote and inaccessible distance, but one cannot determine just what it is. That this style is, perhaps symptomatically, at its worst in Dewey's most important educational writings suggests that his great influence as an educational spokesman may have been derived in some part from the very inaccessibility of his exact meanings. A variety of schools of educational thought have been able to read their own meanings into his writings. Although it is tempting to say that Dewey's work was crudely misread by the most anti-intellectual spokesmen of the new education, it seems fairer to admit that even the life-adjustment educators could have arrived at their use of Dewey through an honest and intelligent exegesis of the master. Lawrence Cremin has observed that, "however tortuous the intellectual line from *Democracy and Education* to the pronouncements of the Commission on Life Adjustment, that line can be drawn." [2]

That it is in fact an unduly tortuous line one may be permitted to doubt. Serious faults in style are rarely, if ever, matters of "mere" style; they embody real difficulties in conception. Far more probable than the thesis that Dewey was perversely distorted by obtuse or over-enthusiastic followers is the idea that the unresolved problems of interpretation to which his work gave rise were tokens of real ambiguities and gaps in thought, which themselves express certain difficulties and unresolved problems in educational theory and in our culture. What many of Dewey's followers have done, with or without complete

[2] *The Transformation of the School,* p. 239.

license from the master himself, is to attack the ideas of leadership and guidance, and the values of culture and reflective life, in favor of certain notions of spontaneity, democracy, and practicality. In this respect they repeat in education some of the themes that were sounded by the egalitarians in politics, the evangelicals in religion, and the prophets of practicality in business. Before attempting to see how Dewey's philosophy lent itself to these uses, let us first look at the essential argument of this philosophy and at the intellectual setting in which it emerged.

· 2 ·

The objectives of Dewey's educational theory, which were closely knit into his general philosophy, comprise a high set of ambitions. In the first instance, Dewey was trying to devise a theory of education—of the development of intelligence and the role of knowledge—which would be wholly consistent with Darwinism. For a thinker born in the year in which *The Origin of Species* was published, and intellectually raised during the flowering of evolutionary science, modern education would be worth nothing if it were not scientific.

Dewey began by thinking of the individual learner as using his mind instrumentally to solve various problems presented by his environment, and went on to develop a theory of education conceived as the growth of the learner. The modern educational system, he saw, must operate in an age of democracy, science, and industrialism; education should strive to meet the requirements of this age. Above all, education should abandon those practices, based upon a pre-democratic and pre-industrial society, which accepted the leisured and aristocratic view that knowledge is the contemplation of fixed verities. Dewey felt that he and his contemporaries must now surmount a series of artificial dualisms inherited from past ages. Primary among these was the dualism between knowledge and action. For Dewey, action is involved in knowledge—not in the sense, as some of his uncomprehending critics charged, that knowledge is subordinated to action and inferior to "practice," but in the sense that knowledge is a form of action, and that action is one of the terms by which knowledge is acquired and used.

Dewey was also trying to find the educational correlates of a democratic and progressive society. How can one construct an educational system that will avoid perpetuating all the flaws of existing society at the root simply by molding children in its own image? If a democratic society is truly to serve all its members, it must devise schools in which, at the germinal point in childhood, these members will be able to cultivate their capacities and, instead of simply reproducing the qualities of the larger society, will learn how to improve them. It was in this sense that he saw education as a major force in social reconstruction. Plainly, if society is to be remade, one must above all look for the regenerative contribution the child is capable of making to society. And this cannot be done, Dewey thought, unless the child is placed at the center of the school, unless the rigid authority of the teacher and the traditional weight of the curriculum are displaced by his own developing interests and impulses. To mobilize these impulses and interests toward learning, under gentle adult guidance, is to facilitate the learning process and also to form a type of character and mind suitable to the work of social reform.

This is an excessively abbreviated statement of Dewey's theory, but it serves at least to show how he stated his problems and to turn attention to the central personage in their solution—the figure of the child. It is here that we may begin, for the conception of the child—no mere intellectual construct but the focus of a set of deep emotional commitments and demands—is at the core of the new education. To anticipate what must subsequently be elaborated at some length, I believe that the conception of the child formed by Dewey and his contemporaries, which later entered into the stream of the new education, was more romantic and primitivist than it was post-Darwinian. This conception of the child, and the related assumptions about his natural growth, made it all the more difficult for Dewey and his followers to resolve those dualisms which he felt should be resolved, and, despite his continuing efforts at clarification, made it difficult also to reconcile the central position of the child with what proved still to be necessary in the way of order and authority in education. Finally, the penumbra of sanctity with which the figure of the child was surrounded made it difficult to discuss with realism the role of democracy in education.

To understand the emotional commitment with which Dewey and his contemporaries approached the child, it is necessary to reconstruct to some extent the intellectual atmosphere around the turn of the century, when his generation began to work its transformation of American education. At this time, both in America and in Europe, there was a quickening of interest in the child and a new turn in sentiment among those professionally concerned with him. It was in 1909 that the Swedish feminist, Ellen Key, wrote her significantly titled book, *The*

Century of the Child, which epitomized the expectations of those who felt that the child had been newly rediscovered. But expressions of this order were becoming common coin. In 1900 the state superintendent of public instruction of Georgia presented at the annual meeting of the National Education Association an inspirational paper entitled "What Manner of Child Shall This Be?" In it he declared: [3]

> If I were asked what is to be accounted the great discovery of this century, I would pass by all the splendid achievements that men have wrought in wood and stone and iron and brass. I would not go to the volume that catalogs the printing-press, the loom, the steam-engine, the steamship, the ocean cable, the telegraph, the wireless telegraphy, the telephone, the phonograph. I would not go among the stars and point to either one of the planets that have been added to our solar system. I would not call for the Roentgen ray that promises to revolutionize the study of the human brain as well as the human body. I would pass over all the labor-saving machines and devices by which the work of the world has been marvelously multiplied. Above and beyond all these the index finger of the world's progress, in the march of time, would point unerringly to the little child as the one great discovery of the century now speeding to its close.

Having thus stated what importance he attached to the discovery of the little child, the school official went on to summarize the progress of the previous century, from the days when, as he imagined, education had been "the exclusive privilege of an autocratic minority" and had been put at the disposal of "an all-powerful democratic majority." Freedom of opportunity had already been given to the American child, but further reforms were still in the making. "Already we Americans have discovered that the old system of education will not fit his case. . . . We have quit trying to fit the boy to a system. We are now trying to adjust a system to the boy." Turning to religious imagery, the official likened American teachers to Christ, in the sense that they were releasing the American child from shrouds and deathly cerements, as Christ released Lazarus, and turning him loose to grow. In the future, he predicted with remarkable prescience, the Christian challenge to the teacher would rise still higher, for the teacher would be expected to save the humblest of God's children: "Time was when

[3] See G. R. Glenn: "What Manner of Child Shall This Be?" N.E.A. *Proceedings,* 1900, pp. 176–8, for this and other quotations.

the power of the teacher was measured by what he could do with a bright boy or a bright girl. From the beginning of this new century the power of the teacher will be measured by what he will be able to do with the dull boy, the defective child. More than ever before in the history of this world the real test of teaching power will be measured, not by what can be done with the best, but by what can be done with the worst boy in the school." [4] The new educational psychology will be "the psychology of the prodigal son and the lost sheep." The "great rejoicings" in American life will come when child study is so mastered and the development of schools so perfected that the educational system touches and develops every American boy. "We shall come to our place of rejoicing when we have saved every one of these American children and made every one of them a contributor to the wealth, to the intelligence, and to the power of this great democratic government of ours."

I have chosen these remarks because, though written by a working educator rather than a theorist, they sum up in brief a number of the convictions prevalent in what was then up-to-date educational thinking. They reflect its Christian fervor and benevolence; its sense of the central place of the child in the modern world; its concern with democracy and opportunity as criteria of educational achievement; its conviction of the importance of the dull child and his demands on the educational system; its optimism about educational research and child study; its belief that education is to be defined essentially as growth; and its faith that a proper education, though focused on the self-realization of the individual child, would also automatically work toward the fulfillment and salvation of democratic society.

The Georgia school official may well have been reading the works of leading contemporaries in the field, for his view of the child is largely in accord with what they were then writing. Dewey, who was in his early forties and just beginning his work in education, was of course one of them; but it is desirable also to look for a moment at the influence, then more ponderable, of two older men who preceded him, the educator Francis Wayland Parker and the psychologist G. Stanley Hall. Parker, whom Dewey once called the father of progressive education, was a man of exceptional vitality, a remarkably effective peda-

---

[4] This was, of course, at odds with the conception of more traditional and less evangelical educators like Charles William Eliot, who once wrote that "the policy of an institution of education, of whatever grade, ought never to be determined by the needs of the least capable students. . . ." *Educational Reform* (New York, 1898).

gogue, and a distinguished school administrator. In the 1870's he remade the school system of Quincy, Massachusetts, achieving results that, by the most impeccably traditional criteria of educational performance, must be considered brilliant. Not long afterward, he went on to the principalship of the Cook County Normal School in Chicago, where he developed more fully his educational theories and his pedagogical techniques. There he undoubtedly set an important example for John Dewey, who was impressed by the Cook County Normal School before he set up his own "Laboratory School" in 1896, and for G. Stanley Hall, who for a time made annual visits to Parker's school "to set my educational watch."

The terms in which Parker cast his educational theory were in many respects too old-fashioned to be in tune with the new currents of thought. For example, they were altogether pre-Darwinian and had no trace of the more sophisticated functionalist psychology which made Dewey's writings so widely appealing. But Parker's view of the child, which was, to a great extent, patterned after Froebel's, was of capital importance. "The child," he said, "is the climax and culmination of all God's creations," and to answer the question: What is the child? is to approach a knowledge of God. "He put into that child Himself his divinity, and . . . this divinity manifests itself in the seeking for truth through the visible and tangible." "The spontaneous tendencies of the child are the records of inborn divinity," he asserted. "We are here, my fellow-teachers, for one purpose, and that purpose is to understand these tendencies and continue them in all these directions, following nature." If the child was the bearer of divinity and "the fruit of all the past and the seed of all the future," it was natural enough to conclude that "the centre of all movement in education is *the child*." One may hazard the guess that Parker's concern with the spontaneous activities of the child were fruitful rather than stultifying partly because he also conceived of the child as omnivorously curious, as having a natural interest in all subjects, as being a sort of savant in the making, and a born artist and handicraftsman as well. Accordingly, he proposed a rather demanding curriculum, and unlike most later progressives, he believed even in teaching grammar in all grades of the elementary school, since he thought it should be "thoroughly mastered."

As Dewey did later, Parker stressed the school as a community: "A school should be a model home, a complete community and embryonic democracy." Properly used, it could be expected to achieve an extraordinary reformation: "We must believe that we can save *every child*. The citizen should say in his heart: 'I await the regeneration of the world from the teaching of the common schools of America.' " [5]

The era in which these words were written was also the era in which G. Stanley Hall, the leader of the child-study movement, said: "The guardians of the young should strive first of all to keep out of nature's way. . . . They should feel profoundly that childhood, as it comes fresh from the hands of God, is not corrupt, but illustrates the survival of the most consummate thing in the world. . . . Nothing else is so worthy of love, reverence, and service as the body and soul of the growing child." It was the era in which Dewey himself said that "the child's own instincts and powers furnish the material and give the starting point for all education." Also: "We violate the child's nature and render difficult the best ethical results by introducing the child too abruptly to a number of special studies, of reading, writing, geography, etc., out of relation to [his] social life. The true center of correlation on the school subjects is not science, nor literature, nor history, nor geography, but the child's own social activities." [6]

It will be apparent that the new education was presented to the world not simply as an instrumentality but as a creed, which went beyond the hope of this or that strictly educational result to promise some kind of ultimate salvation for individuals or for the race. We shall presently see, for example, how G. Stanley Hall foresaw that an education designed in accordance with the nature of child growth would rear the superman of the future. Dewey's early view of the possibilities of education were likewise exalted. Education, he said in his well-titled little pamphlet, *My Pedagogic Creed*, "is the fundamental method of social progress and reform." Hence the teacher must be seen as "engaged, not simply in the training of individuals, but in the formation of the proper social life." Every teacher should accordingly think of himself as "a social servant set apart for the maintenance of proper social order and the securing of the right social growth. In this way the teacher always is the prophet of the true God and the usherer in of the true kingdom of God." [7] Plainly, high expectations like these put a staggering burden upon any proposal for educational reform.

[5] Francis W. Parker: *Talks on Pedagogics* (New York, 1894), pp. 3, 5–6, 16, 23–4, 320–30, 383, 434, 450.
[6] G. Stanley Hall: "The Ideal School as Based on Child Study," *Forum*, Vol. XXXII (September, 1901), p. 24–5; John Dewey: *My Pedagogic Creed* (1897; new ed. Washington, 1929), pp. 4, 9.
[7] *My Pedagogic Creed*, pp. 15, 17.

This creed, this fighting faith, had to be put forward in the face of much stubborn resistance before it could be established as the reigning creed. Men who feel that they must engage in such a crusade are not likely to be greatly concerned with nuances, or with exploring the limits or dangers of their ideas. Unfortunately, what is important in a practical sphere like education is very often not so much the character of a philosophy or creedal commitment as certain questions of emphasis and proportion which arise in trying to execute it; and there is no automatic way of deriving a sense of proportion from a body of ideas. For example, the early spokesmen of the new education demanded that the child be respected, but it was difficult to say where respect might end and a kind of bathetic reverence might begin. Although Dewey himself began to warn in the 1930's against the overuse or the oversimplified use of his theories, he found it difficult to define, even in his later works, the points at which the lines of restraint could or should be drawn without at the same time abandoning certain of his essential commitments.

· 3 ·

Here perhaps the romantic inheritance, quite as much or more than the appeal of post-Darwinian naturalism, may explain the charm of the concept of the child formulated by Dewey and his generation. The most elaborate statements of this concept come from European writers who applied romantic views to the child—on occasion Dewey referred respectfully to Rousseau, Pestalozzi, and Froebel, as he did to Emerson, whose essay "Culture" foreshadowed many of his ideas. The notion of education advanced at the turn of the century by these pedagogical reformers was romantic in the sense that they set up an antithesis between the development of the individual—his sensibility, the scope of his fancy, the urgency of his personal growth—and the imperatives of the social order, with its demand for specified bodies of knowledge, prescribed manners and morals, and a personal equipment suited to traditions and institutions. Theirs was a commitment to the natural child against artificial society. For them, the child came into this world trailing clouds of glory, and it was the holy office of the teacher to see that he remained free, instead of assisting in the imposition of alien codes upon him. They envisaged a child life engaged more or less directly with nature and with activity, and not with absorbing traditions meaningful only to adults or with reading books and mastering skills set not by the child's desires and interests but by adult society.[8]

This view of education began once again to gain currency among Western thinkers at the turn of the century; the United States provided an unusually receptive soil. This country had always had a strong penchant for child-indulgence—it was an extremely common point of observation for nineteenth-century travelers in America. Moreover, American education, being in a singularly fluid state, offered less resistance to such attractive novelties than the tradition-encrusted educational systems of the European countries. The evangelical climate of this country was also a force: the new educators' rhetoric about "saving" every American child, and their implied promise that the child saved would himself redeem civilization, point to this conclusion. It was decades before even so secular a thinker as Dewey lost the confidence evident in the young educational reformer of 1897 who believed that the good teacher would usher in "the true kingdom of God."

If we attend carefully to the overtones of the new educators' pronouncements, with their stress on such terms as spontaneity, instinct, activity, and nature, we become aware of the way in which the problem of education is posed. The child is a phenomenon at once natural and divine—here post-Darwinian naturalism and the romantic heritage link arms—and the "natural" pattern of his needs and instincts becomes an imperative which it is profane for educators to violate.

We are now prepared to appreciate the significance of the central idea of the new educational thought: that the school should base its studies not on the demands of society, nor on any conception of what an educated person should be, but on the developing needs and interests of the child. This does not mean merely that the nature of the child imposes negative limits on the educational process and that it is vain to try to surmount them: to say this would be superfluous. It means that the nature of the child is a positive guide to educational procedure —that the child himself naturally and spontaneously generates the needs and impulses that should animate the educational process.

In a revealing article of 1901, "The Ideal School as Based on Child Study," G. Stanley Hall attempted to say what this guiding principle

[8] One thinks in this connection of Rousseau in *Émile*: "When I get rid of children's lessons, I get rid of the chief cause of their sorrows, namely their books. Reading is the curse of childhood, yet it is almost the only occupation you can find for children. Émile at twelve years old will hardly know what a book is. . . . When reading is of use to him, I admit he must learn to read, but till then he will only find it a nuisance."

would entail. He would try, he said, "to break away from all current practices, traditions, methods, and philosophies, for a brief moment, and ask *what education would be if based solely upon a fresh and comprehensive view of the nature and needs of childhood.*" [9] In short, he would strip away the inherited ideas of what education should be, which are the trappings of an outworn past, and assume that what modern child study has learned is of greater relevance to the purpose. Etymologically, Hall pointed out, the word for school meant leisure, "exemption from work, the perpetuation of the primeval paradise created before the struggle for existence began." Understood in this sense, the school stood for health, growth, and heredity, "a pound of which is worth a ton of instruction."

Because of the natural and sacred character of the child's health, leisure, and growth, every invasion of his time, every demand of the curriculum, must be doubly tried and conclusively justified before we subject him to it:

> We must overcome the fetichism of the alphabet, of the multiplication table, of grammars, of scales, and of bibliolatry, and must reflect that . . . the invention of Cadmus seemed the sowing of veritable dragon's teeth in the brain; that Charlemagne and many other great men of the world could not read or write; that scholars have argued that Cornelia, Ophelia, Beatrice, and even the blessed mother of our Lord knew nothing of letters. The knights, the elite leaders of the Middle Ages, deemed writing a mere clerk's trick beneath the attention of all those who scorned to muddle their wits with others' ideas, feeling that their own were good enough for them.

Of course no one will imagine that Hall, who had received one of the best educations of his generation—and a very traditional one—at Harvard and the German universities, thought that the new education would have as a goal the subversion of literacy.[1] The importance of his views lay in the belief that there is a natural and normal course of child

[9] Hall: op. cit., p. 24; italics added. For quotations in the following paragraphs, see pp. 25, 26, 30, 39. Compare the views of Francis W. Parker: "I wish to have these words written in italics, we do not claim that nature is the center, neither do we claim that history and literature are the center, *we do claim that the child is the center*, that this being, this highest creation of God, with its laws of body, mind, and soul, determines in itself the very nature and condition of its growth." *Discussions at the Open Session of the Herbart Club, Denver, Colorado,* July 10, 1895 (1895), pp. 155–6.

[1] The formulation of this goal had to wait for a later generation of educators. See above, chapter 1, Exhibit L.

development to which bookish considerations should yield. Some of
his particular suggestions were most sensible,[2] and some are still practiced to good effect. It is interesting, too, that just as Parker clung to
the value of grammar, Hall did not think that the study of the classical
languages had been altogether eliminated by this emphasis on natural
development. At least some children might well study languages, Hall
thought; what is especially interesting to a contemporary reader, looking back over the span of seventy years, is that Hall felt that he knew
quite precisely at what points in a child's development the study of
these subjects was "natural." "As to the dead languages, if they are to
be taught, Latin should be begun not later than ten or eleven, and
Greek never later than twelve or thirteen." A generation later, most
proponents of the new education had no use for these languages, and
they would have been horrified to see either of them begun in the primary grades.

Hall's hopes for what could be realized in education through the scientific study of the child were avowedly utopian. With a generous
grant of funds and five years of experimentation, he had "no shadow
of doubt or fear," it would be possible to work out a program that
would satisfy educational prophets and even persuade conservatives,
"because the best things established will be in it."

> But it will be essentially pedocentric rather than scholiocentric;
> it may be a little like the Reformation which insisted that the Sab-
> bath, the Bible, and the Church were made for man and not he for
> them; it will fit both the practices and the results of modern sci-
> ence and psychological study; it will make religion and morals
> more effective; and, perhaps, above all, it will give individuality in
> the school its full rights as befits a republican form of govern-
> ment, and will contribute something to bring the race to the higher
> maturity of the superman that is to be, effectiveness in develop-
> ing which is the highest and final test of art, science, religion,
> home, state, literature, and every human institution.

It will no doubt seem a far cry from Hall's hopes for ten-year-old
Latinists and his call for the superman of the future to the work of the
life-adjustment educators with their campaign against disciplinary sub-

---

[2] I find especially perceptive this recommendation: "The children of the rich,
generally prematurely individualized or over-individualized, especially when they
are only children, must be disciplined and subordinated; while the children of the
poor, usually under-individualized, should be indulged." It suggests a greater sensitivity to the social milieu than Hall's commitment to "natural" patterns might imply.

jects and their recommended class discussions on "How can I get everyone to participate in the activities at the party?" or "Should I have
dates in junior high school?" [3] But utopias have a way of being short-
circuited under the very eyes of their formulators.

· 4 ·

The romantic and Darwinian backgrounds of the new education make
it easier to understand why Dewey should have chosen to define education as growth. In Dewey this conception that education is growth is
no casual act of definition and no idle metaphor: it represents an attempt to locate and restate the very essence of the educational process. There is a frequently quoted passage in *Democracy and Education* which illustrates at once the disturbing quality of Dewey's style
and the importance he attached to the conception of education as
growth. There he wrote: [4]

> We have been occupied with the conditions and implications
> of growth. . . . When it is said that education is development,
> everything depends upon *how* development is conceived. Our net
> conclusion is that life is development, and that developing, grow-
> ing, is life. Translated into its educational equivalents, this means
> (*i*) that the educational process has no end beyond itself; it is its
> own end; and that (*ii*) the educational process is one of continual
> reorganizing, reconstructing, transforming. . . .
>
> Since in reality there is nothing to which growth is relative save
> more growth, there is nothing to which education is subordinate
> save more education. . . . Education means the enterprise of sup-
> plying the conditions which insure growth, or adequacy of life, ir-
> respective of age. . . .
>
> Since growth is the characteristic of life, education is all one
> with growing; it has no end beyond itself. The criterion of the
> value of school education is the extent in which it creates a desire
> for continued growth and supplies means for making the desire
> effective in fact.

The implications of this must be reckoned with: we are not asked to
consider that education resembles growth, or has something in com-

[3] The examples are from Alberty: *Reorganizing the High-School Curriculum*,
pp. 472–3.
[4] *Democracy and Education* (New York, 1916), pp. 59–62.

mon with growth, or may helpfully be thought of as a special form of growth. We are urged to consider that education *is* growth; that growth is life; that life is development; and above all that it is meaningless to try to provide ends for education, since it has no possible further end but more education. "The aim of education is to enable individuals to continue their education." [5]

The idea that education is growth is at first blush all but irresistible. Certainly education is not a form of shrinkage. To say that it is growth seems to assert a desirable connection between the learning process and the world of nature. This concept is refreshingly unmechanical. It does justice to our sense that education is cumulative and self-enlarging and leads toward a mind and character which become larger, more complex, more powerful, and yet finer. But several critics have contended that the notion that education is growth was the source of endless difficulties; and I believe that in the hands of some of Dewey's followers this idea became one of the most mischievous metaphors in the history of modern education. Growth is a natural, animal process, and education is a social process. Growth in the child, taken literally, goes on automatically, requiring no more than routine care and nourishment; its end is to a large degree predetermined by genetic inheritance, whereas the ends of education have to be supplied. In contemplating a child's education we are free to consider whether he shall learn two languages, but in contemplating his natural growth we cannot consider whether he shall develop two heads.

Since the idea of growth is intrinsically a biological metaphor and an individualistic conception, the effect of this idea was of necessity to turn the mind away from the social to the personal function of education; it became not an assertion of the child's place in society but rather of his interests as against those of society.[6] The idea of growth invited educational thinkers to set up an invidious contrast between self-determining, self-directing growth from within, which was good, and molding from without, which was bad. Students of Dewey's philosophy might readily object to any portrayal of his educational thought as oriented excessively toward the biological and individual and as insuf-

[5] Ibid., p. 117. In an earlier work Dewey had said that "the process and the goal of education are the same thing. To set up any end outside of education, as furnishing its goal and standard, is to deprive the educational process of much of its meaning, and tends to make us rely upon false and external stimuli in dealing with the child." *My Pedagogic Creed*, p. 12.

[6] Cf. the criticism by Boyd H. Bode in *Education at the Crossroads* (New York, 1938), especially pp. 73 ff. Among the various critiques, I have found this work and I. L. Kandel's *The Cult of Uncertainty* (New York, 1943) most illuminating.

ficiently mindful of the collective and social. What writer on education, it might be asked, ever spoke more positively about the social character of the educational process and about its ultimate social function?

The problem, however, did not arise from any lack of awareness, on Dewey's part, of the social character of education; it arose from the fact that the concept of individual growth became a hostage in the hands of educational thinkers who were obsessed with the child-centered school. Although Dewey himself did not accept the antithesis between the child and society as a finality—indeed, he hoped to achieve a harmonious synthesis of the two—the historical effect of the conception of education as growth was to exalt the child and dismiss the problem of society, on the ground that the growth of the child stood for health, whereas the traditions of society (including curricular traditions) stood for outworn, excessively authoritative demands. "The authority of society," wrote a leading psychologist in this tradition, "or of any part of society is not presented to the child as a guide to conduct. Reliance is placed on the experience of each individual child. The experience of the race in discovering what line of conduct works out satisfactorily and what does not is utilized only in so far as the child sees fit to appeal to it." [7]

Dewey himself never argued, as critics and followers have often thought, for a directionless education. On this point at least he was painfully clear. He often said in his early as well as his later educational writings that the child himself, unguided, is not capable of spinning out the proper content of his education; that every superficial act or interest, every stray impulse, of the child is not necessarily valuable; that the teacher must somehow, without imposing "external" ends, guide, direct, and develop those impulses of the child which are moving "forward." [8]

Dewey's difficulty was of another order: having insisted that education, being growth itself, cannot have any end set for it save still more

[7] Goodwin Watson, as quoted by I. L. Kandel: *The Cult of Uncertainty*, p. 79.
[8] See almost all of *The Child and the Curriculum* (1902; Chicago ed., 1956), but especially pp. 14–18 and the significant passage on pp. 30–1 in which he pleads that there be some kind of continuous interaction between the child's interest and the direction he gets, so that the two will work in some kind of dynamic harmony. See also *Democracy and Education*, pp. 61–2; also p. 133: "The natural, or native, powers furnish the initiating and limiting forces in all education; they do not furnish its ends or aims." At one point, in 1926, Dewey departed from his customarily benign injunctions to say that the studied avoidance of guidance practiced in some progressive schools was "really stupid."

education, he was unable to formulate the criteria by which society, through the teacher, should guide or direct the child's impulses. The teacher was left with a firm mandate to exercise some guidance, to make some discriminations among the child's impulses and needs, but with no directional signposts.[9] The child's impulses should be guided "forward"—but in which direction? Such a set of criteria presupposes an educational goal, an adult prevision of what the child should know and what he should be. "Let the child's nature fulfill its own destiny," [1] Dewey urged, but the suggestion that the child has a destiny implied an end or goal somewhat removed in time and not envisaged by the child. For this reason, what came to be called progressive education, although often immensely fertile and ingenious concerning means, was so futile and confused about ends; much of what it had to say about teaching methods was of the highest value, but it was quite unclear, often anarchic, about what these methods should be used to teach. Remarkably effective beginnings were made at mobilizing the child's interests for learning, but often these interests simply displaced learning. The more certain progressive education was of its techniques, the less explicit it was about its goals—perhaps in this respect it offered a parable on American life.

Dewey's own vagueness about the curriculum is understandable in the light of this conception of education as growth. Naturally, in the course of his career he wrote a good deal about the curriculum; but it is difficult to discover from his major books on education what he thought a good curriculum should be, or rather what the various alternative curricula should be, in the American school system. This absence of curricular commitments was consistent with his proposition that no ends or goals should be formulated for education, since its only legitimate end is the capacity for still further education. By the time he wrote *Democracy and Education,* Dewey had become convinced that "the curriculum is always getting loaded down with purely inherited traditional matter," and that it therefore needs "constant inspection, criticism, and revision." He was concerned, too, that the curriculum "probably represents the values of adults rather than those of children and youth, or those of pupils a generation ago rather than those of the present day." Here he seems to lend his authority to those who believed that the curriculum should be shaped fundamentally in accord-

[9] "It is as absurd for [the parent or teacher] to set up their 'own' aims as the proper objects of the growth of the children as it would be for the farmer to set up an ideal of farming, irrespective of conditions." *Democracy and Education,* p. 125.
[1] *The Child and the Curriculum,* p. 31.

ance with the expressed desires of children and that it should be largely discontinuous from generation to generation, if not from year to year—for the recommended inspection and revision are not intermittent but "constant." [2]

On one count Dewey was completely forthright: "As long as any topic makes an immediate appeal, it is not necessary to ask what it is good for." Here he favored his readers with one of his rare concrete illustrations: "It is unsound to urge that, say, Latin has a value *per se* in the abstract, just as a study, as sufficient justification for teaching it." Thus far it is easy to give one's assent, but Dewey went on to add that Latin does not need to be justified by having attributed to it some definite use in the future. "When pupils are genuinely concerned in learning Latin, that is of itself proof that it possesses value." [3]

The intention of this was plainly innocent enough, for the context showed that Dewey was simply saying that he set a high value on the spontaneous appreciation by pupils of what they were studying. This did not mean that they were to study whatever was pleasurable. In at least one work he had warned educators against trying to exploit "what is merely pleasure-giving, exciting, or transient." [4] Yet there seems no way of avoiding the conclusion that if the value of every study was to be, as he urged, dependent upon the concrete situation in which the choice of studies was to be made, then the kind of long-range evaluation of subjects which is necessary to the design of curricula becomes inordinately difficult. "In the abstract," said Dewey, "there is no such thing as degrees or order of value." Therefore: "We cannot establish a hierarchy of values among studies." [5]

Again, one may be tempted to agree, if by hierarchy one has in mind the notion that studies are assigned an eternal value equally applicable to all pupils. But it is too easy to conclude from this proposition that any subject is the equal of any other—that, as the N.E.A. later put it, "mathematics and mechanics, art and agriculture, history and homemaking are all peers." A pupil's "genuine concern" to learn Latin was

[2] One is reminded here of the same restless spirit in Francis W. Parker: "Do nothing twice alike. Don't do things you have done before. If the child stood up before, have him sit down now. Whatever you do, do something different. Have no patterns. Uniformity is death—variety is life." N.E.A. *Proceedings*, 1880.

[3] *Democracy and Education*, pp. 283–4.

[4] *The School and Society* (1915; ed. Chicago, 1956), p. 136. The context of this warning was a plea, not for a firm program of academic studies, but rather for a continuous study of what Dewey there called "occupation work." On Dewey's remonstrances against attacks on the orderly organization of subject matter, see Cremin: op. cit., pp. 234–6.

[5] *Democracy and Education*, pp. 280–1.

for Dewey sufficient proof of its value. If for "Latin" one substitutes "driver education" or "beauty culture," considering each as justified if it makes "an immediate appeal," one senses the game that later educators played with Dewey's principles. Dewey himself presumably would not have made such substitutions, but in his philosophy there are no barriers against making them.

The effect of Dewey's philosophy on the design of curricular systems was devastating. Even if one is aware of the conditional and limited character of any hierarchy of values one may establish among subjects, one must have such a hierarchy in mind to design a curriculum that runs over the course of several years, for its lower years must be in some measure conceived as the prerequisite to certain choices in the later years. An urgent desire to learn Latin or any other such subject is not a "natural" impulse in any child. Children can become, in Dewey's words, "genuinely concerned" to learn Latin only if adult society decides that it is good for some of them to have that choice and at what age it should be made possible for them, and only if adult society arranges the prior curricular, social, and intellectual experiences of these children in such a way as to make the choice between learning Latin or not learning it possible and meaningful for them. In short, some part of the adult community must have convictions about the curriculum and be willing to organize it accordingly.[6] Such organization, though leaving the child a considerable margin of choice, would go beyond the classroom "guidance" and "direction" which Dewey explicitly allowed for.

· 5 ·

The ideal of growth was the primary expression of Dewey's concern with the individual; the ideal of education in the service of democracy was the expression of his sense of the social function of education. Although, as I have suggested, the ideal of growth committed many educators to an anti-societal bias, this was not Dewey's view of the matter; he felt that individual growth and the interests of a democratic social order, far from being in any ineluctable antagonism, were susceptible to a completely harmonious synthesis. In his eyes, the new education was to be anything but anarchistic or ultra-individualistic. The child,

---

[6] But see Dewey *per contra*: "In education, the currency of these externally imposed aims is responsible for the emphasis put upon the notion of preparation for a remote future and for rendering the work of both teacher and pupil mechanical and slavish." Ibid., p. 129; cf. the whole passage on aims in education, pp. 124–9.

now released from traditional restraints, would be raised none the less to accept social responsibilities; but these would be defined as responsibilities to his peers and to the future. The new education itself would have social responsibilities more demanding and more freighted with social significance than the education of the past. Its goal would be nothing less than the fullest realization of the principles of democracy. In setting this aspiration, Dewey stood firmly within the American tradition, for the great educational reformers who had established the common-school system had also been concerned with its potential value to democracy; he was also wholly in tune with his times, for the revival and enlargement of American democracy was one of the essential aspirations of the Progressives.

Traditional education, Dewey believed, had been founded upon theories of knowledge and moral development congenial only to pre-democratic society, and, in so far as it was still operative in democratic society, hampered the realization of the democratic ideal. Since the time of classical antiquity, the division of society into a leisured and aristocratic class, which was the custodian of learning, and an enslaved or working class, which was engaged with work and practical knowledge, had encouraged a fatal separation of knowledge and action.[7]

In a democratic society, however, where almost everyone has a function and where there are many shared interests and objectives, it should be possible to surmount this separation and arrive at an understanding of knowledge which does full justice to the element of social action involved in it. A society which is both democratic and progressive "must have a type of education which gives individuals a personal interest in social relationships and control, and the habits of mind which secure social changes without introducing disorder." [8]

Dewey did not at any time fall victim to the delusion that the whole burden of social change could be put on the educational process. Direct instruction and exhortation, he remarked in *Democracy and Education*, could not in themselves bring about changes in mind and character; such changes would also require changes, of a type he did not clearly specify, in "industrial and political conditions." But education could make a vital contribution: "We may produce in schools a projection in type of the society we should like to realize, and by forming minds in accord with it gradually modify the larger and more recalci-

[7] For Dewey's development of this theme, see *Reconstruction in Philosophy* (New York, 1920).
[8] *Democracy and Education*, p. 115.

trant features of adult society." [9] This sentence expresses in brief the essence of Dewey's demand on the schools in behalf of democracy, and at the same time shows a central difficulty in his educational philosophy: he was obliged to assume that there is a kind of pre-established harmony between the needs and interests of the child and "the society we should like to realize." Otherwise it would be necessary either to sacrifice the ideal of education as growth or to abandon the goal of "forming minds" in accordance with an adult, and hence externally imposed, vision of the good society.

Dewey's conception of the manner in which education would serve democracy is different from that formulated by earlier educational reformers. They had expected that a common-school system would enlarge opportunities for the common man while at the same time endowing the whole population with those mental and moral qualities which were deemed necessary to a popular form of government. They were traditional, in the sense that they thought of adult society as formulating the ends of education and devising curricula to suit them. But since this was unacceptable to Dewey, he sought for another, more subtle, more pervasive, and yet more "natural" formulation of the relation between democracy and education. One consequence of this view was that his *Democracy and Education,* for all its generalized discussion of leisure and working classes, had almost nothing to say about the specific class structure of American society, or the relation of educational opportunity to this structure, or the means of extending opportunities to increase social mobility and break down class barriers. In short, his view of the problem of education and democracy was not economic or sociological, or even political, except in the broadest sense of that term; it was largely psychological or social-psychological. In Dewey's theory, the ends of democratic education are to be served by the socialization of the child, who is to be made into a co-operative rather than a competitive being and "saturated" with the spirit of service.

Dewey began with a forceful rejection of systems of education based upon class stratification; for it was the co-existence of a leisured and learned class and an enslaved or working class that led to an unhealthy split between learning and utility. The opposition between learning and utility, between thought and action, can be surmounted only in a democratic educational system which mixes children of varying backgrounds and does not try to reproduce in their schooling the class bar-

[9] Ibid., p. 370.

riers of their society. A democracy, he argued, "is more than a form of government; it is primarily a mode of associated living, of conjoint communicated experience." [1] The problem of the democratic educator is to make of the school a specialized environment, a miniature community, an embryonic society, which will eliminate so far as possible the undesirable features of the larger environment of society. For an enlightened society will try to transmit not simply the whole of its achievements, but "only such as make for a better future society." [2]

And what would be the characteristics of the democratic school community? The teacher, of course, would no longer be a harsh authority imposing external goals through rigid methods. He would be alert to the spontaneous and natural impulses of the children and would take hold of those that led toward constructive ends, giving gentle direction where necessary. The pupils themselves would take an active part in formulating the purposes of their education and in planning its execution. Learning would not be individual or passive, but collective and active; and in the course of their work the students would learn to share ideas and experiences, would develop mutual consideration and respect, and would acquire a capacity for cooperation. These habits, writ large, would some day reshape the larger society itself; for, as Dewey put it in one of his less fortunate sentences: "In directing the activities of the young, society determines its own future in determining that of the young." [3]

Democratic goals would have profound consequences for content as well as method. As soon as the inherited notion of learning as a leisure-class activity is discarded, the style of education it represented also falls under question, being suited neither to democracy nor to industrialism nor to an age of science. The circulation of learning in modern times has relieved it of its class associations. Intellectual stimuli may be found everywhere. "The merely intellectual life, the life of scholarship and of learning, thus gets a very altered value. Academic and scholastic, instead of being titles of honor, are becoming terms of re-

---

[1] *Democracy and Education*, p. 101. While it is quite true that the criterion of democracy can be applied to other social institutions as well as to the apparatus of government, there is much to be lost by encouraging men to think of democracy as a universal and exclusively satisfactory criterion of such institutions as the family and the classroom. I believe Dewey did American education a major disservice by providing what appears to be an authoritative sanction for that monotonous and suffocating rhetoric about "democratic living" with which American educationists smother our discussions of the means and ends of education.

[2] Ibid., pp. 22–4; cf. *The School and Society*, p. 18.

[3] *Democracy and Education*, p. 49.

proach." But we are still trying to throw off the shackles of a "medieval conception of learning"—a conception "which appeals for the most part simply to the intellectual aspect of our natures, our desire to learn, to accumulate information, and to get control of the symbols of learning; not to our impulses and tendencies to make, to do, to create, to produce, whether in the form of utility or of art."

In fact, the intellectual type of education can be of significance only to a minority: "The simple facts of the case are that in the great majority of human beings the distinctively intellectual interest is not dominant. They have the so-called practical impulse and disposition." For this reason, so many youngsters leave school as soon as they have learned the rudiments of reading, writing, and calculating. On the other hand, "if we were to conceive our educational end and aim in a less exclusive way, if we were to introduce into educational processes the activities which appeal to those whose dominant interest is to do and to make, we should find the hold of the school upon its members to be more vital, more prolonged, containing more of culture." Education is already changing in this direction, Dewey remarked, and holds great promise for the future when the new tendencies are put into "complete, uncompromising possession of our school system." "When the school introduces and trains each child of society into membership within such a little community, saturating him with the spirit of service, and providing him with the instruments of effective self-direction, we shall have the deepest and best guaranty of a larger society which is worthy, lovely, and harmonious." [4]

In attempting to realize their social ideals, Dewey and his followers were in time confronted by a certain antagonism between their fear of adult authority and their desire for social reform. Dewey, as I have pointed out, had always endorsed adult guidance in the classroom; what he had opposed was the idea that adults should formulate ends or goals for education, since the principle of growth demanded that it have no end. But the stronger the forces of social reform grew within the ranks of educators, the more evident it became that the ideal of social reform was, after all, an adult end, and that to realize it the co-operation of children could not be automatically counted upon.

[4] *The School and Society*, pp. 24–9. Cf. *Democracy and Education*, pp. 9–10, 46–7, 82–3, 88–9, 97–8, 226, 286–90, 293–305. In a characteristic interpretation by a modern educator who is interested in "developing skills in democratic living": "The democratic life of the school shall be so dynamically related to life outside that the students will be led to understand its meaning, and seek to extend it to all situations in which they are involved." Alberty: *Reorganizing the High School Curriculum*, p. 50.

This truth became particularly evident during the reaction to the great depression. By 1938, when Dewey wrote *Experience and Education*, he felt impelled to warn more sharply than ever that the new education had gone too far when it made teachers afraid to offer suggestions in the classroom. He had even heard of cases in which children were surrounded with objects and materials and then left entirely to themselves because the teacher felt it wrong to indicate what might be done with them. "Why, then, even supply materials, since they are a source of some suggestion or other?" Still, it is the function of the teacher to act only as the leader of the group's activities, and to give such directives as he issues only in the interest of the group, and not "as an exhibition of personal power."

The nagging fear of adult authority remains—the fear of forcing "the activity of the young into channels which express the teacher's purpose rather than that of the pupils." The soundest thing in the new education, Dewey reiterated, was its emphasis upon "the participation of the learner in the formation of the purposes which direct his activities in the learning process." Yet, as he also remarked, "the formation of purposes is . . . a rather complex intellectual operation," and, as he did not remark, it was difficult to show how the very young could take much part in such an operation.[5] He was uneasily aware that the progressive schools were having great difficulty in organizing curricula,[6] but it is uncertain whether he saw that this difficulty had something to do with the expectation that young children could enlist in an operation of considerable intellectual complexity.

Dewey's anxiety about adult authority stemmed from his desire to avoid something which we are still trying with much difficulty to avoid —the inculcation of conformist habits in the child. If there was anything he did *not* want, it was to breed conformist character. But he saw the danger of conformity as arising only from adult society and from its surrogate, the teacher. Speaking of traditional education, he wrote:[7]

[5] *Experience and Education*, pp. 84–5; cf. pp. 4, 59, 64, 66, 77, 80.
[6] Ibid., pp. 95–6.
[7] *Democracy and Education*, p. 60. Dewey's version of traditional education seemed at times to be almost as much a caricature as some of the more savage lampoons of progressivism. Granting that traditional education was frequently rigid and unimaginative, I doubt that Dewey was altogether just in describing it simply as "autocratic" and "harsh," as using "strait-jacket and chain-gang procedures," as opposed entirely to the cultivation of individuality, as offering only "a diet of predigested materials," and as providing a regime under which the individual, while acquiring information, "loses his own soul: loses his appreciation of things worth while, of the values to which these things [items of information] are relative." *Experience and Education*, pp. 2–5, 11, 24, 46, 50, 70.

Since conformity is the aim, what is distinctively individual in a young person is brushed aside, or regarded as a source of mischief or anarchy. Conformity is made equivalent to uniformity. Consequently, there are induced lack of interest in the novel, aversion to progress, and dread of the uncertain and the unknown.

Dewey was so concerned with adult authority as *the* threat to the child that it was hard for him to conceive of the child's peers as also constituting a threat. One can hardly believe that he really intended to liberate the child from the adult world only to throw him into the clutches of an even more omnivorous peer-culture. Yet there was very little place in Dewey's schoolroom for the contemplative or bookish child, for whom schooling as a social activity is not a thoroughly satisfactory procedure. "In social situations," Dewey approvingly wrote, "the young have to refer their way of acting to what others are doing and make it fit in." [8] It was just this kind of activity that provided the participants with a common understanding. Was there not, in his view of the matter, more than a little suspicion of the child who remained aloof or hung back from social activity, who insisted on a singular measure of independence? "Dependence," Dewey wrote,[9]

> denotes a power rather than a weakness; it involves interdependence. There is always a danger that increased personal independence will decrease the social capacity of an individual. In making him more self-reliant, it may make him more self-sufficient; it may lead to aloofness and indifference. It often makes an individual so insensitive in his relations to others as to develop an illusion of being really able to stand and act alone—an unnamed form of insanity which is responsible for a large part of the remediable suffering of the world.

These words are altogether intelligible against the background of nineteenth-century America. The rampant economic individualism that Dewey could see at work in his formative years had created a personal type which was indeed independent, if not to the point of insanity, at least to the point of being anti-social. And in the schoolroom the older education had given scope to the impulses of occasional teachers who were harshly authoritarian. It would probably be too much to expect anyone in 1916 to anticipate the emergence among children of the kind of peer-group conformity that David Riesman has diagnosed in *The Lonely Crowd,* or the decline in adult authority that is observable both

[8] *Democracy and Education,* p. 47.
[9] Ibid., p. 52.

in the classroom and in the regulation of children's lives. Today, when we grow troubled about conformity in children, we are more often troubled about their conformity to the mandates of their peers and to directives from the mass media than we are by their conformity to parents or teachers. We are also aware of the possibility that excessive weakness in adult authority may even create difficulties for children quite as acute as those caused by adult tyranny.

These considerations did not enter into Dewey's world at the time he was formulating his educational theory; but it is possible that his theory itself has helped to bring about a state of affairs which he could hardly have desired. The core-curriculum educators invoke Dewey's principles of immediacy, utility, and social learning when they encourage children to discuss in school "How can I be popular?" or such implicit resistance to parental imperatives as "Why are my parents so strict?" and "What can I do with my old-fashioned parents?" and "Should I follow my crowd or obey my parents' wishes?" [1] Such topics represent the projection of peer-conformity into the curriculum itself in a way that Dewey would surely have found offensive. The problem of conformity and authority was real enough, but it was not solved by reforming the old-fashioned classroom.

Perhaps Dewey somewhat overvalued the social side of learning. He and other thinkers of his generation, notably George H. Mead, were much concerned to establish the intrinsically social character of mind, an effort in which they were eminently successful. In a sense, however, this conception of mind proved almost too much to justify Dewey's view of education. If mental activity is intrinsically social, one may after all claim that the social prerequisities of learning can be met in a wide variety of types of learning, and not merely in the literal social co-operation of the classroom. As the new educators were somewhat reluctant to see, a child sitting alone and reading about Columbus's voyages is engaging in a social experience at least as complex, if of a different kind, from that of a child in the school workshop making model ships with other children. Yet in Dewey's work the important and persuasive idea that a thing gets its meaning from being a social object is at times transmuted into the more questionable idea that all learning has to be overtly shared in social action.[2]

Even more important is a conception of the relationship between the

---

[1] Alberty: op. cit., pp. 470, 474.
[2] See the passage in *Democracy and Education*, pp. 46–8, in which Dewey plays upon the meaning of the term "social."

educational process and its outcome which seems excessively mechanical, especially for one who, like Dewey, hoped always to do justice to to the dialectical fluidity of life. The notion that the authoritative classroom would of necessity produce the conformist mind and that sociable learning would produce the ideally socialized personality is at first appealing, but there is about it a kind of rigid rationality of the sort that life constantly eludes. Did Dewey, for example, really imagine that traditional education had engendered in America, of all places, a mind notably characterized by "lack of interest in the novel, aversion to progress, and dread of the uncertain and the unknown"? Was it necessarily true that education founded upon authority invariably produces a conformist mind, and that there is a one-to-one relationship between the style of an educational system and the nature of its products? There hardly seems to be any place in Dewey's idea of the educational process for the fact that Voltaire was schooled by the Jesuits, or that the strong authoritative structure of the Puritan family should have yielded a personal type so important to the development of modern democracy. To expect that education would so simply produce a hoped-for personal type was to expect more than past experience warranted.

Finally, there are serious difficulties involved in living up to the idea that education should in no way be looked upon as a preparation for the child's future life—what Dewey always called a "remote future"—but rather as living itself, a simulacrum of life, or a sort or rehearsal in the experiences that make up life. The motive of achieving some continuity between school experience and other experiences seems altogether commendable. But Dewey not only held that education *is* life; he went on to say that the school should provide a *selective* environment for the child, an environment that represents so far as possible what is deemed good in society and eliminates what is bad. Yet, the more successful the school was in this task, the less it could live up to the ideal of representing or embodying life. The moment one admits that it is not all of life which is presented to children in school, one also admits that a selective process has been set up which is determined by some external end; and then one has once again embraced the traditional view that education is after all not a comprehensive attempt to mirror or reproduce life but a segment of life that is specialized for a distinct function.

If the new educators really wanted to reproduce life itself in the classroom, they must have had an extraordinarily benign conception of what life is. To every adult, life brings, in addition to some measure of co-operation, achievement, and joy, a full stint of competition, defeat, frustration, and failure. But the new educators did not accept the idea that these things too would be embodied in the little community that was to be organized for children in the school. Quite the contrary, their strongest impulse was to protect children from too acute an awareness of what their own limitations, under adult conditions, might cost them. They were much closer to the argument of Marietta Johnson, one of the pioneers of "organic education" and a founder of the Progressive Education Association, who said: "No child should ever know failure. . . . The school should *meet* the demands of the nature of childhood, not make demands. Any school system in which one child may fail while another succeeds is unjust, undemocratic, uneducational." [3] In her experimental school at Fairhope, Alabama, which was described with enthusiasm by John and Evelyn Dewey in *Schools of To-Morrow*, there were therefore no examinations, no grading, no failures to win promotion; success was measured not by the amount of subject matter learned or the promotions earned but by the effort and joy of the work itself. This view of education may or may not have better effects on children than the traditional school, but that it bears a closer relation to "life" is eminently questionable.

To this objection the new educators had what they felt was a satisfactory answer: the new education was not trying to raise children to know or fit into the life of the past, with its harsh and selfish individualism, but to know and adapt to the life of the present and future, which was hopefully conceived as more social, more co-operative, more humane—to a life that Dewey thought accorded better with "the scientific democratic society of today." [4]

But this answer could only turn attention to the difficulty of designing education to suit the child's growth and at the same time to form society anew. As time went on, some of the new educators themselves began to doubt that Dewey had made a successful synthesis of the idea of education as the child's growth and education as the reconstruction of society. Boyd H. Bode observed in 1938 that the doctrine of growth in its present form "prevents [the teacher] from discovering that he needs a guiding social philosophy." [5] To believe that Dewey's synthesis was successful required a certain credulity about the pre-established

[3] Marietta Johnson: *Youth in a World of Men* (New York, 1929), pp. 42, 261; cf. the laudatory comment on this feature of her school by John and Evelyn Dewey in *Schools of To-Morrow* (New York, 1915), especially p. 27.

[4] *Schools of To-Morrow*, p. 165.

[5] *Progressive Education at the Crossroads*, p. 78.

harmony between child nature and democratic culture which not everyone could share. It seemed to some critics that one would have to give up either the emphasis on child nature and spontaneity or the emphasis on educating for democracy. The child, after all, might feel a natural interest in rebelling at some point or other; but it was impossible to impute to him a natural interest in the reconstruction of society or in having his mind "saturated" with "the spirit of service." During the great depression, the whole school of social reconstructionists tended to recognize quite candidly that this impulse was lacking; that the future good of society required that educators admit that all education embodies a measure of indoctrination; and that "external" ends are inevitably imposed in the educational process.[6] Social reconstructionism in education has not been of much lasting interest, but it did render some service in making progressive educators aware that "external"—that is, adult—objectives are unavoidably dominant in the school. For those who expected that education would be, as Dewey had said in 1897, "the fundamental method of social progress and reform," it would be impossible to leave it as much as he might have hoped in the hands of the child.

· 6 ·

Dewey's educational theory was formulated in the hope that a proper educational synthesis would overcome certain ancient polarities and dualisms in educational thought. The antitheses between the child and society, interest and discipline, vocation and culture, knowledge and action, must all be resolved and ultimately harmonized—as they now supposedly can be in a democratic society which itself has surpassed the aristocratic mental framework in which these antitheses originally appeared. This optimism is vital to Dewey's educational argument: he saw these dualisms in education not as a clue to the nature of human problems but as an unfortunate legacy that could be done away with. The world, as he viewed it when he published his earlier and most influential educational books, was indeed progressing. The age of science and democracy, he thought, would be better, more rational, more intelligent than anything man had known in the past; it would be at once the source and the beneficiary of a better kind of education.

---

[6] Some of the political difficulties in Dewey's theory are penetratingly analyzed by Frederic Lilge: "The Politicizing of Educational Theory," *Ethics,* Vol. LXVI (April, 1956), pp. 188–97.

There was thus a distinct if rather covert utopianism about Dewey's educational thought—and it was the utopian element that so many educational theorists found appealing. Dewey's utopianism was not based upon some portrait of an ideal educational system. He was too wise to draw a blueprint for a finished world, and the very nature of his thesis that education is the continuous reconstruction of experience argued against it. His utopianism was one of method: he believed that the old polarities and dualisms were not, so to speak, qualities in reality that must be resisted, minimized, managed, and confined; but were miscalculations derived from the false way of conceiving the world that had prevailed in the past. One could do better than merely resolve these polarities in various limited and inevitably unsatisfactory ways; in a higher synthesis one could overcome them altogether.

In this respect Dewey echoes an argument against the past which had been sounded by so many American thinkers before him. His language gives the impression that he saw the entire drama of human experience primarily as a source of errors that must be surmounted. To keep alive any current enterprise like education required that one enable it to peel off the residues of the past. "The present," he wrote in an uncommonly eloquent passage in *Democracy and Education,* "is not just something which comes after the past. . . . It is what life is in leaving the past behind it." For this reason, the study of the cultural *products* of the past will not help us understand the present. It is the *life* of the past that counts, the life of which these cultural products are only dead repositories—and that life itself was at its best also a process of surmounting its own past. "A knowledge of the past and its heritage is of great significance when it enters into the present, but not otherwise." To make the study of the past the main material of education is to lose the vital connection between present and past, "and tends to make the past a rival of the present and the present a more or less futile imitation of the past. Under such circumstances," Dewey goes on, scoring what seems to be the climactic point in his argument, "culture becomes an ornament and solace; a refuge and an asylum." [7] It thus loses its capacity to be a transforming agent, one that can improve the present and create the future.

[7] *Democracy and Education,* p. 88. Here I would refer the reader to John Herman Randall, Jr.'s beautifully conceived and not unsympathetic critique of Dewey's interpretation of the history of philosophy, in which he asks: "Would Dewey dismiss out of hand all that imagination has done to make existence endurable, just because the world has not yet through action been made quite wholly new?" P. A. Schilpp, ed.: *The Philosophy of John Dewey* (Chicago, 1939), pp. 77–102, especially p. 101.

It is here that we must return again to the child, for the child is the key to the future; he has within himself the resources to liberate the world from the weight of its past. But before he can do this, the child himself must be freed—and under a proper educational regime really *can* be freed—from the oppressions of the world, from everything that is dead about the apparatus of culture, from the constricting effects of society on the school. Dewey himself was realistic enough to see, to assert and reassert, the limits of the child's spontaneous impulses as a guide to this process. But it was precisely these impulses that interested American educators. Since Dewey aimed at freeing the child from the shackles of the past to the point at which the child could make a reconstructive use of past culture, American educators seized upon his theory as having downgraded past culture and its merely ornamental and solacing "products" and as having finally produced a program to liberate the child for unimpeded growth. Having once put the child so firmly at the center, having defined education as growth without end, Dewey had so weighted the discussion of educational goals that a quarter century of clarificatory statements did not avail to hold in check the anti-intellectual perversions of his theory.

Like Freud, Dewey saw the process by which a society inculcates the young with its principles, inhibitions, and habits as a kind of imposition upon them. But Dewey's assumptions led to a more optimistic calculus of possibilities than that offered by Freud. Freud saw the process by which the individual is socialized as making genuinely impairing demands upon his instincts but also as being in some form tragically inevitable. Society, as Dewey saw it, spoiled the "plasticity" of children, which was the source of their "power to change prevailing custom." Education, with its "insolent coercions, insinuating briberies, and pedagogic solemnities by which the freshness of youth can be faded and its vivid curiosities dulled," had become "the art of taking advantage of the helplessness of the young,"[8] and education itself an art used by society to choke off the best part of its capacity for self-improvement. For Dewey, the world as a source of misery for the child is largely remediable through the educational process; for Freud the two are fixed in an opposition which, while alterable and even to a degree ameliorable in detail, is insurmountable in substance.[9]

[8] *Human Nature and Conduct* (1922; Modern Library ed., New York, 1929), p. 64.
[9] Like Dewey, Freud's thought has had both good and bad consequences for education. In many quarters the educational implications of Freud's views were even more misconceived than those of Dewey. During the 1920's, Freud's psy-

More than a generation of progressive educational experiment confirms Freud's view. Old educational failings have been remedied, often with much success, but other problems have been intensified by the new remedies. Conformity to arbitrary adult wishes has been diminished, but conformity to peers is now seen as a serious problem. The arbitrary authority of the teacher has been lessened, but a subtle manipulation, which requires self-deceit on the part of the teacher and often inspires resentment in the child, has taken its place. The fear of failure in studies has not been removed, but devices introduced to remove it have created frustrations arising from a lack of standards, of recognition, of a sense of achievement.

In his last significant statement on education, Dewey observed that "the drive of established institutions is to assimilate and distort the new into conformity with themselves." While commenting with some satisfaction on certain improvements introduced by progressive education, he ruefully remarked that the ideas and principles he had helped to develop had also succumbed to this process of institutionalization. "In teachers colleges and elsewhere the ideas and principles have been converted into a fixed subject matter of ready-made rules, to be taught and memorized according to certain standardized procedures. . . ." Memorization and standardized procedures once more! It did all too little good, he said, to train teachers "in the right principles the wrong way." With a hardy courage that can only inspire admiration, Dewey reminded progressive educators, once again and for the last time, that it is the right *method* of training which forms the character of teachers, and not the subject matter or the rules they are taught. Pursue the right methods, and a democratic society might yet be created; follow the "authoritarian principle" and education will be fit only to "pervert and destroy the foundations of a democratic society." [1] And so the quest for a method of institutionalizing the proper anti-institutional methods goes on.

---

chology was frequently taken by progressive educators as lending support to a guiding philosophy of instinctual liberation. It also gave rise to a kind of psychologism in education that often diverts attention from the basic instructional task by attempting to make of the educational process an amateur substitute for psychotherapy. It is, of course, hard to draw the line between a legitimate regard for the pupil's psychological needs as a part of the educational process and a tendency to displace pedagogy by psychological concern and even psychological manipulation. The best brief discussion I have seen of Freud's and Dewey's approach to instinct and impulse in their relation to society is in chapter 2 of Philip Rieff's *Freud: The Mind of the Moralist* (New York, 1959).

[1] "Introduction" to Elsie R. Clapp: *The Use of Resources in Education* (New York, 1952), pp. x–xi.

PART 6

Conclusion

CHAPTER XV

The Intellectual:
Alienation and Conformity

❧

· 1 ·

ANTI-INTELLECTUALISM in various forms continues to pervade
American life, but at the same time intellect has taken on a new and
more positive meaning and intellectuals have come to enjoy more acceptance and, in some ways, a more satisfactory position. This new
acceptance sits awkwardly on their shoulders. Being used to rejection,
and having over the years forged a strong traditional response to society
based upon the expectation that rejection would continue, many of
them have come to feel that alienation is the only appropriate and
honorable stance for them to take. What they have come to fear is not
so much rejection or overt hostility, with which they have learned to
cope and which they have almost come to regard as their proper fate,
but the loss of alienation. Many of the most spirited younger intellectuals are disturbed above all by the fear that, as they are increasingly
recognized, incorporated, and used, they will begin merely to conform, and will cease to be creative and critical and truly useful. This is
the fundamental paradox in their position—that while they do resent
evidences of anti-intellectualism, and take it as a token of a serious
weakness in our society, they are troubled and divided in a more
profound way by their acceptance. Perhaps the most divisive issue in
the intellectual community today arises over the values to be placed
upon the old alienation and the new acceptance. Let us look first at the
way this question has been posed in recent years and then at the historical position of the intellectual community for what light it may shed.

For all the popular anti-intellectualism of the 1950's, the intellectuals themselves, especially those of the middle and older generations, were not disposed, as they had been in the 1920's, to wage a counterattack upon American values. Instead, they were ironically engaged in re-embracing their country at the very moment when they were under the most severe attack for being constitutionally disloyal. Even Mc-Carthyism did not quite stop them: the very fear that the senator and his mob might destroy certain values hitherto taken for granted was a reminder that something about American values in the past had indeed been precious. And certain old-fashioned and eminently conservative senators who stood up to McCarthy were much admired as personal monuments to a venerable American integrity.

In 1952, the editors of the *Partisan Review,* which may be taken as a kind of house organ of the American intellectual community, gave a quasi-official recognition of the new mood of the intellectuals when they devoted several issues to a memorable symposium, significantly entitled "Our Country and Our Culture." [1] "American intellectuals," they explained, "now regard America and its institutions in a new way. . . . Many writers and intellectuals now feel closer to their country and its culture. . . . For better or for worse, most writers no longer accept alienation as the artist's fate in America; on the contrary, they want very much to be a part of American life."

The response of the twenty-five contributors to the editors' questions about the relation of the intellectual to America showed that the overwhelming majority not only shared an awareness of a growing *rapprochement* between the intellectuals and their society but also, for the most part, accepted it. If we omitted their qualifications and the accompanying warnings against an excess of complacency, we would risk exaggerating or caricaturing their acceptance; and we might suggest a complacency that was not there. A composite statement of their views, however, shows how much a once intensely alienated segment of the intellectual class had changed its ideas. The habit of "mere exacerbated alienation," most contributors agreed, no longer seemed defensible. Remarks made by several of them about alienation as an historical phenomenon emphasized that alienation had commonly been an ambivalent feeling, and that the great writers and thinkers of the past had combined with their protests against American society a strong affirmation of many of its values and a profound identification with it—that it was indeed the tension between protest and

[1] Reprinted as *America and the Intellectuals* (New York, 1953).

affirmation that had been most often associated with great achievement.

No one doubted that the intellectual's role as a critical nonconformist was of essential value or thought that he ought to give it up to become a mere spokesman or apologist of his society. But it was agreed that American intellectuals no longer look at their country as a cultural desert from which they must flee, or regard it, as one writer put it, with "adolescent embarrassment" when they compare America to Europe. Intellectuals now felt more at home in America than they had twenty or thirty years earlier; they had come to terms with American realities. "We are witnessing a process," wrote one, "that might well be described as the *embourgeoisement* of the American intelligentsia." It was not only intellectuals who had changed; the country had changed too, and for the better. It had matured culturally, and no longer stood in tutelage to Europe. The wealthy and powerful had learned to accept, even defer, to the intellectual and the artist. Accordingly, America had become a reasonably gratifying place in which to carry on intellectual or artistic work, and one in which such pursuits were well rewarded. Even a contributor who found the whole symposium complacent conceded: "The notion that America is uniquely a land of barbarism now seems silly."

· 2 ·

Among the twenty-five contributors to the symposium, only three— Irving Howe, Norman Mailer, and C. Wright Mills—were entirely at odds with the acquiescent mood of the editors' questions; and a fourth, Delmore Schwartz, thought it important to protest against "the will to conformism which is now the chief prevailing fashion among intellectuals." To these dissenters, this re-embracement of America was simply a surrender to current pressures toward conservatism and patriotism, a capitulation to comfort and smugness. The very idea of "*our* country" and "*our* culture" offended them—"a shrinking deference to the status quo," said C. Wright Mills, "a soft and anxious compliance," and "a synthetic, feeble search to justify this intellectual conduct." What seemed to the older intellectuals, whose adult memories stretched back to the cultural controversies of the thirties and in some cases to the twenties, to be no more than a willingness to abandon an oversimplified commitment to alienation into which they had once been misled appeared to somewhat younger men as an incomprehensible moral failure.

The case against the dominant point of view in the *Partisan Review* symposium was put into a formidable statement two years later in the same magazine by one of the dissenting contributors, the critic, Irving Howe, then a professor at Brandeis University. In an article on "This Age of Conformity," [2] Howe asserted that the symposium had been "a disconcerting sign of how far intellectuals have drifted in the direction of cultural adaptation." Capitalism, he said, "in its most recent stage has found an honored place for the intellectuals," who instead of resisting incorporation, have enjoyed returning "to the bosom of the nation." "We are all conformists to one or another degree." Even those who still tried to hold a critical stance had become "responsible and moderate. And tame." The proliferation of new jobs in the mass-culture industries and in the growing college and university system had helped the intellectuals to become absorbed into the permanent war economy. "Intellectual freedom in the United States is under severe attack and the intellectuals have, by and large, shown a painful lack of militancy in defending the rights which are a precondition of their existence."

Howe's counter-ideal to this complacent adaptation was an old one: the community of Bohemia. Flaubert had said that Bohemia was "the fatherland of my breed," and Howe believed that it had also been the basic precondition of cultural creativity in the United States. "The most exciting periods of American intellectual life tend to coincide with the rise of bohemia," he asserted, and then, as though troubled by the difficulties of this proposition, he added: "Concord too was a kind of bohemia, sedate, subversive, and transcendental all at once." Bohemia had been a kind of strategy for bringing artists and writers together in their struggle with and for the world, but now its role had disintegrated. "Bohemia gradually disappears as a setting for our intellectual life, and what remains of it seems willed or fake." The breakup of Bohemia had contributed in an important way to "those feelings of loneliness one finds among so many American intellectuals, feelings of damp dispirited isolation which undercut the ideology of liberal optimism." Once young writers faced the world together. Now they "sink into suburbs, country homes and college towns."

It was not, said Howe, a matter of berating anyone for "selling out" or of calling for material asceticism on the part of intellectuals. What was at issue was the "slow attrition which destroys one's ability to stand firm and alone," which is seen in a chain of small compromises. "What is most alarming is that the whole idea of the intellectual vocation—the idea of a life dedicated to values that cannot possibly be realized by a

[2] *Partisan Review*, Vol. XXI (January–February, 1954), pp. 7–33.

commercial civilization—has gradually lost its allure." The battle against commercial civilization had in his eyes a primary value in its own right. For if the clash between business civilization and the values of art is no longer so urgent as we once thought, he asserted, "we must discard a great deal, and mostly the best, of the literature, the criticism and the speculative thought of the twentieth century."

Howe regretted "the loss of those earlier certainties that had the advantage, at least, of making resistance easy." He was in particular affronted by Lionel Trilling's suggestion in the symposium that the cultural situation of the 1950's, for all its deficiencies, had improved over that of thirty years earlier. "Any comparison," Howe argued, "between the buoyant free-spirited cultural life of 1923 with the dreariness of 1953, or between their literary achievements," was hardly more than a pleasant fantasy. If wealth had accepted the intellectuals, it was only because the intellectuals had become tame, and no longer presumed to challenge wealth, engaging instead in "some undignified prostrations" before it. The intellectuals are more powerless than ever, and most particularly the new realists "who attach themselves to the seats of power, where they surrender their freedom of expression without gaining any significance as political figures." Whenever intellectuals "become absorbed into the accredited institutions of society they not only lose their traditional rebelliousness but to one extent or another *they cease to function as intellectuals.*" Almost any alternative would be preferable to subordination of their talents to the uses of others: "A total estrangement from the sources of power and prestige, even a blind unreasoning rejection of every aspect of our culture, would be far healthier if only because it would permit a free discharge of aggression."

Howe's article was not an entirely personal document, but a kind of manifesto of the intellectuals of the left. Some years later a young historian, Loren Baritz, looking at the social disciplines from a similar point of view, expounded the belief that "any intellectual who accepts and approves of his society prostitutes his skills and is a traitor to his heritage." He asked whether, "by definition, a man of ideas must maintain the posture of the critic, and whether the intellectual who sincerely believes in and approves of the larger movements of his society can reconcile the demands of his mind and those of his society." [3] He

[3] Loren Baritz: *The Servants of Power* (Middletown, Connecticut, 1960); see also the same writer's article in the *Nation*, January 21, 1961, and my own discussion of the issues, "A Note on Intellect and Power," *American Scholar*, Vol. XXX (Autumn, 1961), pp. 588–98.

called for a principled withdrawal of intellectuals from social institutions, from relevance, responsibility, and power: "Let the intellectual be absorbed into society and he runs the grave risk of permitting himself to be digested by it. . . . When he touches power, it will touch him." The right response is a willed estrangement from social responsibility: "When the intellectual becomes socially, rather than intellectually, responsible his mind must lose at least part of the freedom and resiliency which is part of his most fundamental equipment." If the intellectual withdraws to the ivory tower, it is because of "this need for social irresponsibility, for irrelevancy, for the freedom which comes from isolation and alienation."

· 3 ·

As one listens first to the dominant mood of the *Partisan Review*'s symposium and then to Mr. Howe and other dissenters, what one hears are the two voices of an old and familiar dialogue. A self-conscious concern with alienation, far from being peculiar to American intellectuals in our time, has been a major theme in the life of the intellectual communities of the Western world for almost two centuries. In earlier ages, when the life and work of intellectuals had been bound up with the Church or the aristocracy or both, consistent alienation from society was rare. But the development of modern society, from the eighteenth century onwards, created a new set of material and social conditions and a new kind of consciousness. Everywhere in the Western world, the ugliness, materialism, and ruthless human exploitation of early modern capitalism affronted sensitive minds. The end of the system of patronage and the development of a market place for ideas and art brought artists and intellectuals into a sharp and often uncomfortable confrontation with the mind of the middle class. In various ways intellectuals rebelled against the conditions of the new bourgeois world—in romantic assertions of the individual against society, in bohemian solidarity, in political radicalism.

It is natural, for example, that in looking for a great historic precedent, Mr. Howe should turn to Flaubert, who was a tireless connoisseur of the fatuities of the French bourgeoisie.[4] In England, and in a different manner, Matthew Arnold tried to analyze the new cultural situation in *Culture and Anarchy*. In America, the Transcendentalists

---

[4] Flaubert, it must be said, saw some dangers in his role. "By dint of railing at idiots," he once wrote, "one runs the risk of becoming idiotic oneself."

were constantly writing about the difficulty which the individual sensibility experienced in coming to terms with modern society.

Each country had its own variation of this general problem, much as each country had its own variety of bourgeois development. The background of alienation in America made an uncompromising position of alienation seem orthodox, axiomatic, and traditional for twentieth-century intellectuals; for in nineteenth-century American society both the accepted, standard writers and the avant-garde writers were likely to be in the one case at least moderately and in the other intensely alienated. One can truly say of this society that by about the middle of the nineteenth century even those who belonged did not altogether belong. Hence, in our own time, those intellectuals whose conception of their role is formed by the history of this society find it strange and even repellent that intellectuals should experience success or have any association with power.

It was not always so. In our earlier days two groups of intellectuals were associated with or responsible for the exercise of far-reaching social power, the Puritan clergy and the Founding Fathers. Each group in time lost its supremacy, partly because of its own failings, partly because of historical circumstances beyond its control. Yet each also left a distinctive legacy. The Puritan clergy founded the tradition of New England intellectualism; and this tradition, exported wherever New Englanders settled in large numbers, was responsible for a remarkably large portion of the country's dynamic intellectual life throughout the nineteenth century and into the twentieth.[5] The Puritan founders had their terrible faults, but they had at least the respect for mind and the intensity of spirit which are necessary to distinguished intellectual achievement. Where it survived, this intensity often had a wonderfully invigorating effect.

The legacy of the Founding Fathers, itself tinctured by Puritan ideas, was equally important. In the development of new countries, while the people are engaged in liberating themselves from colonial status and forging a new identity, intellectuals seem always to play an important role. The leaders of the American Enlightenment did so with signal effectiveness: they gave the new republic a coherent and

[5] In fact, it is too seldom realized how immensely impoverished the intellectual and cultural life of this large and heterogeneous country would have been, had it not been for the contributions of three cultural strains: the first was that of New England, which dominates the nineteenth century; the second and third are those of the Jews and the writers of the culturally renascent South which have played an important part in the intellectual life of the twentieth century.

fairly workable body of ideas, a definition of its identity and ideals, a sense of its place in history, a feeling of nationality, a political system and a political code.

After about 1820, the old republican order in which the Revolution had been carried out and the Constitution adopted, the order in which both Federalists and Jeffersonians had been reared, was rapidly destroyed by a variety of economic and social changes. With the settlement of the trans-Allegheny West, the development of industry, the rise of an egalitarian ethos in politics, and the submergence of the Jeffersonian South, the patrician class that had led and in a measure controlled American democracy became more and more enfeebled. The laymen and the evangelicals had already dethroned the established clergy. Now a new type of democratic leader with a new political style was to dethrone the mercantile-professional class from its position of political leadership. Soon a new type of industrialist and promoter would completely overshadow this class in business as well.

What was left was a gentlemanly class with considerable wealth, leisure, and culture, but with relatively little power or influence. This class was the public and the patron of serious writing and of cultural institutions. Its members read the books that were written by the standard American writers, subscribed to the old highbrow magazines, supported libraries and museums, and sent their sons to the old-fashioned liberal-arts colleges to study the classical curriculum. It developed its own gentle tradition of social protest, for it had enough of an aristocratic bias to be opposed to the most vulgar features of the popular democracy that was emerging everywhere and enough of a code of behavior to be opposed to the crass materialism of the new capitalists and plantation lords. The most eloquent tradition of moral protest in America is the creation of a few uncompromising sons of the patrician gentry.

But if one thinks of this class as having inherited the austere traditions of the older republican order, the traditions crystallized by the Founding Fathers, one sees immediately the relative weakness of a type that kept the manners and aspirations and prejudices of an aristocratic class without being able to retain its authority. The mental outlook of the leaders of the old republican order, inherited by subsequent generations of patricians, became transformed into something less spirited and less powerful. The culture of the Founding Fathers was succeeded by what I like to call mugwump culture—and by mugwump I refer not just to the upper-class reform movement of the Gilded Age, which is the conventional usage, but to the intellectual and cultural outlook of the dispossessed patrician class. Throughout the entire nineteenth century this class provided the chief public to which the independent and cultivated American mind expressed itself.[6] The mugwump mind, in which the influence of New England was again decisive, inherited from the Puritans a certain solemnity and high intent, but was unable to sustain their passion. From the Founding Fathers and the American Enlightenment it inherited in a more direct and immediate way a set of intellectual commitments and civic concerns. In the mugwump ambience, however, the intellectual virtues of the eighteenth-century republican type dwindled and dried up, very largely because mugwump thinkers were too commonly deprived of the occasion to bring these virtues into any intimate or organic relation with experience. It had been essential to the culture of the Founding Fathers that it was put to the test of experience, that it was forced to cope with grave and intricate problems of power; it was characteristic of mugwump culture that its relation to experience and its association with power became increasingly remote.

The mugwump mind reproduced the classicism of the Founding Fathers, their passion for order and respect for mind, their desire to rationalize the world and to make political institutions the embodiment of applied reason, their assumption that social station is a proper fulcrum for political leadership, and their implicit concern for the decorous exemplification of one's proper social role. But having retreated from the most urgent and exciting changes that were taking place in the country, having been edged out of the management of its central institutions of business and politics, and having chosen to withdraw from any identification with the aspirations of the common people, the patrician class produced a culture that became over-refined, dessicated, aloof, snobbish—everything that Santayana had in mind when he identified the genteel tradition. Its leaders cared more that intellect be respectable than that it be creative. What G. K. Chesterton said in quite another connection may be applied to them: they showed more pride in the possession of intellect than joy in the use of it.

Unlike most Americans, these men had a firm sense of tradition, but

---

[6] I prefer this designation to the term commonly used to evoke this cultural milieu. It is sometimes called Brahmin culture, but this has for my purposes an excessively local New England reference. Santayana's term, the genteel tradition, is more satisfactory, but I believe the expression *mugwump culture* better evokes the broad political implications of this order of society.

for them tradition was not so much a source of strength or a point of departure as a fetish. In the inevitable tension between tradition and the individual talent, they weighted the scales heavily against anything assertive or originative in the individual, for it was an essential part of their philosophy that such assertion must be regarded as merely egoistical and self-indulgent. The tenets of their code of criticism were eminently suited to an entrenched class that is anxious about keeping its position. The business of criticism was to inculcate "correct taste" and "sound morals"—and taste and morals were carefully defined in such a way as to establish disapproval of any rebelliousness, political or esthetic, against the existing order. Literature was to be a firm custodian of "morality"; and what was meant by morality was always conventional social morality, not that independent morality of the artist or thinker which is imposed upon him by the discipline of artistic form or his vision of the truth. Literature was to be committed to optimism, to the more smiling aspects of life, and must not countenance realism or gloom. Fantasy, obscurity, mysticism, individuality, and revolt were all equally beyond the pale.

So it was that Wordsworth and Southey were condemned by an American critic, Samuel Gilman, in the *North American Review* in 1823 for their "disinclination to consult the precise intellectual tone and spirit of the average mass to which their works are presented." Such writers, Gilman thought, had a deserved unpopularity: "Theirs is the poetry of soliloquy. They write apart from and above the world. Their original object seems to be the employment of their faculties and the gratification of their poetical propensities." [7] Of course, the rejection of originality that is justified here is not significantly different from the rejection experienced by many of the best poets of the nineteenth century in Europe. The difference was that the European environment, despite such critical philosophies as those of Gilman's European counterparts, was complex enough to give the writers some room for assertion in its interstices. The American cultural environment was simpler, more subject to domination by the outlook of a single, well-meaning, but limited class.

The discomfort this class felt in the presence of true genius is exemplified at its best and its worst in the relationship of Thomas Wentworth Higginson to Emily Dickinson: he, who was so encouraging and

[7] William Charvat: *The Origins of American Critical Thought, 1810–1835* (Philadelphia, 1936), p. 25. The best evocation of the mugwump literary and intellectual atmosphere with which I am acquainted is that of Perry Miller in the opening chapters of *The Raven and The Whale* (New York, 1956).

so kind to her, even at moments understanding, could never quite rise above thinking of her as another aspiring lady poet and referred to her now and again as "my partially cracked poetess at Amherst." Nor could he resist suggesting to her that she might overcome her loneliness by attending a meeting of the Boston Woman's Club.[8]

For generations, the effort of established criticism was to make writers accede to the sensibilities of a social type which was itself "apart from and above the world." The Puritan intensity of conviction, which had produced fiery dissenters as well as guardians of the laws, was lost; lost too was that engagement with challenging realities and significant power that had helped to form and test the minds of the Founding Fathers. Puritan society, when one pays due regard to its tiny population and its staggering material problems, had laid the foundations for a remarkable tradition of intellectual discipline and had produced a vital literature, first in religion and then in politics. The Founding Fathers, working under exigent political pressures, had given the world a striking example of applied reason in politics, and their generation had made long strides in literature, science, and art as well. Although it drew upon a wealthier society, mugwump culture was notable neither for its political writing nor for its interest in science. It was at its best in history and polite letters, but its coolness to spontaneity and originality disposed it to be a better patron to secondary than to primary talents. It rarely gave the highest recognition to a first-rate writer when a second-rate one was to be found. It passed over the most original native minds—Hawthorne, Melville, Poe, Thoreau, Whitman—and gave its loudest applause to Cooper, its most distinguished figure, and to Irving, Bryant, Longfellow, Lowell, and Whittier. It is easy to yield to the temptation to speak slightingly of the mugwump public, which, after all, provided the support for a large part of the nation's cultural life, but its failure to appreciate or encourage most of the nation's first-rate genius is an ineluctable part of the record.

At any rate, the consequences for American literature of the insulation and deprivation of mind that characterized mugwump culture have long been amply recognized and fervently lamented in American criticism. In 1915 Van Wyck Brooks complained that American literature had suffered from a disastrous bifurcation between the highbrow and the lowbrow; and more recently Philip Rahv, borrowing from D. H. Lawrence, has written of the polarity between the paleface and the redskin, symbolized by Henry James and Walt Whitman. What

[8] George Frisbie Whicher: *This Was A Poet* (Ann Arbor, 1960), pp. 119–20.

these critics had in mind was the divorce in American writing and thinking between sensibility, refinement, theory, and discipline on one side and spontaneity, energy, sensuous reality, and the seizure of opportunity on the other—in short, a painful separation between the qualities of mind and the materials of experience. This separation, traceable to mugwump culture, could be followed through American letters in a number of incomplete and truncated minds. Hawthorne might have been complaining not simply for himself but for almost all of well-bred and thoughtful America in the nineteenth century when he wrote: "I have not lived, but only dreamed of living. . . . I have seen so little of the world that I have nothing but thin air to concoct my stories of. . . ."

All this may help us to understand why the case against intellect took the form it did during the nineteenth century. When the spokesmen for hardy, masculine practicality, the critics of aristocratic and feminine and unworldly culture, made their case against intellect, they had some justification for their point of view. But they mistook the paler and more ineffectual manifestations of intellect that they saw around them for intellect as such. They failed to see that their own behavior had in some measure contributed to making intellect what it was, that intellect in America had been stunted in some part by their own repudiation of it—by the arrant populism, the mindless obsession with "practicality" which they had themselves insisted upon. The case of the anti-intellectualist had taken on the character of a self-fulfilling prophecy. Partly by their own fiat, intellect had become associated with losing causes and exemplified by social types that were declining in vigor and influence, encapsulated by an impermeable world.

· 4 ·

If we turn from consideration of the public to a consideration of American writers themselves, we find that until almost the end of the nineteenth century they were primarily concerned with certain elemental problems of their identity and their craft. They had to find their own national voice, to free themselves from a provincial imitation of English literature and from excessive dependence on English critical judgment, and yet at the same time to steer short of the opposite danger of literary chauvinism. They had to reconcile the aristocratic bias which all but a few of them shared—Cooper was here the most poignant example—with their sympathy for the undeniably appealing energy and hardihood and promise of the American democracy that was developing all around them. The best of them had to come to terms with their own isolation, itself a compelling theme. They had to fashion their own response to the kind of materials which American life offered the creative writer, which were of a different order from the materials available to the European writer. No monuments, no ruins, no Eton, no Oxford, no Epsom, no Ascot, no antiquity, no legends, no society in the received sense of the word—the grievance runs from Hawthorne to Henry James and beyond, though an occasional writer like Crèvecoeur saw merit in being able to dispense with the apparatus of feudalism and oppression, and others like Emerson insisted that only the proper energy of imagination was necessary to see American society in its full potentiality as a literary subject.[9]

There was, again, the sheer necessity of forging a profession for the man of letters (and for the academic too, who taught in colleges which were, most of them, pathetic, libraryless little boardinghouses for drillmasters and adolescent rioters, living under the thumb of this or that sect). Almost no one at first could collect any significant royalties for serious creative work, and in addition to the usual hard economics of authorship, there was the terrible ruthless competition of pirated editions of famous English writers, which, in the absence of an international copyright agreement, unscrupulous reprint houses could pour into the market at low prices. Up to the 1840's, before Longfellow and Whittier struck the public fancy, probably the only authors who made any money to speak of from their creative efforts were Irving and Cooper, but neither of them had much need of his royalties. Practically every man of letters had to have a primary source of income, which his royalties would only supplement, whether it was his patrimony, his wife's trust funds, lectures, college teaching, or an editorial post on a

[9] America, Emerson wrote in the 1840's, had not yet had the genius who could see in the barbarism and materialism of the times another "carnival of the gods" such as anyone could see in the European past from Homeric times to the struggles of Calvinism. "Banks and tariffs, the newspaper and caucus, Methodism and Unitarianism, are flat and dull to dull people, but rest on the same foundations of wonder as the town of Troy and the temple of Delphi, and are as swiftly passing away. Our log-rolling, our stumps and their politics, our fisheries, our Negroes and Indians, our boats and our repudiations, the wrath of rogues and the pusillanimity of honest men, the northern trade, the southern planting, the western clearing, Oregon and Texas, are yet unsung. Yet America is a poem in our eyes; its ample geography dazzles the imagination, and it will not wait long for metres." *Complete Works* (Boston, 1903–4), Vol. III, pp. 37–8.

magazine or newspaper, or, as in the case of Thoreau for several years, manual labor.[1]

During these decades, American writers expressed their protest against the more discouraging side of their condition in a variety of ways—withdrawal, expatriation, overt criticism. But they were more disposed to look upon their estrangement as a consequence of the pursuit of other values than as a value in itself. They were on the whole quite free from one of the most pressing difficulties of the modern thinker, the fact that he is to a painful degree the creature of his own self-consciousness. They suffered at the hands of their society, but they were not overwhelmed by their awareness of their own suffering. (One thinks of the wry and melancholy humor with which Thoreau remarked on the seven-hundred-odd unsold copies of an edition of a thousand of his *A Week on the Concord and Merrimac Rivers* which were stacked in his room: "I now have a library of nearly nine hundred volumes, over seven hundred of which I wrote myself. Is it not well that the author should behold the fruits of his labor?" What contemporary writer, suffering a comparable disappointment, could refrain from spinning out of it a complete theory of modern culture?) When one compares the situation of American writers to a truly bitter case of estrangement—like that, say, of Joyce from Ireland—it seems less than stark. They were in fact quite ambivalent about their America, and later critics, obsessed by their own alienation, could find in these earlier writers texts that would reinforce their feeling of kinship. It became natural to notice Melville's words, "I feel I am an exile here," and to ignore the feeling of identification he expressed elsewhere: "It is for the nation's sake, and not for her authors' sake, that I would have America be heedful of the increasing greatness among her writers. For how great a shame, if other nations should be before her in crowning the heroes of the pen!" On the whole, one must be persuaded by the observation of Richard Chase, in the *Partisan Review* symposium, that he had never believed "that the great American writers of the past felt half so 'estranged' or 'disinherited' as many modern critics have said they did."

After about 1890, however, American writers and other intellectuals became a more cohesive class than they had been, became restless with

---

[1] William Charvat has observed, in his interesting study of the economics of authorship, *Literary Publishing in America, 1790–1850* (Philadelphia, 1959), p. 23: "Not a single literary work of genuine originality published in book form before 1850 had any commercial value until much later, and most of our classics were financial failures. . . ."

the constraints of gentility and conservatism, and took up arms against American society. In the struggle for new freedoms in expression and criticitism that occupied them from about 1890 to the 1930's, the idea of their own alienation became a kind of rallying point, a part of their esthetic or political protest. Before this, intellect in America had been mostly associated with the maintenance of old values. Now, both in historical reality and in the public awareness, it was linked with the propagation of novelty—with new ideas in politics and morals, art and literature. Where the American intellectual had been hemmed in during the nineteenth century by safe and genteel idealism, he now rather rapidly established the right, even the obligation, of the intellectual community to talk realistically about corruption and exploitation, sex and violence. Intellect, for so long considered both by its foes and its exponents as passive and futile, came little by little to be involved in and identified once again with power. Once associated by the public with the conservative classes and with a political outlook well to the right of center, the intellectual class emerged after 1890 as a force standing somewhat to the left, and during the great depression much of it moved to the far left.

This brings us to one of the most poignant aspects of the intellectual's position. Anti-intellectualism, as I hope these pages have made clear, is founded in the democratic institutions and the egalitarian sentiments of this country. The intellectual class, whether or not it enjoys many of the privileges of an elite, is of necessity an elite in its manner of thinking and functioning. Up to about 1890, most American intellectuals were rooted in a leisured patrician class which, whatever its limitations on other counts, had no difficulty in accepting its own identity as an elite. After 1890 this was no longer true in the same degree. The problem of identity once again became a difficulty for intellectuals, because, at the very moment when their sensibilities and concerns were deviating more than ever from those of the public at large, they were trying far more than ever to espouse political causes that supposedly represented the case of the people against special interests—it does not matter for this purpose whether these causes were conceived in the populist, progressive, or Marxist traditions.

Intellectuals in the twentieth century have thus found themselves engaged in incompatible efforts: they have tried to be good and believing citizens of a democratic society and at the same time to resist the vulgarization of culture which that society constantly produces. It is rare for an American intellectual to confront candidly the unresolvable conflict between the elite character of his own class and his democratic aspirations. The extreme manifestation of the general reluctance to face this conflict is the writer who constantly assaults class barriers and yet constantly hungers for special deference. Since any alliance between intellectuals and the people is bound to be imperfect, a loyally democratic intellectual class is bound to suffer acute disappointments from time to time. At moments when the political climate is full of hope and vigor—when some democratic cause is flourishing, as it was in the full flush of Progressivism and in the New Deal—these disappointments may be obscured or forgotten, but such moments do not last. Progressivism was followed by the reaction of the 1920's, the New Deal in time by McCarthyism. Sooner or later, when the public fails to meet the political or cultural demands of the intellectuals, the intellectuals are hurt or shocked and look for some way of expressing their feelings without going so far as to repudiate their popular allegiances altogether. The phenomenon of mass culture has given them a vent for their estrangement from the people. The collapse of hope for socialism, and even, for the moment, of any new movement of serious social reform, has eliminated expectations of any new *rapprochement*. One reason for the fascination of so many intellectuals with mass culture—quite aside from the intrinsic gravity of the problem —is that they have found in it a legitimate (that is, non-political) way of expressing their estrangement from democratic society. And it is significant that some of the bitterest indictments of mass culture have come from writers who were, or still are, democratic socialists. The stridency, even the note of inhumanity, which often creeps into discussions of mass culture may be explained in some part by an underlying sense of grievance against a populace that has not lived up to expectations.

Perhaps the most decisive testimony of the changed situation of twentieth-century intellectuals is that after 1890 it became possible for the first time to speak of intellectuals as a class. As the intellectual community began to detach itself from the leisured class, the whole question of the intellectual and society was reopened. The early nineteenth century had known many men of intellect and a few men who were professional intellectuals; but it had not produced institutions that could forge them into a numerous social order with some capacity for cohesion and mutual communication on a national scale. Only at the end of the century did the country develop a system of genuine universities; great libraries suited to advance research;

magazines with large circulations, receptive to fresh ideas and able to pay writers well; a considerable number of strong and enterprising publishing houses, operating under the protection of international copyright, alert to the possibilities of native writers, and free from genteel inhibitions; well-organized professional societies in various scholarly disciplines; an array of scholarly journals; expanding governmental bureaucracies with a need for trained skills; and, finally, wealthy foundations to subsidize science, scholarship, and letters. Certain types of intellectual careers that had not existed before now came into being on a national scale. To visualize the scope of the change, one must try to imagine, say, muckraking magazines in the 1830's, or the *Harvard Law Review* in Jackson's time, or Guggenheim Fellowships in the Polk era, or the W.P.A. theater project under Cleveland.

At the very time that intellectuals were beginning to become more numerous and effective and more organically involved in American society, in its institutions and its market place, they were becoming more self-conscious about their estrangement. The older awareness of estrangement had taken shape under the particular conditions of mugwump culture. Its basic sources had been lonely and neglected writers or frustrated patricians, and its most eloquent statement, coming at the end of the mugwump epoch, was Henry Adams's *Education*. Adams's book, written earlier but first available for general public circulation in 1918, was, significantly, seized upon by the intellectuals of the post-war era as a document that spoke for them and expressed their sense of their position in American culture; and it appropriately fell to the same generation to rediscover the merits of the long-forgotten Melville. Clearly, the post-war intellectuals responded so much to Adams, not because they shared any of the circumstances of his singular life or his intensely poignant personal disinheritance, but because his indictment of post-Civil War America as a coarse, materialistic, and mindless society fitted their own sense of America in the 1920's. Although the particular setting of mugwump alienation had been altogether different from the avant-garde alienation of this generation, a common consciousness of estrangement and discomfort, failure and lamentation, established a spiritual link between the two. It began to be evident, at least to some, that the "democratic" intellectual would hardly be any more at home in this society than the patrician intellectual.

There is a certain irony in the fact that alienation became a kind of fixed principle among knowing young intellectuals during the years

preceding the war. These were the very years of that "Little Renaissance" in which the literary and political culture of the nation seemed
once again so full of originality and energy as to mock all despairing
assertions about its past. Nonetheless, the alienation of the intellectual
and the artist, long since a ponderable fact, was beginning to congeal
into a sort of ideology, as they fell into a somewhat parochial struggle with their own national inheritance. For American writers what
seemed to count was alienation not from modern society in general or
modern industrialism or the modern bourgeoisie but specifically from
these things as they were manifested *in America*.

The case was best put in Van Wyck Brooks's eloquent early cultural
jeremiads, *America's Coming-of-Age* and *Letters and Leadership*, published in 1915 and 1918. There, with a fervor and persuasiveness that
he would later regret, Brooks exposed what seemed to be the terrible
truth about "a race that has never cultivated life for its own sake."
From the beginning, he thought, the American mind, caught between
the hopeless imperatives of the Puritan code and the stark realities of
business self-assertion, had developed a kind of unwholesome doubleness that militated against the creation or at least the fulfillment of
first-rate artists and thinkers. It had forged, on the one side, a world of
ideals and abstractions uncommitted to any reality, and, on the other,
a world of possession, the soulless accumulation of dollars; caught between them was a thinking class that passed at a frightening pace from
youth to middle age and then to slow, relentless decay. A country
whose life was "in a state of arrested development," "a national mind
that has been sealed against that experience from which literature
derives all its values," had given rise to a gallery of wasted, deformed,
and unrealized talents: [2]

> Poets, painters, philosophers, men of science and religion are all
> to be found, stunted, starved, thwarted, embittered, prevented
> from taking even the first step in self-development, in this amaz
> ing microcosm of our society, a society that stagnates for want of
> leadership, and at the same time, incurably suspicious of the very
> idea of leadership, saps away all those vital elements that produce
> the leader.

American experience had not produced an intellectual tradition or a
sympathetic soil, and in consequence "we who above all peoples need

[2] *America's Coming of Age* (New York: Anchor ed., 1958), p. 99; cf. pp.
91–110 and *passim*.

great men and great ideals have been unable to develop the latent greatness we possess, and have lost [through expatriation] an incalculable measure of greatness that has, in spite of all, succeeded in developing itself." An excessive, rampant individualism had prevented the formation of a collective spiritual life. The pioneering spirit, coarsely bent on acquisition and conquest, had fostered a materialism which was hopelessly opposed to the skeptical or creative imagination; and it had been reinforced by Puritanism, the ideal philosophy for the pioneer, a philosophy whose contemptuous view of human nature simultaneously released the acquisitive side of men and inhibited their esthetic impulses. American business, as it developed in the atmosphere of the pioneer spirit, Puritanism, and frontier opportunities, had indeed become more adventurous and attractive than business elsewhere, but by this very fact it had absorbed and diverted all too much of what was good in the American character. What one had, then, was a society of sorts, but virtually no "organic native culture," and it could hardly be surprising that "our orthodox literary men, whatever models they place before themselves, cannot rise above the tribal view of their art as either an amusement or a soporific."

Brooks's onslaught, which was followed and, in a sense, supposedly documented by his own studies of Mark Twain and Henry James, prefigured the judgment that would be rendered in criticism or literature by writer after writer of his own generation. The same indictment, voiced in more raucous tones and to different ends, ran through the more popular critical diatribes of H. L. Mencken and the literature of Spoon River, Winesburg, and Zenith—those portraits of the mean, stunted, starved lives, the sour little crabapple culture of the American small town, with its inhibitions and its tyrannies.[3] The view of America that had quickened in the pianissimo revolt of the nineties and grown articulate during the Little Renaissance now developed into a fixed conviction, almost an obsession, among the expatriate generation. In 1922, when Harold Stearns edited his volume, *Civilization in the United States,* to which both Brooks and Mencken contributed, the several

---

[3] What an ancient theme this was! In 1837 even Longfellow had said even of Boston that it was nothing but a "great village," where "the tyranny of opinion passes all belief." And three quarters of a century later John Jay Chapman wrote, along the same lines: "No one who has not been up against it can imagine the tyranny of a small town in America. I believe good old fashioned Medicean, or Papal, or Austrian tyranny is child's play compared to it." Samuel Longfellow, *Life of Henry Wadsworth Longfellow* (Boston, 1886), Vol. I, p. 267; Jacques Barzun, ed.: *The Selected Writings of John Jay Chapman* (New York: Anchor ed., 1959), p. xi.

contributors seemed to be trying to outdo each other to prove that there was no such civilization. They spoke for a generation which was to think of American justice as represented by the Sacco-Vanzetti case, American regard for science by the Scopes trial, American tolerance by the Klan, the American amenities by Prohibition, American respect for law by the metropolitan gangsters, and the most profound spiritual commitment of the country by the stock-market craze.

· 5 ·

One of the latent premises underlying the cult of alienation was the idea that the cultural problem in America was not a variation, perhaps more acute, of a universal problem of modern societies, but a case of utterly unique pathology. It was as though other nations did not have their own awkward confrontations of bourgeois philistines and rebellious artists, their unappreciated writers or expatriates. The cult of alienation thus inverted the popular approach to the Europe-America antithesis. In the popular mind, Europe had long stood for oppression, corruption, and decadence, whereas America stood for democracy, innocence, and vitality. Among the intellectuals this rather simple view of things was turned upside down: civilized Europe was counterposed to philistine America. Since the days of Benjamin West and Washington Irving, artists and writers had put this notion into action by expatriating themselves from the United States for large parts of their working lives, and in the 1920's a portion of the intellectual community followed suit by taking off for Paris.

But in the 1930's and afterward, this simple Europe-America antithesis broke down. As time went on, it was painfully apparent that this antithesis was less and less valid, and it was now possible also to see that it had never been wholly valid. European countries had become mechanized and had developed mass societies just as the United States had; and although it was possible for pettish Europeans to refer to this as the Americanization or the Coca-Colanization of Europe, as though mass society were nothing but an American exportation or intrusion, wiser interpreters in the tradition of Tocqueville could see that the United States, being in the vanguard of industrialization and mass culture, foreshadowed rather than created events in Europe.

From the 1930's onward, the cultural antithesis between America and Europe was drastically changed. The depression brought the expatriates home, where they found a new America in the making. By the mid-thirties a wholly new moral and social atmosphere was in evidence. The American political intelligence seemed to have been stung into life and awakened from its torpor by the crash. The New Deal, at first an object of suspicion to the intellectuals, ended by winning the loyalty of an overwhelming majority of them. There seemed to be a new need for the brains of the country, and a new respect for them. The resurgent labor movement promised to be not just another interest group but a force for social reconstruction. The people themselves seemed more appealing than they had been before, both in the urgency of their distress and in the signs of their increasing self-assertion against their old rulers. The air was full of protest and rediscovery. The irritations and lighthearted negations of the twenties seemed altogether passé, its disillusionment and moral anarchy quite inadequate to the needs of the battle against domestic reactionaries and foreign fascists. What seemed to be needed now was a positive creed and a usable past.

Once an old mood has evaporated and a new mood has begun to take form, it is truly astonishing how universal the change becomes—how so many thinkers and writers, quite different in their styles, motives, and points of origin, will begin to regroup themselves and converge around a new spiritual focus. There now began a startling resurgence of literary nationalism, whose character has been so well assessed by Alfred Kazin in the closing chapter of *On Native Grounds*. Intellectuals were seized by a passionate desire to look anew at the United States, to report and record and photograph it. Writers took a fresh and more respectful interest in the American past. For example, whereas a major feature of biographies conceived or written in the twenties had been the task of depreciation—as in W. E. Woodward's cranky assault on Washington, Edgar Lee Masters's merciless assessment of Lincoln, and Van Wyck Brooks's extraordinary critical tour de force on Mark Twain—the characteristic biographical work of the thirties and forties was the type of lavish, tender, full-scale biography whose most massive and sentimental monument was Carl Sandburg's life of Lincoln.

It fell again to Van Wyck Brooks, the eloquent prophet of alienation, to lead the way toward the recapture of America. With *The Flowering of New England* in 1936, he launched one of the most monumental historical labors of our time, his *Makers and Finders* series, which led him to read his way patiently through all the first-, second-, and third-rate figures in American literary history from 1800 to 1915. It seemed now that nothing American was alien to him except his own earlier work, whose strident indictment of the nation's culture he regretted.

He had passed from a relentless assertion of the limitations of important writers to an affectionate search for the importance of limited writers. Like a family historian or genealogist, whose insatiable interest in the clan's past endows him with an endless patience for all the family gossip, he reconstructed almost the whole of American literary history, often with striking insight but rarely with his old critical verve.

Brooks, of course, was not alone. Even Mencken, whose red-nosed prose had long since provided a humorous counterpart to Brooks's solemn indictments of America, could not resist nostalgia. True, his sourly reactionary response to the New Deal stamped him indelibly as a figure of the previous era: his irreverence, which had seemed so completely appropriate to the era of Harding and Coolidge, became merely impertinent under Roosevelt, and his comic gift appeared for the moment to have run out. But when he turned at last to writing the three charming volumes of his autobiography, the work was suffused with a gentle nostalgia that matched Brooks's; and no one who knew what an *enfant terrible* Mencken had been could fail to find something benign, after all, in the environment that had given him so much scope for his unique gift of mockery and provided him with so much personal fulfillment. Sinclair Lewis, too, struck a new note in *Dodsworth*, and by 1938 his Americanism became open and even more complacent, in *The Prodigal Parents*, a dismal novel which seemed nothing more than a vindication of American bourgeois values against youthful rebellion. Finally, he announced to an unbelieving European audience what some American critics had begun to suspect, that he had written *Babbitt* not out of hatred but out of love. Even a younger writer like John Dos Passos, who had been the first to express a distaste for American civilization in radical novels, turned in *The Ground We Stand On* to probing the past for virtues that would yield a new political faith.

Some part of this growing Americanism arose from Europe's gradual loss of its old cultural and moral centrality for American intellectuals. The cultural antithesis between them gradually turned on its axis. T. S. Eliot, Gertrude Stein, and Ezra Pound were the last important American expatriates. The tide of expatriation turned, after the Depression brought the American intellectuals home, when fascism sent refugee artists and scholars in their wake. The United States ceased to be a place men fled from and became a place they fled to. European intellectuals began to think of the United States as a place to go to, not always because they were fleeing for their lives but sometimes simply because they found it a comfortable and rewarding place to live. A trickle had begun even before 1933, and it soon grew into a tidal flow: Aldous Huxley, W. H. Auden, Thomas Mann, Einstein, Schoenberg, Stravinsky, Milhaud, Hindemith, and many lesser figures; whole schools of art historians, political scientists, sociologists. Once the industrial leader, the United States now became the intellectual capital of the Western world, in so far as such a capital could be said to exist.[4] From the point of view of many Europeans, the second of these events was the less forgivable. In any case, the America-Europe antithesis lost most of its cultural meaning on both sides of the Atlantic. The old dialogue between Europe and America became less significant than the idea of Western man and Western society as a whole.

In the 1930's Europe lost its political and moral authority. Fascism revealed a political tyranny beyond anything Americans had known, and the appeasement of fascism by the democratic powers showed the chinks in the entire Western political system. The Nazi-Soviet Pact of 1939, which at last made plain to all but the most credulous that the Bolsheviks conducted their foreign policies with the same ruthlessness as the fascist states, punctured the fellow-traveling mentality and made it impossible to keep up the confusion between populist-liberal and Marxist commitments which had reigned for nearly a decade. It was no longer possible to look to any foreign political system for moral or ideological illumination. Even the gravest American failures of decency paled when, at the end of the war, the full horror of the death camps was disclosed. At the same time, Europe's terrible distress put the responsibilities of the United States in a wholly new light. In 1947, the year when America came to Europe's rescue with the Marshall plan, Edmund Wilson, the least provincial of writers, found it possible to say upon returning from Europe that "the United States at the present time is politically more advanced than any other part of the world," [5] and to speak of our twentieth-century culture as "a revival of the democratic creativeness which presided at the birth of the Republic and flourished up to the Civil War." The twentieth century, he felt, had brought "a remarkable renascence of American arts and letters."

[4] Cf. the recent judgment by Sir Charles Snow: "How many Englishmen understand, or want to understand, that during the past twenty years the United States has done something like 80 per cent of the science and scholarship of the entire Western world?" "On Magnanimity," *Harper's*, Vol. CCXXV (July, 1962), p. 40.
[5] *Europe Without Baedeker* (New York, 1947), pp. 408–9.

· 6 ·

Now we have come chronologically full circle to the time of the *Partisan Review* symposium and to the mood expressed there. For the generation of intellectuals for whom the idea of alienation was associated chiefly with certain excesses of the 1920's and 1930's, that idea had played itself out. But a revival of the old commitment to alienation has taken place among dissenting writers, and it has a strong appeal to the rising generation, strongest perhaps to its most vigorous and critical spirits. The new dissenters argue, and with good reason, that at no time has the need for intelligent dissent and free criticism been greater than it is today, and on this count they find the older cult of alienation still meaningful. These writers do not like the present cultural situation or the political state of the world—and who can blame them?—and on the strength of this dislike they have developed their own conception of the role of the thinker, the artist, the intellectual. It is a conception, however, which I believe oversimplifies history and offers a delusive prescription for the conduct of intellectual life.

The issue these writers pose is whether the task of being enlightening about the state of our society is advanced or impaired by accepting alienation as an overwhelming moral imperative. The burden of their argument shows that, in any case, the intellectual's grievance has changed drastically since the thirties. The old complaint that the role and the task of the American scholar or man of letters were not conceived of as important, or even as legitimate, and that in consequence he lacked recognition, encouragement, and a decent income, has not altogether disappeared. Yet an insistent new note has crept into the writing of the past two decades: one hears more and more that the intellectual who has won a measure of freedom and opportunity, and a new access to influence, is thereby subtly corrupted; that, having won recognition, he has lost his independence, even his identity as an intellectual. Success of a kind is sold to him at what is held to be an unbearable price. He becomes comfortable, perhaps even moderately prosperous, as he takes a position in a university or in government or working for the mass media, but he then tailors himself to the requirements of these institutions. He loses that precious tincture of rage so necessary to first-rate creativity in a writer, that capacity for negation and rebellion that is necessary to the candid social critic, that initiative and independence of aim required for distinguished work in science.

It appears, then, to be the fate of intellectuals either to berate their exclusion from wealth, success, and reputation, or to be seized by guilt when they overcome this exclusion. They are troubled, for example, when power disregards the counsels of intellect, but because they fear corruption they are even more troubled when power comes to intellect for counsel. To revert to Professor Howe's language: when bourgeois society rejects them, that is only one more proof of its philistinism; when it gives them an "honored place," it is buying them off. The intellectual is either shut out or sold out.

To anyone who is willfully unsympathetic, these antithetical complaints may seem perverse or amusing. But in truth they epitomize the intellectual's particular version of the tragic predicament that faces any man who is in one way or another caught between his most demanding ideals and his more immediate ambitions and interests. The discomfort the dissenting writers express is engendered by the fact that American society seems to be absorbing its intellectuals just at the moment in history when their services as an independent source of national self-criticism are most desperately needed. They are to be criticized, I think, not for feeling this discomfort, but for a lack of awareness of the tragic predicament that underlies it.

Among the intellectuals of the Western world, the Americans are probably the most prone to such pricks of conscience, possibly because they feel the constant necessity of justifying their role. British and French intellectuals, for example, usually take for granted the worth of what they are doing and the legitimacy of their claims on the community. But today the burden of guilt that has traditionally afflicted American intellectuals is increased by the power this country has taken in the world and by their legitimate alarm at the peculiar irritating mindlessness and sanctimony to which the canons of our political discourse have been given over. (How many of our politicians dare to talk like adults about the problem of Red China?) But perhaps quite as important as all these contemporary considerations is the fact that, not so very long ago, the tradition of alienation turned into a powerful moral imperative. The older generation of intellectuals first came to terms with this imperative by trying to act in accordance with it; but now, feeling they have been misled by it, they find it no longer binding. They have earned their release by more than two decades of disillusioning experience. Having seen the problem of their own moral position from more than one angle of vision, they can no longer think of it as a simple problem; and like anyone who is given to contemplating the complexities of things, they have lost the posture of militancy. The intellectuals of the younger generation, especially those who take their inspiration directly or indirectly from Marxism, find this unforgivable, and they have begun to condemn it in language that partakes both of the natural cruelty of the young and of the artificial puritanism of the political left.

The young intellectual in the United States today very often feels, almost from the outset of his career, the distractions and pressures attendant upon success, the consequences of a new state of affairs in our cultural life, which is encouraging but also exasperating. The battle waged with such enthusiasm by the intellectual generation that flourished between 1890 and 1914 has long since been won: certain esthetic and political freedoms, the claims of naturalism and realism, the right to deal uninhibitedly with sex and violence and corruption, the right to strike out at authority, have been thoroughly established. But the victories have turned sour. We live in an age in which the avant-garde itself has been institutionalized and deprived of its old stimulus of a stubborn and insensate opposition. We have learned so well how to absorb novelty that receptivity itself has turned into a kind of tradition —"the tradition of the new." Yesterday's avant-garde experiment is today's chic and tomorrow's cliché. American painters, seeking in abstract expressionism the outer limits of artistic liberation, find a few years later that their canvases are selling in five figures. Beatniks are in demand on university campuses, where they are received as entertainers and turned into the esoteric comedians of the sophisticated. In social criticism, professional Jeremiahs like Vance Packard become best-sellers; and more serious writers like C. Wright Mills, who compulsively asserted the most thoroughgoing repudiation of American life in its every aspect, are respectfully reviewed and eagerly read. David Riesman's *The Lonely Crowd*, which can be taken as a depressing account of what the American character has become, is the most widely read book in the history of sociology, and William H. Whyte's mordant analysis of *The Organization Man* is read everywhere by organization men.

It is not hard to understand why many serious minds have come to find these things more discouraging than hopeful. Success that seems to have lost its reality is worse than failure. The large, liberal middle-class audience upon which all this acceptance depends now brings to the work of the intellectuals a bland, absorptive tolerance that is quite different from a vital response. To the writer who has just eviscerated their way of life and their self-satisfying compromises, readers now say "How interesting!" or even at times "How true!" Such passive tolerance can only be infuriating to a writer who looks beyond the size of his royalties and hopes actually to exert some influence on the course of affairs or to strike a note in the moral consciousness of his time. He objects that serious thinking is received as a kind of diversion and not as a challenge. Often he wonders if the fault may perhaps be in himself: whether his own personal compromises—and invariably he has made them—have not blunted the force of his message, whether he has not at bottom become altogether too much like the audience he condemns.[6]

One might hope that this self-probing honesty would yield nothing but good; unfortunately, it leads to a kind of desperation, which may in itself command sympathy but which ends only in the search for a "position" or a pose. Dissenting intellectuals often seem to feel that they are morally on trial for being intellectuals, and their moral responsibility is then interpreted as a responsibility primarily to repudiation and destruction; so that the measure of intellectual merit is felt to lie not in imagination or precision, but in the greatest possible degree of negativism. The responsibility of the intellectual is not seen, in the first instance, as a responsibility to be enlightening about society but rather to make an assertion against it—on the assumption that almost any such assertion will presumably be enlightening, and that in any case it re-establishes the writer's probity and courage.

The prophets of alienation who speak for the left no doubt aim to create a basis for some kind of responsible politics of protest, but when the situation of the intellectual is under consideration their tone becomes strident, and then one hears how much better it is to have "blind unreasoning rejection" than to make moral compromises; the talk is of nostalgia for "earlier certainties that made resistance easy," of the primary need of the intellectual to discharge aggression, of the dangers of becoming a "prostitute" or a "traitor" to the fundamental obligations of the intellectual's role, of the alleged antithesis between social responsibility, which is bad, and intellectual responsibility, which is good. The point here is that alienation in the intellectual is not simply accepted, as a necessary consequence of the pursuit of truth or of some

---

[6] I do not wish to suggest that this tendency is universal; many writers are simply content to rest with the benefits of the situation. As Alfred Kazin remarks: "Too many Americans now want to remain fully attached to our social system and at the same time draw the rewards of a little sophisticated (and wholly external) criticism of it." *Contemporaries* (New York, 1962), p. 439.

artistic vision, but that a negative stance or posture toward society is prescribed as the only stance productive of artistic creativity or social insight or moral probity. The argument does not rest upon the idea that the intellectual has a primary responsibility to truth or to his creative vision, and that he must be prepared to follow them even when they put him quite at odds with his society. It is rather that he must begin with a primary responsibility to repudiate—in Professor Baritz's term —his society. His alienation is seen not as a risk he must have the integrity to run, but as an obligation which preconditions all his other obligations. Alienation has ceased to be merely a fact of life and has taken on the character of a cure or a prescription for the proper intellectual regimen.

One need follow the cult of alienation only a few steps further to come upon other more demanding exponents of alienation of whom the politically left writers would disapprove at central points but whose dedication to alienation as a leading principle is quite similar— men who are, at best, exponents of romantic anarchism and, at worst, of the adolescent rebellion of the beatniks or of the moral nihilism that has been expressed most eloquently by Norman Mailer. And one of the distinguishing features of this literature of alienation is that while its writers aspire to preserve peace and advance democracy and foster culture and release individuality, their discussions of politics and culture are curiously stark and humorless and inflexible, even at times inhumane.

The voices of the political dissenters express an alienation that is at least politically meaningful, and, whatever their excesses, they have engaged in some kind of dialogue with and feel a responsibility to the rest of the intellectual world. Looming behind them, the beatniks today constitute a very considerable public in their own right and a formidable symptom of our cultural malaise. It is impossible to say that the beatniks are to the left of the political dissenters—they are simply, in the current argot, farther out. In the terms in which I have tried to define the intellectual temperament, the political dissenters are frequently overwhelmed by their own piety, whereas the beatniks have let their playfulness run away with them. In their thinking about society they tend to agree with the dissenters about commercialism, mass culture, nuclear armaments, and civil rights; but on the whole they have withdrawn from serious argument with the bourgeois world. The type of alienation represented by the beatniks is, in their own term, disaffiliated. They have walked out on the world of the squares [7] and for the most part have abandoned that sense of vocation which is demanded both by serious intellectual achievement and by sustained social protest.

In their own way, the beatniks have repudiated the path of intellectualism and have committed themselves to a life of sensation—to put it perhaps too sympathetically, as Lawrence Lipton does in the title of his illuminating book about them, *The Holy Barbarians*, to lives of inverted sainthood, marked by an acceptance of poverty and by their willingness to do without the usual satisfactions of a career and a regular income. Not surprisingly, the beatniks, as even their sympathetic commentators are apt to concede, have produced very little good writing. Their most distinctive contribution to our culture may in the end be their amusing argot. Their experimentation, which seems to consist largely of a relaxation of form, does not seem to offer, as the Dadaists did, a new kind of wit or fantasy, or to promise, as a writer like Gertrude Stein did, to set off a new direction in prose. The movement seems unable to rise above its adolescent inspiration. Somehow, when Jack Kerouac advises: "Remove literary, grammatical, and syntactical inhibition," and suggests "no discipline other than rhetorical exaltation and expostulated statement," one feels that he is less close to these earlier literary experiments in expression than to the child-indulgent propensities of the lunatic fringe of progressive education. As Norman Podhoretz has remarked, "the primitivism of the Beats serves . . . as a cover for an anti-intellectualism so bitter that it makes the ordinary American's hatred of eggheads seem positively benign." [8]

In their style of withdrawal, the beatniks are in the Bohemian line of succession, but they seem to have far less humor and self-distance than the older Bohemians, and infinitely less regard for individuality. Harry T. Moore has remarked that "individuals of genius have usually been disengaged, yes, particularly in the arts; but mass disengagement is a different matter. Most of the Beats don't have enough formal knowledge of history or political science to see these matters in perspective, but then they wouldn't want to: it's enough for them that they dislike

[7] Here they have on their side the precedent of Thoreau, who said that he did not care to be counted a member of any society which he had not voluntarily joined. (It is interesting how constantly the anti-institutional theme recurs in American thought.) The difference, of course, lies in Thoreau's sense of his vocation as a writer.

[8] "The Know Nothing Bohemians," in Seymour Krim, ed.: *The Beats* (Greenwich, Conn., 1960), p. 119.

and distrust the world of the Squares. . . ." [9] Their paradoxical creed
of mass disengagement and group inaction is reminiscent of the unfor-
gettable words of an undergraduate in a solemn paper on modern
culture: "The world will never be saved until the individual comes out
of the group *en masse.*" One of the qualities that has so readily subjected the beatniks to mockery in the mass media and the other literature of the squares is this distinctive uniformity—which the beatniks
have carried to the point of having their own dress. They have created
a new paradox: a conformity of alienation. And in so doing they have
caricatured the posture of alienation to a degree that its other exponents
find treasonous and unforgivable.

Quite understandably, then, the beatniks are considered, by sterner
prophets of alienation, to represent an infantile disorder, and they have
been repudiated not only by the angry grandfather of the beat movement, Kenneth Rexroth, but also by such a basically sympathetic critic
as Norman Mailer, who has high regard for the beats' search for
sensation and orgastic satisfaction, but no patience with their passivity,
their lack of assertion. The most forthright case for a really solid kind
of estrangement was made a few years ago by Mailer in a famous piece
in *Dissent* entitled "The White Negro: Superficial Reflections on the
Hipster." Over the beatnik Mailer would elevate the hipster, whose
awareness of the ultimate terrors of life resembles and is derived from
that of the Negro, "for no Negro can saunter down a street with any
real certainty that violence will not visit him on his walk."

This readiness to live with and face violence and death is now the
central virtue, for our collective condition is to face the alternative
between instant death by atomic war and "a slow death by conformity."
What he admired about the hipster, said Mailer, was his willingness to
accept the challenge of death, the challenge "to divorce oneself from
society, to exist without roots, to set out on that uncharted journey into
the rebellious imperatives of the self. In short, whether the life is criminal or not, the decision is to encourage the psychopath in oneself, to explore that domain of experience where security is boredom and therefore sickness. . . ." The hipster has his own "psychopathic brilliance,"
not very easily communicable because "Hip is the sophistication of the
wise primitive in a giant jungle, and so its appeal is still beyond the
civilized man." The importance of hipsters lies not in their numbers—

---

[9] In his postscript on the beats, written for the 1960 edition of Albert Parry's
Garrets and Pretenders: A History of Bohemianism in America (New York:
Dover ed., 1960), chapter 30.

there are, Mailer estimated, not more than a hundred thousand conscious members of the tribe—but in that "they are an elite with the
potential ruthlessness of an elite, and [with] a language most adolescents can understand instinctively, for the hipster's intense view of
existence matches their experience and their desire to rebel."

If the resulting life proves in fact to be criminal, Mailer makes it
clear—if, say, two young hoodlums beat in the brains of a candy-store
keeper—the act is not likely to be brave enough to be "very therapeu-
tic," but at least "courage of a sort is necessary, for one murders not only
a weak fifty-year-old man but an institution as well, one violates private property, one enters into a new relation with the police and introduces a dangerous element into one's life. The hoodlum is therefore
daring the unknown. . . ." [1] Certainly the earlier prophets of alienation in America had never had this much imagination.

· 7 ·

The spokesmen of the beatnik, and the hipster, and the left have their
own quarrels about the proper style of alienation and the limits of its
expression; but they all share a common conviction that there is some
proper style or stance or posture to be recommended which will somehow release the individuality and creativity of the artist, or sustain the
capacities of the social critic and protect him from corruption. Their
conviction that alienation is a kind of value in itself has a double historical root in romantic individualism and in Marxism. For more than a
century and a half the position of creative talent everywhere in the
bourgeois world has been such as to make us aware of the persistant
tension between the creative individual and the demands of society.
Moreover, the more self-conscious the artistic and intellectual communities of the Western world have become about their own position, the
more acutely aware they are that society cannot have the works of
men of genius, or even of distinguished talent, on its own terms but
must accept them as they come. The more one looks at great examples
of creativity, the more evident it becomes that creative minds are not
typically "nice," or well adjusted, or accommodating, or moderate; that
genuis is often accompanied by some kind of personal disorder and
that society must come to terms with this disorder if it wishes to have
the benefit of genius—a problem examined most memorably for our

[1] *Voices of Dissent* (New York, 1958), pp. 198–200, 202, 205; the essay appears also in *Advertisements for Myself* (New York, 1959), pp. 337–58.

time by Edmund Wilson in his discussion of the Philoctetes myth in *The Wound and the Bow*. Our heightened awareness of the alienation of the artist is to a large degree an inheritance from romanticism; the case for the social value of the thinker's alienation was formalized by Marxism, which held that at the focal moment of capitalist crisis the capitalist system would be deserted by many of its intellectuals, who would rather align themselves with the coming movement in history than remain attached to a decaying order.

Once one has accepted the idea that alienation is an inevitable consequence of the assertion of certain artistic or political values, it is easy to slip into the assumption that alienation has a kind of value in itself, much as one may assume that because genius is commonly "temperamental" one can begin to have the manifestations of genius by cultivating temperament. Of course, no one would seriously argue that a young writer, by cultivating, say, a penchant for obsessive gambling, can hope to develop any of Dostoevsky's genius. But so long as such an assumption is not brought into the open, it is easy to drift into the belief that the intellectual cannot fulfill himself unless he cultivates the proper personal style. Just as temperament can be misunderstood as a way to talent, so the proper truculent stance toward the world can be taken as a substitute for the intellectual's critical work. Serious writers on alienation would shrink from defending such a notion, but it asserts itself as a fundamental assumption of their most excited and extreme statements.

Moreover, the culturally constricting aspects of American life have always set American writers upon an imaginative quest for an order of society that could be counterposed to their own as a model, an ideal milieu for intellectual life. Nineteenth-century American academics looked to the German university, artists to French or Italian artistic communities, and writers to the position of the *grand écrivain* in France.[2] For a variety of reasons, these ideals have become tarnished, though they once played a part of real importance in the self-definition and the improvement of American cultural life. Professor Howe is in a very old tradition, then, in his quest for the ideal community in which

[2] Intellectuals outside France still look to that country as an ideal instance of the prestige and influence of the intellectual, but even French intellectuals have their foreign ideals. Once, for Stendhal, it was Italy. Today, for Raymond Aron, it is Britain: "Of all Western countries, Great Britain is probably the one which has treated its intellectuals in the most sensible way." *The Opium of the Intellectuals* (London, 1957), p. 234; cf. his critical comments on the position of the French intelligentsia, pp. 220–1.

the writer may find a refuge from his personal battle with society or a fulcrum for self-confident protest. Since Europe will no longer serve, there remains for him the universal country of Bohemia, which he holds up as a model, now unhappily abandoned, which provides a key to freedom and creativity. But about this, too, some objections must be made. No one would care to deny that Bohemian society has considerable intellectual and political value—but does this value not consist mainly in offering the individual a haven in the earlier transitional phases of his life? For a moment in the life of the young writer or artist, a moment characterized by experimentalism, the search for identity and style, for freedom from responsibility, a Bohemian life can be immensely liberating. But only a small part of the world's important literature has been written by men who were living in Bohemias, and the notion that many intellectuals have spent their mature and productive years there will not stand historical examination. This seems preeminently true of our own national experience. In this country, first-rate writers have been more solitary than lesser ones. Professor Howe's uncomfortable suggestion that Concord was a kind of Transcendentalist Bohemia might be acceptable as a pleasantry, but not as history. Concord was a village refuge from a Boston which Concord intellectuals disliked; but it offered no community of the sort one thinks of in connection with Bohemias, and surprisingly little intellectual society. One need only remember, for example, the truncated relations of Thoreau and Emerson, or of Hawthorne and his neighbors, or Bronson Alcott's lack of organic relations with almost anyone, to realize how true it is that Concord, for all the physical proximity it afforded, hardly constituted an intellectual community.

It is not just that there were no Bohemian revels, which Professor Howe hastens to make clear when he describes Concord's Bohemia as sedate, but that there was very little society. Thoreau reported in his journal that when he "talked, or tried to talk" with Emerson he "lost my time—nay, almost my identity," in a maze of pointless disagreement, and Emerson complained that Thoreau "does not feel himself except in opposition." (Was he aware that since the appearance of "Nature" Thoreau had all but ceased even to read him?) Concerning the Transcendentalists generally, Emerson wrote that "their studies were solitary." [3]

[3] Marcus Cunliffe, in his illuminating survey of *The Literature of the United States* (London, 1954), estimates the situation well when he says (pp. 80–1; cf. pp. 90–1):
    Loneliness and apartness have characterized the American author, from

A certain austere and determined isolation has been more regularly associated with creative work than the distractions of Bohemianism. Solidarity among intellectuals, especially when they are under external pressure, or mutual recognition and encouragement, should not be depreciated; but neither should they be confused with the agreeable face-to-face sociability which is the hallmark of Bohemian life. The truly creative mind is hardly ever so much alone as when it is trying to be sociable. The productive intellectual, rather than relying on Bohemia as a means by which he and others can "face the world together," usually tries to develop the resources by which he can face it alone. Facing the world together is a tactic of politics, but facing it alone seems to be the characteristic creative stance.

Again, for critics concerned with effective political dissent, the history of Bohemia is not encouraging. There was, to be sure, a bright moment in our own history before the First World War when esthetic experimentation, courageous social criticism, and the Bohemian life all seemed to converge—it was represented, for example, by the old *Masses* in Max Eastman's day. But, on the whole, the characteristic Bohemian style has leaned toward personal flamboyance and private rebellion, rather than political effectuality on any considerable scale— and in this respect at least, the beatniks are in the Bohemian tradition. It is dismal to think of doing without Bohemias, but to prescribe a Bohemian life for serious creative or political purposes is to place upon Bohemia a crushing burden of expectation.

· 8 ·

The dislike of involvement with "accredited institutions" exhibited by the prophets of alienation bespeaks a more fundamental dislike of the

---

Poe's day onward. Even the exuberant Americans—Whitman for instance— have had surprisingly few friends with whom to associate, so to speak, professionally. In New England, if we except a circle of Bostonians, this has been especially true. . . . Emerson, Thoreau, and Hawthorne lived for a while in the same village, Concord; and they and other personages pop continually in and out of one another's diaries and letters. Yet it would be less accurate to say that they knew one another than that they knew *of* one another. Each stood somewhat aside, a little critical of his companions, a little derisive, reluctant to commit himself. "But how insular and pathetically solitary," Emerson confided to his journal, "are all the people we know!" In the same source he notes that the happy author is the one who, ignoring public opinion, "writes always to *the unknown friend.*" Of the known, he remarks that "my friends and I are fishes in our habit. As for taking Thoreau's arm, I should as soon take the arm of an elm tree." After Hawthorne's death, he reflects sadly that he has waited too long in the hope that he "might one day conquer a friendship."

association of intellect with power. The frightening idea that an intellectual ceases altogether to function as an intellectual when he enters an accredited institution (which would at one stroke eliminate from the intellectual life all our university professors) may be taken as a crude formulation of a real problem: there is some discord between the imperatives of a creative career and the demands of the institution within which it takes place. Scholars have long since had to realize that the personal costs of working within institutions are smaller than the costs of living without institutional support. Indeed, they have no real choice: they need libraries and laboratories—perhaps even pupils— which only an institution can provide.

For imaginative writers this problem is more serious. The amenities and demands of academic life do not accord well with imaginative genius, and they make the truly creative temperament ill at ease. Moreover, the conditions of academic life are such as to narrow unduly the range of one's experience; and it is painful to imagine what our literature would be like if it were written by academic teachers of "creating writing" courses, whose main experience was to have been themselves trained in such courses. It would be a waste, too, if poets with primary gifts were to spend time as members of committees on the revision of the freshman composition course—hummingbirds, to resurrect an image of Mencken's, immersed in *Kartoffelsuppe*. Still, the partial or temporary support offered by the academy to writer and artist has proved helpful in many careers, and very often the alternative to such support is the creation of a frustrated cultural lumpenproletariat.

However, for intellectuals in the disciplines affected by the problem of expertise, the university is only a symbol of a larger and more pressing problem of the relationship of intellect to power: we are opposed almost by instinct to the divorce of knowledge from power, but we are also opposed, out of our modern convictions, to their union. This was not always the case: the great intellectuals of pagan antiquity, the doctors of the medieval universities, the scholars of the Renaissance, the philosophers of the Enlightenment, sought for the conjunction of knowledge and power and accepted its risks without optimism or naïveté. They hoped that knowledge would in fact be broadened by a conjunction with power, just as power might be civilized by its connection with knowledge. I have spoken of the terms on which knowledge and power were related in the days of the Founding Fathers as being consonant with this ideal: knowledge and power consorted more or less as equals, within the same social circles, and very often within the same heads. But this was not simply because, as some modern critics seem to imagine, the Founding Fathers were better than we are, though they probably were better. It is not simply that Jefferson read Adam Smith and Eisenhower read Western fiction. The fundamental difference is that the society of the eighteenth century was unspecialized. In Franklin's day it was still possible for a man to conduct an experiment of some scientific value in his woodshed, and for the gifted amateur in politics to move from a plantation to a law office to a foreign ministry. Today knowledge and power are differentiated functions. When power resorts to knowledge, as it increasingly must, it looks not for intellect, considered as a freely speculative and critical function, but for expertise, for something that will serve its needs. Very often power lacks respect for that disinterestedness which is essential to the proper functioning of the expert—the governor of a great state once called several distinguished sociologists into conference to arrange a public-opinion poll on a controversial, current issue, and then carefully outlined for them what this poll was to find.

If the typical man of power simply wants knowledge as an instrument, the typical man of knowledge in modern America is the expert. Earlier I observed that it has been largely the function of expertise which has restored the intellectual as a force in American politics. But the pertinent question is whether the intellectual, as expert, can really be an intellectual—whether he does not become simply a mental technician, to use the phrase of H. Stuart Hughes, working at the call of the men who hire him. Here, as in the case of the university and other accredited institutions, I think the answer is not easy or categorical, and a true answer will almost certainly not be apocalyptic enough to please the modern intellectual sensibility. The truth is that much of American education aims, simply and brazenly, to turn out experts who are not intellectuals or men of culture at all: and when such men go into the service of government or business or the universities themselves, they do not suddenly become intellectuals.

The situation of men of real intellectual accomplishment who may also enter the service of power is much more complicated. Do men distinguished for reflective minds cease to be intellectuals simply because they become ambassadors to India or Yugoslavia or members of the President's staff? No doubt certain intellectual responses are no longer possible for men who look at the world from an angle of vision that is close to power and who assume as given those compromises which have to be made when power is attained. But to me it seems to be a personal choice, one that cannot be squeezed into the terms of the forced morality of alienation, whether one is to sacrifice some of one's range of critical freedom in the hope that power may be made more amenable to the counsels of intellect, or even for the Faustian urge to learn something about the world which cannot be so readily learned from the vantage point of the academy.

The intellectual who has relinquished all thought of association with power understands well—almost too well—that his state of powerlessness is conducive to certain illuminations. What he is prone to forget is that an access to power and an involvement with its problems may provide other illuminations. The critic of power tries to influence the world by affecting public opinion; the associate of power tries directly to make the exercise of power more amenable to the thought of the intellectual community. These functions are not of necessity mutually exclusive or hostile. Each involves certain personal and moral hazards, and it is not possible to make the personal choice of the hazards one cares to run into a universal imperative. The characteristic intellectual failure of the critic of power is a lack of understanding of the limitations under which power is exercised. His characteristic moral failure lies in an excessive concern with his own purity; but purity of a sort is easily had where responsibilities are not assumed. The characteristic failure of the expert who advises the powerful is an unwillingness to bring his capacity for independent thought to bear as a source of criticism. He may lose his capacity for detachment from power by becoming absorbed in its point of view. For American intellectuals, so long excluded from places of power and recognition, there is always the danger that a sudden association with power will become too glamorous, and hence intellectually blinding.

What is at stake for individuals is, as I say, a personal choice; but what is important for society as a whole is that the intellectual community should not become hopelessly polarized into two parts, one part of technicians concerned only with power and accepting implicitly the terms power puts to them, and the other of willfully alienated intellectuals more concerned with maintaining their sense of their own purity than with making their ideas effective. Experts there will undoubtedly be, and perhaps also critics capable of stepping mentally outside their society and looking relentlessly at its assumptions, in sufficient number and with sufficient freedom to make themselves felt. Presumably the possibility of debate between them will continue to exist, and the intellectual community will have within it types of minds capable of mediating between the world of power and the world of criticism. If so, intellectual society will avoid the danger of being cut up into hostile and uncommunicative segments. Our society is sick in many ways; but such health as it has lies in the plurality of the elements composing it and their freedom to interact with each other. It would be tragic if all intellectuals aimed to serve power; but it would be equally tragic if all intellectuals who become associated with power were driven to believe they no longer had any connection with the intellectual community: their conclusion would almost inevitably be that their responsibilities are to power alone.

· 9 ·

A few years ago, in a perceptive historical essay, Marcus Cunliffe suggested designations for two types of mind which had figured in our intellectual achievement: the clerisy (a term first used by Coleridge), consisting of writers sufficiently close to the primary assumptions of their society to act in some degree as its spokesmen, and the avant-garde, who are profoundly alienated from these assumptions.[4] The better part of the creative brilliance and the originative power of our intellectual tradition has come from the avant-garde, but the clerisy has had its eminent figures. Franklin, Jefferson, and John Adams were clerisy; and so were Cooper, Emerson (at least in his mature years), the jurist Holmes, William James, William Dean Howells, and Walter Lippmann. The avant-garde names are more imposing, but such is the variety of interesting minds and major talents that there is an impressive third list composed of figures so mixed in their motives that they are impossible to classify: Mark Twain, for example, who embodied extremes of alienation and acceptance in the same riven mind, and Henry Adams, who in a different fashion did the same. No: it is the elusiveness of major talents rather than their susceptibility to facile classification that in the end impresses us most. And true as this is of the problem of alienation, it is still more true of states of mind and styles of life. Here it is not the presence of a single pattern, whether Bohemian or bourgeois, but the range and variety that is striking: one thinks of Emily Dickinson in her Amherst seclusion, Walt Whitman living his many-faceted and robust life, Wallace Stevens in his insurance

[4] "The Intellectuals: The United States," *Encounter*, Vol. IV (May, 1955), pp. 23–33.

executive's office, T. S. Eliot in banking and publishing, William Carlos
Williams in medical practice. The futility of trying to prescribe a pat-
tern may be suggested when one compares, say, John Dewey and
Charles S. Peirce, Thorstein Veblen and William James, William Dean
Howells and Henry James, Oliver Wendell Holmes and Louis D.
Brandeis, Mark Twain and Herman Melville, Emerson and Poe, Henry
Adams and H. C. Lea, Henry Miller and William Faulkner, Charles A.
Beard and Frederick Jackson Turner, Edith Wharton and Ernest
Hemingway, John Dos Passos and F. Scott Fitzgerald.

Before any writer or thinker can look upon himself as a potentially
productive mind, he has already been born into a particular situation in
life and endowed with a character and temperament that are only in
limited respects malleable. This is the range that fate gives him, and
he must work within it. To understand this, we may compare, for example, the lives of Oliver Wendell Holmes, Jr., and Thorstein Veblen—
contemporaries similar in their passionate and wide-ranging intellectualism and in their gift for ironic detachment, but dissimilar in almost
everything else. It would have been futile for either of these men to
try to remake himself at the outset of his career—for Holmes to enter
some kind of Bohemia and cast off his Brahmin inheritance, or for
Veblen to be a good fellow and try to become president of the American
Economic Association. Holmes looked at life rather naturally from the
standpoint of an historically rooted and socially secure class, and he
entered at length into one of our "accredited institutions," where it is
generally acknowledged that he did not cease to function as an intellectual or to do useful work in the world. Veblen, reared on the margin
between a Yankee culture whose values he could never take seriously and an immigrant Norwegian culture which was not really his
own, was fated to remain forever a marginal man, altogether alien to
the prevailing American beliefs. As a scholar, he had to pursue a career
within accredited institutions if he was to have a career at all, but
he succeeded in making himself a source of acute discomfort in every
university he worked at. Some kind of instinctive wisdom, I think,
caused him to keep the world at arm's length, even when it made
friendly gestures. His particular genius, he must have sensed, lay
partly in the same perversity that made constant personal trouble for
him. We may regard it also as the source of much that is vulnerable
in his work, but that perversity kept sharp the biting edge that made
him a kind of ponderous sociological Swift, and one of the most original
minds of his time.

One of the major virtues of liberal society in the past was that it made possible such a variety of styles of intellectual life—one can find men notable for being passionate and rebellious, others for being elegant and sumptuous, or spare and astringent, clever and complex, patient and wise, and some equipped mainly to observe and endure. What matters is the openness and generosity needed to comprehend the varieties of excellence that could be found even in a single and rather parochial society. Dogmatic, apocalyptic predictions about the collapse of liberal culture or the disappearance of high culture may be right or wrong; but one thing about them seems certain: they are more likely to instill self-pity and despair than the will to resist or the confidence to make the most of one's creative energies. It is possible, of course, that under modern conditions the avenues of choice are being closed, and that the culture of the future will be dominated by single-minded men of one persuasion or another. It is possible; but in so far as the weight of one's will is thrown onto the scales of history, one lives in the belief that it is not to be so.

ACKNOWLEDGMENTS

❦

THIS BOOK had its beginning when I was invited to give the first Heyward Keniston Lecture at the University of Michigan on April 27, 1953. That lecture, published in a somewhat expanded form as "Democracy and Anti-Intellectualism in America," *Michigan Alumnus Quarterly Review,* August 8, 1953, left me aware of having raised a variety of unresolved issues, and I found myself impelled to go on with them. It has been helpful to give various parts of the book as lectures: first to a number of undergraduate history societies at Cambridge University, where I was Pitt Professor of American History and Institutions during the academic year 1958–59; then, during the academic year 1961–62, as the Sperry and Hutchinson Lectures at Hiram College, Hiram, Ohio, the Haynes Foundation Lectures at the University of Southern California, and the Ziskind Lectures at Smith College; finally, during the autumn term of 1962–63, when I was Visiting Senior Fellow of the Humanities Council and Class of 1932 Lecturer at Princeton University. To many persons at these institutions I am indebted for their cordial hospitality.

Special aspects of this study were pursued under grants from the Council for Research in the Social Sciences of Columbia University and the program of the Committee on the Role of Education in American History of the Fund for the Advancement of Education. A grant from the Carnegie Corporation made it possible for me to devote a full sabbatical year to this work, and to finish it much earlier and with far more ample research help than I would otherwise have had. Columbia University has been generous in arranging free time, but to mention only this would be insufficient acknowledgment of the many intellectual rewards of my connection with it over a period of twenty-five years, first as a graduate student and then as a member of its department of history.

As always, Beatrice Kevitt Hofstadter has given me textual and sub-stantive criticism of incalculable value. My colleagues, Peter Gay and Fritz Stern, have read the entire manuscript and offered sugges-tions of vital importance. During the years in which this book was be-ing written, my research assistants, Philip Greven, Jr., Carol Gruber, Neil Harris, and Ann Lane, did resourceful work in original materials. Over a period of several years many friends have helped by discussing my notions, offering suggestions, directing me to new material, or reading drafts of chapters, and I wish to thank Daniel Aaron, Daniel Bell, Lee Benson, John M. Blum, Carl Bridenbaugh, Paul Carter, Lawrence Cremin, Barbara Cross, Robert D. Cross, Marcus Cunliffe, Stanley Elkins, Julian Franklin, Henry F. Graff, Robert Handy, H. Stuart Hughes, Edward C. Kirkland, William E. Leuchtenburg, Eric McKitrick, Henry May, Walter P. Metzger, William Miller, Ern-est Nagel, David Riesman, Henry Robbins, Dorothy R. Ross, Irving Sanes, Wilson Smith, Gerald Stearn, John William Ward, C. Vann Woodward, and Irvin Wyllie. Since much of the talk provoked by my ideas took the form of unresolved arguments, it would be especially ironic if any of these persons were assumed to share my views.

An inquiry that covers as much ground as this can be no more satis-factory than the special studies upon which its author must rely. My footnotes indicate, I hope, where my primary obligations rest, but they doubtless fall short of acknowledging the full weight of my indebted-ness to contemporary American historical scholarship. In considering the books and articles upon which I have drawn most heavily, I notice that almost all of them were written during the past fifteen or twenty years, and that taken together they constitute a remarkably formidable body of work. Perhaps this, too, should be thrown in the scales when the state of intellectual enterprise in this country is being assayed.

Index

A NOTE ON THE TYPE

THE TEXT of this book is set in CALEDONIA, a Linotype face designed by W. A. Dwiggins, the man responsible for so much that is good in contemporary book design and typography. Caledonia belongs to the family of printing types called "modern face" by printers—a term used to mark the change in style of type-letters that occurred about 1800. Caledonia borders on the general design of Scotch Modern but is more freely drawn than that letter.

Printed and bound by
The Haddon Craftsmen, Inc., Scranton, Pa.
The typography and binding designs
are based on originals by
W. A. DWIGGINS